Otherworld Journeys

Otherworld Journeys

ACCOUNTS OF NEAR-DEATH EXPERIENCE IN MEDIEVAL AND MODERN TIMES

Carol Zaleski

New York * Oxford
OXFORD UNIVERSITY PRESS
1987

Oxford University Press

Oxford New York Toronto
Delhi Bombay Calcutta Madras Karachi
Petaling Jaya Singapore Hong Kong Tokyo
Nairobi Dar es Salaam Cape Town
Melbourne Auckland

and associated companies in
Beirut Berlin Ibadan Nicosia

Copyright © 1987 by Oxford University Press, Inc.

Published by Oxford University Press, Inc.,
200 Madison Avenue, New York, New York 10016

Oxford is a registered trademark of Oxford University Press

Portions of *I Died Three Times in 1977*, P. M. H. Atwater, reprinted by
permission of the author.

Portions of *Life After Life*, Raymond A. Moody, Jr., reprinted by
permission of Mockingbird Books, Inc.

Portions of *Life at Death: A Scientific Investigation of the Near-Death
Experience*, Kenneth Ring, reprinted by permission of the
Putnam Publishing Group. Copyright © 1980 by Kenneth Ring.

"Prophetic Voices" videotaped interview with near-death experiencers
reprinted with permission of Andrew J. Silver.

Extract from Canto 33 reprinted by permission of the Bodley Head Ltd.
from *Dante's Paradiso*, translated by John D. Sinclair.

"Profile of an Experiencer: Tracy Lovell," *Vital Signs* 1, no. 4,
reprinted by permission of *Vital Signs*.

"St. Patrick's Purgatory," Carol Zaleski. Acknowledgment to
Journal of the History of Ideas XLVI (October–December 1985):
467–85.

Library of Congress Cataloging in Publication Data
Zaleski, Carol Goldsmith.
    Otherworld journeys.
    Bibliography: p.   Includes index.
    1. Near-death experiences—Religious aspects—Christianity.
2. Voyages to the otherworld.
3. Voyages to the otherworld in literature. I. Title.
BT825.Z34 1987 133.9′01′3 86-17983
ISBN 0-19-503915-7

10 9 8 7 6 5 4 3 2
Printed in the United States of America
on acid-free paper

Acknowledgments

THIS BOOK BEGAN several years ago as a dissertation in the Study of Religion at Harvard University. I am grateful for the advice, encouragement, and friendship of my teachers and colleagues, especially Richard R. Niebuhr, Jane I. Smith, William A. Graham, Jr., Margaret R. Miles, Clarissa W. Atkinson, Diana L. Eck, and Wilfred Cantwell Smith.

A doctoral dissertation grant from the Charlotte W. Newcombe Foundation and a residency at the Virginia Center for the Creative Arts allowed me to work on this project without distraction, and the staff of the Harvard Arts and Sciences Computer Services helped me find my way in the labyrinthine other world of electronic text processing. Nicole Galland and Lisa Vines provided valuable eleventh-hour research assistance. Cynthia A. Read's discerning editorial suggestions and Wendy Warren Keebler's vigilant copy editing made the process of revising for publication both edifying and pleasant. John L. Barger deserves credit, too, for his careful work on the index.

Nancy Evans Bush, Bruce Greyson, Raymond and Louise Moody, Karlis Osis, Kenneth Ring, Kimberly Clark, Leslee Morabito, and James Krum were very gracious to me. I would also like to thank those who have taken the risk of publicizing their own experiences in the face of death. Although my perspective is inevitably different from theirs, I hope they will find that this study contributes in some way to our common aim of understanding near-death testimony.

Finally, I wish to acknowledge the wonderful support I received from my family: Philip Zaleski, Morton and Laura Goldsmith, and Berenice Skidelsky. This book is dedicated to them.

A Note on Terminology and Translations

THE TERM "near-death experience," coined by Raymond Moody, applies to the testimony of individuals who have revived from apparent death as well as those who have only come close to death. As I shall indicate in chapter 10, definitions of death, return from death, near-death states, dreams, and visions are often blurry in the material we are considering. Whenever finer distinctions are needed, I supply them; otherwise, for the ease of the reader I use such terms as *near-death experience, near-death vision, otherworld journey, otherworld vision, deathbed vision,* and *return from death* almost interchangeably.

Translations are my own, unless otherwise noted. For the sake of brevity, I have not reproduced the original Latin or vernacular European texts, but I have indicated where these sources can be found. Latin editions of many works cited here are included in the *Patrologia latina* series edited by J.-P. Migne, indicated in the notes by the abbreviation *PL*. Biblical passages are taken from the Revised Standard Version or, in some cases, the Douay-Rheims edition. For apocalypses and other extracanonical texts, I have relied most often on *The Old Testament Pseudepigrapha*, edited by James H. Charlesworth.

Contents

PART II
MEDIEVAL CHRISTIAN RETURN-FROM-DEATH STORIES: A THEMATIC TREATMENT

PART III
THE MODERN NEAR-DEATH NARRATIVE: A THEMATIC AND COMPARATIVE TREATMENT

Otherworld Journeys

Introduction

IN NEARLY ALL cultures, people have told stories of travel to another world, in which a hero, shaman, prophet, king, or ordinary mortal passes through the gates of death and returns with a message for the living.

In its most familiar form, this journey is a descent into the underworld. Countless figures of myth, sacred history, and literature are said to have ventured underground to the kingdom of death, to rescue its shadowy captives or to learn its secrets.

The voyage to the underworld—portrayed in religious epics and enacted in rituals, dramas, and games—is often associated with initiatory death and rebirth. To represent states of ecstasy, divinization, and royal or prophetic consecration, on the other hand, many traditions favor the symbolism of ascent to higher worlds. Thus, legend attributes to the Prophet Muhammad a heavenly journey that sealed his status as God's messenger and established the model for later Islamic literature on the path of souls at death or in mystical rapture. So, too, the prophetic powers of Zarathustra and Mani, Enoch and St. Paul find expression in vivid tales of ascent to celestial spheres. In many different societies, moreover, ritual and spiritual practices aimed at achieving transcendence imaginatively act out or imitate the heavenly journey. The shaman dons an eagle feather or mounts a sky pole to achieve what Mircea Eliade calls a "breaking of the plane," and to recover the primordial human condition of free access to heaven.[1] The Mithraic initiate, like Blake's sunflower, counts the steps of the sun, ascending a seven-runged planetary ladder from darkness to light. The philosopher of antiquity disdains the mud-ball on which he stands and contemplates the superlunary and ideal world, launching a mental "flight of the alone to the Alone."[2]

3

A third variety of otherworld travel, neither so lofty as celestial ascent nor so profound as descent into the abyss, but perhaps just as lively in its appeal to the imagination, is the fantastic voyage. From the fabled wanderings of Odysseus and St. Brendan to the fanciful travelogues of Sir John Mandeville, to the chronicles of Marco Polo, Columbus, and Ponce de León, this genre has provided great scope for the interplay of the historical and the mythic imagination. The protagonist of a fantastic journey tale sets forth to find another world by exploring the remote reaches of this world: the far east or west, the edge of the ocean, the Ultima Thule. He returns to tell of hidden treasures and elusive Edens, of fabulous prodigies, monsters, ghosts, demons, and angels that inhabit the periphery of normal life.

From these three types of otherworld journey narration arise a multitude of overlapping forms and a vast array of mythical, mystical, dramatic, ritual, poetic, allegorical, and even satirical expressions. If there is such a thing as "otherworld journey studies," it is thus a field whose materials are almost endlessly varied and whose contributors, approaching from their separate disciplines, rarely see eye to eye.

Scholars have investigated otherworld journey motifs in primitive and tribal religion; in Oriental, Mesopotamian, and Greek mythology; in the works of Homer, Plato, and Vergil; in the multiple strands of Hellenistic religion; in Jewish and Christian apocalyptic literature; and in Zoroastrian, Islamic, and medieval Christian traditions. During the nineteenth century, there developed within Dante scholarship a whole industry devoted to mining the otherworld vision stories of Christian, Zoroastrian, and Islamic literature and folklore in the search for sources of the *The Divine Comedy*. So many precursors were found and championed over the years that one might imagine that Dante needed little besides scissors and paste to construct his poetic journey.[3]

The best scholarly treatments of otherworld journey literature focus on particular historical contexts, making use of comparative insights but keeping a fairly tight rein on speculative interpretation. Too often, however, generalizations about the otherworld journey come from authors who view all its varied forms according to a single model, whether taken from shamanism, psychoanalysis, depth psychology, or psychedelia. More taxing, but much more worthwhile, would be to build an interpretive theory on the basis of detailed historical and cross-cultural study, just as, for example, Victor Turner has done for pilgrimage. Despite the profusion of scholarly and informal writings on the other world, this comprehensive work has yet be done.

For one who does not wish to tackle such an ambitious task, however, there remain smaller uncharted areas. Since no general theory of otherworld journey narration can be complete that fails to recognize its latest manifestations, we might search for contemporary parallels or vestiges. Perhaps the otherworld journey motif is "camouflaged"(as Eliade would put it) in the modern lore of space travel which, like the fantastic voyage legends of the past, exemplifies what might be called the lure of the edge.

Another possibility is that otherworld journey accounts might be found in contemporary culture, not only in camouflaged or self-consciously literary forms, but also in "literal" forms that claim to describe actual events. Indeed, this is true of at least one tenacious variety of otherworld journey narration, in which the protagonist dies and yet survives to tell the tale. Such eyewitness accounts of life after death can be found throughout the folklore and religious literature of the world. In Western culture, return-from-death stories developed within and alongside the apocalyptic traditions of late antiquity, flourished in the Middle Ages, declined during the Reformation, and reappeared in connection with some of the evangelical, separatist, and spiritualist movements of the nineteenth century. Today these tales have returned in full force in the form of "near-death" testimony, first popularized in the early 1970s by Raymond Moody's best-selling book *Life After Life*, and kept in the public eye since then by a flood of books, articles, talk shows, and films on the subject.

Let us consider the opening statements of two accounts of visionary near-death experience:

> My heart had stopped. . . . Everything was just completely black . . . this void became the shape of a tunnel, and then before me was the most magnificent light; it's The Light in capital letters, and it's—very bluntly—the essence of God.

> Four days ago, I died and was taken by two angels to the height of heaven. And it was just as though I rose above not only this squalid earth, but even the sun and moon, the clouds and stars. Then I went through a gate that was brighter than normal daylight, into a place where the entire floor shone like gold and silver. The light was indescribable, and I can't tell you how vast it was.

The first of these narratives comes from Tom Sawyer, a heavy-equipment operator who lives in Rochester, New York. He is describing, to the audience of the television feature show "20/20," what he experienced during fifteen minutes in which he lay crushed under the weight of his pickup truck.[4] The second passage has been attributed to Salvius, a sixth-century holy man who, according to the author of the *History of the Franks*, spent a night lifeless on a funeral bier, but revived when God sent him back to serve the Church as a bishop.[5]

Are these two accounts describing essentially the same experience? Are the differences between them merely incidental? What do the similarities and differences between these narratives, fourteen centuries apart, tell us about the history of otherworld journey narration, its recurrent features, its social function, and its ultimate significance?

Such questions can be answered adequately only by examining accounts like those of Tom Sawyer and Salvius in historical context, so that they no longer appear either monolithically similar or, because of different idioms, completely unrelated. A closer look will reveal, for instance, that Salvius's vision is a work of hagiography and, as such, differs from many return-from-death narratives of the same period which feature the visit of a sinner or penitent to hell. Tom Sawyer's account has not been reworked into a literary form, but he nonetheless tells a story that, as the present study will show, reflects modern assumptions and concerns.

The purpose of this study is to examine the return-from-death story in two widely separated settings: medieval Christendom and modern "secular" and pluralistic society. Comparative study will highlight features that are not otherwise obvious, putting into sharper relief the elements that are culturally specific and at the same time drawing attention to perennial aspects of otherworld journey narration. It will disclose some of the ways in which the otherworld journey narrative is shaped by the social and historical situation in which it occurs. Although this will not tell us the whole story about otherworld journeys, it will provide a new perspective on the question of how we might interpret the literature of otherworld visions.

Part I begins with a step backward, to get an overview of the otherworld journey as it recurs throughout the history of the world's religious traditions. The second chapter provides a more detailed introduction to its Western Christian forms, as represented by four classic and influential narratives: the Vision of St. Paul, the *Dialogues* of Gregory the Great, the Vision of Drythelm, and the *Treatise on the Purgatory of St. Patrick*. Part II is a thematic treatment of the medieval return-from-death story, beginning with the exit from the body and following the journey through the other world and back to life. The last chapter of this section considers the complexities of the relationship between the medieval visionary and his or her culture, and between the visionary experience and its literary expression.

The material covered in part II ranges from the sixth to the early thirteenth centuries; after that period, the otherworld vision story tends to become a deliberate literary construction, self-conscious and systematic in its allegorical themes and classical allusions, and without the connection it formerly had to experience-based reports. Although it is scarcely possible to determine the authenticity of any given account, this study is concerned primarily with medieval and modern narratives that at least make the claim that they represent actual experience.

The medieval narratives examined here correspond to what historian Peter Dinzelbacher calls the first phase of medieval Christian vision literature (lasting until the mid-thirteenth century), in which the visionary travels out of his or her body to visit heaven, hell, and purgatory, and returns to life transformed.[6] In the second phase, which Dinzelbacher dates from the mid-twelfth century, most of the visionaries are well-known saints (usually women religious) for whom mystical and allegorical apparitions are a chronic experience. As Dinzelbacher shows, these seers play a more passive role, receiving otherworldly visitations rather than traveling out of their bodies to exotic realms. Readers who seek a more complete grounding in the social dynamics and demographics of medieval vision literature than the present comparative study can provide will find it valuable to consult Dinzelbacher's work, along with the writings of Jacques Le Goff on the evolution of purgatory in the religious imagination of Western Christian society.

I have not attempted to write a continuous history of return-from-death narratives in Western culture, but rather to present two periods of peak interest in this subject and to learn from the contrasts and continuities between them; part III therefore shifts to the twentieth century, to examine contemporary near-death literature and its recent precursors. As a parallel to the thematic treatment in part II, part III traces the modern visionary's journey from apparent death to recovery, and from recovery to telling the story. Here, as in the chapters on medieval vision lore, we will learn of sudden exit from the body; travel across tunnels, paths, or fields; encounters with luminous guides and spirits; glimpses of heavenly bliss; reluctant reentry into life; and an aftermath of psychological and spiritual transformation. Yet we will find striking differences as well: gone are the bad deaths, harsh judgment scenes, purgatorial torments, and infernal terrors of medieval visions; by comparison, the modern other world is a congenial place, a democracy, a school for continuing education, and a garden of unearthly delights.

If we are to succeed in negotiating the labyrinth of medieval and modern otherworld journey accounts, we must do more than simply tabulate these recurrent and contrasting motifs. We must search for a common thread that will not be deflected by variations in content and will help us to account for both similarities and differences without prejudice. That common thread is story: the otherworld journey is a work of the narrative imagination. As such, it is shaped not only by the universal laws of symbolic experience, but also by the local and transitory statutes of a given culture. The present study is intended to fix our attention on the narrative and imaginative character of otherworld visions, for only by holding on to this thread can we avoid the blind alleys down which so many discussions of religious visions and life after death have led.

In part IV, I attempt to meet the problem of interpretation head-on. How do we evaluate the visionary testimony of individuals who believe that they have returned from the gates of death? The current wave of interest in near-death experience makes this a live issue. We can no longer treat otherworld journey narration as a cultural fossil, buried safely in the past. With so many people turning to near-death literature in the hope of gaining insight into the meaning of death, theologians and scholars of religion have a responsibility to put this material in historical perspective and to reflect on its ultimate significance. To refuse the challenge to interpret near-death literature is only to widen the gap between academic theology and popular religious concerns. The result is a loss for both sides; not only does the public lose the benefit of historically informed discussion, but theology is deprived of a potentially revitalizing connection to contemporary experience.

It would be premature at this stage to announce a comprehensive theory of otherworld visions. Instead, this study reviews the interpretations that have already been advanced—from medieval Christian vision theory to the current debate over explanations of near-death experience—and suggests some alternative views. Chapter 10 is an attempt to mediate between the near-death researchers and the critics who are determined to debunk their work; I propose a nonreductionist approach which gives credit to individual testimony while still taking into account the physiological, psychological, and cultural conditions that shape visionary experience in the face of death.

In chapter 11, I offer some reflections on the symbolic character of otherworld visions and on the visionary and imaginative aspects of religious thought in general. If, as William James asserts in "The Sentiment of Rationality," the role of philosophy is to define the universe in a way that gives people a warrant and a point of reference for the use of their innate capacities, then it must also make a place for our imaginative powers.[7] The traditional way to accomplish this has been to define the universe as an object that religious images describe. Unfortunately, for those who think critically about science, history, and world religions, such simple acceptance of religious imagery no longer seems to be a reasonable option. We can still say that the religious imagination guides us through life and as far as the threshold of a wider life, but we cannot claim that it supplies us with direct maps of an afterlife. Without attempting to pronounce the final word on this complex subject, the last chapter indicates some directions for future exploration.

PART I

ORIENTATION

CHAPTER 1

A Wide-Angle View

THE RECORD OF human origins is the record of human attitudes toward death. We can pick up hints of this as far back as half a million years ago: the skulls left behind by Peking Man, a *homo erectus* type discovered in the 1930s in China, have been severed from the spinal cord in such deliberate fashion as to lead some paleoanthropologists to speculate about ritual cannibalism, or at least to entertain the thought that these early hominids took care in the way that they disposed of their dead.[1]

If it is true that Peking Man devoured the brains of his enemies or heroes, or cherished the skulls of his ancestors, then he may have been much like us: a creature baffled by death and a spinner of dreams and tales about another life. Yet the skulls found at Choukoutien cave are mute, and there is no consensus on their meaning or function. For more articulate evidence of ritual behavior toward the dead, we can turn to the fossil legacy of the Neandertals, early *homo sapiens* peoples who ranged across Europe and the Near East during the last great glacial age, until they were supplanted by the Cro-Magnon ancestors whom we call, so emphatically, *homo sapiens sapiens*.

Interestingly, the sites that have yielded the richest fossil harvest of Neandertal technology have been, in effect, their cemeteries.[2] At Le Moustier, the cave in the Dordogne that gave its name to the "Mousterian" cultures, famous for skillful stonework, a teenage boy reclines with head on arm at the bottom of a burial pit, surrounded by flint pieces, a stone axe, and the remains of what may have been a funeral meal or food offering. At Teshik Tash in Uzbekistan, a child lies within a corona of ibex horns, his skeleton painstakingly stripped of its flesh. The most inviting of these Middle Paleolithic burial sites, however, is preserved in a 60,000-year-old layer of Shanidar cave in Iraq, where analysis of pollen in the sediment suggests that the body may have been lovingly laid to rest on a bed of multicolored flowering herbs.

During the more recent Cro-Magnon period, from 35,000 to 10,000 years ago, the funeral industry appears to have established itself in widely separated regions around the world. Corpses are curled and bound in fetal position, as if to restrain them from returning to disturb the living or to prepare them for a second birth; they are adorned with cowrie shells and painted with red ochre, as if to warm them with the tint of blood and fire; and they are supplied with weapons, food, statues of the mother goddess, and other goods which might be needed for a happy sojourn in the grave or a safe voyage to the other world.

As intriguing as the fossil record may be, it tells us little about Paleolithic views of death unless we supplement it with a disciplined exercise of imagination, drawing on analogues in primitive and modern cultures of our own age.[3] The ceremonial behavior toward the dead which we see embedded in the earth we excavate is nearly universal in historic times; and wherever one finds burial with grave goods or ritual cremation, sacrificial meals or prescribed acts of mourning, such practices are but satellites of a much larger system of myths and rites that portray and sustain the cycles of life, death, and rebirth.

If we permit ourselves to speculate backward, then, viewing our Paleolithic forerunners in the mirror of our world's living cultures, we can affirm that they took pains to bury their dead because they shared with us an awareness of death that transcends the instinctive fascination and aversion displayed by our primate cousins. Perhaps this knowledge of death, as a force that impinges on the individual, the community, and the cosmos, is what marks our species as, potentially, wise. Indeed, homo sapiens—whose name, taken literally, means "man tasting"—is not just the tool-maker, fire-tamer, and master of words. He is also, as the world's scriptures tell us, a creature familiar with the taste of death.[4] We know that we will die, and that knowledge invades our consciousness, shapes our artifacts, arts, and sciences; it will not let us rest until we have found ways, through rituals and stories, theologies and philosophies, either to make sense of death or, failing that, to make sense of ourselves in the face of death.

If it is true that the prospect of death "concentrates the mind wonderfully,"[5] it is also true that it galvanizes the imagination, giving rise to some of the most vivid images in our cultural repertoire: the danse macabre, the winged skull on a Puritan headstone, the pale gentleman who likes a good bet, the "conqueror worm," and, above all, the visionary journey to the other world, with which the present study is concerned.

A gallery tour of otherworld journey images throughout history might begin as far back as Upper Paleolithic times, with the enigmatic murals that adorn the Ice Age cave sanctuaries of France and Spain.[6] In the shaft of the Lascaux cave, for instance, a bird-faced man is depicted falling backward or lying dead in the path of a wounded bison. Some paleoanthropologists and historians of religion, who wish to see more in this painting than a prosaic hunting scene, have proposed that the man is a prehistoric shaman of sorts, embarked on a trance-induced journey to other worlds; close by, a pole with a bird perched on top resembles a widespread shamanic image of ascension and flight.[7] Whether this shamanic reading is justified cannot be decided here, but it is tempting to imagine that the world's first art may have been intended to portray, along with hunting emblems and fertility icons, scenes of visionary transcendence of death.[8]

The shaman is, in fact, the prototypical otherworld traveler, and it is in the shamanic lore of Central Asia and Siberia, and other tribal cultures, that we find the most compelling enactment of this motif. Mircea Eliade writes:

> . . . the shaman is above all the specialist in ecstasy. It is owing to his capacity for ecstasies—that is, because he is able, at will, to pass out of his body and undertake mystical journeys through all the cosmic regions—that the shaman is a healer, and a director of souls as well as a mystic and visionary. Only the shaman is able to pursue the wandering soul of the sick person, capture it and bring it back to the body: it is the shaman who accompanies the souls of the dead to their new dwelling-places, and he, again, who embarks on long, ecstatic journeys in Heaven to present the soul of the sacrificed animal to the gods, and implore their divine benediction.[9]

The shaman inaugurates his career as a "specialist in ecstasy" by a symbolic encounter with death, whether brought on spontaneously by illness or seizure, or deliberately courted through ritual mimesis or psychophysical techniques. His initiation may involve a harrowing ordeal such as having his flesh devoured by demons or ancestor spirits. Reduced to his skeletal or spiritual essence, he is ready to set forth for the other world. The journey takes many forms: in some Australian tribes, the medicine man descends into a dark cave where he is dismembered by spirits and ingests magic crystals which lift him to the sky;[10] the Igulik Eskimo shaman travels to the ocean floor to propitiate the capricious mother of the sea beasts, who rules the souls of the dead and guards the marine animals on which human livelihood depends;[11] the Altaic shaman ascends to the sky through the smoke hole of his tent, or climbs a tree pole notched to represent the seven levels of heaven.[12] In recent years, scholars have become increasingly aware of the shamanic elements adhering to the otherworld journey motif in its varied manifestations in world literature. For example, Walter Burkert has shown the kinship between hunting rituals in which shamans set out to conquer or placate the master of the beasts and Greek myths in which heroes travel to another world.[13]

The shamanic otherworld journey survives in the modern world not only as a tribal religious phenomenon, but also in new forms born from the mingling of diverse religious and cultural systems. Perhaps the best-known modern record of visionary travel to the other world is related in *Black Elk Speaks*, the life story of a Lakota Sioux holy man.[14] In his youth, Black Elk set out on a traditional shamanic path, but later participated in the Messiah movement that swept the plains, and eventually became a Catholic catechist. His first visionary experience came to him when he was struck down at the age of

nine by an unexplained paralysis. While he lay apparently dead, he was sum-
moned out of his body by two thunder beings who escorted him to a tipi in
the clouds. There the six grandfathers—the powers of the sky, the earth, and
the four quarters—gave Black Elk the gifts of healing and spiritual insight.
After this initiatory experience, Black Elk could no longer live the life of a
normal child; like the visionaries we will meet later in these pages, he
returned from death transformed, with new powers and a special role to play
in his community.

There are countless variations on the shamanic visionary journey, but if
we look beyond the shamanic experience as such to the manifestations of the
otherworld journey motif as it has evolved in the major religious traditions
and cultures of the world, the prospect becomes truly dizzying. A global history of the otherworld journey would involve examining not only funeral
practices and views of the afterlife, but also rites of passage, pilgrimage and
travel lore, prophetic and apocalyptic literature, and mystical and ecstatic
visions.[15] Here, however, we will only glance at a few of the highlights of this
yet-to-be-written history.

The legacy of the ancient Near East is rich in otherworld journey
themes. One of the earliest known literary narratives of descent to the underworld belongs to the cult of Inanna, the Sumerian goddess of fertility. In the
Descent of Inanna, she boldly seeks to storm the gates of Arallu, the land of
the dead, ruled by her evil sister Ereshkigal; but her powers as queen of
heaven do not avail Inanna in this shadowy, dust-choked realm.[16] At each of
the seven gates, she is forced by a guard to strip off one of her garments.
When she arrives, naked and powerless, before the throne of death, a baleful
glance from her sister is enough to reduce Inanna to a rotting piece of meat.
The god Enki revives her by sending down the water and food of life; in the
end, however, Inanna purchases her freedom only by delivering her lover, the
vegetation god Dumuzi, into the hands of death.

Like Persephone, Dumuzi is permitted to spend six months of each year
in the world of the living, alternating as a hostage with his sister, the wine
goddess. Scholars have seen reflected in the legend of Inanna's descent the
cycles of agricultural death and rebirth: Dumuzi, elsewhere a shepherd god,
here plays the part of the grain which dies each spring at harvest time; in the
fall, his sister dies with the harvesting of grapes. According to another interpretation, suggested by Thorkild Jacobsen, the descent of Inanna depicts the
dwindling of meat in the storehouse, to be replenished every spring by the
sacrifice of flocks in the person of the divine shepherd Dumuzi.[17] Rather than
seeking to transcend death, the Descent of Inanna, like other agricultural
myths of underworld descent, incorporates it within the life-cycle. Inanna
comes back to life, but she fails to break the power of death: Arallu remains
the "land of no return."

The route to the Mesopotamian underworld is mapped even more fully
by the cycle of tales about Gilgamesh, the legendary ruler of the city-state of
Uruk, and his comrade Enkidu. Oral and written accounts of their heroic

exploits and their encounters with the netherworld circulated for more than a thousand years before taking final shape as the Babylonian and Assyrian Epic of Gilgamesh. The presence of death is felt early in the epic, when Enkidu has a premonitory dream of being carried off by a dark being:

> To the road which none leave who have entered it,
> On the road from which there is no way back,
> To the house wherein the dwellers are bereft of light,
> Where dust is their fare and clay their food.[18]

When the dream comes true and Enkidu meets his death, Gilgamesh goes wild with grief. Mourning for his lost companion is secondary, however, to the dread Gilgamesh feels for himself. No longer satisfied with the surrogate immortality conferred by royal lineage and heroic accomplishments, he sets out on an obsessive quest for the antidote to death. He journeys westward, tunnels through the underground realm where the sun travels at night, crosses the corrosive sea of mortality, and struggles toward the paradise of the flood hero Utnapishtim, whom the gods have singled out for eternal life.

On his journey, Gilgamesh meets Siduri the barmaid. At once temptress and wise woman, she counsels him to abandon his quest with words that foreshadow the advice of Proverbs and Ecclesiastes:

> "Gilgamesh, whither rovest thou?
> The life thou pursuest thou shalt not find.
> When the gods created mankind,
> Death for mankind they set aside,
> Life in their own hands retaining.
> Thou, Gilgamesh, let full be thy belly,
> Make thou merry by day and by night.
> Of each day make thou a feast of rejoicing,
> Day and night dance thou and play!
> Let thy garments be sparkling fresh,
> Thy head be washed; bathe thou in water.
> Pay heed to the little one that holds on to thy hand,
> Let thy spouse delight in thy bosom!
> For this is the task of [mankind]!"[19]

Gilgamesh fails in his effort to escape our common fate. Given the test of staying awake for six days and seven nights, he succumbs to sleep, thus proving himself unfit for the eternal wakefulness he seeks. Utnapishtim takes pity and tells Gilgamesh about a plant that restores youth. Yet even this boon is lost; while Gilgamesh bathes in a well, a serpent steals the prize. In the end, Gilgamesh returns to the world of mortals resigned to the wisdom of the barmaid Siduri.

The Assyrian version of the epic preserves a Sumerian legend which gives further, though no more cheering, details concerning the state of the dead. In a mythical time at the beginning of the world, Gilgamesh accidentally drops some sacred objects, which fall into the underworld. When Enk-

idu goes down on a mission of retrieval, death seizes him; yet his ghost returns
to tell Gilgamesh how dreary it is to be devoured by vermin and reduced to
dust along with rulers and commoners alike.

Similar ideas recur throughout the literature of the ancient Near East:
the dead lead a listless half-life, cramped together in dark, dusty, or swampy
quarters beneath the earth. The Psalmist of the Hebrew scriptures reminds
God that "in death there is no remembrance of thee; in Sheol who can give
thee praise?"[20] And Job laments:

> Are not the days of my life few?
>   Let me alone, that I may find a
>   little comfort
> before I go whence I shall not return,
>   to the land of gloom and deep
>   darkness,
> the land of gloom and chaos,
>   where light is as darkness. (Job 10:20–22)

Of course, the same Job also cries out, "I know that my Redeemer lives"
(Job 19:25), and we must bear in mind that the prophets of Israel believed
that the god of their fathers and mothers was preparing a special destiny for
his people.[21] But the fact remains that in most of its ancient Near Eastern
manifestations, the motif of journey to the underworld neither symbolized
nor encouraged hope for eternal life.

In the very different climate of pharaonic Egypt, however, the otherworld journey became associated early on with elaborate conceptions of judgment, reward, and punishment after death.[22] During roughly the same period
in which the hero Gilgamesh was said to have made his fruitless journey to
the land of the dead (at least a thousand years before his story was written),
the kings of Egypt were devising ways to secure for themselves a prolonged
sojourn in the afterlife.[23] At first they were buried in underground stone
chambers (*mastabas*); here the dead ruler resided in an imperishable house,
accepted visits and offerings from the living, and survived through the
remembrance of his name. The pyramids, dating back to the beginnings of
the third millennium B.C., performed this function on a grand scale, willing
permanence into being by sheer mass. Their outward shape traced an image
of the cosmic mountain or the heavenly ladder by which the pharaoh
ascended to the sky. Inscribed on the walls within were instructions, incan-
tations, and prayers whose aim was to guide the pharaoh into the company
of the sun, or to identify him with Osiris, the dying-and-rising god who
became the lord of the dead.

The Pyramid Texts leave the impression that the road to the other world
was paved only for the ruling class; the pharaoh's survival after death helped
to guarantee the social and cosmic order, but offered no promise of an eternal
life in which his subjects might share. A more "democratic" picture of the
afterlife emerged during the Middle Kingdom, however, after a period of
social upheaval in which it became obvious that the pyramids were not inviol-

able; from then on, anyone who could afford the burial rites could journey to the western or underworld realm of Osiris, there to be judged and admitted (if all went well) to a happy afterlife in the Field of Reeds.

The Coffin Texts, the Book of the Dead, and other mortuary manuals from this period paint vivid portraits of the otherworld journey and the dread proceedings before the divine tribunal. In these works, we get an early glimpse of the perilous river-crossing, the weighing of the heart or deeds on a scale, and other ordeals and obstacles which were to become standard features of Western otherworld iconography. Most important, the Egyptian texts suggest that it is the idea of a postmortem judgment, in which the dead are ranked according to merit or ritual preparedness, that gives the other world its definite features; otherwise, the realm of the dead would remain as faceless and undifferentiated as the Mesopotamian "house of dust."

The story of Setme and Si-Osiri, a popular Egyptian wisdom tale, illustrates this point.[24] One day in Memphis, the prince Setme chances to witness the splendid funeral procession of a wealthy man, followed by the miserable disposal of a poor man. Setme expresses the wish that his end may be like that of the rich man. In response, his son Si-Osiri, who is the reincarnation of an ancient sage, takes him on an educational tour through the seven halls of the underworld, down to the judgment seat of Osiris, where they witness the recording and weighing of deeds and the doom of the wicked. The rich man has failed the test and now lies at the entrance to the fifth hall, his right eye transfixed by the pivot of the gate. The poor man, however, sits in glory next to Osiris, clothed in the rich man's finery. This visionary journey tale, similar in many ways to the New Testament parable of the rich man and Lazarus (Luke 16:19–25), departs radically from the common ancient Near Eastern wisdom sayings that find a moral lesson in the fact that death levels rich and poor alike. The story of Setme and Si-Osiri emphasizes the distinctions of merit and status in the other world, and provides a correspondingly graphic depiction of its many mansions.

In Greco-Roman myths and mysteries, we find an assorted crowd of otherworld journey motifs: images of Hades as a shadowy subterranean zone compete for space with detailed maps of descent into a labyrinthine underworld, exotic allegories of ascent to celestial spheres, and fanciful romps in Elysian resorts.

The journey to Hades appears several times in Homeric literature, notably in the eleventh book of the *Odyssey*, in which the wandering hero voyages beyond the world-circling river Ocean to visit the dead seer Tiresias. Like Gilgamesh, Odysseus finds the dead to be a singularly cheerless lot; they come forward one by one, too weak even to speak of their dismal condition until they have fed on the blood of a sacrificed sheep. With the exception of a few anomalous scenes of postmortem punishment, the Homeric Hades resembles the Mesopotamian Arallu or the Sheol of the Psalmist; and it conveys a similar *carpe diem* message: in the words of the shade of Achilles, it is better to be a hireling and alive than to be lord over all the dead.[25]

In the mystery traditions, a more differentiated picture of life after death emerges, reflected in soteriological dramas in which the participant submits to flagellation, fasting, and other ordeals in imitation of death, or ritually links himself or herself with a divine or heroic being—Heracles, Persephone, Demeter, Dionysus, Orpheus, Isis, Mithras—who has made the descent to the underworld. It has been suggested that initiates in the mysteries of Eleusis acted out the journey to Hades by climbing down from the second story of the Temple of Demeter (the *telesterion*) and tunneling through a dark passage to emerge in a bright meadow.[26] Unfortunately, evidence is lacking to support such a reconstruction (which conjures up images of the haunted house at an amusement park), but the initiatory pattern of death and rebirth is clear.[27] The *Homeric Hymn to Demeter* recommends the rites of Eleusis as the sole guarantee of postmortem contentment: "Happy is he among men upon earth who has seen these mysteries! But he who is uninitiate and who has no part in them, never has lot of like good things once he is dead, down in the darkness and gloom."[28] A saying attributed to Plutarch inverts this idea: "the soul [at the point of death] has the same experience as those who are being initiated into the great mysteries . . ."[29]

Rehearsal for death, in this sense, is an acknowledged purpose of the mysteries. Thanks to ritual preparation, initiates will not be taken by surprise when their last hour arrives. The landscape disclosed by death will look familiar to them; they will know which path to choose in order to arrive at a transcendent state of being. We may suppose that a similar intention lies behind the practice of burying explicit instructions with the dead, such as those found inscribed on gold plates in graves scattered throughout southern Italy and Crete:

> Thou shalt find to the left of the House of Hades a spring,
> And by the side thereof standing a white cypress.
> To this spring approach not near.
> But thou shalt find another, from the Lake of Memory
> Cold water flowing forth, and there are guardians before it.
> Say, "I am a child of Earth and starry Heaven;
> But my race is of Heaven (alone). This ye know yourselves.
> But I am parched with thirst and I perish. Give me quickly
> The cold water flowing forth from the Lake of Memory."
> And of themselves they will give thee to drink of the holy spring,
> And thereafter among the other heroes thou shalt have lordship.[30]

These intriguing grave tablets, which some have linked with Orphic or Orphic-Pythagorean schools, reflect a deep-rooted tendency in the religious traditions of archaic and classical Greece to equate the experience of death with the rigors of spiritual training and to portray both under the symbolism of the otherworld journey.

For Plato, the purificatory rites associated with the Orphic brotherhoods supply a ready metaphor for the philosophic life; philosophy, Plato tells us, is a "preparation for death," in that the pursuit of wisdom demands detachment from the body and training of the soul.[31] If, as the Orphics taught, the body is a "tomb" for the soul, then the exercise of our higher reasoning powers is no less than a journey beyond the grave.[32] In several of his dialogues, Plato expands this analogy into full-blown otherworld journey narratives, drawing on conventional mythic treatments of postmortem judgment as well as on Orphic or Pythagorean notions of transmigration.[33] He appears not to take these eschatologies literally, saying only that "something like this must be true," yet he prefers them to the characteristically Homeric view of Hades because their stratified picture of the other world is more suitable for allegorical and didactic interpretation.[34] As Plato understands it, the Orphics and Pythagoreans were the first to suggest that the soul at death faces a "forking of the roads" leading either to beatitude or to torment and wearisome rebirth.[35]

At the close of the *Republic*, Plato relates a return-from-death story in which this symbolism of the two paths is prominent. A soldier named Er, slain in battle, comes back to life on the funeral pyre and describes his visit to the next world. He tells of leaving his body and journeying with a great throng to the place where souls are judged; the righteous ascend through an opening in heaven, while the wicked travel downward and to the left to meet their punishment. All souls eventually return to choose their next lives; this choice is governed partly by character and partly by the celestial mechanics of Necessity and Chance. The moral of the story, which Er has been sent back to proclaim, is that only those who have led an "examined life" will be able to turn fate to their advantage; only an ardent dedication to the pursuit of wisdom can combat the stupefaction (symbolized by the effects of drinking from Lethe) to which all flesh is subject.

While Plato entertained several different ways of imagining the destiny of wisdom-loving souls, ascent to higher worlds became a central symbol for the Platonic, Stoic, and Neopythagorean schools that followed him. Cicero concludes his *De re publica*, in homage to Plato, with a visionary narrative allegorizing the philosophic life as an astral journey, and Plutarch wages his battle with the Epicureans in the form of dialogues on the soul's ascent, escorted by its daimon, to its home in the empyrean.[36]

Despite the philosophical attractions of relocating the realm of the blessed dead from the underworld to the sky, descent to Hades remains a pervasive theme in classical literature down to the Christian era. The visit of Aeneas to the shades of the underworld is closely akin to that of Odysseus. Perhaps because of his Platonic and Stoic leanings, however, Vergil differentiates the fate of the dead, hinting at Elysian fields in the air and painting graphic tableaux of torment under the earth; indeed, it was for this that he won the honor of escorting Dante on his trip through hell.[37]

In the Hellenistic world of late antiquity, however, ascent motifs predominate. As Alan Segal has shown, the heavenly journey provides a mythic "constellation" or structural pattern for nearly all the manifestations of Hellenistic religion, including the imperial cult; mystery religions; prophetic, sectarian, and apocalyptic movements in Judaism; the early Christian movement; Gnosticism; and later forms of Jewish mysticism.[38] In these diverse settings, as Segal's examples show, the heavenly journey functions as a vehicle for theodicy; a cosmic endorsement of the authority of prophets, priests, or rulers; a defense of threatened ideologies; and a preview of the afterlife.

The most dramatic (though not the earliest) instances of this pattern occur in the Gnostic literature of the Hellenized Near East, where we find a dazzling assortment of otherworld journey legends, brilliantly reflecting a syncretic alloy of Persian dualism, Babylonian astrology, Jewish apocalyptic, Christian or pre-Christian soteriology, and Greek philosophy from the Orphic-Pythagorean-Stoic-Platonic vein.[39] These tales are shaped by the conviction that the world is the work of a malevolent demiurge (sometimes identified with the god of the Hebrew scriptures), whose fondest wish is to trap spirits in the prison of matter and prevent their return to the fullness (*pleroma*) of divine being. From the Gnostic point of view, birth itself is a descent into the underworld, recapitulating the primordial fall of the World Soul. During its descent to earth, the spirit (*pneuma*) acquires the vices associated with the seven planetary spheres and dons the coarse vestments of body and personality. What we think of as our waking life is diagnosed by the Gnostics as the end result of this downfall: a state of sleep, amnesia, and intoxication. Death, potentially, is the antitoxin; but it has this virtue only for those who have been awakened by the teachings of a divine ambassador (the Gnostic Christ, the serpent of Genesis, Mani).

Even so, as Vergil says in another context, the descent is easier than the ascent.[40] Classical texts (such as Pindar, fragment 129) locate scenes of Elysian bliss in brighter pockets of the underworld; but Gnostic otherworld journey narratives place ordeals and torments even in the heavens. Typically, a ruling *archon* stands guard at each of the planetary stations, ready to thwart the spirit in its attempt to divest itself of its dark coverings and pass beyond the cosmos into the zone of light. The texts that describe this hazardous postmortem journey are also guidebooks for its safe completion, disclosing the names of the planetary *archons* and suggesting techniques for making the spirit invisible or invulnerable to their attack:

> The Lord revealed to me what the soul must say when ascending into heaven, and how she must answer each of the upper powers: "I have come to know myself, and I have collected myself from everywhere, and I have not sown children to the Archon but have uprooted his roots and have collected the dispersed members, and I know thee who thou art: for I am of those from above." And thus she is released.[41]

Otherworld journeys abound in the literature of the Jewish apocalyptic movement, of which some consider Gnosticism to be a radical branch.[42] As the term apocalypse suggests, this literature takes the form of visionary disclosures, unveiling the cosmic significance of historical events, or looking ahead to the collective death and renewal toward which all creation is journeying.[43]

More world-affirming than Gnosticism but more intensely eschatological than earlier prophetic works, the Jewish apocalypses were composed in response to crises (such as the Babylonian exile, the cultural encroachments of Hellenism, and the Roman destruction of the second Temple) which led religious leaders to despair of traditional remedies. No longer was it enough to turn each disaster into a call for national repentance. Thus, the seer of 4 Ezra, recoiling from the devastation of the Temple in A.D. 70, learns in a vision that the earth, now irrevocably corrupt, is hurtling toward a final cataclysm:

> and the sun shall suddenly shine forth at night
>   and the moon during the day.
> Blood shall drip from wood,
>   and the stone shall utter its voice;
> the peoples shall be troubled,
>   and the stars shall fall.[44]

The seer of 4 Ezra goes on to predict that the earth will return for seven days into the primeval condition of chaos and silence; out of that chaos shall be born the age to come.[45] As in other apocalyptic works, the presence of mythic elements—titanic battles, scenes of cosmic destruction and renewal, dragon conquests, sacred weddings, images of the royal cult—is more striking than in the older prophetic literature.[46] This dramatic imagery, much of it borrowed from the neighboring cultures of Canaan, Mesopotamia, Persia, and Egypt, brings with it an increasing reliance on the otherworld journey as one of the common vehicles for visionary disclosure.

Among the most vivid of the apocalyptic otherworld journeys are the narratives concerning Enoch, the antediluvian patriarch who was the first to ascend directly to heaven without dying: "Enoch walked with God; and he was not, for God took him" (Gen. 5:24). Apocalyptic writers filled in Enoch's itinerary, sending him on a series of visionary tours. In the oldest extant account, Enoch begins his journeys with a dream:

> I saw in my sleep what I will now tell with the tongue of flesh and with my breath which the Great One has given to men. . . . Behold clouds called me in the vision, and mist called me, and the path of the stars and flashes of lightning hastened me and drove me, and in the vision winds caused me to fly and hastened me and lifted me up into heaven. And I proceeded until I came near to a wall which was built of hailstones, and a tongue of fire surrounded it, and it began to make me afraid.[47]

Enoch faints, and a vision within the vision brings him to an immense house of burning marble, where he meets God face to face. Archangels then escort him through the cosmos, showing him the storehouses of stars, storms, and winds; the pillars of heaven; the abyss where the rebel angels are punished; and the hollow places where the dead dwell in anticipatory torment or delight, awaiting the final day of judgment.[48] On a second journey, Enoch learns the secrets of heaven (ranging from meteorological lore to the names of the angels of the divine presence), sees the Son of Man, and witnesses the future resurrection and judgment of the dead.[49]

To tour the cosmos, then, is to travel ahead in time. Although a great deal of apocalyptic literature looks backward, describing past events in symbolic cipher, the visionary journey form of apocalypse looks to the future: the seer visits the coming age in its preexistent pattern in the other world. It was in the context of apocalyptic visions of a future eschatological crisis that Jewish and early Christian writers experimented with elaborate conceptions of resurrection and judgment, moving far beyond terse Old Testament promises of a vindication for Israel. These texts portray not only the collective destiny of the nation, but also the fate of individuals on the day of judgment; in some cases, they describe the interim period between death and resurrection, thus paving the way for the return-from-death stories with which this study is concerned. Bernard McGinn, who has traced the development of apocalyptic themes in the medieval Christian West, points out that after the "classical" period of intertestamental Judaism and early Christianity, this literature branched out into two distinct genres: visionary accounts of the experience of individual souls in the afterlife, and apocalyptic texts that interpret historical and contemporary events in the light of an impending judgment.[50]

Visionary travel to the other world is a core symbol in the literature of Merkabah mysticism, an esoteric movement (related to both apocalypticism and Gnosticism) which developed within rabbinic Judaism in Palestine and Babylonia. This literature extols the glory of the heavenly court and describes elaborate psychophysical and spiritual techniques for ascent (or, paradoxically, descent) through the seven spheres to the *Merkabah*, the divine throne-chariot.[51] The medieval Kabbalistic schools, a later phase of Jewish speculative mysticism, contemplated endlessly on the soul's exile, transmigration and return—a theme rendered especially poignant by the expulsion of Jews from Spain.[52] In later rabbinic literature, thanks to the influence of these diverse apocalyptic, Merkabah, and Kabbalistic traditions (and despite some hostility to the exotic teachings and practices they represent), the otherworld journey found favor as a way to embellish the legends of biblical prophets and patriarchs; Moses' vision of the promised land (Deut. 34) became, in medieval midrashic narratives, a full-fledged tour of heaven and hell.[53] The otherworld journey also survived—indeed, flourished—as a theme of popular Jewish storytelling, especially in the eighteenth-century Hasidic communities of Eastern Europe. Many examples can be found in the *Shivhei ha-Besht (In Praise of the Baal Shem Tov)*, a collection of Hasidic anecdotes, which begins with the assertion that "in earlier days when people revived after lying in a coma close to death, they used to tell about the awesome things they had seen in the upper world."[54]

Strange as it may seem, the Christian otherworld journey does not depend directly on the pattern of Christ's death, resurrection, and ascension. The early church taught that Christ died and rose again as the "first fruit" of a collective resurrection, rather than as the model for the individual soul's journey from the body at death; although believers might share in Christ's redemptive ascent, they could not imitate his descent as a divine mediator from heaven to earth. For an advance scout to the other world, one would have to look to earlier prophetic or apocalyptic seers; thus, we shall see that the Christian return-from-death story, like its Jewish counterpart, evolved from apocalyptic precursors into didactic tales about ordinary men and women who were sent back from the other world. In addition, among other influences on these narratives should be counted the indigenous folklore and pre-Christian myths of the European continent and the British Isles, including Celtic legends of travel to lands beneath the waves or beyond the mist, and Germanic accounts of Hel, Valhalla, and the perilous crossings between them.[55] To get an idea of the abundance of otherworld journeys in folklore, one has only to glance at Stith Thompson's *Motif Index of Folk-Literature*, which catalogues an extraordinary range of such tales.[56]

A wealth of otherworld journey lore can be found in Zoroastrian eschatological traditions, which are closely related to Judeo-Christian visions of life's end. The classic Zoroastrian return-from-death story is the Book of Arda Viraz, in which a Persian priest volunteers to take a narcotic and embark on an intelligence-gathering mission to the other world.[57] Viraz's report, like those of other seers, conforms to and confirms his inherited expectations. After a seven-day coma, in which his body is laid out like a corpse, he comes back to life and tells of seeing the Bridge of the Separator (where each soul meets its own conscience); the weighing of deeds; the place of the "mixed" (where those of neutral merit dwell); the heavenly stations of the stars, moon, and sun (where good thoughts, good words, and good deeds are welcomed); the radiant paradise of eternal life; the turbulent river swollen by tears of mourning; and the dark pits of hell, where the wicked huddle in despair.

In the Islamic world—following, in part, Judeo-Christian and Persian precedents—the otherworld journey has flourished as a much-loved way to represent Muhammad's privileged relation to God and his role as intercessor for the community. According to prophetic and devotional traditions, the Prophet was miraculously transported from Mecca to Jerusalem one night; from Jerusalem he ascended on a winged steed to visit the seven heavens (and, in some accounts, the fires of hell) in the company of the angel Gabriel.[58]

Some scholars have seen shamanic elements in this legend; in several versions, before his magical flight (also described as the mounting of a "ladder"—*mi'raj*—to the sky), Muhammad is visited by three angels who cut open his body and cleanse his internal organs.[59] There are, however, other features which tie the *mi'raj* legend to the traditions of prophetic monotheism and "book religion."[60] In the Qur'an, Muhammad's opponents are quoted as saying that they will not give him credence until he ascends into heaven and will not believe in his ascent until he brings down a book (Sura 17:92–95). The *mi'raj* stories may be construed as an attempt to answer this challenge: they show Muhammad being greeted at each of the heavenly gates by his forerunners (Adam, John the Baptist and Jesus, Joseph, Enoch, Aaron, Moses, and Abraham, according to Ibn Ishaq) and then rising above them to the divine throne. God greets Muhammad as "friend" (*wali*), accepts his plea for a reduction in the number of obligatory prayers, and sends him back to humanity as the first universal prophet.[61]

In addition to establishing the Prophet's credentials, the *mi'raj* accounts
provide instruction on what to expect at death. In Ibn Ishaq's retelling,
Muhammad says that the ladder on which he mounted to heaven was "that
to which the dying man looks when death approaches."[62] This idea is embellished in medieval eschatological treatises such as *The Precious Pearl*, according to which the soul at death is escorted by angels through the seven heavens
to the divine throne, where it receives a preliminary reckoning before returning to the grave to await the day of judgment.[63]

Although Muhammad's ascension, considered strictly, was a unique
privilege, it became common for religious writers to speak of devotional practices (from ordinary ritual prayer to the ecstatic invocations and dances of the
Sufi brotherhoods) as ways to accompany the Prophet on his journey to
heaven. The *mi'raj* was a favorite theme of Sufi poetry and art, beginning in
the ninth century with al-Bistami's description of his own meditative rapture.[64] Jalal al-Din Rumi, the thirteenth-century Sufi poet, declares that the
aim of spiritual life is to "die before you die" and, like Muhammad, to ascend
to that intimacy with God which he has withheld from angels and yet granted
to his servants and lovers.[65]

In these examples we have seen, briefly and from a remote height, a few
of the landmarks in the history of Western otherworld journey narration. If
we were to look for otherworld journey motifs in the religious traditions of
India and the Far East as well, we would encounter many of the same recurrent themes. These traditions also see death as a journey whose final goal is
the recovery of one's true nature, even if its immediate effect is a temporary
sojourn in paradises or hells or a return to existence in a new body; they agree,
moreover, that awareness of death is a precondition for wisdom and that it is
necessary to prepare—morally, spiritually, or imaginatively—if one is to die
well.

The Katha Upanishad, for example, retells an ancient Indian legend of
underworld descent as the basis for an edifying narrative about a young Brahman who descends to the abode of Yama, god of death, and brings back to
the land of the living knowledge of the fire-sacrifice and the meditative disciplines by which one can win release from the cycle of rebirth and redeath.[66]

In ancient China, Lao Tzu, the legendary founder of philosophical
Taoism, is said to have left his body inert and lifeless in order to go "for a
stroll at the origin of things";[67] among later Taoist sects an essential mark of
the holy man was the ability to take flight, fueled by alchemical elixirs or
special breathing methods, and wander freely through enchanted islands,
sacred mountains, or celestial spheres. "Ascended to Heaven at the height of
the day" was, according to Max Kaltenmark, the standard epithet for a Taoist
sage who had won the prize of immortality.[68]

Despite the Buddha's unwillingness to speculate about the afterlife, Buddhist literature teems with other worlds, from celestial paradises like the Pure
Land of Amitabha, with its bejeweled trees and fragrant streams, to fiery hells
where sinners are hammered on anvils and barbecued by grinning devils.[69]
There are many popular legends of *bodhisattvas* who fulfill their vow to save

all sentient beings by journeying to retrieve sinners from the deepest hells. In an early Mahayana tale, one of the Buddha's chief disciples, Maudgalyayana, visits the six realms of rebirth (the hells, and the abodes of hungry ghosts, animals, humans, titans, and gods) and returns to warn people of the sufferings to which we are bound by our deeds (*karma*).[70] The Chinese version of this tale, in which the hero (called Mogallana or Mulien) rescues his mother from her purgatorial discomforts in the other world, is celebrated in the yearly festival of the hungry ghosts.[71] The legend is known in Japan as well, where it complements ancient indigenous traditions such as the descent to the underworld of the Shinto creator gods Izanagi and Izanami, and reinforces shamanistic practices of visionary and mimetic journey to other worlds.[72] The same story is told in Tibet, where Buddhist eschatology, joined with local shamanic lore, has given rise to an elaborate literary tradition devoted to mapping the intermediate states (*bardos*) through which we pass in our illusory migrations through existence.[73] These *bardo* manuals—known to the West as *The Tibetan Book of the Dead*—are recited to the deceased in order to help them to recognize that the blinding lights and the peaceful and wrathful deities that they encounter are but projections of the mind's own intrinsic splendor. To realize this is to escape from the wheel of becoming and dying; failing that, the *bardo* manuals advise the deceased to take refuge in a tutelary deity and aim for an auspicious rebirth.

The *bardo* is an appropriate place to bring this brief survey to a close; although the Tibetan manuals are unsurpassed in the detail they provide about the other world, their purpose is to cut the journey short by calling attention to the sublime emptiness of its forms. It is tempting to wander further in these phantasmagoric realms, but enough has been said to indicate how pervasive in world literature is the theme of otherworld travel. In the next chapter, therefore, we will make our exit from the *bardo* of global motif-collecting, in order to become acquainted with some of the distinctive features of the return-from-death story in the literature of the medieval Christian West.

CHAPTER 2

Four Models of Christian Otherworld Journey Narration

The Otherworld Journey as Apocalypse: The Vision of St. Paul

THE PIONEER OF Christian otherworld journeying is St. Paul, who hinted in a letter to the church at Corinth that he had been privileged with a brief visit to heaven:

> I must boast; there is nothing to be gained by it, but I will go on to visions and revelations of the Lord. I know a man in Christ who fourteen years ago was caught up into the third heaven—whether in the body or out of the body I do not know, God knows. And I know that this man was caught up into Paradise—whether in the body or out of the body I do not know, God knows—and he heard things that cannot be told, which man may not utter. (2 Cor. 12:1–4).

Paul apparently struggled against the temptation to exult in this revelation, but his followers were under no such restraint; as early as the third century, a Greek text was circulating that purported to tell the whole story of his adventures in the other world. Eventually the text acquired a preface claiming that the narrative had been discovered along with a pair of shoes in a sealed marble box left behind, like a time capsule, by the apostle himself. Translated into Latin and vernacular languages, this Vision (or Apocalypse) of St. Paul enjoyed immense influence, dampened only slightly by St. Augustine's refusal to believe that the apostle would have disclosed the very secrets that he himself had deemed "unlawful to utter."[1]

The oldest versions of the Vision ignore Paul's own apparent uncertainty about the nature of his experience ("whether in the body or out of the body I do not know, God knows") and cast him as a prophetic seer in the tradition of Enoch and Elijah, who ascended bodily into heaven to receive God's commission and descended bodily into hell to win respite for souls in torment. Like the legends of Muhammad's ascension, the Vision confirms Paul's apostolic role; and like other Judeo-Christian apocalypses, it shows through the eyes of the visionary that the earth is on the verge of incineration in the fires of its own corruption.

For medieval readers, however, much of the Vision's glamour derived from its vivid depiction of the experiences that are in store for individuals at death and in the period before the final judgment. Although Paul himself does not die, he observes the departure of three souls from their bodies and witnesses their journeys after death: the soul of a just man exits his body in the company of shining angels who defend him against the hostile powers of the air and escort him to the heavenly court to be vindicated and welcomed by God; a wicked man is dragged roughly from his body by "angels without mercy," harassed by his animating spirit, claimed as a fellow traveler by the hostile powers, and consigned to torment in the outer darkness; a second wicked man, after spending seven days before his trial on a forced tour of the cosmos, faces conviction when his own guardian angel turns state's evidence, producing a manuscript record of his sins and bringing forward the souls of those he had murdered or betrayed.

The judicial assessment of deeds, beginning on the deathbed and consummated at the divine tribunal, became a regular feature of medieval Christian "art of dying" manuals and depictions of the other world. As in many other traditions, death provides the occasion for a dramatic unmasking, in which one's true character (often represented by the triad of "thoughts, words, and deeds") is externalized for all to see; this may take the form of a record or mirror of deeds, a weighing of the soul or its works, a confrontation between the evildoer and his or her victims, a public display of stolen objects, or a symbolic duel between the soul's good and evil impulses. Whatever its guise, the review of deeds is essentially an encounter with oneself; and I shall argue below that it is the most telling episode in the journey, providing a key for interpreting the imaginative laws at work in visions of the other world.

In the Vision of St. Paul, however, the severity of this postmortem judgment is balanced by the weight given to repentance. God overlooks the youthful sins of a certain man, asking to see a record covering only the past five years. If he had repented in this time, his previous transgressions would be erased. The threat of condemnation combined with the hope for forgiveness provides a double incentive toward righteousness, avoiding the extremes of despair and vain confidence. Similarly, medieval vision narratives and treatises on the "art of dying" juxtapose accusation and acquittal. If they seem inconsistent or unsystematic, that is because their purpose is to inspire efforts, not to explain the relative proportions of justice and mercy in God's plan. The chapters to come will show that it is characteristic for otherworld journey narratives to be didactic rather than theoretical in intent.

In the long versions of the Vision of St. Paul, the apostle turns from his clairvoyant inspection of deathbed and judgment scenes and embarks on a visit to paradise, the promised land, and the city of Christ, followed by an edifying tour of the regions of torment. The medieval redactors who abbreviated the Vision were interested primarily in Paul's visit to the realms of punishment; heaven is conspicuously absent from these abridgments, but the pains of hell are described with great relish. Sinners swing by their ears from flaming trees, revolve like Ixion on a fiery wheel, and stand immersed in an infernal river where their flesh is nibbled by monstrous creatures; those beyond hope suffer confinement in the dark pit "sealed with seven seals," which is opened momentarily for Paul so that he can savor its stench.[2] In case all this is not impressive enough, Paul is told, in words borrowed from Vergil's *Aeneid*, that "there are 144,000 pains in hell, and if there were 100 men speaking from the beginning of the world, each one of whom had 104 tongues, they could not number the pains of hell."[3]

Like the protagonists of medieval otherworld journey tales, Paul is charged with the task of reporting the grisly details of postmortem punishment for the sake of those who are still alive. As Theodore Silverstein has pointed out, however, the Vision of St. Paul is a transitional work.[4] Rather than describing the return from death of an ordinary monk or layman, it glorifies the otherworld journey of a divinely favored apostle, who successfully petitions God to arrange a Sabbath respite for the sufferers in hell. Among Judeo-Christian apocalypses the Vision of St. Paul was the foremost source of otherworld imagery for the Middle Ages, but these images would undergo revision in the light of new understandings of purgatory, intercession, and penance, and would take on different meanings in the service of new or reformed religious communities.

The Otherworld Journey as Miracle Story: The Dialogues of Gregory the Great

Moving beyond early Christian precedents, our next stop en route to the medieval other world is with Gregory the Great, the sixth-century pope and spiritual writer whose *Dialogues* helped to set the standards for medieval discussion of miracles and visions.[5] A collection of entertaining and edifying wonder-tales, the *Dialogues* attempt to demonstrate, in the face of epidemics, Lombard invasions, and schism, that a providential order underlies events and that the age of great saints and signs from heaven has not passed. The fourth and final book of the *Dialogues* is devoted to "last things"; here Gregory offers "proofs" of the soul's immortality and demonstrates—through an assortment of deathbed visions, ghostly apparitions, and eyewitness accounts of the other world—the reality of postmortem punishment and the efficacy of masses and pious works on behalf of the dead.

Of the forty-two anecdotes in book 4, three held a special fascination for medieval readers. The first concerns a hermit who revived from death and testified that he had been to hell, where he saw several powerful men dangling in fire. Just as he too was being dragged into the flames, an angel in a shining garment came to his rescue and sent him back to life with the words (echoed in several medieval visions): "leave, and consider carefully how you will live from now on." After his return to life, the hermit's fasts and vigils bore witness, Gregory tells us, that he had indeed seen the terrors of hell; this too would become a common formula for the transforming effects of an otherworld journey.[6]

A second memorable tale of return from death came to Gregory firsthand, from a prominent businessman named Stephen, who died while on a trip to Constantinople.[7] Stephen confessed to Gregory that he had never believed the stories about hell and punishment but that his brief visit to the infernal court had changed his mind. Fortunately for him, the judge sent him back, saying, "I ordered Stephen the blacksmith to be brought here, not this man." Stephen regained consciousness immediately, and his testimony was confirmed by the death, in that very hour, of a blacksmith of the same name. Although this story clearly belongs to the common stock of tales of death by mistaken identity, Gregory insists that such apparent mixups occur "not as an error, but as a warning."[8] Gregory here shows his genius for adapting such material to his own didactic purpose; without significantly changing the story, he introduces a providential element, thereby transferring it from the realm of folklore to that of religious instruction. His example would be followed closely by later generations of otherworld journey narrators.

The most influential of Gregory's anecdotes of return from death is the story of a soldier who died and revived, and whose visionary testimony sheds additional light on the destiny of Stephen the businessman. The reverberations of this account in medieval vision literature will be discussed in chapter 4 below; because it is such an important source, I translate it here in full:

Three years ago, as you know, this same Stephen died in the virulent plague which devastated this city [Rome], in which arrows were seen coming down from the sky and striking people dead. A certain soldier in this city of ours happened to be struck down. He was drawn out of his body and lay lifeless, but he soon returned [to life] and described what befell him. At that time there were many people experiencing these things. He said that there was a bridge, under which ran a black, gloomy river which breathed forth an intolerably foul-smelling vapor. But across the bridge there were delightful meadows carpeted with green grass and sweet-smelling flowers. The meadows seemed to be meeting places for people clothed in white. Such a pleasant odor filled the air that the sweet smell by itself was enough to satisfy [the hunger of] the inhabitants who were strolling there. In that place each one had his own separate dwelling, filled with magnificent light. A house of amazing capacity was being constructed there, apparently out of golden bricks, but he could not find out for whom it might be. On the bank of the river there were dwellings, some of which were contaminated by the foul vapor that rose up from the river, but others were not touched at all.

On the bridge there was a test. If any unjust person wished to cross, he slipped and fell into the dark and stinking water. But the just, who were not blocked by guilt, freely and easily made their way across to the region of delight. He revealed that he saw Peter, an elder of the ecclesiastical family, who died four years ago; he lay in the horrible slime underneath the bridge, weighed down by an enormous iron chain. When he asked why this should be, [the soldier] was given an answer that called to our minds exactly what we know of this man's deeds. He was told, "he suffers these things because whenever he was ordered to punish someone he used to inflict blows more out of a love of cruelty than out of obedience." No one who knew him is unaware that he behaved this way.

He also saw a certain pilgrim priest approach the bridge and cross it with as much self-command in his walk as there was sincerity in his life. On the same bridge, he claimed to have recognized that Stephen of whom we spoke before.[9] In his attempt to cross the bridge, Stephen's foot slipped, and the lower half of his body was now dangling off the bridge. Some hideous men came up from the river and grabbed him by the hips to pull him down. At the same time, some very splendid men dressed in white began to pull him up by the arms. While the struggle went on, with good spirits pulling him up and evil spirits dragging him down, the one who was watching all this was sent back to his body. So he never learned the outcome of the struggle.

What happened to Stephen can, however, be explained in terms of his life. For in him the evils of the flesh contended with the good work of almsgiving. Since he was dragged down by the hips and pulled up by the arms, it is plain to see that he loved almsgiving and yet did not refrain completely from the carnal vices that were dragging him down. Which side was victorious in that contest was concealed from our eyewitness, and is no more plain to us than to the one who saw it all and then came back to life. Still, it is certain that even though Stephen had been to hell and back, as we related above, he did not completely correct his life. Consequently, when he went out of his body many years later, he still had to face a life-and-death battle.[10]

Compressed into this brief vision story are several motifs that recur throughout medieval otherworld journey literature: the river of hell, the flowery meadows of paradise, the white-clothed throngs in heaven, the test-bridge, and, above all, the externalization of deeds. Gregory makes it plain that the vision should be understood symbolically: the real meaning of the house built with bricks of gold is that those who give alms generously are constructing their eternal abodes in heaven; and the houses blackened by foul vapors were prefabricated, he implies, by the unsavory deeds of those destined to dwell in them. It was thanks largely to this widely read account that the bridge—as the setting for a *psychomachia* or symbolic confrontation with deeds—became such a prominent feature of the medieval otherworld landscape.

The anecdotes in book 4 of Gregory's *Dialogues* mark a turning point in the history of Western otherworld journey narration. Even more than the Vision of St. Paul, Gregory's vision stories focus on the interim period between death and resurrection. This does not mean that apocalyptic eschatology had relaxed its grip on the imagination of sixth-century Christians;

Gregory speaks with urgency about the approach of Doomsday and suggests that otherworld visions are on the rise because the world to come is drawing near and mixing its light with the darkness of the present age.[11] In the *Dialogues*, however, Gregory is concerned with the eschatological crisis that begins with the hour of death; he seems to find more edification in contemplating the purgatorial or punitive torments that await the average sinner than in making apocalyptic predictions about the experiences that will befall the human race in its last days.[12]

Gregory also departs from the classic apocalyptic model of otherworld journey narration in that the visions he relates come from relatives, neighbors and fellow monks, rather than from remote biblical heroes. These are cautionary rather than dramatically revelatory tales; the protagonists are either sinners who revive only long enough to warn the rest of us about the penalties awaiting transgressors, or penitents mercifully sent back to amend their own lives. For this reason, Gregory's visionary anecdotes cannot lay claim to the prestige that attaches to pseudepigraphic works. But Gregory compensates for the absence of exalted credentials by offering corroborating details; almost like a psychical researcher, he interviews witnesses, provides character references, and sets each story in familiar locales that will inspire his audience's trust; wherever possible, he cites circumstantial evidence such as the confirmation of Stephen's vision by the death of Stephen the blacksmith. Indeed, it was partly through Gregory's influence that empirical verification became a hallmark of the medieval otherworld vision.

The Otherworld Journey as Conversion: The Vision of Drythelm

While Gregory could be described as father to the whole family of medieval Christian otherworld journey tales, his influence is especially marked in what I call the Drythelm line, a literary tradition that can be traced back to the Vision of Drythelm related by the eighth-century Anglo-Saxon monk and scholar Bede in his *Ecclesiastical History of the English People*.[13] As Bede informs us, Drythelm was a pious Northumbrian family man who died one evening after a severe illness but revived the next day at dawn, terrifying his mourners by sitting up abruptly on his deathbed. He related what he had seen in the other world to his wife, and later to a monk who repeated the story to Bede.

Though similar in many respects to the narratives we have already considered, the Vision of Drythelm is far more developed as a journey and gives a fuller account of otherworld topography, even foreshadowing the purgatorial landscapes of the twelfth and thirteenth centuries. It therefore serves well as an introduction to the medieval form of the otherworld vision. At the beginning of the story, Drythelm meets a man "of shining countenance and bright apparel" who escorts him to an enormous valley, one side of which roars with flames while the other rages with hail and snow.[14] Countless misshapen souls are tossed to and fro between fire and ice. Appearances suggest that this is hell, but Drythelm's guide explains that it is a place of temporary torments, reserved for deathbed penitents who can be released from their punishments by masses, prayers, alms, and fasts performed by the living on their behalf.

To reach the mouth of hell, the two travel through a land of darkness, in which Drythelm can make his way only by keeping his eyes fixed on the bright silhouette of his guide. Hell is a bottomless, stinking pit. From it leap tongues of fire (in diabolic parody of Pentecost, perhaps) on which damned souls are cast upward like sparks only to fall back again amidst mingled sounds of laughter and lament. Drythelm sees malign spirits dragging the unhappy souls of a priest, a layman, and a woman into the abyss. The demons threaten Drythelm with their tongs, but are put to flight by his guide, who appears just in time in the form of a bright star.

They travel southeast to a realm of clear light, where they encounter a vast wall. Suddenly they are on top of the wall, in a bright, flowery meadow. Here Drythelm meets "many companies of happy people" and supposes that he is in heaven, but learns that it is only an antechamber for the not quite perfect. As he approaches the kingdom of heaven, he hears sweet singing and enjoys a fragrance and light even more glorious than before. Despite his longing to remain, Drythelm is dispatched back to his body, with the promise that a life of vigilance will eventually win him a place among the blissful spirits. Upon revival, he tells his astonished wife:

> Do not be afraid, for I have truly risen from the death by which I was held fast, and have been permitted to live again among men; nevertheless, from now on I must live not according to my old habits, but in a much different manner.[15]

Accordingly, he distributes his property, retires to a Benedictine monastery, and takes up a life of austerity and devotion, fasting, and cold baths.

For Bede, the most impressive part of Drythelm's story is its ending; like Gregory, Bede holds that "it is a greater miracle to convert a sinner than to raise up a dead man."[16] And it is a greater miracle yet if the tale of a dead man's recovery and spiritual transformation changes the hearts of its hearers; these authors value the otherworld journey narrative primarily for its power as a model for conversion and its usefulness in advertising the cause of particular religious institutions and ideas. Whatever role Drythelm may have played in the development of the narrative, Bede's account of the vision can be read as a manifesto for Benedictine monasticism, ascetic discipline, and intercessory masses for the dead. The vision also reflects the eschatology of the Anglo-Saxon church of Bede's time; by intimating a purgatorial state distinct from hell, it departs from earlier Celtic Christian traditions and conforms to the orthodoxy of Rome.[17]

All of these features recommended the Vision of Drythelm to Anglo-

Saxon spiritual writers and homilists of the ninth to eleventh centuries, who faithfully retold or creatively embroidered the return-from-death stories related by Gregory and Bede and whose endorsement contributed to the success of visions of the Drythelm line. The full flowering of this tradition, however, occurred in the period from the tenth to the mid-thirteenth centuries, which saw both the development of long, almost novelistic accounts of journey to the beyond and back, and increasing mention of otherworld visions in chronicles, sermons, and books of *exempla* for preachers. During that time, the otherworld journey found favor with monastic and clerical authors as a way of expressing their views on penance, intercession, and religious vows. It also played a part in what Jacques Le Goff calls the "spatialization" of purgatory, which went hand in hand with standardization of the rites by which the living purged their faults, prepared for death, and petitioned for the welfare of their departed kin.[18]

Despite such changes in its social function and eschatological content, however, in many respects the return-from-death story remained the same, preserved by literary imitation, by the pious conservation of traditional forms of expression, and by the universality of its themes. Thus it is possible to make some generalizations about the Christian otherworld journey—to identify groups or types that cut across regional boundaries and persist throughout the long centuries that we loosely call the Middle Ages.

Part II of this book will pay special attention to a group of long narratives from the twelfth and thirteenth centuries that follow the Drythelm pattern of death, revival, and conversion. Among them are the visions of Adamnán, Alberic, the Boy William, Tundal, and the Knight Owen (St. Patrick's Purgatory). Although they depend on sources shared by all medieval otherworld journey narratives (the Bible, apocalypses, legends of martyrs and desert saints, Gregory's *Dialogues*, and classical works such as Vergil's *Aeneid* and Plutarch's *Moralia*), the narratives in this group display a remarkable similarity in their choice of which set phrases and images to borrow. Typically the visionary is told, after viewing purgatorial torments and mistaking them for the punishments of the damned, that there are far worse sights to come (Drythelm, Tundal, Owen); he sees souls tossed between fire and ice (Thespesius, Drythelm, Tundal) and rising like sparks from the pit of hell (Drythelm, Alberic, the Boy William, Tundal); he is temporarily deserted by his guide (Thespesius, Drythelm, the Boy William, Tundal); he finds paradise surrounded by or on top of a wall, which he surmounts without knowing how (Drythelm, Adamnán, Alberic, the Boy William, Tundal, Owen); at the end, after a brief taste of heavenly joys, he is compelled against his will to return to life (Drythelm, Tundal); and after he revives, his newly austere mode of life testifies to the authenticity of his vision (Drythelm, Alberic, and Tundal borrow Gregory's phrasing for this). In addition, the test-bridge, whose history will be discussed in chapter 4, recurs with many similarities in the visions of Adamnán, Alberic, Tundal, and Owen.

These and other parallels suggest the presence of a literary tradition that is at least partly deliberate in its conformities. Yet the "Drythelm line" is far from an exact designation. One cannot determine the sequence of literary transmission or discover its causal mechanism merely by arranging similar narratives in chronological order.[19] Nor would such a linear history of motifs do justice to the complexities of interpretation. Each text has a unique functional significance within its particular social milieu. Beyond that, it seems likely that at least some of these narratives reflect actual experience and as such cannot be reduced to a matter of mechanical literary dependence; I will have more to say in future chapters concerning the experiential basis of vision literature.

The Otherworld Journey as Pilgrimage: St. Patrick's Purgatory

The "spatialization" of purgatory is nowhere more evident than in the cycle of tales about a sacred site in Lough Derg, County Donegal, which achieved fame in the Middle Ages as a goal for pilgrims and a doorway to the other world. Here, according to legend, St. Patrick converted the pagan Irish by means of a graphic demonstration of the pains of the damned and the joys of the blessed.

Located in a cave or cavelike cell on a barren archipelago in the mysterious red waters of Lough Derg, far in the northwest of Ireland, this holy site was hospitable to pagan and Christian Celtic traditions that placed the realm of the dead in the west, beneath the waves, beyond the mist, or on a remote island. There are traces of an early Celtic monastic settlement and hints of a more ancient pre-Christian past. By the twelfth century, however, the sacred places of Lough Derg had come under the control of a community of Augustinian canons regular, who administered the rites of entry and departure.[20] Thousands of pilgrims traveled to Lough Derg to be locked inside the Purgatory, where they might see extraordinary visions extending their pilgrimage into the other world. Those who survived this ordeal were said to be exempt from the pains of purgatory after death, and they returned to their parishes and monasteries with vivid stories of the terrors and wonders to be found on the other side of life's threshold.

Despite several attempts to dismantle the site, the Purgatory has a nearly continuous history up to the present day; since the final destruction of the cave in the eighteenth century, however, it has become a setting for penitential exercises rather than otherworldly excursions. Today, St. Patrick's Purgatory draws close to fifteen thousand pilgrims and tourists each year, having become, according to Victor and Edith Turner, "a kind of national totemic center."[21]

During the period we are considering, the journey to St. Patrick's Purgatory received its greatest publicity in England and on the Continent, where hearsay accounts of the pilgrimage were amplified and transformed into works of didactic literature in the tradition of Gregory's *Dialogues* and the Vision of Drythelm. In this form, the Purgatory legend played a major role in the development of medieval conceptions of the otherworld journey; I will therefore conclude this chapter by examining it in detail.

The most famous account of this pilgrimage is the *Treatise on the Purgatory of St. Patrick*, relating the vision of the Knight Owen. Composed near the end of the twelfth century by an English Cistercian monk who calls himself H. of Sawtry, it was translated into nearly every European vernacular language, set to verse, and retold in chronicles, saints' lives, and sermons.[22] The *Treatise* prospered because of its unique combination of didactic and popular appeal: it was at once a romantic tale of knightly adventure and a cautionary tale destined to be read from the pulpit; in addition, it rode in on the wave of enthusiasm for St. Patrick that followed the "discovery" of his relics and their solemn translation to Downpatrick in 1186.[23] Although it was written with a monastic audience in mind, the story of Owen's visit to Lough Derg became, during the thirteenth century, a vehicle for lay religious instruction, gleefully employed by the preaching friars, who specialized in evoking dread of purgatory.[24]

The apparently inexhaustible subject of travel to the other world by way of St. Patrick's Purgatory was also treated in countless letters, diaries, and poems by various other pilgrims to Lough Derg, both fictional and historical.[25] Not surprisingly, the legend extended its influence far beyond the Middle Ages—Ariosto mentioned the Purgatory in *Orlando Furioso*, and Shakespeare alluded to it by having Hamlet say, "Yes, by Saint Patrick ... Touching this vision here, / It is an honest ghost, that let me tell you."[26] Rabelais treated it in a satiric vein, and Erasmus described it as a distant echo of the cave of Trophonius. In seventeenth-century Spain, Montalvan retold the H. of Sawtry account in his *Vida y Purgatorio de S. Patricio*, and Calderón turned it into a play (*El Purgatorio de San Patricio*), which so affected Shelley that he saw a strange vision after reading it. Robert Southey made the legend the subject of his ballad, "Sir Owen"; as late as 1844, Thomas Wright felt entitled to ask, "who has not heard of St. Patrick's Purgatory?"[27]

The widespread influence of the *Treatise* makes it worth our while to review its content.[28] Its most striking feature is the way it links terrestrial to extraterrestrial topography: the protagonist steps through a physical doorway into the other world; he insists that his was not the visionary experience of an ecstatic.[29] This peculiar detail seems to set the Purgatory legend apart from other Christian tales of rapture and return-from-death visions. H. of Sawtry says in a preface, however, that his account of Owen's journey simply follows the precedent of Gregory's *Dialogues*, and later commentators rarely discriminate between the testimony of the Knight Owen and that of the visionaries. Despite its idiosyncrasies, the *Treatise* can be read as a typical medieval vision story.

Like the visions of Drythelm, Tundal, and others, the *Treatise* is essentially a conversion narrative, in which the hero is a sinner who changes his way of life after a visit to the other world. The Knight Owen, a crusader under King Stephen (1134–54), returns to his native Ireland after a successful campaign and is suddenly seized with chagrin for having devoted his life "to violence and plundering, and, what he regretted more, the desecration of churches and theft of ecclesiastical property. . ."[30]

To repair his rupture with God and society, Owen has only to submit to the machinery of the twelfth-century penitential system, with its pre-scribed tariffs and austerities. For crimes like Owen's that threatened the social order, pilgrimage would be considered an appropriate punishment. A form of banishment, the obligatory pilgrimage temporarily rid society of a menace who, ideally, came back reformed.[31]

Not content to follow the routine, however, Owen tells his bishop, "Since, as you assert, I have offended my maker so greatly, I will assume a penance more severe than all other punishments. . . . I wish to go down into the Purgatory of St. Patrick."[32]

Although the prior and canons in charge of the Purgatory attempt to dissuade him, Owen keeps his resolve, and after a fifteen-day retreat he has himself locked into the cave for the night. As is common in visionary topo-graphies, this chamber, which appears small from outside, turns out to be cavernous within. Tentatively, Owen makes his way through a long, dark passageway, following a distant glimmer of light which finally brings him to a vast open cloister. Here he meets twelve men clothed in white and recently shaven, who look like monks. Like the canons on the earthly side of the threshold, these mysterious figures play an initiatory role: they warn Owen of the perils to come and instruct him to use the name of Jesus as a protective prayer; then they abandon him to his fate. The instant they leave, a cataclys-mic uproar shakes the ground; it sounds as though the entire human and ani-mal kingdoms were screaming in unison. Only by invoking the divine name does Owen preserve his sanity. He is then carried off on a tour of infernal sightseeing.

Owen visits four fields of punishment where, as in earlier visionary and apocalyptic accounts, sinners are devoured by dragons, set upon by serpents and toads, fixed to the ground with red-hot nails, baked in furnaces, immersed in boiling cauldrons, and hooked to a flaming version of Ixion's wheel.[33] Mov-ing south, Owen and his demonic guides come upon a well from which naked bodies shoot upward like sparks and then fall back into the sulphurous flames. "This is the mouth of hell," the demons say, and they cast Owen in. He falls endlessly, for this well is none other than the realm of utterly lost souls, the bottomless pit described in Rev. 20:1–3 and featured in the visions of St. Paul, Drythelm, and Alberic. No longer a mere spectator, Owen descends into a state of deadly oblivion, forgetting to call on the name of Jesus. At the last minute, however, a divine intervention causes Owen to remember the invo-cation, and he is lifted to safety on a tongue of flame.

From the well, the party travels to a river of fire and sulphur, spanned by a bridge which Owen must cross. If he should fall off, he will land in the clutches of demons and be dragged down to hell. The bridge has three great shortcomings: it is too slippery to stand on, it is too narrow to gain a foothold on it, and it rises to a vertiginous height. As Owen ventures to cross, however, he finds the bridge widening at every step, until there is enough room for two carriages to pass. Readers familiar with Western otherworld journey traditions will recognize that this bridge is at once test and testimony; Owen can make it across only because his harrowing tour through the realms of punishment has already cleansed him of his sins. He easily attains the other shore, leaving the demons shrieking in impotent rage.

His ordeals behind him, Owen walks up to a jeweled gate, which opens in welcome, leading him to a land of light more dazzling than the sun, where he meets a procession of clergy carrying crosses, banners, candles, and golden palm branches, singing an unearthly harmony. Two archbishops take Owen on a tour of the delightful meadows adorned with flowers, fruit, grass, and trees, "on whose fragrance he felt he could subsist forever." There is no night, no darkness, no heat, no cold—negatives are employed where superlatives are inadequate to describe fully the delights of this region.[34] Yet this is only the earthly paradise, an intermediate realm where those who have been purified by purgatorial suffering await God's call to ascend to heaven. Owen's guides remind him that although everyone must undergo purgatorial torments after death, the duration and severity of the punishment can be lessened by the masses, prayers, and alms of the living. Only those confined in the well are beyond help. Thus the *Treatise*, like the otherworld visions related by Gregory and his successors, serves to promote not only private acts of penance and spiritual reform, but also liturgical practices that link the living with the souls of their departed kin."

The archbishops conduct Owen to the top of a mountain and bid him look up at the sky, which is the color of gold burning in a furnace. Here, at the entrance to the heavenly paradise, Owen receives his first taste of heavenly food. A flame comes down from heaven and irradiates each person.

> It descended on the head of the knight and entered him just as it entered the others. Then he felt such a sweet sense of delight in his body and his heart that he could scarcely tell, for the delight of the sweetness, whether he was living or dead; but the time passed in an instant.[36]

Just when Owen is thinking that he wants to stay there forever, his guides tell him it is time to go back. If he lives well, they promise, he will return to this place when he dies. If not, he knows what is in store for him. Owen is afraid that if he returns to earth he will relapse into his old ways. Against his will, they lead him through the gate and close it after him: having begun his journey by being locked into the Purgatory, Owen ends it by being locked out of heaven.

Nothing remains for Owen but to go back the way he came. Fortunately, his ordeal has purified him; as he retraces his steps, the demons flee in dismay. Back at the starting point, Owen meets the twelve men who initiated his journey. They joyfully give him absolution and urge him to hurry to the doorway, which he reaches at dawn, just in time to be set free by the canons. After another fifteen-day retreat in the church, he takes a cross on his shoulder and sets out for Jerusalem, now a pilgrim rather than a crusader. Upon his return, he asks the king for permission to take up the religious life and is assigned to serve as interpreter for the Cistercian monk Gilbert of Louth on his mission to found a new abbey in Ireland. An eager recruit, Owen replies, "It is a joy to serve monks of the Cistercian order, and you should welcome them to your land since I own that in the other world I saw no others in such great glory as I saw them."[37]

During their stay in Ireland together, Owen confides his experiences in the Purgatory to Gilbert. Once Gilbert returns to England to become abbot of Basingwerk, he cannot keep so edifying a story to himself. He spreads the word before large audiences, including the monk of Sawtry, who finally commits it to writing. Owen stays in Ireland, not suspecting his imminent rise to fame. This conforms to the principle set forth by Gregory in the first book of his *Dialogues*: for his own merit the visionary should wish to conceal his experience, but for the sake of others the story should be told. This twofold convention—the reticence of the visionary and the didactic purpose of the narrative—is a standard feature of medieval visions and one which we will have reason to compare to modern accounts.

C. M. van der Zanden has shown that the *Treatise* is in part a Cistercian manifesto, depicting the white monks as the best qualified to inherit St. Patrick's task of taming Ireland. As van der Zanden points out, the twelve men in white, whom other scholars have compared to the twelve apostles or the *doucepers* of the Charlemagne legend, look very much like Cistercians.[38] When Owen returns from the Purgatory, he is convinced of the Cistercians' superior rank in heaven; he displays his rehabilitation by becoming a humble servant for the Cistercian mission to Ireland. H. of Sawtry also makes a point of showing the king's support for the Cistercian order.

This is not the first case in which Cistercian bias has shaped the content of an otherworld journey narrative; in fact, the Cistercians were especially sensitive to the propaganda value of an otherworld journey and contributed more to this genre than did any other religious order. Like Gregory and Bede, they turned the otherworld journey story into a conversion narrative, putting great emphasis on the transformation of the visionary after his return from death. During the twelfth and early thirteenth centuries, a period of intense controversy over competing vows and observances, they portrayed this transformation in an especially partisan light.[39] The visions of Gunthelm and the Monk of Melrose and the Cistercian stories collected during the early thirteenth century by Peter of Cornwall offer visionary evidence for the favored position of Cistercians in heaven and for their especially intimate relation to the Virgin Mary.

Another remarkable feature of the story of Owen, as of all accounts of St. Patrick's Purgatory, Cistercian or otherwise, is the way in which it dramatizes one of the central religious conceptions of the Middle Ages: the idea that life is a pilgrimage. It is well known that the high Middle Ages witnessed a virtual craze for pilgrimage discourse. After the lull in the barbarian inva-

sions of the ninth and tenth centuries, travel became somewhat less dangerous, and interest in the symbolic value of pilgrimage kept pace with the
increasing number of pilgrims on the road. This is not to say that pilgrimage
as a metaphor was a medieval invention. The early Fathers often spoke of
the church as a pilgrim or exile in the world, embarked on a collective journey
through the *saeculum* to the day of judgment.[40] In the high Middle Ages,
however, pilgrimage became a symbol for the individual's journey through
life and death. Romance and legend celebrated the solitary seeker: the desert
hermit, the Irish seafaring saint, the knight on a quest, the courtly lover, the
traveling penitent.[41]

The Knight Owen is just such a solitary hero. The *Treatise* underlines
his loneliness. First, the canons lead him to the door, lock him inside, and
desert him. Then he is met by a reception committee of sorts, but they can
only point the way and warn of its dangers; they cannot accompany him. A
brief episode of desertion by the guide is a common feature of medieval
visions, but Owen is one of the few who must travel the whole distance
unescorted.

The purgatorial teaching of the *Treatise* also tends toward individualism.
Each person's progress through the regions of the other world is governed by
a separate timetable:

> No one who is in torment knows how long he will stay there. . . . And when
> they come to this land, they do not know how long they are to remain. . . .
> Here, as you can see, we dwell in great peace and joy, but after a certain period
> determined by God, each one of us will go beyond. Daily the number of our
> society increases and daily it decreases. For just as some come to us daily from
> the torments, having been purged, so some of us ascend from the earthly par-
> adise to the heavenly paradise.[42]

Inevitably, Christian pilgrimage came to be identified with the ultimate
passage of death. Comparison of death with pilgrimage is found in pilgrim
narratives with no explicit otherworld content as well as in vision narratives
that do not concern actual travel. The St. Patrick's Purgatory accounts, which
combine pilgrimage with otherworld vision, merely enlarge upon an already
natural association. The usual pilgrim's goal is the tomb of a martyr or saint
or the shrine that houses holy relics: in short, a visit to the venerated dead.
In preparation for this journey, the pilgrim is instructed to fast, keep vigils,
and put on special clothing (tunic, pouch, and staff) that separates him or her
from ordinary life. He or she is now, in effect, "dead to the world."

During the period we are considering, moreover, a common purpose of
pilgrimage was to work off one's debt of purgatorial suffering. In the drama
of pilgrimage, with its real and mimetic ordeals, the penitent played the part
of a soul in purgatory; and if he or she died before fulfilling the vow, under-
studies could step in: friends or relatives could perform the pilgrimage as
proxies. In a number of medieval ghost stories, the dead return to berate their
families for shirking the obligation to help one's kin in purgatory.[43] Thus, as

Victor Turner notes, "if pilgrims are companions to the dead, it is to the dead of the church suffering; and if pilgrims are equivalent to the dead, it is to the dead in Purgatory."[44]

Those who entered St. Patrick's Purgatory followed an initiatory routine that amounted to a ritual imitation of death. Antonio Mannini, who visited the Purgatory in 1411, describes it thus in a letter he wrote to a friend soon after his experience:

> Having placed me flat on my back as though I were dead, he closed my eyes and commanded me not to open them until the office was over; he crossed my hands upon my breast, and having said over me the vigil and all the Office of the Dead, he signed me three times with holy water, with the same prayers and solemnity as is used for the dead, neither more nor less. Then he opened my eyes with his own hands, put the cross in my right hand, and made me stand up.[45]

Given the hazards of travel in the Middle Ages, there were practical as well as symbolic reasons to equate preparation for pilgrimage with preparation for death. The author of a sermon for one of the feasts of St. James advises pilgrims to Compostela to settle their affairs before they set out:

> If one is legitimately intent on reaching the threshold of St. James, then before the journey begins he forgives those who have injured him, confesses and makes amends for every encroachment of which his neighbors or his own conscience accuse him, obtains permission from his parish priest, his lord, his spouse, or anyone else to whom he is obligated; if he can, he gives back whatever is not rightfully his, finds a peaceful solution for the conflicts that are within his control, accepts appropriate penance, puts his house in good order, and on the advice of his parish priests, distributes his property, setting aside a certain amount for alms in the event of death . . .[46]

The pilgrim is singularly well prepared to travel the road to heaven because the perils of his or her earthly journey— treacherous bridges, flooded rivers, robbers, tariffs—have trained him or her to withstand the trials that must be faced after death. In the twelfth-century Vision of Tundal, the only soul who crosses the test-bridge with ease is a priest who holds a palm branch, signifying that in life he had gone on pilgrimage to Jerusalem; this reprises the episode quoted above from Gregory's account of the vision of a soldier in Rome. The pilgrim's letters of permission and safe conduct also have their otherworld counterparts: the Knight Owen relies on the name of Jesus as a kind of password to protect him from demonic assaults and to help him cross the test- bridge; and among the souvenirs of later visitors to St. Patrick's Purgatory, one finds official passports for travel to Lough Derg along with protective formulas, usually "Lord Jesus Christ, son of the Living God, have mercy upon me a sinner," to secure safe passage once they have entered the Purgatory cave.[47]

It was common for spiritual writers to compress pilgrimage and otherworld journey into a single, densely packed image, which would symbolize the ordeals encountered on the soul's itinerary through life. As we have seen,

Gregory reads the perilous crossing in moral terms, interpreting Stephen's struggle on the test-bridge as a conflict of virtues and vices; and the author of the pilgrimage sermon quoted above compares the arduous journey to Compostela to the narrow road that leads to life:

> The pilgrim's path is rich in goodness, but it is also a difficult strait. For strait is the way that leads man to life, and wide and broad is the way that leads to death. The pilgrim's path goes directly forward, for it is the departure from vices, the mortification of the flesh, the disclosure of virtues, the absolution of sinners, the fulfillment of penitence, the way of the just, the delight of the saints; it is faith in the resurrection and reward of the blessed; it is distancing from hell and drawing near to heaven.[48]

Monastic authors of the Middle Ages were adept at allegorizing both pilgrimage and otherworld journey in order to express their conviction that the monk who stays in his monastery is in fact the celestial pilgrim par excellence. St. Bernard, who preached the Second Crusade, nonetheless told his monks, "Jerusalem is your cell," and Catherine of Siena urged a Carthusian monk who had been denied permission to visit St. Patrick's Purgatory to seek its finer analogue in spiritual exercises.[49]

A vivid example of the allegorical treatment of travel can be found in the Vision of Gunthelm, a twelfth-century Cistercian tale designed to show that monastic vows are more sacred and binding than the vocations of crusader or pilgrim. Gunthelm, a worldly crusader-knight like Owen, repents of his sins and vows to make a penitential pilgrimage to Jerusalem. He consults a Cistercian abbot who persuades him to join the white monks instead. Although he is a dedicated novice at first, Gunthelm has second thoughts about breaking his pilgrimage vow and makes secret plans to depart for Jerusalem. That night a demon, in the guise of a monkey, appears at his bed and shakes him senseless. For three days, while his body lies near death, Gunthelm visits heaven and hell under the guidance of the archangel Raphael and St. Benedict (who better to teach him the value of monastic stability?). Benedict brings the frightened novice before the Virgin, who asks him to make up his mind whether he will keep his promise to stay in her house and serve her. Gunthelm renews his vow before the altar, and when he returns to life his wanderlust is entirely quenched.

In another account, also of Cistercian authorship but apparently oriented toward lay piety, the otherworld journey is offered as consolation to a peasant who cannot afford the expense of an earthly pilgrimage. Thurkill, an impoverished Essex farmer, is so hospitable to pilgrims and so devoted to St. James that his patron favors him with an aerial version of the pilgrimage to Compostela. Thurkill meets St. James in a basilica without walls which is both a heavenly replica of the shrine at Compostela and a gathering place for the dead; he also sees the test-bridge, the weighing of souls, the theater of hell, the Mount of Joy, and other spectacles, which he describes very much in the style of a pilgrim diary.

The Vision of Thurkill strongly suggests that otherworld journey nar-

ratives resemble pilgrimage narratives in content because they resemble pilgrimage in social form and function. The pilgrim who visits Canterbury or
Calvary recreates and participates in events of cultural significance—as do all
pilgrims in every period and society. So, too, the visit of a solitary knight to
St. Patrick's Purgatory is a far from isolated affair; he explores a landscape
whose contours are culturally formed. Imaginative rehearsal enables pilgrim
and visionary alike to learn the roles they must play in order to live and die
meaningfully.

The dual theme of pilgrimage–otherworld journey retained its orienting
function when it passed from the literature of monastic propaganda and popular homily into the literature of spiritual allegory; this long-lived tradition
reaches from *The Divine Comedy* to *Pilgrim's Progress* and still has its occa-
sional representatives among modern works of symbolic fiction (René Dau-
mal's *Mount Analogue* comes to mind). St. Patrick's Purgatory stands apart,
perhaps, for the peculiar way in which it links inner and outer pilgrimage.
Nonetheless, it seems to share a common purpose with these other and bet-
ter-known accounts of spiritualized outer journeying or visualized inner
travel: the overcoming of moral and spiritual dislocation. The protagonist
who has lost his way in the "wilderness" or "dark wood" of an aimless life
recovers his path by an imaginative pilgrimage through the culturally shaped
regions of the other world. As a symbolic guidebook, the legend of St.
Patrick's Purgatory belongs to an immense family of visionary and spiritual
writings that seek to locate humanity in a divinely and socially sanctioned
cosmic hierarchy and to map the perilous journey through life and death.

The four narratives considered in this chapter correspond roughly to
four phases in the development of the Christian otherworld journey. The
Vision of St. Paul brings apocalyptic narrative within the compass of the
deathbed vision; the miracle tales of Gregory the Great celebrate experiences
of ordinary folk sent back to life; the Vision of Drythelm expands the return-
from-death story into a full-blown visionary journey, resuming some apocalyptic themes; and the Vision of the Knight Owen, which represents the most
fully realized form of the otherworld journey, gives us a sense of the narrative
complexities attained by this genre during its peak years in the high Middle
Ages.

PART II

MEDIEVAL CHRISTIAN RETURN-FROM-DEATH STORIES: A THEMATIC TREATMENT

CHAPTER 3

The Other World: Medieval Itineraries

Exit from the Body

ENOCH, ST. PAUL, and the pilgrims to St. Patrick's Purgatory may have visited the other world while still in the flesh, but the typical medieval traveler to heaven and hell finds it necessary first to discard his or her mortal clothing. The otherworld journey narrative usually begins by describing how the soul is severed from the body before departing for the next world. Through illness or injury, ecstasy or dreaming, the tie to the body is loosened. Whether extracted by an angel or demon or departing of its own accord, the soul exits through the gateway of the mouth and sets out for the other world. After a symbolic time lapse—usually one night ("from sunset to cockcrow") or three days—the soul returns to reanimate its lifeless body.[1]

In the seventh-century Vision of Barontus, the story is told from two viewpoints: that of the monks who hover solicitously around the inert body, and that of Barontus as he contemplates his soul's labors from within. Struck down by a fever after divine office, Barontus is found writhing on the floor, gesturing at his throat. A colleague interprets this frenzy as an incursion of malign spirits and rushes to disinfect the room with holy water. Suddenly an unseen force chokes Barontus into unconsciousness. From three in the morning until vespers, the monks chant and pray for their brother's recovery. At vespers they observe the signs of death and begin to pray instead for his heavenly welfare. When the cock crows, however, Barontus revives, sits up, and praises God.

Barontus tells the astonished mourners what befell him. First, two loathsome demons accosted him, grappled him by the throat (as his frantic pan-

tomime suggested), and dragged him toward hell. At three in the morning—
the moment when his community began to pray for him—the archangel
Raphael flew to his defense and contended with the demons for jurisdiction
over his soul. Finally, at vespers, the archangel declared, "I will take this soul
[*animam*] with me before the tribunal of the eternal judge, but will leave his
spirit [*spiritum*] here in the body."[2] Thus, like the modern near-death experiencer, Barontus entered a comatose state in which vital signs were absent,
but resuscitation was still possible; though he appeared dead, the thread of
life was sustained by an imperceptible "spirit" (understood here as an animating principle, akin, as its etymology suggests, to "breath"). Similarly, the
thirteenth-century visionary Thurkill retained a connection to his lifeless
body through the breath: whenever his soul coughed in the other world, his
body coughed on earth.

   At the moment of death (or near-death), Barontus felt himself rent asun-
der: "Raphael touched my throat and I, wretched, suddenly sensed my soul
torn out of my body."[3] It is not clear, however, whether this suffering was
caused by his illness, by the moral faults that made him susceptible to
demonic attack, or by the intrinsically violent character of death.

   To the question raised by this ambiguous episode—is death a friend or
an enemy?—Christian thinkers have advanced no single answer. A survey
would show that Christian responses to the prospect of death have covered
the spectrum from philosophical conceits about the natural immortality of the
soul to the view that body and soul are intrinsically united and that death is
therefore an unmitigated calamity.[4] One rarely encounters either of these
extreme viewpoints in its pure form; in visionary accounts of the soul's exit
from the body, they are often mixed indiscriminately, without regard for theoretical coherence. Spiritual and didactic writers make a virtue of such inconsistencies by speaking of two deaths: the pleasant death of the saint, who is
as glad as any Platonist to win release from the body and travel to his or her
celestial home, and the painful death of the wicked, whose punishments begin
with the agony of separation from the body and are consummated in spiritual
and "corporeal" torments after death. For the third class of souls, neither
saints nor mortal sinners, death has a double face, promising both suffering
and bliss.

   The literary sources for the medieval picture of the exit from the body
can be found in apocalyptic literature; apocryphal accounts of the deaths of
biblical figures such as Adam, Abraham, Moses, and the Virgin Mary; and
legends of the lives and deaths of the desert fathers.[5] Like the literature of
martyrdom, these narratives celebrate the victorious death (or victory over
death) of the religious hero. In some cases, following a tradition that origi-
nated in the early Christian communities of Egypt and Syria, this is contrasted with the unsavory death of the sinner. Thus, as Theodore Silverstein
notes, the Vision of St. Paul (especially in its Syriac version) details "the allur-
ing manner in which the psychopomps remove the soul of the good . . . and
the violence with which the wicked soul is seized."[6] Echoes of this idea recur
in countless later works of eschatology and religious instruction. Its popularity

as a cautionary theme is understandable; there can hardly be a more effective way to dramatize the contrast between the fate of the righteous and that of the reprobate than to translate the spectacle of postmortem reckoning from the celestial court to the familiar setting of the deathbed.

The tradition from which the two deaths theme derives is complex. In the apocrypha and pseudepigrapha, the patriarchs are often portrayed as unwilling to die, despite their expectation of a painless death and a heavenly reward. In the Testament of Abraham, for example, when God commissions the archangel Michael to give the patriarch polite advance notice of his death, Abraham refuses to hand over his soul. As if to buy time, he requests a tour of the universe, but the excursion ends all too soon, with Abraham still unprepared to relinquish his flesh. As a last resort, God sends Death, disguising him as an archangel in order to spare Abraham the sight of his terrible countenance. In this encounter, Abraham exhibits a full range of human reactions to death: fear, curiosity, enervation, rebellion—everything but acceptance. Even after Death discloses his true form, Abraham continues to resist his fate. But a trick decides the issue: when Abraham accepts a friendly embrace, his soul adheres to the hand of Death.[7]

The motif of reluctance to die might be seen as the vestige of a typically Egyptian or Semitic outlook which cannot imagine life except in an embodied form. But it appears even in early monastic writings that, in other respects, are marked by affinity to Cynic and Stoic ideals of heroic detachment from the demands of the flesh, and by a seemingly dualistic understanding of the relationship between body and soul.[8] One account in the *Lives of the Fathers* tells of a desert monk granted the vision of the last hours of a sinner and a saint. He saw that even a holy pilgrim might resist death:

> And when it came time for him to fall asleep, the brother [who was watching] saw Michael and Gabriel coming down for his soul. One sat at his right and the other at his left and they asked his soul to come forth. But it did not go out, as though he were unwilling to leave behind his own body. Gabriel said to Michael: Take this soul now so that we might go. Michael answered him: We have been commanded by the Lord to expel [this soul] without pain, therefore we cannot tear it out with force. Michael then cried out in a loud voice saying: Lord, what is your will for this soul seeing that it does not yield to us and depart? But a voice came to him: Behold I send David with his cithara and the whole chorus that sings to God in Jerusalem, so that when he hears the psalm in their voice he will come forth. And when they all came down around that soul singing hymns, the soul came forth into the hands of Michael and was carried up with joy.[9]

This story was retold at the turn of the tenth century by Aelfric, the Anglo-Saxon homilist, and appears in the *Exempla* of Jacques de Vitry.[10] For the most part, however, medieval renditions of the two deaths theme treat resistance to death as a sign of guilt. Thus, in an influential Latin homily which takes the two deaths theme from the Vision of St. Paul and Egyptian sources, a visionary witnesses the death of an unjust man whose soul cowers in his mouth, afraid to exit because it can see demons waiting to ensnare

it.[11]The extraction of the good soul is by contrast a gentle, pleasantly lubri-
cated process. Once the element of unwillingness to die has dropped out, in
fact, the death of the just man is so free of conflict as to be devoid of dramatic
interest, and it is excluded from all but one version of the homily. Silverstein
shows that the history of the Vision of St. Paul texts reveals the same preference for description of the unjust soul's departure from the body. This is
but one instance of the way in which vision narratives are shaped by a concern for dramatic appeal.

In otherworld journey literature, only those destined for hell, like Tundal, cling to life. For the just, separation from the body frees the soul from its
cares. The monk of Wenlock, whose vision was narrated by St. Boniface in
the early eighth century, reports that his departure from the body was like
the lifting of a veil. From his liberated vantage point, he saw clearly that his
body was alien to his spirit:

> His own body, while he was outside it, was so exceedingly horrid to him that
> in all those visions he saw nothing so hateful, nothing so contemptible, noth-
> ing except for the demons and the malodorous fire, that exuded such a dreadful
> stench as his own body.[12]

Similarly, the young recluse whose otherworld journey is retold by Caesarius
of Heisterbach describes with disgust the uninviting spectacle of her body
lying on the floor, bloodless and pallid.[13] Of course, attitudes toward the flesh
vary according to context: hagiographic narratives extol the fragrance and
incorruption of the saint's body after death; late medieval *memento mori*
tracts dwell on the repulsiveness of the corpse as it moulders in the tomb.
The human body commands respect in the Christian tradition because of the
Incarnation, and in medieval piety tender feelings toward the human Jesus,
as an infant in swaddling or suffering on the cross, would seem to call for a
general truce in the hostilities between body and soul. But the need to struggle against captivity to sensual urges and vicious habits was more pressing to
many Christian thinkers than any other concern; and it was this need that led
them to depict the body in such a bad light in works that have a moral or
spiritual aim.

Belief that body and soul are inveterate enemies finds its most vivid
expression in a series of poems that detach the two deaths theme from its
original visionary context and cast it in the form of an address to the body by
the condemned soul or a debate between the two. The earliest examples are
the Old English *Soul's Address to the Body*, the late-twelfth-century Latin
poem known as the Royal Debate, and the early-thirteenth-century *Dialogus
inter corpus et animam*, which was the basis for several popular Middle
English poems.[14]

In *The Departing Soul's Address to the Body*, the soul stands outside the
body, weeping. But the lament soon turns to reproach. Lifelong pursuit of
wealth, status, and pleasure has brought the body no further than the grave,
"a doorless house,/ where worms possess/ all that was most honoured/ of the

foul dead carcase."[15] Repeating the famous *ubi sunt* formula ("where now are all your former glories?"), the soul blames the body for their mutual downfall:

> Alas! thy foul will
> hath wrought my woe.
> Thou foul food for worms,
> why hast thou deceived me?
> For thy wicked sin
> I shall now in hell
> suffer there a wretched time,
> all for thy wicked life;
> yet I will flee thee
> and thy dreary fate.[16]

In the debate poems, the body chides the soul for attempting to pass the buck:

> Where was I, by wood or way,
> Where sat, stood, or did aught amiss,
> But thine eye was on me aye?
> Well thou knowst that sooth it is.
> Whither went I, up or down,
> And did not bear thee on my back?
> Under thy rein, from town to town,
> Still thou hadst me for thy hack,
> But thou it in my ear didst rown,
> Never thing I did or spak;
> This proof assoils me, thou must own,
> Now I lie here so blue and black.[17]

Before the argument can be decided, the soul hears the hounds of hell approaching; soon it will know the torments of the damned, while the body decomposes in the grave until they are reunited for the final reckoning.

This split personification of body and soul is a dramatic device that should not be interpreted as philosophical dualism. The soul laments the infidelity of the body, not its physicality. Since the contest is a draw and the question of blame is never settled, the debate poems highlight the complexities of the human will even while making a simple didactic point about the wages of sin.

In the rare cases in which the soul of a good man addresses its body, the words are friendly. The good soul, while not struggling against death, regrets that it must disrupt the conjugal bliss it enjoyed with its body. It praises the body for its moderate habits and looks forward to their eventual reunion.[18] According to *The Departing Soul's Address to the Body*, babies cry because they have a presentiment that the union of their spirit and flesh will one day be severed.[19] Similarly, Caesarius of Heisterbach, who gives many examples of the easy deaths of saints, nonetheless sees death as a violation of the pristine unity of body and soul:

> Through the transgression of the first-created, death entered into the world.
> Hence death [*mors*] received its name from "biting" [*morsus*]. As soon as man
> bit [*momordit*] the apple of the forbidden tree, he incurred death and sub-
> jected himself as well as his whole posterity to its necessity. Death is also said
> to have come from "bitterness" [*amaritudine*], because, as it is said, no pain in
> this life is more bitter than the separation of body and soul.[20]

In the late medieval "art of dying" literature, on the other hand, the
bitterness of death goes unmentioned, as the intention is to teach people how
to "die willingly," in a composed and grateful state of mind. *The Book of the
Craft of Dying* begins with this "commendation of death":

> Death is nothing else but a going [out] of prison, and an ending of exile; a
> discharging of an heavy burden, that is the body; finishing of all infirmities; a
> scaping of all perils; destroying of all evil things; breaking of all bonds; paying
> of the debt of natural duty; turning again into his country; and entering into
> bliss and joy.[21]

As these examples show, the history of Christian evaluation of death
comprises the whole range of possible responses, from "my God, my God,
why hast thou forsaken me?" to "Crito, I owe a cock to Asclepius." Some
modern interpreters of the Christian message have tried to separate the
Christian (or Hebrew) position on death from distorting Platonic influences,
but the result never seems to do justice to this complex religious heritage, in
which Athens and Jerusalem have been mingled from the very beginning. It
is important, in any case, to recognize that expressions of antipathy to the
flesh, or dualistic conceptions of body and soul, are presented with didactic
intent and should be understood in that light. When attempting to warn people away from sin or to console them in the face of death, one sets aside
philosophical subtleties in favor of ideas and pictures that appeal to the imagination. The two deaths motif thrived because it expressed spiritual principles in the guise of *agon*, or conflict between personalities. Its dualism is dramatic and practical rather than metaphysical; as I shall say below, this has
implications for our interpretation of visionary narratives.

So, too, the soul is conceived in a way that animates it for the imagination. In the Vision of Barontus, for example, we are told that his separated
soul "seemed so small that it was like a tiny bird just hatched from the egg."[22]
Although his five senses remained intact, he felt disoriented and lacked the
breath necessary to produce sound: "My little soul . . . could not speak until,
when it came time for discussion, it received a body of air similar to the one
I had left behind."[23] With his "body of air and light," Barontus was able to
journey through heaven and hell.[24]

According to the Barontus story, the soul requires the vehicle of an airy
or ethereal body in order to negotiate the regions of the other world during
the nebulous period before the day of judgment. This idea finds its warrant
in patristic commentaries that interpret the parable of Dives and Lazarus
(Luke 16:19–31) as evidence that the soul is a "similitude of the body."[25] As

Christians began to think of the afterlife as a period of activity rather than a state of repose, a sharper image of the soul emerged; in order to be recognizable as a person, the soul assumed the lineaments of the body.

Thus, in the third-century Narrative of Zosimus, the hermit-visionary discovers that the blessed "see the shape of the soul as a shape of light, perfect in all the body apart from the distinction of male and female."[26] A medieval poem in Old French portrays the soul as a naked child-sized figure, tinted with the color of its besetting vice.[27]

The conventional picture of the soul as a homunculus ultimately owes more to the popular religious imagination than to theological reflection. In popular works of literature and art, it seems to matter little whether Athens or Jerusalem sets the stage—the "somatomorphic" image steals the show. On the tympana of cathedrals, in colorful miniatures illustrating the lives of the saints, in bas-relief on the tombs of princes, and in the "art of dying" woodcuts, the naked and childlike soul is extracted from the body by angels who carry it up to heaven in a linen napkin, or by demons who drag it down to hell, while around the deathbed the pious mourners or greedy expectant relatives gather.

Of course, there are exceptions to the somatomorphic rule: the soul is sometimes visualized as a bird or as a bright or fiery sphere.[28] According to Caesarius of Heisterbach, the abbot of Morimond discovered in his visit to the other world that his soul was shaped like "a glassy spherical vessel, with eyes before and behind, all-knowing and seeing everything at once."[29] Another visionary cited by Caesarius found that his soul was "a spiritual substance, spherical in nature, like the globe of the moon." Caesarius explains that to mortal eyes souls, like angels, have bodily form, but to those free of flesh the soul appears as these two visionaries describe it—a luminous sphere whose gaze extends to all directions.[30] Drythelm, Tundal, and Edmund of Eynsham saw souls ascending in the form of sparks, and their precursor Thespesius saw bubbles which rose and burst to disclose the forms of men and women. Usually, though, such alternative images of the soul are presented consciously as similes, while the homunculus gets by without the encumbrance of an "as if."

For theologians both medieval and modern, the tendency to make the soul impersonate the body has been an embarrassment. Regardless of how one conceives the distinction between spirit and matter, somatomorphism violates it; it is primitive, crude, even idolatrous. Yet, as both medieval and modern otherworld journey literature attests, the tendency is irresistible. Before dismissing it out of hand, then, we should make an effort to discover its strengths; it may offer something that is missing from our more sophisticated conceptions.

A study of otherworld journey narratives reveals that, for all its crudity, somatomorphism appears to obey a fundamental law of the imagination. As we have seen in the Vision of Barontus, the protagonist—a separated soul—invariably visits the other world in a bodily form. If accounts such as this are the product of the imagination, then for "other world" we may read "domain

of the imagination." Through this minor "Copernican revolution," the principle that a disembodied soul cannot function in the other world becomes the
principle that an abstraction cannot act in the imagination.[31] This overturns
our usual cognitive hierarchy; we are accustomed to consider corporeal
images too coarse and heavy to stay aloft in the stratosphere of our spiritual
ideas. Yet in the domain of religious imagination, the reverse is true: abstractions are too thin and bloodless to breathe in the lush atmosphere of the imagination. To come to life in the imagination, spiritual entities must take on
visual, organic form. We may regret this "despotism of the eye,"[32] but we
cannot escape it; and we shall see that it rules modern near-death narratives
as well as medieval accounts.

Fortunately, some contemporary religious thinkers are helping to correct
the common view that imagination is a tyrannical and capricious deceiver of
those who seek truth.[33] Sympathetic students of the history of Christianity
are coming to appreciate the corporeal imagery that is an undeniable part of
this religious heritage and is nearly as pervasive as ever today. This new sensitivity to symbol and image has the potential to revitalize theology; for when
the pendulum of religious discourse moves too far from the concrete and vital,
then it must either swing back—or stop.

The Guide

Medieval visions that portray the departing soul in the form of a child seem,
from one point of view, to illustrate Jesus' teaching that "unless you . . .
become as little children, you shall not enter the kingdom of heaven" (Matt.
18:3). *Puer* ("boy") signifies *purus* ("pure"), Caesarius of Heisterbach tells us;
so it is not surprising that when a certain monk caught a visionary glimpse of
his own soul, it seemed to take the form of a young boy, not yet contaminated
by vicious adult ways.[34] From another point of view, the childlike appearance
of the soul connotes not purity, but powerlessness. Naked or swaddled in a
shroud, sexless, juvenile, and almost featureless, the soul is effectively
stripped of status. It retains—just barely—a personal form, but it lacks a social
identity. These medieval images of the naked departing soul invite comparison with the Mesopotamian legend of Ishtar's descent, Gnostic soul journey
narratives, Platonic allegories, and other works of philosophy and myth in
which the journey to the underworld or upper worlds of the dead requires
removing garments, discarding the flesh and its passions, and leaving behind
the insignia of earthly status.[35]

Mere departure from the body does not suffice to make the soul a full-
fledged citizen of the next world; in medieval Christian as in many other
eschatological traditions, the newly deceased soul is pictured as lingering by
the body for a brief interregnum during which it belongs to neither world.[36]
In Victor Turner's phrase, the soul is "betwixt and between." Those on the

earthly side of the threshold can help through funeral rites and prayers for the dead, but an otherworld guide is needed as well to usher the immigrant soul into its new surroundings. In the return-from-death story, the soul's assimilation into the other world is, by definition, incomplete; yet the temporary visitor would be lost without the services of an experienced escort, capable of interpreting alien sights. The advent of a guide is therefore a crucial event for most medieval otherworld visions.

Like other features of visionary journey literature, the guide is at once an archetype, or universal motif, and a theme with a specific literary history. For the texts we are considering here, that history begins with the apocalyptic literature of late antiquity.[37] In the Vision of St. Paul, for example, there are three different sorts of guides: an angelic intermediary and interpreter who escorts the apostle through the other world (the archangel Michael in most of the Latin versions), a company of guardian angels who defend just souls before the divine tribunal, and two groups of angelic psychopomps, one benign and the other horrific, who see to the removal of souls. These three roles—instructor, protector and soul-taker—can be found in medieval accounts as the combined function of a single guide.

Throughout medieval vision literature, the guide is consistently portrayed as shining, splendid, dressed in dazzling white robes. The Vision of Drythelm, as we have seen, describes the guide, in biblical terms, as a luminous being. "I was guided," Drythelm reports, "by someone of shining countenance and bright apparel."[38] This effulgence soon becomes all-important, for they enter a realm so dark that Drythelm can see nothing except the light radiating from his guide's clothing. Later, when Drythelm is about to be carried off to hell, the demons are put to flight by a bright star that turns out to be the guide.[39] Similarly, at the end of the ninth century, Charles the Fat makes his way through the infernal maze tethered to a ray of light (a gleaming version of Ariadne's thread) held by his angelic escort.

With the appearance of the guide, the vision narrative takes the form of a dialogue. Beginning with the simple command, "Follow me," the dialogue progresses through a series of questions and answers, culminating in the delivery of particular messages, commissions, or warnings, and concluding with the command to return to the body.[40] As in *The Divine Comedy*, the colloquy of visionary and guide may be accomplished partly in silence. When Drythelm gazes stupefied at the terrible valley of fire and ice, his guide remarks, "do not assume so; this is not hell as you imagine."[41] The twelfth-century Cistercian novice Gunthelm receives telepathic instruction from St. Benedict and the archangel Raphael. The author of Laisrén's vision relates that "the angel answered at once, in the way that the (guardian) angel has always answered thoughts and reflections."[42]

In his role as interpreter and instructor, the guide often seems to be reading the mind, not of the visionary, but of his amanuensis, the author of the account. As the guide identifies the souls of various sinners and reveals the rationale for their particular torments, his voice blends with that of the narrator. The otherworld landscape is a text, and it is the guide's responsibility to gloss this text, pointing out the lessons embedded in its strange features. Thus, Drythelm's guide explains the valley, pit, and meadow in moral rather than topographic terms, as evidence for the value of repentance and intercession. In the ninth-century Vision of Wetti, recorded by Heito and Walahfrid Strabo, the angelic guide is a mouthpiece for the convictions of the authors; he praises the efficacy of Psalm 118 in words that suggest support for the liturgical reform of Benedict of Aniane, he delivers long diatribes on the corruption of the clergy, and he derives a political and moral lesson from the sufferings of Charlemagne in purgatory.[43] Similarly, in the twelfth-century Vision of the Monk of Eynsham, St. Nicholas echoes the opinions of Bishop Hugh of Lincoln in words borrowed from the biography of Hugh composed by the Vision's author, Adam of Eynsham.[44] And in the thirteenth-century Vision of Thurkill, the guides extol precisely those values—hospitality, pilgrimage, and honest tithing—that appear to be the chief concerns of the author.

As protector and guardian angel, the guide figure is related to Greek and Roman ideas of the personal *daimon* or tutelary *genius*.[45] Walahfrid Strabo, author of the Vision of Wetti, derives his portrait of the guide from the Christianized *genii* described by the second-century *Shepherd* of Hermas.[46] At once soul-taker and instructor, the guide reveals himself near the end of the vision as Wetti's guardian angel: "I am he who was ordered to watch over you." He praises Wetti for his chaste boyhood and penitent old age and expresses displeasure with his dissolute youth, in a speech that, as David Traill notes, resembles the angel's lecture to Hermas in the fifth Vision.[47]

In several medieval accounts the guide is a saint rather than an angel, and his relation to the visionary is one of patronage. Because Barontus belongs to the abbey of St. Peter of Longoretus, Raphael summons St. Peter himself to take his place as the visionary's advocate, saying, "the demons are accusing one of your little monks, and won't let him go."[48] By the time of the twelfth-century vision of Edmund, the monk of Eynsham, the patronage relationship has taken on a distinctly feudal cast; because the monk is a parishioner of St. Nicholas, the saint takes him by the hand and "adopts" him into his heavenly entourage. Edmund addresses Nicholas as "my duke." Together they encounter the soul of a drunken goldsmith who has been rescued from perdition by the patronage of Nicholas, as well as the soul of a harlot who has been saved because of her devotion to St. Margaret. This advocacy is presented in explicitly feudal terms, as protection in exchange for service. Thurkill is guided through the other world by the saints (James, Julian, and Domninus) who are the beneficiaries of his vow to go on pilgrimage to Compostela, and Cistercian visionaries often find themselves under the generous auspices of the Virgin. In contemporary near-death accounts, we will find little to compare to this feudal compact of the soul with the patron saint; it has been replaced by more democratic, less hierarchical forms of solidarity and protection, such as that afforded by family members and friends.

As defender of the soul, the guide snatches the visionary out of monstrous jaws, makes pathways through hellfire, and fends off demonic attacks. The demons, rigorists when it comes to God's law, confront the soul with an exact record of its misdeeds, which the guide must counter by enumerating the soul's virtues, vouching for its repentance and appealing to mercy.[49]

However powerful the guide's protection, at some point the visionary may find he has to go it alone. In Plutarch's account of the otherworld journey of Thespesius, the protagonist is deserted by his guide just as they enter the region of torments; as if to parody the role of the guide, a band of hideous goblins starts to shepherd him around. Similarly, Drythelm tells us plaintively, "when my guide had brought me to this place [the edge of the pit of hell], he suddenly disappeared and left me alone in the midst of the darkness and of the horrible scene."[50]

In a nearly identical episode, the Boy William is inexplicably abandoned by his guide. And Tundal, who as a sinner merits a particularly traumatic tour of hell, is more than once left to his own devices. The guardian angel whose advice he spurned in life intends that Tundal should experience a few of the punishments he has earned. Tundal is therefore swallowed by a beast but then rescued. When they reach the lower hell, where demons and souls rise and fall on tongues of flame that dart from a bottomless cistern in the midst of unimaginable cold, stench, and darkness, the guide disappears once again, leaving Tundal in despair. The demons taunt, "He who led you here deceived you . . . for there is no one who would care or be able to deliver you from our hands."[51] But just as they are leading him away on hooks, the guide reappears as a "spirit of light" and banishes the minions of darkness with the consoling news that Tundal will henceforth be treated with mercy rather than strict justice.

In a variety of guises, the guide thus serves both as an echo of the author's voice and as a narrative expedient— describing, interpreting, and impelling the action. At the same time, the presence of the guide is a sign of continuity between the otherworld journey and the spiritual path in life. Although one may exchange this world for the next, one remains under the protection and tutelage of the same guardian angel or patron saint. The need for a guide may be felt regardless of whether one enters the other world by dying, dreaming, or trance; for just as Hermes, in Greco-Roman myth, doubles as psychopomp and dream-escort, so the Christian guardian angel or patron saint guides souls who have wandered into the other world through the gate of sleep. In this respect, the dream-visions of Sunniulf, Charles the Fat, Laisrén, and Ansellus Scholasticus do not differ from apparent death stories; evidently the vision narratives are telling us that a spiritual guide is as necessary for the living as for the dead. We shall see that this sentiment persists even in modern accounts, despite uncertainty as to who might fill such an important role.

The Journey

In addition to the guide who helps the soul find its bearings in the other world, a symbolic conveyance or path of approach is required to account for the mystery of transition from this life to the next. Medieval vision narratives offer a variety of vehicles and pathways which, though less elaborate than Elijah's chariot, Alexander's griffon, or Muhammad's heavenly steed, nonetheless pass muster as forms of spiritual transportation. Baldarius in the seventh century and Alberic in the twelfth are raised aloft by doves, Gunthelm follows his guide up a ladder to the realm of ether, St. Benedict treads a bright carpet to heaven, and a neighbor of Gregory's, on the point of death, sees a ship waiting to take him to Sicily, a land of volcanic openings to hell.[52] The last thought before death is also a vehicle of sorts, said to transport souls swiftly to their appropriate final destination.[53]

Paths toward or within the other world come in two main varieties: the delightful way (*via amoena*) and the dark or thorny path. In a late-ninth-century vision, the young Ansgar dreams that he is stuck in a slippery mire, much like Bunyan's Slough of Despond; over against this is a "most delightful path" along which the Virgin Mary and his mother approach. Ansgar, however, cannot extract himself from the mud. In order to attain that bright path, he must return to life and disavow his childish frivolities. St. Boniface describes the journey of an anonymous visionary who travels over a rainbow that connects the three heavens; and Wetti's guide leads him "through a very bright path of exceeding delightfulness."[54]

Several vision narratives describe the dark path in terms that recall Vergil's description of the descent of Aeneas into the underworld: "They went darkly through the gloom under the lone night."[55] Thus, Drythelm, approaching the pit of hell, walks "through the shades under the lone night."[56] Thorny paths recur, as H. R. Patch points out, in the *Shepherd* of Hermas, the visions of Gottschalk and Alberic, and elsewhere.

A somewhat different use of the two paths theme is based on the scriptural metaphor of the narrow road that leads to life and the broad path to perdition.[57] We have seen how this analogy was applied in the context of pilgrimage. In vision literature, the two paths take literal form without losing their original symbolic meaning and may be converted back into metaphor or allegory in the commentary of narrator or guide. Caesarius describes a novice who, like Gunthelm, felt tempted to leave the monastery but was dissuaded by a nocturnal vision. In this thirteenth-century narrative, the novice finds himself before two roads that enter a wood, one on the right and the other on the left. Uncertain about which to take, he asks the advice of an old man who suddenly appears at his side, and learns that the road on the right is troublesome and thorny but leads to a "most delightful flowery field." The path on the left presents no difficulties but ends in a hideous field of rocks and mud. As Caesarius interprets the vision, the difficult road is the monastic path leading through the wood of earthly life to the meadows of Paradise, while the left-hand path, a pleasant and well-traveled easy street, leads straight to damnation.[58]

Within the other world the visionary may traverse a wide field, desert waste, or dark forest, or surmount obstacles such as walls of fire, curtains of mist, and guarded doorways. His approach may be a laborious or perilous passage up a ladder or across a slippery bridge, or he may find himself effortlessly spirited to the other side of a fiery river or the summit of a forbidding mountain.[59] As in the The Divine Comedy, the traveler follows a specific route through the other world, imaginatively surveying and mapping its picturesque terrain. Unlike The Divine Comedy, however, these roughly hewn narratives generate only fragmentary maps.

The contrast to The Divine Comedy is worth considering. In Dante's lucidly reasoned, symmetrical cosmology, the nine heavenly spheres, from the Primum Mobile through the fixed stars and planets to the moon, enclose our world in a sturdy Ptolemaic package. The continents and oceans occupy a hemisphere that stretches from Gibraltar in the west to the Ganges in the east, with Jerusalem at the center. Below it lies an inchoate hemisphere of water whose horizon is broken by a single mountain directly opposite Jerusalem. Hell is an inverted cone beneath the earth's crust, wide enough at the top to allow access through any terrestrial opening, be it Lake Avernus or St. Patrick's Purgatory, and narrowing to a point in the innermost core of the earth, where Satan is immobilized upside down in a lake of ice. A tortuous tunnel leads from this cryosphere of despair to the mountain of Purgatory, on whose summit sits the earthly Paradise, Jerusalem's counterpart. From here, Dante ascends through the spheres to the empyrean.

The route of the medieval visionary is not so easy to trace, nor are the locations of hell and purgatory clearly defined. The visionary may ascend or descend, go north to the realm of punishment and south to the abode of the blessed (Paul and Drythelm), west to hell (Adamnán), east to paradise (Baldarius), southeast to purgatory (Owen), or, like Thurkill, he may find himself in the middle of the world with hell, purgatory, and heaven gathered close at hand. One reason for the inconsistencies in otherworld topography is that belief in a definite infra- or extraterrestrial location for purgatory, as distinct from hell, is a comparatively late development in Christian thought. The Irish church was especially slow to abandon the older eschatology according to which both the utterly reprobate and those who can be saved through intercession are confined together in hell; thus, in Irish visions up to the twelfth century, as in the earlier Anglo-Saxon visions, hell is divided into an upper and lower region (following a hint from St. Augustine), or a valley and a pit, where the different classes of sinners—the almost good, the half wicked, and the totally wicked—may receive their appropriate punishments.[60]

Interest in purgatorial experience was strong throughout the Middle Ages, but Jacques Le Goff has argued that it was not until the late twelfth century that Christian thinkers began to picture themselves as tenants of a three-tiered cosmos in which purgatory occupied its own separate sphere. Le Goff sees a connection between this eschatological development and the rise of "middle classes," which introduced ternary rather than binary divisions in feudal society and led to the "wholesale revision of the maps of both this world and the other."[61] This imaginative revision took hold only gradually; as late as 1220, Caesarius of Heisterbach suggested that purgatory might exist in several places at once.[62]

By the time Dante wrote, however, purgatory was more solidly established. The letter of Pope Innocent IV in 1254 and the Second Council of Lyon in 1274 had given official recognition to purgatory as a place, thus taking it from the realm of folklore and popular religious instruction and making it a subject of scholastic curriculum and commentary. The detailed cosmological scheme of *The Divine Comedy* reflects this scholastic phase, during which newly translated works of Aristotelian and Arabic science—which appealed to the intellectual's passion for system-building as well as to the thirst for natural knowledge—helped to shape what is now often assumed to have been a standard and unvarying medieval world-picture.

In the less tidy universe of medieval return-from-death stories, however, there are variations even on the time-honored theme of descent into hell. Despite classical precedents, the widespread Christian belief that hell is located within the bowels of the earth, and the powerful symbolism of Christ's harrowing of hell, few medieval visionaries reach the other world by traveling downward. Among medieval narratives, the only notable reenactment of Christ's legendary descent to hell is the tenth-century journey of Ansellus Scholasticus, one of the few visionaries to be guided by Christ himself. The subterranean adventures of such pilgrims to St. Patrick's Purgatory as Raymond de Perelhos, who slid through the cave like Alice falling down the rabbit hole, seem as close in spirit to the descent of Aeneas and the legend of Trophonius's cave as to the account in the Gospel of Nicodemus of Christ's sojourn among the dead. Strangely, though medieval visions are more concerned with the realms of punishment than with heaven, they speak more often of ascent than of descent.

One reason for the predominance of ascent in narratives of the apparent death variety is that the initial separation of soul and body is itself an ascent; before the soul can set out for any otherworldly destination, it must rise up out of the body. From this point there are several options: an aerial tour of the planet, a journey to one of the four directions, or a heavenly ascent. The simple vertical ascent of a holy soul is represented in the Vision of Salvius:

> Four days ago, when the cell shook, and you saw me lifeless, I was taken by two angels and carried up to the height of heaven, and it was just as though I had beneath my feet not only the squalid earth, but also the sun and moon, the clouds and stars. Then I was brought through a gate that was brighter than our light, into a dwelling-place where the entire floor shone like gold and silver; there was an ineffable light and it was indescribably vast.[63]

Spiritual writers often relate this kind of heavenly journey to interior ascent through the faculties to the summit of contemplative intelligence.

Such untroubled ascent is rare, however, even in hagiographic narratives. In one of his well-publicized journeys to heaven, St. Fursa finds the way blocked by demons who assail him with carping accusations, casting back at him "his deeds, his idle words and even his thoughts."[64] After an extended debate between legalistic demons and angels who advocate mercy, Fursa manages to pass unharmed, only to be threatened by the fire of doom surrounding the earth. Young Alberic's nine-day journey begins when a dovelike bird draws his soul out of his mouth and carries him "as high above the earth as the stature of a man."[65] After this preliminary ascent, Alberic tours the regions of punishment as far as "the tartarean place and the mouth of the infernal abyss."[66] From there he proceeds to a "most delightful field" in the midst of which lies paradise and finally arrives in the first heaven.

Even the hell-bound begin their journey by ascending to a higher vantage point from which they may look down at the body they are leaving behind. Tundal, a prodigious sinner, finds himself above his body in the company of demons who would drag him down to the "unquenchable fire" were it not for the intervention of his guardian angel. In his hair-raising visit to purgatory and hell, however, there is no hint that Tundal descends beneath the earth. Instead, this vision follows the model of Adamnán, whose ascent through the seven heavens includes a tour of the hells, and thus preserves a trace of the apocalyptic tradition of a dangerous journey to heaven.[67] Scenes of torment in the heavens also occur in the visions of Barontus, Fursa, the Monk of Wenlock, Turpin, Laisrén, Wetti, and Tundal.

Again, the contrast with *The Divine Comedy* is instructive: just as Dante follows the classical model in depicting descent into hell, so his ascent to the empyrean has a Stoic and Platonic flavor, adapted to the contemplative theology but strikingly different from the popular vision literature of the Middle Ages. In return-from-death stories, a trace remains of ancient beliefs about evil spirits, ordeals, and places of punishment in the heavens; though originally inseparable from the very idea of a plurality of heavens, these beliefs fell into disrepute because they were associated with Gnosticism. Yet their influence survived in certain half-digested fragmentary forms, still recognizable not only in vision narratives, but also in the doctrine of seven cardinal sins, the astrological principle of three benign and three malefic planets, and the deathbed confrontations that occur in body-and-soul poems and "art of dying" manuals.[68]

R. H. Charles has argued that the effort of orthodoxy to expel evil spirits from the heavens destroyed the rationale for their sevenfold or tenfold division.[69] With respect to the medieval return-from-death story, his point seems well taken. Just as the elimination of struggle from the exit of the good soul from the body put the death of the wicked soul in the spotlight, so the purging of conflict and evil from the heavens appears to have led to a greater interest in hell. The fullest descriptions of the heavens are found in those narratives that preserve the element of struggle, such as Irish visions, where horrific as well as sublime aspects of the heavens survive intact.[70]

Although Dante gives equal treatment to heaven, it has become a commonplace to say that the *Paradiso* is less engaging than the other two canti-

cles of *The Divine Comedy* because of the absence of conflict or sharply
defined personalities. This assessment seems to me unjust, however. Dante's
heaven is neither static nor undifferentiated; rather, it appeals to the medieval
love of hierarchy by portraying heaven as a dynamic hierarchy of love ("the
love that moves the sun and the other stars," canto 33).

For medieval audiences, the ranking of the blessed in a series of concen-
tric but ascending heavens, like the ranking of the nine orders of angels,
derived its plausibility—or, rather, its imaginative power—from the fact that
it reflected and affirmed the social order and provided an emblem for the
structure of human intelligence. There have been modern parallels to this
hierarchical conception of the other world, notably in the visionary treatises
of Emanuel Swedenborg, in the spiritualist literature he influenced, and
among theosophists and other self-consciously esoteric intellectuals. For
many people in our own day, however, the plurality of heavens seems at last
to have lost its rationale; the very notion of ranking souls offends democratic
instincts. Contemporary near-death accounts show that the modern imagination is satisfied by the mere assurance of an afterlife in heaven, and prefers
to regard it as a place of continual progress without sharply demarcated levels
of spiritual attainment, much less ordeals.

CHAPTER 4

Obstacles

From Whinny-muir when thou may'st pass,
  Every nighte and alle,
To Brig o' Dread thou com'st at last;
  And Christe receive thy saule.
                          A Lyke-Wake Dirge

ONCE HE OR SHE has left the body, the medieval visionary must face a bewildering variety of obstacles and ordeals. For every test passed, wall surmounted, or accuser put to flight, there seem to be several more to take its place. According to S. G. F. Brandon, the multiplication of obstacles—a universal feature of vision literature—is an expression of pervasive anxiety.[1] Viewed more positively, it demonstrates the fertility of the religious imagination. Imagination, according to Coleridge, is an "esemplastic" power, a capacity "to shape into one"; but the history of religion shows that it is also polyplastic, giving rise to a rich diversity of forms.[2] Nowhere is this imaginative abundance more evident than in accounts of the trials that await souls after death.

In eschatological traditions that emphasize an ultimate reckoning, this proliferation of imaginative forms for judgment poses a problem. For example, despite repeated insistence in the Qur'an on belief in judgment at the end of time, Islamic literature abounds in intermediate and supernumerary judgment scenes. Islamic traditions pile redundance upon redundance, depicting the moment of death as both trial and execution of sentence, and following this with a rigorous interrogation in the grave, which determines whether souls will await the resurrection in torment or in comfort; it appears as though, by the time of the final reckoning, the outcome will already be

61

known. In Christian eschatological literature as well, the multiplication of judgment scenes makes it difficult to determine when, if ever, a decisive post-mortem trial takes place.

We can see this principle of redundance at work in the second-century *Testament of Abraham*, a Jewish text reshaped by Christian hands.[3] As he enters the first heaven, Abraham sees two paths, one broad and the other narrow, leading to broad and narrow gates. Adam sits between the two gates and weeps at the sight of masses of souls entering through the broad gate, laughing for joy when he sees one in seven thousand (or one in seven, as a shorter version more generously suggests) go in the narrow gate to salvation.[4] As if this did not suffice to separate the sheep from the goats, an elaborate trial follows in which Abel considers the evidence inscribed in a great book and pronounces sentence while an angel on the right records the soul's good deeds and an angel on the left writes down its sins. At the same time, the bright archangel Dokiel weighs the soul (or, in a later passage, the soul's deeds) in a balance, and the merciless archangel Purouel tests the soul (or its deeds) with fire. Moreover, this is only the first round; at the *parousia* (which Christian readers would understand as a reference to the second coming of Christ), souls will be judged by the twelve tribes and finally by God.

In this chapter, we shall see that medieval visions exhibit a similar profusion of barriers, obstacles, trials, and judgment scenes. My aim is not to systematize this material into a rational theology of judgment, but rather to examine the prominent forms of expression, in order to appreciate the imaginative experience they convey.

When death is visualized as a journey, it is natural to portray judgment in the form of topographic obstacles; thus, in many medieval narratives the visionary's first ordeal is to confront some forbidding feature of the other-world terrain. The barriers that serve a cartographic purpose—marking boundaries between different realms of the other world—also serve as dangerous thresholds, where the soul must prove itself worthy to proceed to happier realms. To emphasize this point, rivers are fiery, fetid, or filled with knives; gates are locked and guarded; walls rise to dizzying heights; and mountains are steep and lashed by ferocious winds.[5] The very act of crossing such hazardous borders constitutes a trial by ordeal, entailing an intrinsic judgment and penalty. The terrors of formal judgment thus blend with the more familiar perils of long-distance travel.

Border obstacles are of two kinds: artifacts like walls and bridges, and natural features like rivers and mountains. Perhaps most common is the river, that creator of terrestrial boundaries which is a universal means of organizing cosmic territory. The landscape of medieval visions is irrigated by the biblical waters of Eden, the four rivers of Hades, and countless unnamed infernal streams swollen with filth or flame, where, according to the visions of St. Paul, Sunniulf, the monk of Wenlock, Wetti, Charles the Fat, Alberic, and Owen, among others, sinners suffer immersion to the extent of their demerit. These rivers demarcate the provinces of punishment and bliss and measure the progress of the soul, but except in the Vision of Adamnán and a few others that betray Gnostic influence, there is no precise correlation between other-world rivers and the zones of planetary or cosmic space; in most of the accounts we are considering, only a nuance remains of the cosmological function of the river.

Fire

The rivers of medieval visions seem to acquire their greatest cleansing powers not from water but from fire. This can be attributed, in part, to natural symbolism; in domestic and ritual practices, from cooking to cremation, incensing to smoke-curing, metalsmithing to alchemy, fire is an agent of purification, used to destroy coarse elements and restore the original underlying essence. Even a world-destroying fiery cataclysm can share this cathartic significance, since it prepares the way for a new creation. As an Anglo-Saxon homily puts it, "Heaven and Earth will pass away and yet will continue because they will be cleansed, by fire, from the hue which they now have."[6]

In Christian eschatology, the fiery river was originally a feature of the day of judgment, rather than of individual postmortem experience. In this context, fire serves to test, to punish, or to purge—three distinct functions that often seem confused in biblical and apocalyptic narratives, perhaps because the imagery is a patchwork, derived from heterogeneous sources.[7] Jewish and early Christian conceptions of a trial by fire are apparently related to the Zoroastrian eschatological tradition that foresees a final judgment in which all humans will pass through a burning river swollen by the volcanic meltdown of all the mountains on earth. This ordeal will reveal the righteous for what they are; as a ninth-century work puts it, they will find the molten river as pleasant to wade through as warm milk. For sinners, it will be a torment; but eventually all will make it across, and the world will emerge cleansed of the dross of wickedness. Some scholars have suggested that this imagery is based not only on the practice of testing metals in fire, but also on the actual use of fire or molten metal for trial by ordeal.[8]

In the Jewish and Christian eschatological literature of late antiquity, there are many instances, though no coherent tradition, of a cathartic fire of judgment that discriminates between saints and sinners. The Testament of Isaac, for example, describes a fiery river that recognizes and spares the just souls who pass through its flames, and in the History of Joseph the Carpenter, Joseph pleads for safe passage through a cathartic sea of fire. Similarly, many patristic and medieval Christian authors comment on the capacity of the fire to burn sinners according to their degree of guilt while bringing no harm to the saints.[9] Among otherworld journey narratives, the saint's relative immunity to the fire of doom is illustrated most clearly by the Vision of Fursa. In the course of his heavenly ascent, Fursa sees the fires that are destined to consume the world at the end of time in a conflagration fueled by the poisonous vapors of human vice. The flames draw alarmingly close to Fursa, but his angelic guide reassures him, quoting Isaiah: "What you have not kindled will not burn you. For although this seems to be a vast and terrible funeral pyre, its purpose is to test each person according to the merits of his deeds, and to burn away illicit desire."[10] The river of fire that Adamnán encounters in the second heaven similarly cleanses souls in proportion to their stains. By the time of the late medieval funeral ballad, A Lyke-Wake Dirge, the "intelligence" of the fire of doom is well known:

> If ever thou gavest meat or drink,
>   Every nighte and alle,
> The fire sall never make thee shrink;
>   And Christe receive thy saule.

> If meat or drink thou ne'er gav'st nane,
>   Every nighte and alle,
> The fire will burn thee to the bare bane;
>   And Christe receive thy saule.[11]

The four fiery rivers of Hades passed from Greco-Roman myth into Christian eschatological literature; they are mentioned by name in otherworld journey narratives from the Vision of St. Paul to Dante. In addition, classical authors such as Vergil and Macrobius bequeathed to the Latin Middle Ages an aerial and allegorical version of the passage through flames after death.[12] Under the influence of this tradition, Fursa sees four fires rising up from the four corners of the world; like the four streams of Hades, they correspond to four principal human passions.[13] This correlation of the four fires and four sins is an instance of the much larger enterprise of drawing correspondences between the colors, directions, metals, heavenly bodies, and inner qualities.

Unlike classical allegorists, however, Christian interpreters of the fire ordeal hold the literal and the figurative meanings together. Commenting on St. Paul's statement that human works will be tried by fire—a favorite prooftext for early discussions of purgatorial experience—Gregory says that the fire can be understood as symbolizing suffering undertaken as penance in this life. In case this metaphorical blaze should not suffice to cauterize our sins, however, Gregory is economical enough to propose that what is symbolic in this life may be actual in the next, so that evildoers can expect a corporeal burning in the other world.[14] Thomas Aquinas would later point out that the prospect of a soul being punished by physical fire after death is no more difficult to understand than the torment it experiences while inhabiting a body in life.[15]

The vision narratives show, however, that Christian eschatology sets strict limits on the use of fire imagery. The idea of universal salvation did not win the approval of the Latin church, and as a consequence the Christian fire of doom lost some of the virtues of its Persian counterpart. Thus, patristic writers such as Hilary and Ambrose speak of a fire through which all must pass at the end of time, but they reserve its restorative power for those destined to be saved. Gregory is even more cautious; following Augustine, he warns that this fire can only cleanse the minor faults of good souls.[16] As the doctrine of purgatory developed, some of the cathartic qualities originally attributed to the fire of doom were transferred to the various fiery streams that souls might encounter in the intermediate period between death and resurrection; but here, too, the same restrictions applied: for the damned the fire could be an agent only of punishment, never of purgation.[17]

The Test-Bridge

Passing from the natural elements of water and fire to man-made features of otherworld topography, we move from the imagery of catharsis to that of construction, from the recovery of paradise to the building of the city. Artifacts such as the test-bridge, the balance, the book, and the various edifices of the other world measure what one has done rather than what one is, one's history rather than one's nature. Perhaps this tells us why, in medieval visions, the bridge became as important as the fiery river it spans.

As Arnold van Gennep has shown in his studies of rites of passage, the symbolic or ritual crossing of a border can provide a way to come to terms with the critical transitions of life and death. In the test-bridge of medieval vision literature, this motif appears in a particularly concentrated form. Although it symbolizes safe passage, the bridge also intensifies the dangers of crossing otherworld boundaries. Whoever sets foot on its narrow planks is singled out for the attention of forces seeking the soul's downfall.

Those of us who, in the course of a daily commute, cross over or tunnel through abysses of sewage-filled water, may take for granted the technical wizardry involved. At a time when such feats of civil engineering were rare, however, bridges had a supernatural import. G. A. Frank Knight attributes the mystique of bridges to a widespread primitive belief that bridge-building encroaches on the domain of the river-spirit who, deprived of drowning victims, must be appeased through sacrifice.[18] There is evidence that ancient Roman bridge-builders placated the divinity of the Tiber by casting humans or effigies into the river. In European folklore, as Knight points out, the tutelary river deities are Christianized into demons, every bit as hungry for human victims as were their pagan counterparts. Hints of bridge-sacrifice are preserved in popular folktales in which the devil claims the first soul to cross a new bridge, and also in the children's game called "London Bridge."[19]

In Christian Europe as in ancient Rome, bridge-building was seen as a sacred as well as dangerous undertaking, and the upkeep of bridges was entrusted to clergy.[20] Symbolically, the supreme clerical bridge-builder of Western Christendom was the pope, who became "Pontifex Maximus" in place of the Roman and Christian emperors who had inherited this title from the official charged with conserving the Pons Sublicius. During the high Middle Ages, bridge-building acquired a new practical importance as a consequence of the rise of pilgrimage. An order of "Fratres Pontifices" took care of building hospices and pilgrim bridges, using alms and indulgence payments collected from those who wished to build themselves a bridge to heaven. That this industry enhanced the effectiveness of bridge symbolism is evident in the lore associated with pilgrimage to the shrine of St. James at Compostela. According to legend the first pilgrims who carried the body of St. James to its sepulcher were miraculously rescued from a bridge that broke under their feet. Conflated with later reports of supernatural adventures on bridges, this tale led to rumors about a mysterious "bridge that trembles," which became a regular feature of medieval accounts of pilgrimage to the shrine of St. James.[21] Here, as in the sermon called "Veneranda dies" (quoted in chapter 2), the analogies between pilgrimage and otherworld journey form a loop that permits a continual exchange between literal and metaphorical, this-world and otherworld signification.

The literary history of Western eschatological bridge symbolism takes us back again to ancient Persia, to the pre-Zoroastrian tradition that souls must cross a perilous bridge in the other world. In Zoroastrian sacred writings, which vividly dramatize the experience of moral choice, this ordeal becomes an occasion to test whether the soul's allegiance is to *asha* ("truth") or to *druj* ("the lie"). As the earliest Zoroastrian hymns (the Gathas) describe it,

> Thus does the evil one's conscience forfeit the assurance of the straight
> (path);
> His Soul (?) stripped naked (?) shall be afraid at the Bridge of the Separator.[22]

According to the standard Zoroastrian picture of postmortem experience—developed in the sixth to tenth centuries but drawing on much earlier traditions—several forms of reckoning take place at this Bridge of the Separator (*Chinvato Peretu*). First the soul's deeds are weighed in a balance, and then it attempts to cross the bridge; for the wicked soul, the bridge narrows to a razor's edge, making downfall a certainty. On the bridge, the soul may also meet its own deeds (*daena*, also translated as "conscience"), appearing in the form either of a beautiful maiden or of an ugly hag who escorts it to its proper mansion in heaven or in the depths of hell.[23] This tradition embellishes Zarathustra's own warning to those in power: "They shall be tortured by their own soul and their conscience when they come to the Bridge of the Separator. . . ."[24]

The earliest Western portraits of the test-bridge—in Gregory's *Dialogues*, the Vision of Sunniulf, the Vision of the Monk of Wenlock, and a twelfth-century version of the Vision of St. Paul—share many of the characteristics of the Chinvat bridge. In Gregory's account of a soldier's vision, as we have seen, the otherworld bridge is the scene of struggle for the soul and encounter with one's deeds in an externalized form. The river of hell below resembles its Persian counterpart in that it is dark and foul-smelling rather than fiery.[25] As on the Chinvat bridge, the just cross easily to the meadows on the opposite shore, while the unjust cannot keep their footing and fall into the clutches of demons waiting below. In Redaction 4 of the Vision of St.

Paul the test-bridge appears again, with emphasis on its separating function: the wicked who attempt to cross the bridge are punished in groups according to their sins, following Gregory's exegesis of Christ's declaration, "Bind them in bundles to be burned."[26] Redaction 4 also brings in the motif of graded immersion, transferring this punishment from the fiery river described in the long Latin version of the Vision of St. Paul to the dark and fetid river spanned by the test-bridge.

The prestige of Gregory's *Dialogues* and of the medieval versions of the Vision of St. Paul ensured the success of the test-bridge; in Christian visions and allegories, it became a standard way to extend the narrow path theme into the other world. While neither Gregory nor Redaction 4 of the Vision of St. Paul explicitly mentions the narrowness of the bridge, Gregory comments that "he saw the just crossing over a bridge to a beautiful place, because the road that leads to eternal life is extremely narrow."[27] Other bridge texts treat the theme of narrowness in greater detail, either by developing the hints supplied by Gregory the Great or, perhaps, by drawing on sources that included all of the features of the Chinvat bridge. The Vision of Sunniulf, for example, portrays a fiery river in which victims are immersed to varying degrees and which is spanned by "a bridge so narrow that it could scarce take the width of one footstep."[28] An even more dramatic treatment of the narrow bridge appears in a medieval Vision of Ezra:

> . . . he saw a fiery river and over it a great bridge and the just came and crossed with joy and exultation. And sinners came and the bridge was turned back into the fineness of a filament of thread, and they fell into the river confessing their own sins. . . .[29]

From the time of Gregory the Great until at least the fifteenth century, the test-bridge is a recurrent feature of Western vision literature. Rather than developing in a direct sequence from the formative accounts described above, however, the bridge tradition grows in the fashion of a banyan, at times branching out widely and at other times dipping back to its own roots. An exhaustive account of its ramifications would have to include the kindred stock of Norse otherworld bridge lore (the Gjallar of the underworld and the Bifröst which, like a rainbow, reaches to the sky) and the numerous bridges of medieval allegory and romance; for discussion of the sword bridge, the active bridge, and others, both perilous and benign, in this literary context, I refer the reader to the final chapters of H. R. Patch's *The Other World*. Intriguing parallels in Islamic and Far Eastern religious traditions would also have to be taken into account. Islamic eschatological tradition assigns to the day of judgment the trial of crossing *al-Sirat*, a bridge that is thinner than a hair, sharper than a sword, and, in some versions, set with hooks and thorns; the righteous cross easily to the Garden, but the wicked find the bridge slippery and dark, and after expending thousands of years in the attempt to cross, fall into the Fire below.[30]

It is obviously beyond our scope to chart the full history of Western bridge lore, but we can classify medieval otherworld bridges according to a few recurrent types. The form of the bridge—slippery, spiked, narrow, broad, or changing in width to suit the occasion—varies according to its function, and its function is determined in part by teachings about purgatory. For the bridge is a purgatorial as well as an infernal symbol; it suggests both the possibility of passage to safety and the potential for downfall. In the vision of Gregory's soldier, the bridge has a double function: to separate the saved from the damned and to test and refine those destined to be saved. Most subsequent bridge narratives follow Gregory's model in this respect, and the Irish visions elaborate on it in their depiction of the "active bridge"[31] that divides souls into three or four classes and intensifies the purgatorial ordeal.

The first of the Irish active bridges occurs in the tenth-century Vision of Adamnán. While visiting the nethermost hell, Adamnán sees a vast, high bridge spanning a fiery glen. The righteous, whose presence in hell is not explained, find the bridge spacious and easy to cross. An intermediate group of souls, those who late in life converted from grudging to willing obedience to God, have a more anxious journey; the bridge is narrow at first, but eventually it widens. For sinners, however, the bridge starts out wide and then narrows until they fall into the jaws of "eight red-hot serpents" waiting below.[32]

Occasionally the infernal river has cathartic properties, and the entire bridge episode is purgatorial. During his tour of paradise, the monk of Wenlock stops at a "way-station" before heaven, where souls venture onto a slippery log placed over a river of fire and pitch.[33] Those who fall off are immersed by degrees in the river, but everyone eventually emerges, cleansed, on the opposite bank. Lest this suggest universal salvation, St. Boniface explains that only minor sins are purged in the river.[34] The elaborate bridge episode in the twelfth-century Vision of Alberic seems to combine these purgatorial features with elements from the Vision of Adamnán. Alberic sees a wide iron bridge across a river of burning pitch. Some souls cross quickly and easily while others, weighed down by guilt, make only sluggish progress. When sinners reach the middle of the bridge it appears to shrink to the size of a thread. They fall into the river, are tormented, and clamber back up until eventually they manage to reach their goal. St. Peter informs Alberic that the bridge "has the name of purgatory."[35] In addition to this purgatorial bridge, the Vision of Alberic features a burning iron ladder which is equivalent to a hell-bridge. The ladder is 365 cubits high, apparently representing the days of the year; the souls forced to climb it are those who neglected to observe Sundays and feast days. Because of their failure to adhere to the liturgical calendar, they lose their grip on the ladder and fall into the basin of oil, pitch, and tar at its foot.

In two bridge episodes, the twelfth-century Vision of Tundal resumes the themes central to Gregory's account: the narrow path, the pilgrim priest, the confrontation with one's sins, and the double function of the bridge. In the first episode the bridge extends across the valley of the proud, at the bottom of which is a sulphurous stream. From this bridge, one thousand paces long and one pace wide, Tundal sees many souls fall to their doom. Only the pilgrim priest with his palm branch and tunic makes it across. Seeing this "narrow path" and the destruction below, Tundal asks his escort, "who shall deliver me from this road of death?"[36] In the realm of thieves and plunderers, Tundal sees another bridge, which is two miles long and only one palm wide. Like Sunniulf's bridge and Perpetua's ladder, it is fixed with sharp iron spikes. Those who fall off are devoured by fire-breathing beasts. This is the first extended episode in which the visionary is forced to travel over the bridge unaided. To make matters worse, Tundal must bring with him a cow he had stolen from his godfather. He makes his way across, now slipping from the bridge and clinging to the cow, now dragging the cow along as it dangles from the bridge. Halfway to the end, Tundal meets a soul who, like himself, is guilty of robbing churches. The soul is carrying sheaves of corn, possibly representing an unresolved debt of tithes.[37] Burdened as they are, they cannot pass each other, and neither is willing to give way. They face each other and weep until, without knowing how, they find themselves at opposite ends of the bridge.

Soon after Brother Marcus recorded Tundal's vision, another Cistercian monk described the otherworld journey of an Irish knight who, like Tundal, was a sinner and violator of churches. As we have seen, the Knight Owen's bridge is high, narrow, slippery, and every bit as versatile as the bridge seen by Adamnán and Alberic, for it widens as soon as he invokes the name of Jesus.

From Adamnán to Alberic to Tundal to Owen, Gregory's bridge is passed down the Drythelm line to the Vision of Thurkill, where it appears as part of a densely furnished purgatorial environment. In a corridor of fire bounded by high walls, souls linger for a period proportionate to how black and spotted they are. From the fire they proceed to an icy salt lake, where they suffer graded immersion and cross a bridge at speeds ranging from an instant to many years, depending on their deeds and the number of masses performed on their behalf. Because of stakes and thorns that pierce their feet, they first walk on their hands and then roll until they reach the opposite shore bleeding from head to foot.

Encounter with Deeds

In the accounts we have considered, such traditional ordeals as the contest for the soul and the weighing of deeds often take place on or near the bridge, compounding the hazards of crossing. This follows a precedent set by the vision of Gregory's soldier, in which the otherworld bridge becomes a stage for a "psychomachy," or battle between the soul's good and evil impulses. In a manner that recalls the Chinvat bridge legend, Gregory transmutes the old motif of harassment of the journeying soul by external powers into a morally instructive self-encounter.

Gregory is the first and most influential Western Christian author to focus explicitly on the inner significance of obstacles in the other world; but the iconography of confrontation with deeds was well established long before his time in the Jewish and Christian vision literature of late antiquity. The Vision of St. Paul, as we have seen, depicts the soul's exit from the body as a critical moment in which a lifetime's accumulation of acts and intentions becomes externally visible. The soul is either embraced or disowned by its guardian angel and challenged by evil spirits who look for traces of their influence; its merits and demerits, hidden during life, are now disclosed. Again, at the divine tribunal, the soul's deeds are displayed in the form of victims who come forward to testify against it. The familiar image of a book of deeds—implicit in God's daily review of human actions—is more explicit in Redactions 3 and 4. All versions agree, however, that one's character will be externally manifest at death; in the long Latin version, an angel asks Paul, "Have you believed and known, that whatever each one of you has done, he sees in the hour of his need?"[38] The Vision of St. Paul, along with the Testament of Abraham and the *Dialogues* of Gregory the Great, presented medieval readers with all the essential features of the encounter with deeds: the bridge, the externalization of deeds, the book, and the balance.

Biblical sources can be found for much of the imagery of encounter with deeds, but the significance of this imagery is altered when it appears in the context of visions of a personal afterlife. In the Bible, the book of life gathers the names of the elect into an honor roll prepared for the judgment of nations at the end of time.[39] In pseudepigraphic works such as 1 and 2 Enoch and the Testament of Abraham, in rabbinic literature, and in medieval visions of the other world, on the other hand, books of deeds record the righteous and wicked acts of individuals who will face judgment after death. The vision narratives make a clear connection between the ordeal of reading this document and the various other obstacles and challenges that interrupt the soul's ascent. Bede tells of an unrepentant sinner who at the point of death sees his good deeds in "a very beautiful but exceedingly small book" presented by two handsome youths, while his evil deeds appear starkly inscribed in an enormous tome wielded by demons. As they drag him away, the evil spirits cry, "This one is ours!"[40] The struggle between St. Peter and the demons over the soul of Barontus takes the form of a debate in which each party recites an itemized list of his good or evil deeds. Winning the contest, St. Peter says, "He is not your comrade, but ours."[41] The same formula occurs in the body-and-soul poems and the "art of dying" books, which transfer the confrontation motif from the other world to the deathbed. As is evident in St. Fursa's vision, in which devils pelt him with the record of his thoughts, words, and deeds, the book of deeds, like the perilous bridge, is a vestige of the ancient theme of confrontation with evil spirits.

Far from being a book of life, then, the medieval record of deeds is often a writ of indictment, brandished gleefully by demons. Through God's mercy or the efforts of an intercessor, on the other hand, the soul's bad marks may be overlooked. In order to prove that "none should despair because of the magnitude of his crimes," St. Peter tells Alberic of the deathbed vision of a rich man who, after failing to seduce another man's wife, later repented and helped to rescue that man from Saracen captivity.[42] As he was dying, he saw a demon with a great book inscribed with all his sins. At the last moment, however, an angel appeared with a vial filled with tears the rich man had shed for the imprisoned husband and in contrition for his own sins. These tears, sprinkled on the book, erased a third of his sins.[43] In the "art of dying" illustrations, demons flaunt the record of deeds in order to tempt the dying man to despair; the corresponding inspiration to hope relies on consoling images of salvation by grace, rather than a counterbalancing record of virtues. Thus, by the fifteenth century, the book of deeds had been transformed from a symbol of impartial justice into a reminder of the need for mercy and intercession.

One can trace a similar development in the medieval Christian image of the weighing of souls. Originally, at least in the biblical tradition, weighing in a balance was a metaphor for the exact and impartial measurement of a person's worth: "thou art weighed in the balance and found wanting."[44] In medieval art and vision literature, however, the weighing of the soul or its deeds changed from a trial into a contest. On the Last Judgment tympana of many cathedrals, Michael, the soul's champion, appears holding the balance while a devil tries to tip it; in some cases angelic or saintly intercessors are shown exerting their influence on the soul's side of the scale.[45] In the balance scene of the Vision of Thurkill, impartiality is quite beside the point: when a certain priest's evil deeds outweigh his virtues, St. Paul throws an aspergillum onto the scale, knocking the incriminating weights out of the pan and onto the foot of the devil, who hops off in a rage, waving his ineffectual roll of deeds.[46] Similarly, in the near-death vision of John, dean of Aix, described by Caesarius, the scale of judgment is brought in by demons, "who always inflict themselves upon the dying."[47]

As these examples show, the theme of a weighing or recording of deeds became associated with a "pharisaic" or demonic legalism, mercifully overruled by Christ or by the saints and angels who act as instruments of the new law of grace. E. P. Sanders has demonstrated, however, that this pervasive Christian view of rabbinic Judaism as a religion of legalistic "works-righteousness" rests on a misreading of the Jewish iconography of judgment. In rabbinic texts, the imagery of the book and the balance is intended to support moral exhortation and theodicy; it does not represent an account-book soteriology according to which salvation can be earned by amassing a greater number of merits than debts.[48] Here is an obvious instance in which unnecessary theological and historical misunderstandings have resulted from a failure to recognize the dramatic and didactic character of images of the afterlife.

Just as evil deeds are revealed externally in the other world, so good deeds may appear in a material form to assist and comfort the soul. Among the good deeds rewarded in heaven, almsgiving lends itself particularly well to concrete visualization, in such forms as the golden mansions seen by Gregory's soldier. Medieval visions appear to take the idea of redemption literally, linking it with the ancient notion that the dead must pay the ferryman; those who sacrifice their wealth in this world pass through the gate of heaven as easily as if they had bribed a customs official. Conversely, when Barontus meets St. Peter he finds himself momentarily embarrassed for funds because he held back a secret cache of twelve gold coins when he joined the monastery. The monk returns to life, under orders to give one coin to a poor pilgrim every month for a year, so that finally, as St. Peter puts it, "you will buy yourself passage to the heavenly country."[49] The systematization of penitential practices during the Middle Ages could only encourage such financial analogies.

The idea that we are building our future dwellings through our actions in life extends beyond almsgiving to include all kinds of deeds. Medieval visions often depict houses that demonstrate the worth of their owners by their relative strength, purity, and opulence. So, too, do evil deeds contribute to the architecture of the other world, enclosing usurers in infernal counting-houses and seating tyrants on fiery thrones.

In the Vision of the Monk of Wenlock, the visible manifestation of deeds is not unlike the Zoroastrian *daena*:

> And he heard all the particular sins with which he had disgraced himself from his youth on, and had either neglected to confess, forgotten, or not known to be sinful. Each in its own voice cried out against him and accused him most dreadfully, and each specific vice came forward as if in person, one of them saying: "I am your greed, by which you have so often desired things that are illicit and contrary to God's precepts. . . ."[50]

The parade of vices continues, as the monk makes the acquaintance of his vainglory, falsehood, idle speech, disobedience to superiors, sluggishness, wandering thoughts in church, and so on.[51] Then evil spirits, "joining in the chorus of accusation," bring forward one of his victims, a living man whose very wound and blood cry out against the monk.[52] He is defended, however, by his personified virtues—obedience, fasting, prayer, chanting of psalms—each the monastic antidote for one of his sins.

The personification of deeds takes a particularly novel form in the Vision of Thurkill. While in hell, the visionary attends a theater whose fiery seats are constructed by sins and dismantled by penance and alms. Here sinners are forced to imitate themselves for the entertainment of the demons. A proud man who struts about self-importantly, puffing his cheeks in indignation, provides endless merriment for the infernal spectators. It appears that the demons have staged an elaborate "type satire," as several stereotyped characters come forward in succession to act out their sins.[53]

The accounts we have just considered are notable for their use of the narrative technique of personifying abstract qualities. Whether considered as a device of allegory, as a strategy by which the imagination brings unconscious contents into consciousness, or as a process embedded in language itself, personification imagery is a fascinating and complex subject. To do it justice would take us outside the context of otherworld journeys, for even in medieval literature personification does not always involve a visionary framework. Indeed, compared to *Piers Plowman* and similar allegorical works, the use of personification imagery in return-from-death stories is fairly restrained. The monk of Wenlock encounters vices that are particular to him as well as generally relevant to monastic life. Although hardly idiosyncratic, they do not correspond to any standardized lists of the sins. By the fifteenth century, however, the systematization of medieval views of sin and penance is evident in vision narratives. The late-fourteenth-century Vision of Lazarus echoes Vergil's saying that the pains of hell cannot be numbered, but then reduces them to seven, to match the seven cardinal sins. In the same period, two accounts of pilgrimage to St. Patrick's Purgatory, one fanciful and the other in a veridical style, bring the infernal landscape into conformity with the same catalogue of the seven sins.[54] This standardization is a sign of the decline of the genre. By the fifteenth century, the otherworld journey is primarily a vehicle for allegory or romance; as a result, the vision framework is explicitly conventional, and stereotypes are preferred to personal details.

In our discussion of obstacles encountered in the other world, a few notable characteristics have come up repeatedly. We have seen that the perilous bridge-crossing and the encounter with deeds reflect an older tradition concerning the soul's dangerous journey and the challenge by evil spirits and that, for didactic purposes, such external ordeals are often interpreted as manifestations of an internal state of affairs. This permits Gregory, Caesarius, and others to make the point that judgment is partly an intrinsic process, the self-assessment of souls whom death or doomsday has unmasked. In the encounter with deeds, the protagonist is, in effect, turned inside out; his inner state, the acts and impulses that were hidden even to himself, are projected outward onto the stage of the other world. The encounter with deeds is in this respect perhaps the most significant moment, even the epitome, of the otherworld journey; never is it more clear that the other world is the domain of the imagination. Some implications of this observation will become evident in part IV, when we approach the interpretation of near-death visions.

Our consideration of obstacle scenes thus brings to light a feature to which we will have reason to return; it reveals one way in which the other world functions as a reference point for symbolic or metaphorical discourse. The idea of being weighed down by guilt or attachment, for instance—a natural corollary of Christian or Platonic ascensional spirituality—is illustrated by the vision narratives in ways that range from abstract metaphorical statements to concrete visualization. Gregory speaks of guilt as blocking the passage of sinners across the bridge, while the Vision of Alberic develops the image into a picture of souls whose progress on the bridge is slowed down by their heavy cargo of bad deeds. Occasionally the image is even more externalized: the burden is an object one has stolen or a victim one has injured. Setting these obstacle texts side by side, we can see a common thread that runs from sophisticated to cruder, more dramatic expressions, from the Augustinian theme of the soul's gravity to Tundal dragging along his godfather's cow.

This study yields a general rule for the interpretation of religious or visionary literature: we should avoid the premature separation of "literal" from "spiritual" significance. Gregory is sensitive to this principle when he moralizes the encounter with deeds without abolishing its literal sense; for him the other world is a place where inner values take on external forms, which must be understood symbolically even while they are experienced "corporeally." At the same time, even outside the context of vision literature, symbols of judgment, such as the weighing of deeds, and symbols of spiritual journey, such as the two paths, seem to derive their vitality from our capacity to place them imaginatively in the other world. The common saying that "the road to hell is paved with good intentions," in contrast, has limited force because we know that it is only metaphorical; we no longer see it as a feature of otherworld topography. Thus, the other world is a repository for our symbols; as the opposite pole to this world, it makes possible the alternation of current, or exchange of meaning, by which a symbol lives.

CHAPTER 5

Reentry

THE ACCOUNTS WE are considering provide so comprehensive a tour of the realms of punishment that the reader is inclined to think he or she has peered into every cavity of Leviathan's mouth; yet the sight of heaven, usually saved for last, is almost coquettishly brief. As Caesarius of Heisterbach puts it:

> . . . a bitter potion tasted beforehand makes a sweet one taste sweeter, and an undercoat of black paint makes the white shine more brightly. Read the visions of Wetti, Gottschalk, and others to whom it was granted to see the pains of the wicked and the glory of the elect: the vision of punishment always comes first.[1]

This observation is confirmed by the visions of Drythelm, the monk of Wenlock, Alberic, Edmund, the Boy William, Tundal, Owen, and Thurkill.[2] The hell-first itinerary is a sign that the otherworld journey account has become a form of conversion narrative: the protagonist progresses from a deathlike state through hell or purgatory to a state of transformation. Whether it is depicted as the experience of a change of heart or as the decision to enter a specific religious order, conversion is the main theme of most twelfth- and thirteenth-century vision narratives. For this reason, there is no need to describe a long interlude in heaven; once the visionary has imbibed the bitter potions served up in hell, a mere taste of heavenly bliss is enough to prove that it is worth the effort to live well enough to win a place there. Transformation is expressed by the visionary's return to the body to take up a new way of life.

Shortly upon arriving in heaven, then, the visionary learns that it is time to go back to the world, whether to benefit others with tidings of the afterlife,

to profit by a second chance to atone for sins, or to carry out a special assign-
ment. Salvius is in the midst of enjoying the fragrance of heaven when a voice
interrupts to say, "send this man back into the world, since he is necessary to
our churches."[3] Salvius does not welcome the decree, however:

> Alas, alas, Lord, why have you shown me these things, if I was to be cheated
> of them? Behold! Today you are casting me out from your face, to return to
> the perishable world, so that in the end I won't have the power to come back
> here.[4]

Reassured of God's guardianship, Salvius nonetheless weeps his way back to
life, sits up on the funeral bier, and laments his return.

Similarly, Drythelm finds his journey cut short after he has toured the
purgatorial valley of fire and ice, the pit of the eternally lost, the flowery
abode of the near-perfect, and is on the point of crossing the threshold of
heaven. Pulling him back down to the meadow, his guide explains,

> Now you must go back to the body and live among men again; but if you strive
> to examine your actions more carefully and to keep your ways and words in
> righteousness and simplicity, you will gain for yourself a dwelling-place after
> death among these rejoicing multitudes of blessed souls whom you behold.[5]

It is no sooner said than done; Drythelm discovers, to his great dismay, that
he has suddenly returned to life.

The command to return to life, as formulated in visions of the Drythelm
line, is clearly modeled on Gregory's account of the vision of the hermit
Peter, which ends with the command, "Leave, and consider carefully how
you will live from now on."[6] The same formula occurs in the visions of Adamnán, the Boy William, and Owen. William's guide tells him, "This will be
your place if you have lived well."[7] In the seventh-century vision related by
Valerio of Bierzo, the monk Maximus is told, "Go immediately and return
to your home, and if you behave well, then as soon as you come back again I
will take you into this place of delight and you will remain with me until
eternity."[8] Like Salvius, Maximus begs to remain but has no choice; a
moment later, he opens his eyes to find himself confined in his "little body"
(*corpusculum*), undergoing funeral rites.

Adamnán, too, finds his visit abruptly concluded:

> But when he bethought him to rest and tarry in that land, he heard, through
> the veil, the angel's voice, enjoining him to return again into that body whence
> he had departed, and to rehearse in courts and assemblies, and in the great
> congregations of laymen and of clerics, the rewards of Heaven and the pains
> of hell, even as his guardian angel had revealed them unto him.[9]

The author suggests that Adamnán's subsequent career as saint and scholar
simply reflected his effort to enact this command.

The Vision of the Monk of Eynsham paints a vivid picture of the baffle-
ment of the onlookers as the dead man revives, and of the visionary's distress
at finding himself in the flesh again. The monk Edmund begins to stir, his

eyelids quiver, tears stream down, and he sighs and mumbles, gradually forming words of lament: "O holy Mary, for what sin do I lose so great a joy?"[10] When the brothers ask him how he is feeling, he replies, "truly was I well until this moment, but now I am truly ill." Edmund recalls that St. Nicholas sent him back so that he might persevere and win the rewards he has seen. Yet even though he revives on Easter eve to the cheering sound of heavenly bell-ringing, he weeps for days over the misfortune of his unasked-for resurrection.

Tundal, sent back because he does not deserve to remain, similarly asks his angelic guide, "Lord, what great evils have I ever done that I must go back to my body, leaving behind such glory?"[11] The angel only warns him to remember what he has seen and strive to abstain from his former behavior. Then, without any lapse of time, Tundal feels his soul dragged into the heavy orbit of its body.[12] Gottschalk's soul, also, "endeavored with all its might to avoid the grip of the body."[13]

Visitors to St. Patrick's Purgatory are among the few who, in contrast, appear pleased to return to the world. In the account of Raymond de Perelhos, for example, the Purgatory is depicted as a dangerous subterranean labyrinth, from which one is fortunate to escape; the prior in charge attempts to dissuade Raymond from entering by echoing the warning Vergil's Sibyl gives to Aeneas: "Truly, I confess that to descend into the Purgatory is easy, but to recall one's steps, this is the task, this the toil."[14] In spite of this, however, Raymond returns to the world as abruptly as the other visionaries.

The Visionary Transformed

Although the journey back to the body is usually effortless and instantaneous, it is an axiom of medieval vision literature that those who return from the other world are never the same again. As we saw in chapter 2, Drythelm revives from death with the conviction that "from now on I must live not according to my old habits, but in a much different manner." Distributing his goods among his wife, his sons, and the poor, he retires to the monastery of Old Melrose, where he finds spiritual solace in prayer, fasting, and soaking in an icy river, a self-imposed ordeal that recalls some accounts of the torment of graded immersion. Asked how he can bear the bitter cold, he replies, "I have seen colder things," and to those who wonder that he should volunteer for such harsh penance, he declares, "I have seen harsher." Bede adds further testimonials of Drythelm's transformation:

> Until the day of [his] death, he persevered in such penance of mind and body that even if his tongue had kept silent, his life would have proclaimed that he had seen many things, either dreadful or desirable, that have been hidden from others.[15]

This description, like the formula for the command to return, appears to be modeled on Gregory's account of the vision of the hermit Peter:

> After the voice [telling him to return to life], warmth gradually stole back into his limbs and, waking from the sleep of eternal death, he related everything that had gone on around him. And from then on he chastened himself with such vigils and fasts that even if his tongue had kept silent, his way of life would have proclaimed that he had seen and been terrified by the torments of hell.[16]

This formula echoes throughout the Drythelm line. Commenting on Alberic's vision, Peter the Deacon describes the aftermath by patching together phrases from Gregory and Bede:

> He prevails today in such great abstinence and gravity of manner that no one doubts that he has witnessed and been terrified by the pains of sinners, and has seen the glory of the saints. For from that time until now, God willing, he has consumed neither meat, nor fat, nor wine; he has never worn shoes, and to this day he has persevered in this monastery of Monte Cassino in such penance and humility of heart and body that even if his tongue kept silent, his life would proclaim that he had seen many things, either dreadful or desirable, that were hidden from others.[17]

The theme of the visionary's transformation held special attraction for Cistercian writers, in part because they were fascinated with the penitential significance of purgatory and in part because, as R. W. Southern points out, "they were the last generation of medieval men to believe that it was good for all men to be monks."[18] Owen, Gunthelm, and Tundal display their transformation by seeking refuge in the Cistercian order, thus suggesting that a general "conversion of mores" is insufficient guarantee of heavenly reward. Caesarius of Heisterbach, who counts "a foretaste of the pains of hell" among the chief motivations for entering a Cistercian monastery, relates several vision stories that sanction conversion to the white monks.[19] Helinand de Froidmont retells the Drythelm story with the same idea in mind, translating the visionary from a seventh-century Northumbrian who becomes a Benedictine monk into a twelfth-century Englishman who becomes a Cistercian.[20]

The otherworld journey leaves its mark not only in conversion, austerities, and other signs of reform, but also in long-lasting physical and emotional effects. Caesarius states, as if it were a commonly held opinion, that those who come back from the dead never laugh again. In his account of the otherworld visions and subsequent conversion of the abbot Morimond, he offers confirmation of this theory in the words of a reliable witness:

> Know that I myself watched him closely for that, but I never detected any tendency to levity in his manner, such was his seriousness and forbearance; I never even saw him smiling or uttering frivolous words.[21]

Jacques de Vitry claims the same transformation for penitents who survive a journey through St. Patrick's Purgatory.[22]

In addition, the visionaries return to life afflicted (or blessed) with a variety of symptoms, some related to their illness, others of supernatural origin. Fursa sweats on cold days, and the monk of Wenlock is blinded for a week and suffers memory loss. Gottschalk returns with three "witnesses of the vision"—pain in the head, the side, and the feet—but also finds that he is immune to fire.[23] Orm temporarily loses the power of speech, and Alberic is so stupefied that for several days he cannot recognize his own mother.

Old wounds are healed, or new scars appear. Fursa bears a permanent burn mark on his shoulder and jaw from a flaming soul flung at him by a demon; Bede finds it quite wonderful that "what the soul suffered in secret, the flesh showed openly."[24] On the other hand, Edmund of Eynsham finds upon his recovery that an open wound on his leg has disappeared without a trace. In a letter to a friend, Antonio Mannini describes the effect of his visit to St. Patrick's Purgatory: "The bearer of this will tell you how I came out marked, for I showed him so that he might tell you about it; and perhaps I shall carry the mark forever."[25] This supernatural branding may be the visionary's counterpart to the medieval pilgrim's badge.

Perhaps the most peculiar souvenir, however, is the one acquired by Alberic. Just before sending the youth back to his body, St. Peter produces an enormous document covered with minute inscriptions, folds it into a tiny page, and makes him swallow it. Here, presumably, are his instructions for life, delivered in a form that will not fade with time; as the apostle says, "you will not be allowed to reject it, and your blood will not dissolve it."[26] Not long afterward, the capsule takes effect, for Alberic gives up all his property and enters the monastery of Monte Cassino.

The Visionary as Messenger

Just as Er must forgo the waters of Lethe in order to be "the messenger to mankind to tell them of the other world," so the medieval visionary is obliged to remember the journey and bring back a report to the living. According to Bede, this is the purpose of Drythelm's journey: "in order to arouse the living from spiritual death, a certain man, already dead for some time, rose up again in his body and related many memorable things that he had seen."[27] The monk of Wenlock receives explicit orders:

> . . . the blessed angels admonished the man who saw and heard all these things in spiritual contemplation while rapt out of the body, that he was to go back to his own body without delay. He must not hesitate to reveal the things he had been shown to believers and those asking with a pious intention, but must refuse to discuss them with scoffers. To a certain woman who lived in a far-off place, he was to expound the sins she had committed one by one, and intimate to her that by offering satisfaction she could propitiate herself to God if she wished. To a certain priest named Begga, he was to disclose all these spiritual visions and afterwards proclaim them to men just as the priest instructed him.[28]

Wetti's atonement consists in proclaiming publicly, along with the general theme of punishment and reward after death, pointed criticisms of negligent monks, priests, counts, and emperors. In a *roman à clef*, partly unlocked by Walahfrid Strabo's acrostics spelling out the culprits' names, Wetti describes the postmortem sufferings of the once mighty Charlemagne, and delivers ultimata to several living political and clerical figures. The emperor Charles the Fat sees his father, uncle, and cousin, who urge him to learn from their mistakes. Edmund of Eynsham sees Henry II. Thurkill watches the devils make sport of a judge well known for his corruption. Such description of particular individuals, rather than groups of anonymous sinners, is an innovation which, according to David Traill, can be dated to the sixth century.[29]

Yet, while some visionaries feel a compulsion to tell their tale akin to the obsession of Coleridge's Ancient Mariner, there is also a certain taboo against publishing the secrets of heaven. After giving in to his brothers' entreaties to describe his experience, Salvius cries,

> Woe is me, that I have dared to reveal such a mystery. For behold, the sweet fragrance which I was drinking in from the holy place, and by which I was sustained for these three days without any food or drink, has receded from me. And my tongue is covered with horrible sores, and is so swollen that it seems to fill my whole mouth. Now I know that it was not well pleasing to the Lord my God that these secrets should be publicized.[30]

Fursa and Drythelm will tell their visions only to sincere penitents, and Alberic, Tundal, and Edmund of Eynsham, who publicize their experiences widely, remain as tight-lipped as St. Paul about the celestial paradise.[31] Adamnán and Antonio Mannini say that what they experienced cannot be revealed because it is ineffable, and Thurkill fears that he is too simple-minded to play the preacher. Caesarius and many other authors warn that the visionary who parades his gifts is flirting with the deadly sin of vainglory.[32]

On the other hand, to account for the existence of the narrative, someone must step in to overrule the bashful visionary. When Wetti protests that he is too lowly to be the herald of such momentous tidings, his angelic guide scolds him, "What the supreme judgment of God orders, you, held back by lazy sluggishness, have not the nerve to proclaim?"[33] Similarly, according to the Roger of Wendover version of the Vision of Thurkill, St. Julian visits Thurkill in a dream in order to prod him out of his hesitation, reminding him that "he had been taken out [of his body] just so that he might publish those things that he heard."[34] Thurkill obediently sets out the next morning on a highly successful lecture tour, moving audiences to tears in parish after parish, and amazing those who once thought him an inarticulate rustic.[35] Here the otherworld journey narrative reproduces, on a less noble scale, the motif of the illiterate or the stutterer who, like Moses, suddenly becomes an eloquent prophet.

Often it is a superior on earth who persuades the visionary to tell his story. We have seen that the monk of Wenlock learned his role as a messenger from coaches on both sides of life's threshold—the priest Begga, who probably helped to shape the monk's story, and the angelic guides, whose instruction dovetailed nicely with the author's interests. In the Vision of the Monk of Eynsham, Edmund reminds his prior that it was obedience alone that loosened his tongue:

> I have related to you as concisely as I could the things that were revealed to me . . . since I was coaxed by the love and compelled by the command of your holiness.[36]

The Narrator as Messenger

The reticence of the visionary is matched by the narrator, who portrays himself as equally unwilling to display his poor talents except under a superior's orders. H. of Sawtry explains that however much he would like to edify people, he would not dare to retell Owen's story were it not for his abbot's insistence.[37] Adam of Eynsham excuses his presumption by saying that "great men" (Thomas the prior and St. Hugh the bishop of Lincoln) commissioned him to put his brother's vision in writing. Ralph of Coggeshall claims that he was "compelled by the importunity" of fellow monks to record the Vision of Thurkill.

This modest posture no doubt reflects the real pressures of the system of intellectual patronage and of life under monastic discipline; in some narratives, however, it is evidently a literary conceit. Even though, as David Traill tells us, Walahfrid's poem helped him win a place as tutor to Charles the Bald, the young author insists that, far from seeking advancement, he was "forced to break [silence] and impelled, as if by a goad, to keep on writing." For Walahfrid, as for Adam of Eynsham and Ralph of Coggeshall, the claim of writing under protest is intended to disarm in advance the objections of skeptics. Traill points out that expressions of reluctance to publish in classical and medieval literature are frequently only pro forma; he suggests that Walahfrid, at least, is deliberately imitating the stylish prefaces of Jerome and other accomplished Latinists.[38]

A close look at the narrators' remarks in the longer vision stories reveals an intricate set of literary conventions, woven together to form a defense of both the style and the content of the narrative. The clearest examples of this can be found in the Vision of the Monk of Eynsham as narrated by Adam of Eynsham, the Vision of Owen, and the Vision of Thurkill composed soon afterward by Ralph of Coggeshall. Each of these narratives begins with a similarly worded argument for the authenticity of the vision. The authors refer to biblical passages on visionary experience in the future life (1 Cor. 13:9-12; 2 Cor. 3:13-16, 4:6; 1 Thess. 5:4-5; and Heb. 1:1), reinterpreting these passages in ways that will support their claims. Echoing Gregory's opinion that visions have become more frequent because the world is already partially illuminated by Doomsday's aurora, they review St. Paul's contrast between our present condition of dark, enigmatic understanding and the eschatological hope for a face-to-face vision of God.[39] Adam of Eynsham declares:

> Those things that the fathers perceived in a mirror and an enigma, but not in open revelation, are now actually seen by some people, and are understood with greater certainty by others, since they have heard them from those who have seen. Many things previously unheard-of and hidden from mortal eyes, have been brought into the light; things that once were doubted have become certain, and things that lay completely concealed have been set out in clear view.[40]

Ralph of Coggeshall similarly introduces Thurkill's story with the claim that the coming of Christ has ushered in a new era in which God speaks to his people by means of direct revelation rather than obscure and enigmatic hints about the future life; and he cites the visions of Owen, Tundal, and Edmund of Eynsham in order to show how common this experience has become in his time.

In part IV, we shall see that contemporary near-death literature is shaped by conventions comparable to those we are considering here. One such convention, the vigorous protestation of honesty, is a standard feature of medieval return-from-death narratives. The twelfth-century monk Alberic prefaces the revised account of his vision with a letter declaring that it is "better to say nothing of all this than to relate something false and fabricated"; he anathematizes the editors who have added fanciful elements such as the height of the gates of hell, a conversation between Moses and God, and Adam's postmortem menu.[41] Adam of Eynsham protests, perhaps too much, that he would rather keep silent forever than commit the sin of lying; and Ralph of Coggeshall also vouches for the veracity of Adam's account:

> Another vision, which took place in the year 1196 in the monastery of Eynsham, has been splendidly set down in an accurate account which Adam, the subprior of that monastery, an extremely serious and religious man, wrote in an elegant style, just as he heard it from the mouth of him who had been taken out of his body for two days and nights. I do not believe that such a man, so religious and so learned, would have decided to commit [these things] to writing unless they had been investigated and supported by credible evidence; especially since he was at that time chaplain to Hugh, Bishop of Lincoln, a very holy man.[42]

Ralph reports that he personally interviewed the former prior of Eynsham, who assured him that "he had no more doubt of the truth of this vision than of the crucifixion of our Lord Jesus Christ," and supplied additional proofs.

Beyond literary convention, however, there seems to have been a real campaign to win support for Adam's account of Edmund's vision. Ralph of Coggeshall remarks that "the reason I am reporting all this is that many of his own brothers reject the vision. . . ." Interestingly, the copy of this vision in the *Book of Revelations* (compiled by Peter of Cornwall a short while before the appearance of the Vision of Thurkill) is defaced by crosses that have been partially erased. Peter explains:

> Thinking that this vision could not be true, I, Peter, crossed it out of this book, but afterwards I proved it to be entirely authentic through witnesses who were truth-telling and well acquainted with the matter.[43]

What were the proofs that persuaded Peter of Cornwall to change his mind and so impressed the author of Thurkill's vision? In a final chapter, added later, Adam supplies evidence that he considers decisive. Along with some secret effects, which Adam does not disclose, Edmund's story was confirmed by a number of external signs. As if throwing down a gauntlet to potential detractors, Adam presents these signs. He asks the skeptics to consider whether anyone could feign as strange an illness as Edmund's. Could someone known to be afflicted with sleeplessness lie stiff as a board for two days, not stirring even when bystanders made loud noises and pricked him with goads? When the monk's eyes sank back into his head, their lights extinguished, and his breath faded, leaving only a tenuous fluttering in his veins, was this just a "cunning deceit"? When to all these "manifest proofs" are added the miraculous healing of the monk's leg and his constant tears, even those of weak faith must acknowledge that "these things were made known to believers not by human fabrication but by divine command."[44]

If Adam of Eynsham and others harp on evidence, it may be because the mundane settings in which medieval visions occur highlight their extraordinary character in a way that strains credulity. Jewish and early Christian revelations are authorized by the exalted status of the visionary, in his pseudonymous guise as antediluvian hero, king, patriarch, prophet, or apostle; but the medieval Christian vision is a more democratic affair. A close brush with death, in the Middle Ages as today, is the poor man's mantle of prophecy— it can happen to anyone. The criteria for judging authenticity are therefore partly empirical: the credentials of the visionary and his witnesses, and the signs or aftereffects that corroborate his account.

The credentials of the visionary vary according to his place in society. He may be a sinner who could have nothing to gain by disclosing the punishments he has been forced to sample.[45] He may be a penitent or saint with no interest in fame, like Salvius, who favored seclusion, or Owen, who sought an obscure post with the Cistercians in Ireland. Or he may be a simple peasant, like Orm, Gottschalk, or Thurkill, too naive to concoct an elaborate fraud. Several of the visionaries are children—Baldarius, Ansgar, Orm, Alberic, the Boy William—who, even if they are not exactly innocent little lambs, are thought unlikely to feign conversion. Indeed, far from representing a state of sinlessness, these youthful visionaries stand for the Christian penitent who, like a child, must be reared with threats and promises, and will never learn to behave until he sees a graphic picture of heaven and hell.[46]

These visionaries are not figures from the legendary past, but contemporaries, neighbors, and colleagues, who display individual characteristics even when they serve as ideal types. What the medieval otherworld journey narrative loses in scriptural authority, then, it gains in familiarity. Personal details such as Thurkill's flooded fields, his problems with tithing, his cough, his search for his mother, and his confrontations with his father and landlord, help to ground his story, however universal its themes, in concrete history. The narrative persuades not only because it has the right credentials, but also because the reader can identify with it.

If, as in many non-hagiographic vision stories, the protagonist is too obscure to command recognition and respect, the narrator often compensates by interviewing witnesses and invoking the good reputation of his sources, as we have seen Gregory the Great and Ralph of Coggeshall do. In some cases, the narrator even seeks out the visionary himself, so that he can say, like Christ's disciples, "what need we any further testimony? for we have heard it from his own mouth."[47] And, as we have seen, the author makes a great point of minimizing his own role, insisting that he is just a reporter presenting the unvarnished story without fancy rhetoric.

In addition to these testimonials, medieval authors offer external proofs that are remarkably similar to the kind of evidence brought forward in contemporary near-death literature: the transformation of the visionary, unusual physical and emotional symptoms, signs that he was truly dead, and extraordinary powers, such as the ability to predict his own death or that of others, or to know things that he could not have found out through normal means. Gregory the Great, the authors of the Vision of Wetti, and others cite evidence of the sort modern psychical researchers have termed "crisis apparitions," in which the visionary sees another soul just at its moment of death, and "cross correspondences," in which certain details are confirmed by another person's vision, even though the two visionaries have no knowledge of each other.[48]

Finally, our authors frequently appeal simply to the virtue of faith. For example, Ralph of Coggeshall compares those who reject Thurkill's vision to the scoffers who populate biblical miracle stories:

> ... it is written of the Lord our Savior's many miracles on earth that "some said he is a good man, and others said no, but he seduces the people" [John 7:12]. No wonder, then, that a certain vision which took place in the year 1206 in our parts, should be rejected and held worthless by some. But since many people of sounder mind, keener intellect, and more religious life put faith in this vision, both because of the simplicity and innocence of the man to whom it befell, and because many have profited to no small degree from hearing this vision narrated, being inspired to choose a more perfect way of life; and since I have been asked by some of my comrades—nay rather compelled by their importunity—I have taken the trouble to commit briefly to writing the vision of a simple man in simple words, just as I have heard it from his mouth.[49]

Educated medieval readers surely noticed the literary posturing, the conventional claim of simplicity and concern for the rustic, the familiar ring of such phrases as "even if his tongue had kept silent," as well as the repetition in the narrative of standard otherworld scenes. Apparently, however, they did not consider these grounds for rejecting an account. This brings up a fundamental difference between medieval and modern canons of interpretation. Whereas modern readers might doubt the veracity of a narrative filled with easily recognized conventions, medieval readers considered the recurrence of well-known motifs a sign of authenticity. We tend to search for unprecedented elements, as if these were the kernels of truth masked by husks of borrowed formulas, but medieval readers believed that after all the proofs have been tallied, there is no better index of an account's validity than its edifying qualities and its conformity to tradition. That is why our authors so often point unabashedly to the precedents they have followed, saying as Guido does in his prologue to Alberic's vision, "what we describe is neither new nor incredible."

Vision and Revision

From otherworld visions to tales of terrestrial exploration, from devotional and contemplative writing to allegories, medieval imaginative literature thrives within, rather than despite, the constraints of genre and convention. We should not dismiss recurrent images and formulas as a sign of mechanical literary formalism. Such inherited patterns as the motif of reluctance to publish are more than merely decorative; in narratives based on actual visions they simultaneously mold and express the experience of the visionary.

A case in point is the Vision of Thurkill. Paul Gerhard Schmidt attempts in an article on this narrative to distinguish the literary contribution of the author, Ralph of Coggeshall, from the original experience of the visionary; he suggests that Thurkill's own report is responsible for particularized features, such as the presence of the little-known saint Domninus and of St. Osith, patron of the visionary's home county, while the more stereotyped characters—the dishonest miller, the adulterer, and the proud man who perform in the theater of hell—reflect the literate interests of the author.[50] The influence of Ralph of Coggeshall might also be seen in the emphasis this vision places on the virtues of hospitality and honest tithing. But the narrative contains other elements that, in view of the popular diffusion of pilgrimage and otherworld vision lore, either Thurkill or Ralph of Coggeshall could equally well have contributed. If, as Schmidt believes, both were familiar with the Vision of Gunthelm, then they may share the responsibility for adapting the portrait of Adam and the sinners' theatrics from this earlier account.[51]

The situation is complicated by the fact that the vision story does not jump in one bound from the visionary's oral report to the narrator's pen. The Vision of the Monk of Eynsham, like many other literary records of return from death, appeared long after Edmund reportedly had his vision. And Paul Schmidt has shown that Thurkill's story evolved over a period of weeks dur-

ing which he met with his parish priest, family, and neighbors. As H. L. D.
Ward says,

> [Thurkill] told it by snatches at first: and no doubt it grew. One can imagine
> him telling a monk of St. Osith's how Roger Picoth lamented his standing
> debts to his workmen (an idea that would naturally occur to a humble tenant
> of the Picoths) and the monk's rejoining, "did he say nothing of his dues to St.
> Osith's?"[52]

Thurkill's audience stood to gain a great deal from his report that their
departed landlord wished his son to pay off his debts; leading questions may
also have been responsible for his indictment of a local judge and for the
special messages he brought back to his neighbors, revealing how many
masses their deceased relatives needed to win release from purgatory.[53] C. J.
Holdsworth sums it up:

> In the longer accounts it is pretty obvious that the amanuenses affected the
> development in many ways. One can at times almost hear them prompting
> the seer, "And what happened next? did you see your parents? what had hap-
> pened to the last abbot we had before this one? and how was the late king
> faring who so often burdened Mother Church with unjust taxes to support his
> lust for glory?"[54]

In short, we cannot simply peel away the literary wrapper and put our
hands on an unembellished event. Even when a vision actually did occur, it
is likely to have been reworked many times before being recorded. The vision
is a collaborative effort, produced by the interaction of the visionary with
neighbors, counselors, the narrator, and other interested parties. One cannot
point to the moment when the vision changed from a matter of personal
confession into a public project; rather, it is built up in layers placed over one
another like a series of transparencies. Though a bottom layer of actual experience may be present in some (but certainly not in all) vision stories, its contours are nearly indistinguishable from those of the superimposed images
through which we discern it.

Even the hypothetical bottom layer—the visionary's own experience—
has a collective aspect. Artistic and literary depictions of the deathbed reveal
that dying in the Middle Ages was a social event, an occasion for interaction
with family or clergy—as well as invisible hosts—through liturgy, prayer, set-
tling of property claims, and vocal reading. It is in a deathbed setting of this
sort that Wetti calls for Gregory's *Dialogues* to be read aloud. No doubt this
helps to orient him for his journey to the next world; some would say that
the text fuels his febrile hallucinations. When Wetti comes back to life, the
social interaction immediately resumes, as his brothers press to hear his
report.

In a sense, the visionary's interaction with his neighbors never ceases.
His very experience of the other world is shaped by expectations, both conscious and subliminal, that he shares with his peers, and he draws upon a
common treasury of images from scripture, folklore or literary tradition, and

religious art. During the time in which he is seeing the unseen and hearing the unheard-of, the visionary is inwardly engaged in the kind of interpretation, comparison, and discussion with others that accompanies all of our experience and is inseparable from it. A second transparency slides easily over the first, as the vision is further articulated through give and take with the audience.

The third transparency, which appears when the vision is committed to writing, reflects a more deliberate effort to bring the vision into conformity with preexistent models, from Ixion's wheel to the Easter chronology. The author will shape the vision into a vehicle for hagiography, didactic prose, political satire, allegory, or other special aims. If the narrative is successful, subsequent redactors will overlay it with transparencies of their own, suppressing unnecessary details and adapting the account to fit the genre in which it appears, as do Gregory the Great, Bede, Aelfric, Roger of Wendover, Caesarius of Heisterbach, Helinand de Froidmont, Vincent of Beauvais, Jacques de Vitry, and many others.

Finally, although the bottom layer of personal experience may be imponderable, personal appropriation of the story can occur at any level, adding to the vitality of the narrative. Alberic did this when he revised his vision after a few years of monastic education, and collaborated with Peter the Deacon to produce what he considered a more truthful account.[55] Rather than degenerating as it becomes further removed from its source, an account may gain in authenticity if it falls into the hands of an author who understands, from experience or artistic intuition, what it may have to offer. A narrative like the Vision of Alberic is saturated with actual experience; to attempt to dig down to its bottom layers may be almost as much beside the point as hunting for the man from Porlock, Beatrice, or the dark lady of the sonnets.

On the other hand, our authors, unlike Dante, insist on the factuality of their accounts, and their objective value as visible evidence of unseen truths. Adam of Eynsham is vehement in condemning fabrication, even though he obviously has reworked Edmund's vision; several times the angelic guides utter the same edifying phrases that Adam attributed, in an earlier biography, to St. Hugh of Lincoln.[56] Should we conclude that Adam of Eynsham, along with Gregory the Great, Alberic, Ralph of Coggeshall, and Peter of Cornwall, were deliberately deceiving their audience while pronouncing anathema against anyone who would tamper with their testimony?[57] Did they feel that their pious mission justified spinning any tale that might trick the infidels into faith? Such questions are likely to occur to modern readers struck by the contrast between their protestations of exact truth-telling and their free handling of the material they present.

To give our authors a fair hearing, however, we need to reexamine what they meant by verification. In one sense, they seem to be concerned with marshalling objective evidence to convince unbelievers that there is life and retribution after death. Gregory tells us that this is why he wrote the fourth book of the *Dialogues*, and Peter of Cornwall explains that he composed the *Book of Revelations* because "there are still some who believe that there is no God and the world is ruled by chance, and many who only believe what they see."[58]

Beyond these remarks, however, there is little evidence that our authors are trying to instill new beliefs in the minds of diehard skeptics. The unbeliever to whom they submit their proofs is a straw man; by conquering his doubts, they hope to bring their message home to those lukewarm or vacillating believers who make up their real audience. Gregory's proofs for survival of death appear in the context of a literary dialogue with a monk who agrees to "impersonate the weak." Similarly, Adam of Eynsham writes that he is supplying the proofs of Edmund's vision in case "the infidelity, or to put it more fairly, the infirmity, of some people be such that they do not credit what I have said."[59] Both authors suggest that unbelief is not a "tough-minded" or neutral position, in which the intellect demands hard evidence and reserves judgment until the facts are in; rather, it is a weakness, a disease or deformity of the will. Their target, therefore, is the de facto skeptic, who simply lacks the moral energy of his or her inherited convictions.

In this respect, the vision narratives we are considering are similar to many other works of Christian apology and instruction. The Christian philosophical proof of God or immortality—best exemplified by St. Anselm's argument with "the fool who says in his heart there is no God"—usually aims to attract an assent of the will, rather than to sway a disinterested intellect.[60] This important characteristic is easily overlooked by modern readers under the influence of the intellectualist outlook that prevails in our post-Enlightenment era; it becomes evident to us only when we fix our attention on the story, dialogue, or devotional narrative in which a proof or argument is embedded. Thus, Anselm's "ontological argument" for the existence of God is but an interlude in an extended narrative prayer. To debate the merits of this proof, extracted from the rest of the text, is certainly to misunderstand and impoverish it. So, too, when we consider narrative context, we see that the empirical arguments accompanying otherworld vision stories present a moral and imaginative challenge rather than a scientific one. The keynote is edification, even if the constant refrain is proof.

Indeed, our authors suggest that the visionary proof, taken in isolation, is an inferior way to approach the truth, unnecessary for the pure in heart or for the trained contemplative. Gregory reminds his readers that proofs of the soul's immortality are easy to come by, and therefore superfluous, for those who are taught directly by love.[61] Bede shares this sentiment; therefore, as Benedicta Ward points out, he would like us to think of his miracle and vision stories as "signs" that manifest truth to those who seek it, rather than as "proofs" of a previously doubted proposition.[62]

Interpretation of Visions

Medieval literature thus sends us mixed signals about the value of visionary testimony as evidence for the unseen. Even though Gregory, Adam of Eynsham, H. of Sawtry, and Ralph of Coggeshall speak of proofs and proclaim a new age of open revelation, they do not recommend that their readers seek visionary experiences of their own; they only wish to persuade us to take to heart the messages that other visionaries bring back. Far from touting visionary experience, these monastic authors show themselves well aware of the delusions, "vainglory," and morbid symptoms that can afflict the visionary.

In a passage frequently cited and echoed by medieval authors, Gregory cautions readers of the *Dialogues* that dreams and visions are often unreliable:

> What we must recognize, Peter, is that dream-images reach the soul in six ways. They arise from a full stomach or from an empty one, from illusion or from thought combined with illusion, from revelation or from thought combined with revelation.... But surely, since dreams are affected in turn by so many different conditions, one should believe them only with great difficulty, inasmuch as their source is hard to bring to light. Holy men, however, by a certain inner awareness, can discern which of the voices and images of their visions are illusions and which are revelations. Thus, they know whether something they perceive comes from the good Spirit, or whether they are experiencing an illusion. For if the mind does not put up a guard against these things, it will lose itself in countless vanities produced by the deceiver, who is accustomed to foretell many true things so that he can prevail in the end by ensnaring the soul on a single falsehood.[63]

As a pastoral theologian schooled in classical and Augustinian epistemology Gregory distrusts visions, and as a contemplative he is persuaded that in its highest capacity the soul rises beyond images. Even at its most sublime, Gregory believes, visionary experience involves the activity of an intermediate mental capacity, in which divine illumination mixes with sensory impressions.

Although Gregory believes that the dying can have visions while in a state of full awareness as well as in dream, he maintains that all communicable experience of the other world is symbolic:

> Repartus saw a pyre of wood, not because wood is burned in hell, but in order to be able to narrate to the living the nature of the burning of the wicked. He saw the fuel with which the living are familiar, so that through familiar things his listeners might learn what unfamiliar things they ought to dread.[64]

Gregory does not say that Repartus interpreted the unfamiliar in familiar terms for his listeners, but that he actually saw it that way; the content of his visionary experience appears to be determined by the didactic purpose of the narrative it will generate. Similarly, Gregory explains a dying man's vision of a ship waiting to take him to Sicily by treating the image as a pedagogical device; only in this way could he grasp the reality of his spiritual journey to the other world: "through images, Peter, we learn to appreciate the real significance of [our] situation."[65]

Although they usually spare their audiences the epistemological niceties, medieval vision narratives follow Gregory's lead in suggesting that what the protagonist saw, though real, should not be accepted too literally. In his intro-

duction to the *Treatise on the Purgatory of St. Patrick*, H. of Sawtry explains
that Owen saw things "as if in a corporeal form and likeness" simply because
he was a corporeal and mortal man.[66]

Sophisticated remarks of this sort abound in vision narratives, but they
do not yield a coherent rule for the interpretation of visions. Many ambigui-
ties remain, all related to a central question: was the visionary still attached
to a body, and, if so, what bearing does this have on the validity of the vision?
The case of St. Patrick's Purgatory is unique, perhaps, because the visionary
sets out for the other world in his body; but the authors of St. Patrick's Purgatory accounts do not say whether this physical entry is an advantage or an
obstacle to exploration of the other world. Laurence Rathold, a fifteenth-century pilgrim to the Purgatory, reports that he saw things "corporeally, but not
in themselves."[67] Does this mean that, had he discarded his body, he would
have encountered what philosophers since Kant have called the "thing-in-
itself"? More likely, he would be like the other visionaries about whom we
have read, neither in the body nor in the spirit but rather in the imagination,
and subject to influences from both. Those who appear to have attained a
"face-to-face" vision find that it slips away in the recoil to normal life, or that
in retelling it must be translated into the clumsy corporeal images of our mental repertoire. The problem is eschatological as well as corporeal; much
depends on how one interprets the "then" of Paul's "now in an enigma, then
face to face." Many Christian thinkers have maintained that the face-to-face
vision is reserved for the resurrection.

Only a few vision narratives attempt to describe what we might call transcendent or mystical experience in the context of the otherworld journey.
One model for this is Gregory's account of a visionary experience attributed
to St. Benedict. While watching the departure of a dying friend's soul, Benedict suddenly saw the whole world gathered before his eyes in a flood of light.
What intrigues Gregory about this episode is not Benedict's clairvoyance,
but his contemplative vision of the whole, which Gregory attributes to an
"enlarging" and "raising up" of the mind:

> ... anyone who has seen a little of the light of the Creator finds all of creation
> small, because the innermost hidden place of the mind is opened up by that
> light, and is so much expanded in God that it stands above the world. In fact,
> the soul that sees this is even raised above itself. Rapt above itself in the light
> of God, its inner powers are enlarged. When it looks down from above, it finds
> that what it formerly could not grasp is now small. ... Of course, in saying
> that the world was gathered before his eyes, I do not mean that heaven and
> earth shrunk, but that his spirit widened. He who is rapt in God can see with-
> out difficulty everything that is below God. Therefore in that light that was
> shining before his exterior eyes, there was an inner light in his mind, which
> lifted his spirit to the heights and showed him how paltry were the things
> below.[68]

The critical glance back at the earth is a common episode in otherworld
journey narratives, while the vision of all creation fused into one occurs more
often in mystical literature. Both motifs appear in the *Paradiso*. When Bea-

trice bids Dante to "look down and see how much of the universe I have already put beneath thy feet," the poet reports, "With my sight I returned through every one of the seven spheres, and I saw this globe such that I smiled at its paltry semblance."[69] And a unifying vision very much like the one Gregory attributes to Benedict is described in the final canto:

> O abounding grace, by which I dared to fix my look on the Eternal Light so long that I spent all my sight upon it! In its depth I saw that it contained, bound by love in one volume, that which is scattered in leaves through the universe, substances and accidents and their relations as it were fused together in such a way that what I tell of is a simple light. I think I saw the universal form of this complex, because in telling of it I feel my joy expand.[70]

Something analogous takes place in the otherworld journey of the seventh-century monk Baldarius who, just before returning to his body, sees the whole world collected before his eyes and in one glance can make out cities, rivers, buildings, and countries, as well as individual people.[71] Alberic relates that "while I was standing in the first heaven, everything above and below me seemed lucid and transparent."[72] Adamnán, Alberic, and Tundal discover that the inhabitants of the highest heaven can see all sides of everything without turning; they face one other and are surrounded by the countenance of God in every direction. These are but a few of many variations on the theme of comprehensive vision.

In interpreting Benedict's vision of the whole, Gregory indicates that both exterior and interior light are involved, and does not tell us where corporeal vision leaves off and spiritual vision begins. Like Augustine, he believes that physical seeing is in itself a spiritual activity, in which the mind takes note of impressions gathered through intentional acts of seeing. Spiritual vision, in turn, draws on such sensory forms as bridges, ships, houses, fragrance, music, and light. Thus, there seems to be a continuity between sense-based imaginative experience and spiritual or contemplative vision. Nonetheless, Gregory often sounds a more dualistic note, insisting on the categorical difference between these two modes of knowing.[73]

If this is an inconsistency, it is one that is endemic to medieval religious and philosophical literature. Although they rarely indulge in theoretical discussion, our narrators share an ambivalence toward the imaginative aspect of visions that reflects not just Gregory's teachings, but the whole tradition of medieval psychology and epistemology, in its elaboration of principles derived from classical and patristic thought.[74]

According to both classical and medieval psychology, dreams and visions are perceived through the soul's image-making power, *imaginatio* or *phantasia*, a capacity midway between sense and reason that shares some of the qualities of each. The twelfth-century theologian Hugh of St. Victor says of imagination what Gregory says of his age: it is "shadow mixed with light"— shadow because it deals in "phantasms" extracted from sense experience, light because it collects these images and offers them to the higher cognitive powers, thus performing a service indispensable to reason.[75] Although its primary function is to copy sensory impressions, medieval thinkers agree that imagination can also act independently, conjuring up images from its own storehouse and recombining them in new ways, bound by neither the laws of sense nor of reason. It is the poet's and the dreamer's license, permitting us to entertain such fancies as a creature "maad of a lions heed, of a gootis bodi, and of a dragons tail."[76] By constructing possible future scenarios (including images of punishment or reward after death) out of the building blocks of past memories, it can assist moral deliberation.[77] But its freedom from the senses also makes imagination seem dangerous to medieval writers; not only playful fancies, thought experiments, prophetic dreams, and artistic reveries, but also deranged or diabolical illusions find entry here. In addition, as Richard of St. Victor vividly portrays it, imagination is a compulsive talker, whose incessant babble, even when it makes no harmful suggestions, can seriously hinder self-recollection.[78] When we imagine, writes Achard of St. Victor, we see things through a veil rather than as they are in themselves.[79] The direct contact with reality for which the soul longs and which it pursues vainly in sense experience is possible only in the highest degrees of contemplation, when the soul adheres to its object without intervening images. In the present life such an experience is like an unexpected flash of light, instantly forgotten and essentially incommunicable because it is alien to our mortal and imaginative nature. The sensory terms (especially seeing and tasting) that proliferate in medieval spiritual writings are intended to represent the absolutely simple and unmediated quality of communion with God, rather than to suggest its congruence or continuity with ordinary experience.[80]

It is thus partly in deference to the contemplative disparagement of imaginative vision that the texts we have considered reveal so much of hell and purgatory and so little of heaven. This, too, is the reason that the visionary is often reluctant or unable to communicate the secrets of the third heaven, which, according to Augustine, are the arcana of intellectual vision.[81]

Nowhere are these ideas more clearly illustrated than in *The Divine Comedy*. In the first two canticles, Dante summons his memory and imagination to portray hell and purgatory, but in the third canticle he laments that they are unequal to their task.[82] Paradoxically, with the final words of the *Paradiso*, the poet exercises his imaginative power to its limit in order to convey an experience that, in his view, surpasses it:

> Bernard signed to me with a smile to look upward, but already of myself I was doing what he wished; for my sight, becoming pure, was entering more and more through the beam of the lofty light which in itself is true.
>
> From that moment my vision was greater than our speech, and memory too fails at such excess. Like him that sees in a dream and after the dream the passion wrought by it remains and the rest returns not to his mind, such am I; for my vision almost wholly fades, and still there drops within my heart the sweetness that was born of it.
>
> ... Like the geometer who sets all his mind to the squaring of the circle and

for all his thinking does not discover the principle he needs, such was I at that strange sight. I wished to see how the image was fitted to the circle and how it has its place there; but my own wings were not sufficient for that, had not my mind been smitten by a flash wherein came its wish. Here power failed the high phantasy; but now my desire and will, like a wheel that spins with even motion, were revolved by the Love that moves the sun and the other stars.[83]

With these final words, Dante gave supreme expression to an outlook that was shared by most of the authors of visionary and contemplative literature from the time of Gregory the Great to the scholastic period. Among writers of the long return-from-death narratives of the high Middle Ages, Adam of Eynsham, H. of Sawtry, and Ralph of Coggeshall are the most articulate on this subject; though they sometimes suggest that clear sight has replaced enigmatic knowledge, they nonetheless acknowledge that the visionary, as well as his audience, can grasp the realities of this world and the next only through "corporeal" symbols. This very limitation of our mortal condition gives imagination, at least temporarily, a sacramental value. But the authors of these narratives adhere to the wider spiritual and philosophical tradition in considering imaginative experience at best a way-station, at worst a diabolical trap set in the path to the eschatological goal of meeting reality face to face.

Few of these writers attempt a synthesis of the sort achieved by *The Divine Comedy*, however, with its fusion of visionary and contemplative discourse, and its equal treatment of hell, purgatory, and heaven. More often the territory is divided: vision literature, a didactic genre, concentrates on hell and purgatory, while contemplative writings specialize in what Jean Leclercq calls "devotion to heaven."[84] This division of labor, though not absolute, reflects a widespread assumption that graphic images are appropriate for infernal or purgatorial subjects, but incommensurate with transcendent, heavenly experience.

In the twentieth-century vision literature to which we shall now turn, we again encounter some of the questions to which our medieval narrators have supplied such ambiguous answers. Paul's famous uncertainty, "whether in the body or out of the body I know not, God knows," recurs in new forms in contemporary discussion of near-death and "out-of-body" experience. And though the criteria have changed, the evaluation of the imaginative or symbolic element in visions remains as great a problem today as it was in the medieval context. In both periods, there is a popular assumption that one has only to leave the body to be able to see natural and supernatural reality directly. In the Middle Ages, this idea was challenged on eschatological grounds; today it is called into question by the findings of social science and comparative history of religion. Current views of religion as a "cultural system" make it untenable to treat symbolic discourse as a side effect of being in the flesh.[85] Debate goes on as to whether the visionary actually leaves his body, but the more telling question has become "whether in my culture or out of my culture, I know not, God knows." This question calls for a comparative or cross-cultural approach; my hope is that the comparative study of medieval and modern otherworld journey narratives, separated by a half-millennium of cultural change, will provide a fragment of the Rosetta stone that is needed to decipher the language of contemporary visions.

PART III

THE MODERN NEAR-DEATH NARRATIVE: A THEMATIC AND COMPARATIVE TREATMENT

CHAPTER 6

From Deathbed Visions
to Life After Life

TABLOID HEADLINES PROCLAIM, "LIFE IN HEAVEN: Incredible new eyewitness accounts by 12 who came back from the dead."[1] Raymond Moody's *Life After Life*, advertising itself as "actual case histories that reveal there is life after death," has sold over three million copies in the United States alone. Elisabeth Kübler-Ross, the revered but scandal-haunted apostle of humane treatment for the dying and their families, tells the world in countless interviews that the visionary testimony of her patients proves "beyond a shadow of a doubt" that death is but a doorway to a better world. In great demand on the talk-show circuit is the "near-death experiencer" who appears, escorted by sympathetic psychologists, as a latter-day Lazarus bearing clinically tested tidings of the afterlife.[2] Every year the theme of revival from "clinical death" resurfaces in novels, documentary films, and fantasy or horror movies—complete with special effects.[3] As one television commentator put it, "Now in the twentieth century it's fashionable to be dead and come back and talk about it."[4]

A glance at the bibliography will confirm the impression that we are in the midst of a widespread revival of popular interest in return-from-death stories and deathbed visions. But the chapters to come will show that this is more than a mere craze; we are witnessing what Eliade calls a "cultural fashion," which should claim our attention because it has something to teach us about the direction our society is taking.[5]

Nineteenth- and Twentieth-Century Precursors

Now in his early forties, Raymond Moody is considered, somewhat to his dismay, the "grandfather" of what appears to be a radically new method of

97

investigating the possibility of life after death. As Moody freely acknowledges, however, this is not entirely justified; although *Life After Life* and its
progeny break with the past in some ways, they cannot help but inherit the
traits of older generations of explorers.

A little digging at the roots of this family tree reveals, for example, that
the mid-1800s witnessed a spate of books combining visionary testimony of
the hereafter with edifying descriptions of death. The ancient theme of the
"two deaths"[6] returned in the context of religious revival, taking such forms
as *Deathbed scenes; or Dying with and without Religion; designed to Illustrate the Truth and Power of Christianity*, compiled by a Methodist minister
who revels in the contrast between the sweet demise of Wesley and his followers and the final agonies of Voltaire.[7] Modern heirs to this tradition, such
as the born-again cardiologist Maurice Rawlings, publish explicitly Christian
versions of near-death testimony, designed to counteract the secular human-
ism conveyed by *Life After Life*.

More direct inspiration for contemporary near-death literature can be
found in the early work of the British and American psychical researchers. In
1903, F. W. H. Myers included several accounts of deathbed visions in his
massive two-volume book on *Human Personality and Its Survival of Bodily
Death*. James H. Hyslop wrote on "Visions of the Dying" in the first issue of
the *Journal of the American Society for Psychical Research* in 1907, and did
so again in 1918, proposing a census of deathbed visions that would allow
investigators to search systematically for evidence in support of spiritualist
claims.[8] In 1926, Sir William Barrett, a prominent British physicist and co-
founder of the Society for Psychical Research, published *Deathbed Visions*,
a study of apparitions and glimpses of the next world described by the dying
with their last breath. In our own day, Karlis Osis of the Parapsychology
Foundation and the American Society for Psychical Research is continuing
Barrett's work on a grand scale. Since 1959, he has been collecting physicians'
and nurses' reports of deathbed phenomena. With the help of Erlendur Haraldsson, an Icelandic psychologist and parapsychologist, he has extended this
study to India, looking for patterns that cut across cultural differences. His
work is solidly within the discipline of parapsychology; like his colleague Ian
Stevenson (who is especially interested in verifying reincarnation memories),
Osis believes that the evidential weight of deathbed and "come-back" visions
is enhanced by their convergence with mediumistic phenomena, out-of-body
reports, and other staples of psychical research.[9] In contrast, *Life After Life*
and the studies that followed it tend to disassociate near-death research from
traditional parapsychology.

Nonetheless, the reasons for the appeal of contemporary near-death literature are similar to those that swelled the ranks of the spiritualist movement in the second half of the nineteenth century and attracted public attention to the work of the early psychical researchers. Like spiritualism in its
heyday, near-death studies give the impression of being nondogmatic, rational, empirical, even naturalistic. Only the obsolete aspects of spiritualism are
discarded: its naive cosmologies, its discredited apparatus of spirit-trumpets,

gauzy ectoplasm, and pseudo-Indian "controls." In place of these worn-out tricks, near-death literature offers fresh and apparently more plausible testimony of the afterlife. The purpose remains the same, however; experiential reports of life after death are popularly considered to be practical evidence which, when verified in the lab, will yield scientific confirmation of religious hopes. Moreover, near-death reports, like the literature of mediumship and psychical research, are well suited to the peculiar blend of anxiety and optimism that characterizes the modern secular or liberal religious mentality.

Another approach to near-death experience is found in the medical and psychiatric studies of response to the threat of death. This began, as Russell Noyes shows, with the nineteenth-century "euthanasia" books, forerunners of the hospice movement, which present personal testimony and medical observations to show that dying need not be painful.[10] In 1892, the study of visionary experience at death received a boost when Swiss geologist and Alpinist Albert Heim published accounts from mountain climbers who survived nearly fatal falls. Heim sought to reassure bereaved families that death by falling is a more dreadful experience for onlookers and relatives than for the victim. The thirty survivors he interviewed reported feeling calm, detached from the scene of danger, and joyful: "They had, so to speak, fallen into heaven."[11] Oskar Pfister, a Swiss minister, lay psychoanalyst, and friend of Freud, published an interpretation of Heim's findings in 1930. He theorized that the victims were evoking infantile fantasies in order to evade the unacceptable prospect of death.[12] R. C. A. Hunter followed the same line of explanation in an influential article, "On the Experience of Nearly Dying," published by the *American Journal of Psychiatry* in 1967.

Today psychiatric evaluation of near-death experience is the specialty of Russell Noyes, Jr., a professor of psychiatry, and his collaborator, Roy Kletti, a clinical psychologist, at the University of Iowa. Though less dogmatic than Pfister and Hunter, Noyes and Kletti treat near-death experience as a variation on the "depersonalization" syndrome. Since Noyes and Kletti admit that near-death experience has positive as well as pathological aspects, most near-death researchers respect and draw upon their work, even while taking exception to some of their interpretations. The chapters that follow will therefore refer occasionally to Noyes's and Kletti's findings along with those of Moody and his followers, and in chapter 10 I will discuss the merits of the depersonalization theory.

Scattered magazine articles and popular books predating *Life After Life* have dealt with the return-from-death theme. Among them are Jean-Baptiste Delacour's *Glimpses of the Beyond* (published in English translation in 1974 from a 1973 German original), which features the testimony of movie stars and other celebrities who came back from apparent death; *Return from Tomorrow*, the "clinical death" conversion experience of psychiatrist George G. Ritchie, Jr.; and *The Vestibule*, an anthology of afterlife testimony by Jess E. Weiss, a former World War II infantryman whose gradual recovery from combat injuries led him into Christian Science.

Aside from these precedents, new interest in the experiences of dying patients was sparked by the writings of Elisabeth Kübler-Ross and by the quieter efforts of thanatologists and other medical and social workers who struggle with our culture's avoidance of death. Of special interest to near-death researchers is the work of Czechoslovakian psychologist Stanislav Grof and anthropologist Joan Halifax, who investigated the use of psychoactive drugs as a therapeutic aid for dying patients. The "rebirth" experiences described by Grof and Halifax in *The Human Encounter with Death* have much in common with current accounts of near-death visions.

Current interest in death and dying also reflects a widespread tendency to interpret life as a series of stages or "passages." Kübler-Ross organizes the experience of dying into five stages like those used by George Vaillant, James Fowler, Gail Sheehy, and other academic and popular psychologists, to describe the developmental crises of life. Often the purpose of contemporary books on the life-cycle is to recover the significance of periods of growth and struggle—principally "mid-life crisis," aging, and facing death—which seem to be neglected because of the prestige of youth and the linear, goal-oriented outlook of modern society.

Perhaps a less culturally specific reason for the appeal of near-death reports is that they include personal testimony of mystical experience, a subject of perennial interest. And finally, as this book is meant to illustrate, the current fashion for near-death literature is an instance of the periodic resurgence of otherworld journey narration. Although it addresses persistent hopes and fears concerning death, otherworld journey narration is a "wave" phenomenon rather than a constant. It seems to recur when it is needed most, that is, when the way society pictures itself and its surrounding universe is so changed as to threaten to dislocate the human being.

A more ambitious work might show that this has been the case for most categories of otherworld journey narrative, for Judeo-Christian apocalypses and Islamic *mi'raj* traditions, for *The Divine Comedy* and the Zoroastrian *Book of Arda Viraz*, and for such modern American movements as Mormonism, Shakerism, spiritualism, and the Ghost Dance religion. Proof of life after death has not always been the purpose of such literature; that particular interest is characteristic of our own doubt-ridden and science-bitten culture. But one aim, though usually implicit, seems to be universal: to survey and reappraise the imagined cosmos, and to return to society with a message about our human place in it, about how we should live.

Life After Life: A New Phase

Despite its many precursors, the publication in 1975 of *Life After Life* launched a new phase of near-death research and popularization. Raymond Moody was the first to cast his net widely enough to reach people who ordinarily ignore both the technical literature of parapsychology and the mass-market paperbacks and lurid tabloid articles about psychic phenomena. This, no doubt, is one reason for the commercial success of his book.

The packaging of *Life After Life* helped to ensure this wide appeal by artfully combining the commonsense with the sensational. On the back cover, Elisabeth Kübler-Ross announces that the book "will confirm what we have been taught for two thousand years—that there is life after death." While the publishers court the public with exciting blurbs, Moody establishes trust by his reasonable and affable tone. In his opening remarks he backs off from such extravagant claims: "I am not trying to prove that there is life after death. Nor do I think that a 'proof' of this is presently possible."[13]

Moody modestly admits his bias: "This book, written as it is by a human being, naturally reflects the background, opinions and prejudices of its author." We learn that he is a liberal Methodist with a deep curiosity about life and death, but no dogmatic opinions. Without condemning psychical research, he disavows any connection with bizarre fringe movements: "I write as a person who is not broadly familiar with the vast literature on paranormal and occult phenomena."

As we shall see, Moody presents near-death phenomena in naturalistic terms, setting the picture of the other world within a frame of cautious reservations, and leaving readers free to draw their own, perhaps more triumphant, conclusions. Like the medieval narrators who seek to disarm the skeptics in their audience, Moody invites us to test his findings: "All I ask is for anyone who disbelieves what he reads here to poke around a bit for himself."

In another book-jacket endorsement, Richard Bach, the author of *Jonathan Livingston Seagull*, calls attention to the reassuring normality of *Life After Life*: "I'm delighted to read straight honest research that dissolves ancient fear and mystery." In effect, Raymond Moody domesticates life after death; here is evidence for survival that can be found, as Moody puts it, "not in darkened rooms in circumstances contrived by witch doctors, but in the bright light of emergency and operating rooms, presided over by physicians."[14] Moody's precedent is followed by Michael Sabom, Kenneth Ring, and other near-death researchers who consider themselves medical or psychological investigators rather than psychic sleuths.[15]

Moody first learned of near-death experience from George Ritchie, whose tale, published under the title *Return from Tomorrow*, became a best-seller in the inspirational book field.[16] When they met in 1965, Moody was an undergraduate philosophy major at the University of Virginia, and Ritchie, a former Army doctor, was teaching psychiatry at the School of Medicine. Ritchie relates in his book that in 1943, when he was a private in the Army, he contracted double lobar pneumonia, suffered cardiac arrest, and apparently died. Nine minutes after he was pronounced dead, however, he was resuscitated by an adrenaline injection.

Ritchie recalls that in the first minutes of this crisis he found himself outside his body, staring in confusion at the dead form which he could recognize only by a fraternity ring on one of its fingers. He fled the hospital, heading toward Richmond, Virginia, to keep an appointment, but was so distressed by his discarnate condition that he soon returned to search for his body. When he finally found himself again, he was at a loss as to how to reenter the flesh. Just at that moment, the room filled with light and he felt himself in the presence of Christ, who directed him to review all the thoughts and deeds of his life. Christ then conducted him on a tour of several regions of misery and bliss, realms "vastly different" from our own world though they occupy the same space.[17] After a brief glimpse of luminous streets and edifices and shining throngs, Ritchie fell asleep and woke up in his hospital room. Since then, Ritchie says that his life has been ruled by a longing to see Christ again, and a conviction that he was sent back to life in order "to become a physician so that I could learn about man and then serve God."

Moody records that he was impressed by Ritchie's warm personality as well as his unusual story; but he did not pursue the subject until after he had obtained his Ph.D. in philosophy and was teaching at East Carolina University. In classes on Plato's *Phaedo*, he found that discussions of philosophical arguments on immortality prompted a few students to come forward with personal anecdotes similar to Ritchie's. In 1972, when Moody entered medical school with the aim of teaching philosophy of medicine, he began collecting such stories. *Life After Life* is based on 150 accounts from people who approached Moody after hearing him lecture or reading articles about his study, and from patients referred to him by physicians.[18] Although most cases involved revival from apparent or "clinical" death, Moody coined the term "near-death experience" to include unusual episodes reported by survivors of life-threatening danger who were not physically harmed, as well as secondhand accounts of deathbed experience.

From this mass of anecdotal material, Moody sifted out fifteen elements that seemed to recur most frequently. *Life After Life* presents them in roughly chronological order, suggesting that they represent events in a coherent sequence. They are listed in the table of contents as follows: (1) Ineffability, (2) Hearing the News, (3) Feelings of Peace and Quiet, (4) The Noise, (5) The Dark Tunnel, (6) Out of the Body, (7) Meeting Others, (8) The Being of Light, (9) The Review, (10) The Border or Limit, (11) Coming Back, (12) Telling Others, (13) Effects on Lives, (14) New Views of Death, (15) Corroboration. On this chronological skeleton, Moody constructed a "theoretically 'ideal' or 'complete' experience which embodies all of the common elements, in the order in which it is typical for them to occur." This composite portrait, with its neat progression from the deathbed to the hereafter and back again, has been so influential that it merits quotation in full:

> A man is dying, and as he reaches the point of greatest physical distress, he hears himself pronounced dead by his doctor. He begins to hear an uncomfortable noise, a loud ringing or buzzing, and at the same time feels himself moving very rapidly through a long dark tunnel. After this, he suddenly finds himself outside of his own physical body, but still in the immediate physical environment, and he sees his own body from a distance, as though he is a

spectator. He watches the resuscitation attempt from this unusual vantage point and is in a state of emotional upheaval.

After a while, he collects himself and becomes more accustomed to his odd condition. He notices that he still has a "body," but one of a very different nature and with very different powers from the physical body he has left behind. Soon other things begin to happen. Others come to meet and to help him. He glimpses the spirits of relatives and friends who have already died, and a loving, warm spirit of a kind he has never encountered before—a being of light—appears before him. This being asks him a question, nonverbally, to make him evaluate his life and helps him along by showing him a panoramic, instantaneous playback of the major events of his life. At some point he finds himself approaching some sort of barrier or border, apparently representing the limit between earthly life and the next life. Yet, he finds that he must go back to the earth, that the time for his death has not yet come. At this point he resists, for by now he is taken up with his experiences in the afterlife and does not want to return. He is overwhelmed by intense feelings of joy, love, and peace. Despite his attitude, though, he somehow reunites with his physical body and lives.

Later he tries to tell others, but he has trouble doing so. In the first place, he can find no human words adequate to describe these unearthly episodes. He also finds that others scoff, so he stops telling other people. Still, the experience affects his life profoundly, especially his views about death and its relationship to life.[19]

For the investigators whom Moody inspired, this narrative has become a template against which to measure future near-death reports. Even when their findings do not fit this picture exactly, the near-death researchers are conscious of differing with Moody and look for ways to account for the discrepancy. On the other hand, a growing number of evangelical Christian books about near-death experience are casting Moody in a diabolical role, as an emissary of that being of light who is none other than Satan in disguise, or as a member, along with Robert Monroe and Elisabeth Kübler-Ross, of an insidious New Age conspiracy.[20] Contemporary near-death literature thus seems to say of Moody what was once said of the formidable Immanuel Kant: you can think with him, or you can think against him, but you cannot think without him.

Moody himself is uncomfortable with his conspicuous role. In a recent interview he remarked that press reports were inflating the importance of his evidence for life after death by a circular logic: "The argument was that these findings were enunciated by the eminent Dr. Moody. And why was I the eminent Dr. Moody? Because I enunciated these findings!"[21] Moody withdrew from the lecture circuit when he began to feel that such publicity was drawing attention away from more scientific studies. He told a Charlottesville conference on near-death studies in October 1982, "If you want to read anything on the subject and haven't, I would not recommend my books now, but rather defer entirely to Kenneth's and Michael's books."[22] He has gone on to complete his psychiatric residency at the University of Virginia, and to write on topics related only indirectly to near-death experience: a book on madness in our society and a book on humor as therapy with the self-parodying title of *Laugh After Laugh*. He remains active in the field of near-death studies, however, working vigorously to persuade those in clinical practice of the need to listen and respond with sympathy to their patients' near-death testimony.

In the wake of *Life After Life*, several psychologists and physicians embarked on more systematic studies designed to test Moody's results. Except for Karlis Osis, whose cross-cultural study of deathbed observations began well before and proceeded independently of Moody's work, all of the prominent current investigators were first motivated by reading *Life After Life*. The remainder of this chapter will consider their work.

The Researchers

Of the researchers whose work was inspired by Moody's book, perhaps the best known is Kenneth Ring. A professor of psychology at the University of Connecticut, Ring was interested in out-of-body reports, mystical experience at death, and other "altered states of consciousness" long before he read *Life After Life*.[23] In a preface to his book *Life at Death: A Scientific Investigation of the Near-Death Experience*, however, he credits Moody's book with redirecting his career. He tells us that the effect of reading *Life After Life* was more than academic; it lifted him out of a serious depression: "I remember feeling spiritually adrift, as if I had somehow lost my way."[24] Volunteer work at a convalescent home did not help Ring to recover a sense of purpose, as he had hoped it might; and philosophical brooding only intensified his inner paralysis. When he read *Life After Life* during this critical period, he discovered a way to move beyond fruitless speculation; he began to seek out near-death survivors, "mostly ordinary people" who, thanks to their extraordinary experience, seemed to hold an answer for him.

> The effect, combined with a certain quality of luminous serenity which many near-death survivors display, made me feel that I myself was undergoing an extended spiritual awakening. In any event, as my interviews continued, I found that I was no longer oppressed by the spiritual deadness that had ... provided the initial impetus to my research. In fact, my feeling was becoming just the opposite.[25]

Ring's description of the way a book was able to rescue him from despair is reminiscent of William James's account of the spiritual tonic he discovered in Renouvier's defense of free will. An even closer analogue may be found in the annals of the psychical research movement; the search for evidence of life after death has often served as a way of resolving personal crises.[26] The notion that the otherworld journey has the power to reorient is also prominent in medieval vision literature. Readers of *The Divine Comedy* will recall that Dante's narrative journey begins with a similar crisis, in which he discovers, midway through life, that he has lost the right path. So, too, by imaginatively participating in the pilgrimage of "ordinary people" to the other world, Ring found his own way back to life. He tells us that he wrote *Life at Death* in order to extend the same benefit to his audience:

> It is my personal hope that many readers, on finishing it, will find that they, too, have been moved and inspired by having the opportunity to listen to the accounts of those who have returned from the brink of death to tell the rest of us what it is like to die.[27]

To this manifesto for the inspirational value of near-death testimony, we can compare Bede's comment that Drythelm died and revived "in order to arouse the living from spiritual death." In chapter 8, we will consider accounts which suggest that the very act of narrating otherworld journey tales can have a healing power.

Like Moody, Ring was impressed above all by the "single pattern" or "common program" disclosed when one compares a number of near-death reports. Yet he felt that a systematic study, founded on more objective data, was needed to bolster the informal presentation in *Life After Life*. In addition to collecting anecdotes that resembled Moody's, he introduced up-to-date psychological sampling and testing methods to measure the frequency and demographics of near-death experience, the influence of medical circumstances, the role of religious expectations and prior knowledge of near-death literature, and the psychological aftereffects for survivors.

With the help of medical staff, clergy, and administrators at several hospitals in Connecticut and Maine, Ring came up with fifty-four patients who had recovered from near-death crises and were willing to be interviewed. To enlarge the sample of accident and attempted-suicide survivors, however, Ring also wrote to psychiatrists, advertised in local newspapers, and accepted a few subjects who referred themselves after learning of the study. Interview sessions followed a standard form. Ring or an assistant would introduce himself, "take whatever time is necessary to establish rapport with the patient," explain the project, and promise confidentiality. The interviewer was to encourage his subject to speak freely, by making reassuring remarks that verged on gentle coaching:

> The first thing I should say is that some people—not necessarily everyone, though—appear to experience unusual things when they have a serious illness or when they come close to dying. Sometimes these things are a little puzzling and people are somewhat hesitant to talk about them. (Be a little jocular here; try by your manner to put the patient at ease.) Now please don't worry about this in talking with me! I just want you to feel free to tell me *anything* you can remember—whether it makes sense to you or not. OK?[28]

After listening to the patient's story, the interviewer would probe for features of Moody's composite near-death experience, following a list of such pointed questions as: "Did you actually think you were dead?" " . . . were you ever aware of *seeing* your physical body?" "Did you at any time experience a light, glow, or illumination?" "Did your life—or scenes from your life—ever appear to you as a mental image or memories?"[29] On this evidence critics may consider that, despite scientific intentions, the near-death report is as much a collaborative effort as the medieval vision narrative.

Ring's results nevertheless deviate from Moody's model in some respects. The buzzing or ringing noise, the sense of having a second body, and the approach to a border occur rarely in Ring's narratives. Rather than speaking of tunnels, Ring's subjects report drifting through a dark void.[30] For Moody's "being of light," Ring's findings indicate a "presence" who is felt and heard more often than seen. Aside from these discrepancies, which Ring considers minor, *Life at Death* puts greater emphasis on the chronological sequence in which near-death experiences appear to unfold.[31] Instead of listing "elements," Ring describes five "stages" of near-death experience: peace, body separation, entering the darkness, seeing the light, and entering the light. Although it is rare for a report to include all five stages, Ring finds, as one might expect, that "deeper" or more intense experiences are more complete, and that the earlier stages are reported more frequently.[32] Following this chronological pattern, Ring proposes his own model near-death experience:

> The experience begins with a feeling of easeful peace and a sense of well-being, which soon culminates in a sense of overwhelming joy and happiness. This ecstatic tone, although fluctuating in intensity from case to case, tends to persist as a constant emotional ground as other features of the experience begin to unfold. At this point, the person is aware that he feels no pain nor does he have any other bodily sensations. Everything is quiet. These cues may suggest to him that he is either in the process of dying or has already "died."
>
> He may then be aware of a transitory buzzing or a windlike sound, but, in any event, he finds himself looking down on his physical body, as though he were viewing it from some external vantage point. At this time, he finds that he can see and hear perfectly; indeed, his vision and hearing tend to be more acute than usual. He is aware of the actions and conversations taking place in the physical environment, in relation to which he finds himself in the role of a passive, detached spectator. All this seems very real—even quite natural—to him; it does not seem at all like a dream or an hallucination. His mental state is one of clarity and alertness.
>
> At some point, he may find himself in a state of *dual awareness*. While he continues to be able to perceive the physical scene around him, he may also become aware of "another reality" and feel himself being drawn into it. He drifts or is ushered into a dark void or tunnel and feels as though he is floating through it. Although he may feel lonely for a time, the experience here is predominantly peaceful and serene. All is extremely quiet and the individual is aware only of his mind and of the feeling of floating.
>
> All at once, he becomes sensitive to, but does not see, a presence. The presence, who may be heard to speak or who may instead "merely" induce thoughts into the individual's mind, stimulates him to review his life and asks him to decide whether he wants to live or die. This stock-taking may be facilitated by a rapid and vivid visual playback of episodes from the person's life.

At this stage, he has no awareness of time or space, and the concepts themselves are meaningless. Neither is he any longer identified with his body. Only the mind is present and is weighing—logically and rationally—the alternatives that confront him at this threshold separating life from death: to go further into this experience or to return to earthly life. Usually the individual decides to return on the basis, not of his own preference, but of the perceived needs of his loved ones, whom his death would necessarily leave behind. Once the decision is made, the experience tends to be abruptly terminated.

Sometimes, however, the decisional crisis occurs later or is altogether absent, and the individual undergoes further experiences. He may, for example, continue to float through the dark void toward a magnetic and brilliant golden light, from which emanates feelings [sic] of love, warmth and total acceptance. Or he may enter into a "world of light" and preternatural beauty, to be (temporarily) reunited with deceased loved ones before being told, in effect, that it is not yet his time and that he has to return to life.

In any event, whether the individual chooses or is commanded to return to his earthly body and worldly commitments, he does return. Typically, however, he has no recollection *how* he has effected his "reentry," for at this point he tends to lose all awareness. Very occasionally, however, the individual may remember "returning to his body" with a jolt or an agonizing wrenching sensation. He may even suspect that he reenters "through the head."

Afterward, when he is able to recount his experience, he finds that there are simply no words adequate to convey the feelings and quality of awareness he remembers. He may also be or become reticent to discuss it with others, either because he feels no one will really be able to understand it or because he fears he will be disbelieved or ridiculed.[33]

Despite Ring's effort to listen impartially to the evidence, this description suggests that he wishes to reconcile his findings with those of Moody. The sound, the tunnel, and feelings of loneliness are features that occur only rarely in the reports Ring collected; yet he includes them in his model narrative, buffered with "mays" and "ors" as if they were options he is unwilling to rule out, if only out of loyalty to his predecessor.

Although Ring agrees with Moody on the main features of the "core experience," he ventures much further when it comes to speculating about the meaning of near-death experience. In the final chapters of *Life at Death*, and in a sequel called *Heading toward Omega* (based on a three-year study of 100 survivors), Ring claims to see in near-death reports signs of an emerging holistic and "holographic" awareness. Advances in medical resuscitation techniques are producing a growing population of near-death survivors; in Ring's eyes, they form a spiritual vanguard whose reports of mystical and paranormal experience have no less than planetary and prophetic significance.[34] At a recent conference in Charlottesville, he unfurled the New Age banner, speaking with the ebullient rhetoric favored by transpersonal psychologists:

Near-death experiences collectively represent an evolutionary thrust toward higher consciousness for humanity as a whole. . . . People who have had near-death experiences, as well as many other people whose lives have been transformed by one or more deep spiritual experiences, all these people as a totality represent in effect a more highly advanced human being; no longer *homo sapiens*, but maybe *homo noeticus*. . . . These are people whose consciousness has been flooded with a . . . higher kind of awareness, a higher spiritual illumination; they know things from a different level than most of us do. And more and more of these people are coming into being. . . . To my thinking, the emergence of this new strain of human being, if this hypothesis is right, on the planet now, signals a possibility that the dawning of the New Age is indeed upon us.

Fortunately, Ring keeps his interpretive flights separate from his investigative footwork, leaving the rest of us free to lag behind. The other near-death researchers usually stop short of such optimistic augury; many are content if only they can find indications that would justify returning to old-fashioned soul-talk.[35] Ring's speech has its echoes in earlier otherworld journey literature, however. Gregory the Great and several of those who followed him also considered return-from-death cases to be on the increase, thanks to the dawning of, not Aquarius, but Doomsday. Ring's discourse revives this link between otherworld journey narrative and apocalyptic prophecy; but he and other researchers with a humanistic bent imagine that the advent of the New Age, like the individual passage from life to death, will be a peaceful evolutionary development. It will be achieved, if all goes well, by gradual realization of human potential, rather than by catastrophic change. Indeed, Ring believes that the New Age mentality is our one hope for averting the sheer destruction of a nuclear apocalypse.

Simultaneously with Ring's investigation, cardiologist Michael B. Sabom (now a professor at Emory University and a staff physician at Atlanta Veterans Administration Medical Center) began a major study of near-death experience. In his book *Recollections of Death: A Medical Investigation*, Sabom tells us that he started out as a hard-headed scientist who, though a churchgoer, had little use for notions of life after death. While studying clinical cardiology at the University of Florida in 1976, however, Sabom attended a Methodist adult Sunday School class and heard Sarah Kreutziger, a psychiatric social worker, give a talk on *Life After Life*. Sabom comments: "My indoctrinated scientific mind just couldn't relate seriously to these 'far-out' descriptions of afterlife spirits and such."[36] Kreutziger nonetheless persuaded him to take part in a larger presentation of near-death reports for which he would answer medical questions. In preparation, they interviewed some of their own patients who had survived close brushes with death. To Sabom's surprise they found two who recalled experiences very similar to those Moody describes. This prompted Sabom to attempt a systematic study, aimed at either verifying or falsifying Moody's findings in a scientific manner. With Kreutziger as his assistant, he began a five-year investigation of near-death experience in two hospitals at the University of Florida; Sabom interviewed patients in medical intensive care units, while Kreutziger concentrated on the kidney dialysis unit where she normally worked.[37]

In the hope of producing an impeccably controlled sample, Sabom and

Kreutziger chose subjects solely on the basis of their medical records. They did not solicit volunteers through letters or advertisements; in addition, they rejected any potential subjects who were considered mentally or emotionally disturbed, and separated the reports of "prospectively" selected patients from those who had been referred. Finally, they set aside cases involving anesthesia, and were left with a group of seventy-eight victims of cardiac arrest, coma, or accident, thirty-four of whom reported mystical or out-of-body states while they were close to death.[38]

As interviewers, Sabom and Kreutziger had the advantage of being able to blend into hospital routine, since they were already identified as regular medical personnel. They approached each patient with normal medical questions about the critical episode, and did not betray their exotic interests until they came to ask whether the patient could recall any experiences while unconscious. To those whose curiosity was piqued by this line of questioning, they would explain:

> I am interested in the experiences and reactions of patients who have survived critical medical illnesses. Some patients have indicated that they have experienced certain events while unconscious and quite ill. I am sincerely interested in any such experiences, no matter what they may be.[39]

The patient would then have a chance to speak freely; but after hearing the narrative, Sabom or Kreutziger would proceed, as Ring did, to delve for the elements described in *Life After Life*.[40]

Apart from a few differences to be discussed below, the results appear to agree with Moody's findings. Sabom concluded from his study that the fundamental features of near-death experience are ineffability, timelessness, conviction that the experience is real rather than hallucinatory or dreamlike, feelings of peacefulness and release from pain (occasionally preceded by brief pangs of anxiety or loneliness), and separation from the body. If the experience progresses, according to Sabom, the subject may either stay on the scene looking down upon the body and watching rescue efforts, or depart altogether, traveling to a luminous realm, where he will encounter spirits and evaluate his life. The local out-of-body state Sabom calls an "autoscopic NDE," to set it apart from the otherworld journey or "transcendent NDE."[41]

If the validity of transcendent near-death experience can be tested only in its transforming effects, autoscopic visions can at least be checked against medical records and doctors' recollections. Here Sabom saw an opportunity to make the most of his clinical setting:

> I had known from the beginning of my study that the majority of the patients I would be interviewing regarding the NDE would have been resuscitated from cardiac arrests. At this stage in my career, I had personally directed and participated in well over a hundred such procedures. I knew what a resuscitation consisted of and how it would appear to an onlooker. I had been eagerly awaiting the moment when a patient would claim to have "seen" what had taken place during his resuscitation. Upon such an encounter, I had intended to probe meticulously for details which would not ordinarily be known to

nonmedical personnel. In essence, I would pit both my experience as a trained cardiologist and the description of the resuscitation in the medical chart against the professed visual recollections of a lay individual.[42]

Sabom writes that he was astonished to find several patients whose reports of what went on while they were unconscious or "dead" held up to his scrutiny. It was enough to make him reconsider the relationship between mind and brain. Sabom does not turn to radically new models of conscious-ness as Ring does, however. He draws instead on the work of Sir Charles Sherrington and Wilder Penfield, who propose to dust off the old dualistic model, restore its luster with the latest mysteries of neurological medicine, and bring it back into service, at least until a better theory comes along.[43]

From 1976 on, while the tidings of *Life After Life* were being trumpeted through the media, many other near-death research projects began to appear. John Audette, who became Moody's research assistant after hearing him lec-ture in 1974, started his own study at two hospitals in Peoria. Ian Stevenson, a University of Virginia parapsychologist known for his investigation of rein-carnation memories, turned to near-death research in the hope that this might win for his beleaguered discipline the respect and interest of the medical profession.[44] Stevenson's former assistant, psychiatrist Bruce Greyson, who says that "reading . . . *Life After Life* . . . opened up a new world," began an extensive study of near-death reports among survivors of suicide attempts.[45] Craig Lundahl, a New Mexico sociologist, made a collection of Mormon return-from-the-dead stories. Fred Schoonmaker, a Denver cardiologist, sur-faced with the results of a fifteen-year study of 2300 survivors of cardiac arrest, 1400 of whom, he claimed, had transcendent or "peak" experiences to report. Karlis Osis, former director of research at the Parapsychology Foun-dation and at the American Society for Psychical Research, added consider-ably to the momentum of near-death research by publishing the results of his studies of deathbed visions in India and America, in a widely distributed book that one reviewer called "the beginning of an alliance between survival researchers and the lay public."[46]

Moody saw to it that the principal researchers, who had written him admiring letters, got in touch with one another. Thanks to his introductions, John Audette, Kenneth Ring, Bruce Greyson, Michael Sabom, and others met in Charlottesville in November 1977 and decided to join forces. In August 1978, they formed the Association for the Scientific Study of Near-Death Phenomena, which later changed its name to the International Asso-ciation for Near-Death Studies (IANDS). John Audette was the first presi-dent, presiding over a post-office box and mimeograph machine in East Peo-ria. But the group quickly grew from 98 to over 700 members, incorporated as a nonprofit organization, and found an office at the University of Con-necticut under the leadership of Kenneth Ring, with Michael Sabom as vice-president, Bruce Greyson as secretary, John Audette as treasurer and execu-tive director, Raymond Moody as honorary president, a salaried office manager, maroon T-shirts, and a logo that combines the tunnel image with the Taoist yin-yang symbol.[47] The board of directors is made up of thanatologists, psychiatrists, parapsychologists, physicians, entrepreneurs, and people who have had near-death experiences, along with a few critics of near-death research. The board of advisors includes U.S. Senator Claiborne Pell, Elisabeth Kübler-Ross, and George Gallup, Jr. Through *Vital Signs*, a quarterly newsletter, and *Anabiosis*, a semiannual journal, as well as IANDS-sponsored conferences, videotapes, and films, members learn of the latest projects and hear personal testimony, philosophical reflections, theoretical explanations of near-death experience in terms of holography or "hyper-space," and hardheaded debunkings.

The quarterly issues of *Vital Signs* speak enthusiastically of the expansion of IANDS from a shoe-string volunteer effort into a thriving organization that has sponsored national research conferences as well as countless workshops for physicians, nurses, and counselors. According to a recent count, over fifty members are now working on their own near-death research projects. Bruce Greyson has received a grant from the University of Connecticut Research Foundation to continue his studies of the effect of near-death experience on death anxiety and suicide ideation; others are investigating such topics as near-death experience in children, "negative" experiences at death, and near-death reports in Japan and Guam. Encouraged by these successes, IANDS now seeks to raise $100,000 to create a research endowment and a new center for conferences, counseling, educational programs, and archives.

A British branch of IANDS has been established by Margot Grey, a humanistic psychologist who is herself the survivor of a transforming near-death experience. In *Return from Death*, she presents the results of an eighteen-month study—which she calls cross-cultural—comparing the testimony of American subjects selected from the IANDS archives with that of British near-death survivors. In her methods and results, Grey follows Kenneth Ring almost exactly, finding the same core experience with its five phases, the same spiritual and paranormal effects, and arriving at the same conviction that we are about to witness an "evolutionary" transfiguration of our species. Although it was written before *Heading toward Omega* appeared, Grey's book not only reflects a shared New Age ethos, but also appears to have been shaped by Ring's article on "Precognitive and Prophetic Visions in Near-Death Experiences."

Not all studies of near-death experience take place under the auspices of IANDS. Recently, the Gallup Poll organization has entered the field, adding questions about near-death experience to its periodic surveys of American religious beliefs and attitudes toward death and the afterlife. In *Adventures in Immortality*, a widely publicized book based on the results of these surveys, George Gallup, Jr., estimates that 15 percent of the population has had a close brush with death and that 34 percent of these people can remember feelings of peace and painlessness, separation from the body, a sense of being in another world, or a life review.

Aside from some polemical accounts produced by conservative Christians, most current near-death research projects have been yielding compatible results; it is therefore possible to consider near-death narratives thematically, noting important exceptions along the way, as I have done for medieval Christian vision stories. To simplify discussion, I will take the narratives at face value, without speaking like a court reporter ("the alleged out-of-body experience") or burdening the reader with repeated protestations of detachment. Yet my thematic presentation, unlike that of Moody and his colleagues, makes no claim to identify the essential features or "common program" of near-death experience per se. As I have already suggested, we can only study the literary and oral retelling, not the direct experience; the themes that will be examined here belong to what might be called a narrative tradition in the making. In part IV, I will evaluate the claims of near-death researchers, but in the next two chapters I am concerned primarily with classifying and comparing the motifs that recur in contemporary near-death literature.

CHAPTER 7

The Other World: Modern Itineraries

Attitudes toward Death and Dying

IN BOTH MEDIEVAL and modern narratives, scene one of the otherworld drama is set on the deathbed. Here, according to Christian tradition, the dying rehearse their future judgment: the sinner exits in agony and the saint glides away in peace. These two deaths mark the first forking of the road all souls must follow—to heaven or hell, to Christ's right hand or his left.

Today, however, we hear a great deal about good deaths and very little about bad ones. The two deaths theme, a hardy perennial of Christian didactic literature, has wilted in the climate of secular optimism. Enlightened minds no longer find it edifying to contemplate a grisly end; pain is something to avoid at all costs, to drown in a "Brompton cocktail" of potent narcotics, or to deny. As if embarrassed by the idea of gruesome death, popular writings on near-death experience and "conscious dying" shift attention to "beautiful" deathbed scenes, suffused with a rosy glow of acceptance, ornamented with sublime visions, and set apart from the ordinary by paranormal insights and premonitions that defy medical prognosis.[1] Karlis Osis summarizes the traits of this exemplary death:

> Although most patients apparently drift into oblivion without awareness of it, there are some, clearly conscious to the end, who say they "see" into the beyond and who are able to report their experiences before expiring. They see apparitions of deceased relatives and friends. They see religious and mythological figures. They see nonearthly environments characterized by light, beauty, and intense color. These experiences are transformative. They bring with them serenity, peace, elation, and religious emotions. The patients die a

"good death" in strange contrast to the usual gloom and misery commonly expected before expiration.[2]

Although this description recalls the deathbed scenes of patristic and medieval hagiography, readers of *At the Hour of Death* will notice that the requirements for sainthood have been greatly relaxed; all sorts of people may enter the beatific circle. The gift of being able to predict one's time of death, for instance, no longer seems to depend on one's moral, spiritual, or social standing.[3]

Elisabeth Kübler-Ross is even more generous; she insists that everyone, however ill or deranged, becomes lucid and blissful at death.[4] In her view, pain is not death's mischief, but rather a symptom of the struggle to live.[5] If there is such a thing as "death," Kübler-Ross assures us that it is a soothing transition, a happy homecoming, a birth without pangs, "like the butterfly coming out of a cocoon."[6]

In declaring that "there is no death," Kübler-Ross is directly in line with her spiritualist predecessors. Consider the words of Andrew Jackson Davis, the clairvoyant prodigy who in 1845, at age nineteen, dictated from "magnetic sleep" a massive volume that became the *Summa theologica* of the spiritualist movement. Death is dreaded, Davis declares, only "in consequence of wrongly apprehending the process of dying, and of not knowing the ineffable beauties that surround the living man when it escapes the outer form."[7] He goes on to use the butterfly analogy, an image with a classical pedigree, which became pervasive in spiritualist writings:

> The butterfly escapes its gross and rudimental body, and wings its way to the sunny bower, and is sensible of its new existence.... The body dies on the outer, or rather changes its mode of existence while the spirit ascends to a higher habitation, suited to its nature and requirements. And as it is with these, so it is with me, and the transitions which I continually experience.... Death, or the transition so termed, is ... of all things the most to be admired, and its prospect is the first thing to be cherished and appreciated.[8]

As Russell Noyes shows, the authors of the "euthanasia" manuals of the nineteenth century were the first to suggest as a matter of medical observation that dying need not be painful. They encouraged the physician to take the place of the priest in practicing "obstetrics of the soul"; as such, his role was to ensure a comfortable death by dispensing narcotics along with spiritual solace.[9] Today, Lewis Thomas and other medical writers are proposing that a pain-free passage from life is in some sense our natural birthright.[10] That the good death has lost its cautionary counterpart is partly the result of advances in pain control; but it also reflects modern attitudes toward the significance—or lack of significance—of human suffering.

Near-death narratives eulogize the good death in words that recall the medieval "art of dying" tracts. The author of *I Died Three Times in 1977*, for instance, explains that "dying is a release from pain, like getting out of prison."[11] In a critical episode following an attack of thrombosis, she found herself floating up to the ceiling, looking down at her motionless frame:

> When I was satisfied that it was dead, there came a joyous euphoria, like a prisoner being released from a long jail sentence. I danced and danced around the lightbulb, singing like a child. It was finally over. I was free![12]

Some report feeling so wonderful while "dead" that they resent the fuss being made to revive them. A victim of anaphylactic shock writes that from her vantage point above the telephone wires, the spectacle of firemen trying to slap the breath back into her frame looked "cosmically comic." When their efforts finally succeeded, she felt a "sense of imprisonment and degradation" at being forced to reenter the body which "now seemed like a foreign substance."[13]

Like the medieval visionaries who paused in their ascent to glance back at earth and "smiled at its paltry substance," the near-death subject looks down upon the scene of crisis with an attitude of clinical detachment, as if it were a mildly interesting avant-garde play:

> I could see my own body all tangled up in the car amongst all the people who had gathered around, but, you know, I had no feelings for it whatsoever. It was like it was a completely different human, or maybe just an object.[14]

Once set free, the mind may take offense at the body's insolent claim to represent the self. One of Moody's informants recalls that he "didn't like being around this thing that looked like a dead body—even if it was me!"[15] Sabom records a similar response: "I recognized me laying there . . . about like looking at a dead worm or something. I didn't have any desire to go back to it."[16]

Even family ties may lose their value: "It was like all relations were cut. . . . Everything was just so—technical."[17] Such descriptions of being cut off and detached correspond well to the tenth tableau of the medieval "art of dying" block-books, in which an angel protects the dying man from temptation to attachment by concealing his family and possessions from his eyes.[18] Some patients report an echo-chamber effect, or a sense that friends and relatives gathered by the bed are receding or shrinking away.[19]

Psychologists Russell Noyes, Jr., and Roy Kletti attribute the feeling of remoteness to an affective disorder known as depersonalization, in which the world and one's body may appear distant, empty, or unreal. In the face of extreme danger or imminent death, they point out, depersonalization may have an adaptive value. Those with a chance to survive are shielded from panic so that they can lucidly calculate the best course of action; at the same time, disengagement from earthly ties cushions death's blow to the ego.[20]

The depersonalization theory has several strengths, to be discussed below, but it does not do justice to the joyful tone of near-death testimony. According to most reports, it is only in contrast to the blissful sensations and expanded vision of near-death experience that the body seems worthless and alien and normal life narrow and degraded. While all the color drains out of the flesh and its environs, near-death subjects say they are attracted to a new focus of irresistible interest, another world more real than the one they left behind. As Noyes and Kletti acknowledge, this goes far "beyond the mere numbing of depersonalization."[21]

Whether we call it transcendence or depersonalization, survivors of near-death experience often say that it has made them less preoccupied with their bodies and with material things:

> ... after this, my mind was the main point of attraction, and the body was second—it was only something to encase my mind. I didn't care if I had a body or not. It didn't matter because for all I cared my mind was what was important.[22]

It sounds strange to hear such dualistic, if not pessimistic, views of the body quoted with relish by researchers who are otherwise relentlessly "holistic" in their outlook. Yet, just as we saw in the medieval context, this experience-based or imaginative dualism does not amount to a philosophical position. Especially in the current intellectual climate, the dualistic language of near-death reports is unlikely to presage a revival of world-renouncing asceticism.

Similarly, we should not take contemporary accounts of the "thrill of dying" entirely at face value. Some critics, theologians among them, fear that the publicity being given to blissful near-death experience may lead to a "cultlike exaltation, sentimentalization, and even worship of death."[23] Yet survivors of mystical near-death experience neither run to a monastery nor run off a cliff; their expressions of apparent zest for death are accompanied by greater appreciation of physical life. Indeed, a life-affirming outlook is the central message of near-death narratives, as we shall see below.

Images of the Soul

As in the medieval narratives, many modern visionaries find that they are clothed in an airy or ethereal body. In a study conducted by Bruce Greyson and Ian Stevenson, 58 percent of those who reported near-death experience said that they sensed themselves in a new body, the same size and age as its physical counterpart, but lighter in weight.[24] Most of Moody's informants also felt that they had a body of some sort, taking shape as a mist, cloud, or sphere, or mimicking the contours of the physical form.[25] For Elisabeth Kübler-Ross, the spiritual body is an exact replica of the physical body, lacking only its defects; and she offers this image of postmortem rehabilitation as a utopian pledge:

> In a near-death experience, the body becomes perfect again. Quadriplegics are no longer paralyzed, multiple sclerosis patients who have been in wheelchairs

for years say that when they were out of their bodies, they were able to sing and dance.[26]

Neurologists suggest that the feeling of physical wholeness is an extension of the "phantom limb" disorder that tricks the senses into receiving signals from missing or dead extremities;[27] it is as if a Platonic demiurge tampers with our neural circuitry, forcing the body image to conform to an archetypal pattern. But regardless of the neurological or psychological conditions, in otherworld journey narration "somatomorphism" is almost an inevitable imaginative device. For as we have seen with medieval examples, the otherworld journey is above all a dramatic form, shaped by rules of narrative imagination, in which the abstract "soul" or "spirit" must be personified or embodied in order to play its part effectively.

Ways of embodying the self may vary, however, and a comparison of medieval and contemporary near-death narratives reveals some remarkable changes in popular imagery for the soul. Several of Moody's and almost all of Ring's informants are content to speak of "me" without elaborate somatic analogies.[28] The most striking way in which contemporary accounts differ from their medieval counterparts, however, is their introduction of quasi-scientific vocabulary borrowed from electricity and magnetism. A columnist in *Vital Signs* writes, "It's like we were light or energy shaped somewhat like a body but not a body."[29] Some sense themselves as an "energy pattern" or "wave length," resembling the body in form, but composed of finer or faster "vibrations."[30]

This new kind of corporeal imagery for the soul is in part a legacy of the nineteenth- and early twentieth-century spiritualists and occultists. The spiritualists combined traditional and sometimes crude soul-body dualism with a notion that the body is a matrix for the development or "emanation" of spirit. Underlying this conception of the relation between body and spirit was an assumption that matter and spirit exist on a continuum, differing in degree rather than in kind. Popularized through the influence of von Reichenbach, Mesmer, Bulwyer Lytton, and Swedenborg, this metaphysical doctrine appealed to the discoveries of electricity, magnetism, and "ether" for empirical evidence that spirit is but a rarefied form of matter, and matter a condensation of spirit.[31]

According to this view, the grossest physical objects are linked to the highest spiritual essences. One consequence is that however worthless the vacated body may seem, there can never be an absolute antagonism between body and soul. Hence, the spiritualist variation on the chain of being theme serves even more effectively than its medieval counterpart to mitigate the pessimistic implications of soul-body dualism; it provides a metaphysical rationale for the notion that departure from the body is inevitably a smooth transition. The essential compatibility of spirit and matter means that passage from one level to the next, from physical to nonphysical body or from earth to "Summerland," can occur without great trauma. In this respect, near-death accounts are in complete agreement with spiritualist cosmology and with mediumistic and clairvoyant descriptions of the afterlife.

In the writings of Andrew Jackson Davis, for example, we can see the way this optimistic cosmology reshapes and reinvigorates the old idea that the soul discards its body like an outworn garment. While attending the death of one of his patients, he found himself able to perceive the departure of her spirit:

> Now the head of the body became suddenly enveloped in a fine, soft, mellow, luminous atmosphere; and, as instantly, I saw the cerebrum and the cerebellum expand their most interior portions; I saw them discontinue their appropriate galvanic functions; and then I saw that they became highly charged with . . . vital electricity and vital magnetism. . . .
>
> Now I saw, in the mellow, spiritual atmosphere, which emanated from and encircled her head, the indistinct outlines of the formation of another head! . . . This new head unfolded more and more distinctly. . . . I saw, unfolding in their natural, progressive order, the harmonious development of the neck, the shoulders, the breast, and the entire spiritual organization.
>
> While this spiritual formation was going on, which was perfectly visible to my spiritual perceptions, the material body manifested, to the outer vision of observing individuals in the room, many symptoms of uneasiness and pain; but these indications were wholly deceptive; they were wholly caused by the departure of the vital or spiritual forces from the extremities and viscera into the brain, and thence into the ascending organism.
>
> . . . I learned that the correspondence between the birth of a child into this world, and the birth of the spirit from the material body into a higher world, is absolute and complete—even to the umbilical cord, which was represented by the thread of vital electricity, which for a few minutes, subsisted between, and connected the two organisms together.
>
> . . . I saw her begin to breathe the most interior or spiritual portions of the surrounding terrestrial atmosphere. . . . And now I saw that she was in the possession of exterior and physical proportions, which were identical, in every possible particular—improved and beautified—with those proportions which characterized her earthly organization. That is to say, she possessed a heart, a stomach, a liver, lungs, etc., just as her natural body did previous to (not her, but) its death. This is a wonderful and consoling truth! But I saw that the improvements . . . were not so particular and thorough as to destroy or transcend her personality; nor did they materially alter her natural appearance or earthly characteristics. So much like her former self was she, that, had her friends beheld her (as I did) they certainly would have exclaimed . . . "Why how well you look! How improved you are!"
>
> . . . I saw her pass through the adjoining room, out of the door, and step from the house into the atmosphere! I was overwhelmed with delight and astonishment when, for the first time I realized the universal truth that the spiritual organization can tread the atmosphere which, while in the coarser earthly form, we breathe—so much more refined is man's spiritual constitution.[32]

Similarly, interpreters of near-death experience suggest that the separation of body and soul should be seen in a context of "energy materialism,"[33] rather than as an illustration of harsh disparity between spirit and matter.

Compared to clairvoyant and mediumistic accounts of the past century, however, contemporary near-death narratives are free of metaphysical pretension, preferring commonsense figures of speech to exotic terms like "astral body" and "etheric double." There is no trace of ectoplasm, and the electrical umbilical cord mentioned by Davis (or the "silver cord" favored by spiritualists and theosophists) seems to have gone out of style.[34] Kübler-Ross, who has closer ties to mediumship and occultism than do the other near-death researchers, is the only one to emphasize the notion of a cord linking the spiritual body to its physical dwelling; indeed, she speculates that one day there will be a machine somewhat like a geiger counter to measure when the cord is severed.[35]

By discarding most of the terminology that has become explicitly identified with spooks and seances, while retaining the use of scientific and quasi-scientific vocabulary, near-death literature moves even further in the direction of naturalism and empiricism. The effort of spiritualists to create a plausible cosmology is also brought up to date in near-death visions; the spheres of the other world are no longer identified with specific planetary or atmospheric zones, but are characterized—as in George Ritchie's account—as "dimensions" or regions of inner space.

Liminality

Having made an exit, often through the traditional gateway of the head, near-death subjects find themselves hovering above the body in "liminal" condition, often gravitating toward the light bulb or a corner of the ceiling.[36] A number of unusual sensory effects accompany this phase. Bruce Greyson and Ian Stevenson found reports of warmth and analgesia in nearly three quarters of their sample; half of the near-death survivors they surveyed saw lights and auras and heard strange sounds—ranging from Moody's bells and buzz-saws to cathedral choirs.[37] Though sight and hearing become more vivid, taste and smell usually disappear; modern visionaries miss out on the heavenly perfumes and manna banquets that grace medieval paradise scenes.[38] The kinesthetic sense that registers weight, motion, and position also vanishes, according to Moody and Ring.[39]

Aside from the neurological conditions that may help to explain these oddities, it is possible that sensory impressions are selected for their cognitive or affective connotations, for their link to the sense of self. Warmth can bring with it or be interpreted as a message of security and love. Vision and hearing are intimately associated with knowing. Smell, taste, kinesthesia, on the other hand, seem less important as supports for identity. Both medieval and modern vision stories suggest that the soul must be stripped of nonessential attributes; in order to experience reality directly, it becomes an undiscriminated organ of knowledge and affection. The distinctions between sensation, emotion, and cognition melt away, and only the minimal traits required to make a person are retained.

Temporal perception is also strangely distorted during this liminal phase.[40] The newly separated self, like a Kurt Vonnegut hero, gets "unstuck in time": thoughts speed up as the surrounding scene slows down.[41] According to Noyes and Kletti, this is another depersonalization effect, commonly reported by people in extreme danger as well as by survivors of near-death crises.[42] Desynchronization can be a great help to someone who has a split second to make a hairpin turn or grab hold of an onrushing branch. For those who are physically on the point of death, however, it marks the transition to a state in which time, from all reports, loses its meaning altogether.[43]

If timelessness is a universal feature of mystical experience, altered time is a characteristic mark of the visionary journey and as such has recurred throughout Western culture, from the Seven Sleepers of Ephesus to Friar Felix (the Rip van Winkle prototype who consumed three hundred earth years enjoying a momentary reverie of heaven), to the modern near-death experiencer who relives his past in the instant between heartbeats.[44] Temporal mutation is also a feature of otherworld adventure stories that involve actual travel, from the voyage of Brendan the Irish seafaring saint to the scientific lore of modern space travel.

Often, feelings of peace, warmth, painlessness, and altered time surface only after the struggle to live is abandoned. By embracing his fate, the victim is transformed; the cold sweat of panic turns into an oceanic bath of assurance. A nurse who nearly died from a penicillin reaction revealed under psychoanalysis that her ecstatic near-death experience began when she surrendered to death:

> In the car, when her breathing began to become difficult, she realized what was happening and she experienced frantic fear, which, however, soon passed. (She would never fear dying again, she said.) . . . She remembered a "last violent reaction" in which she fought desperately against it, but she was not afraid, and then she had given in, knowing she wanted it (death).[45]

The progression from desperate struggling to joyful surrender is especially characteristic of those who suddenly face extreme mortal danger, as Noyes and Kletti point out. Yet the testimony of survivors who were physically near death is remarkably similar to that of accident victims who only expected to die. Albert Heim's summary of the reactions of falling mountain climbers speaks for both groups of near-death subjects:

> . . . no grief was felt, nor was there paralyzing fright of the sort that can happen in instances of lesser danger. . . . There was no anxiety, no trace of despair, nor pain; but rather calm seriousness, profound acceptance, and a dominant mental quickness and sense of surety.[46]

Although it is a commonplace of spiritualist literature that the newly dead are dreamy, confused, and unaware that they have died,[47] near-death reports indicate that such disorientation is rare and transient. Like the accident victims Heim describes, today's near-death subjects feel their senses sharpen and their minds clear the very moment they disengage from the body. An out-of-body experience, or even a vague sense of remoteness from the crisis, seems to disentangle the mind from the failing flesh, allowing it to function unimpaired. A survivor of anaphylactic shock recalls: "I was fully aware of what was happening both physically and in the minds of those in the emergency room until I was revived, at which point I was very confused."[48]

In the near-death testimony collected by Moody, Ring, and Sabom, only a few subjects indicate that, like Tundal, they tried at first to reenter the body.[49] Moody suggests that momentary feelings of loneliness and frustration quickly dissolve as the experience progresses, either because help arrives or because the visionary is flooded with positive feelings which overwhelm any anxieties. Near-death survivors insist that the experience was vivid and coherent rather than dreamlike; they felt more capable of rational deliberation and less likely than usual to misread their situation.[50]

The Journey

If it is pleasant to be cut adrift from the body, reports nonetheless indicate that this is just the threshold of a full near-death experience. To embark on the otherworld journey proper, some visionaries—today as in the Middle Ages—rely on symbolic vehicles and pathways of approach. An Indian woman whose return from apparent death was investigated by Karlis Osis rode to heaven on the back of a bespangled cow; her American counterpart, a victim of cardiac failure, hailed a taxicab.[51] And Kenneth Ring interviewed a woman who was "ferried across the River Styx."[52]

More often, however, near-death survivors say they were propelled or drawn along a path by an invisible force, without the aid of chariots, boatmen, or beasts of burden. The standard picture of this passage to the other world, etched into the popular imagination by *Life After Life*, is a dark tunnel that leads to a welcoming light.[53] According to some accounts, the soul is squeezed through this tunnel toward its bright destination as if by the contraction of uterine walls:

> . . . I entered head first into a narrow and very, very dark passageway. I seemed to just fit inside of it. I began to slide down, down, down.
> . . . I was in a narrow, v-shaped passage, like a trough, about the width of this chair. It just fit my body, and my hands and arms seemed to be at my side. I went head first, and it was dark, dark as it could be in there. I moved on through it downward . . .[54]

Critics have seized upon such reports because they seem readily explained as stress-triggered fantasy; near-death experience, they argue, is just a replay of the inaugural descent down the birth canal into the glare of the

delivery room and the clutches of white-garbed godlings.[55] Sympathetic interpreters, on the other hand, say that it is only fitting that life should end with
a reminiscence of its beginning. For this reason Stanislav Grof, who for years
administered psychedelic death and rebirth to terminal patients, considers
the tunnel experience the epitome of near-death transfiguration.[56]

Yet not all tunnel narratives symbolize birth so obviously. Moody and
his colleagues have catalogued many variations on the theme: walking
through immense calverts or pipes, spinning in vertiginous spirals, descending into caves or wells. Also classed with tunnel episodes are accounts that
resemble the medieval visions of the Drythelm line, in which the protagonist
follows a luminous guide through a dark valley or narrow path to a realm of
light; a few refer explicitly to the biblical valley of the shadow of death.[57]

Moreover, as apt as the tunnel image may be to mark entry into new
life, Ring and Sabom count few instances of it. According to their studies, a
more common vehicle of transition is the sensation of floating through a black
void toward a glowing light.[58] In his interviews with dying patients, Charles
Garfield found some who felt they were fluctuating between narrow confinement and boundless drifting.[59]

Paradoxically, there seems to be an affinity between these opposite
effects. A cardiac arrest survivor, writing in *Anabiosis*, speaks of being "propelled through a cylindrical void."[60] In some accounts, it is the sensation of
movement that creates the impression of a tunnel:

> There was total blackness around me. I want to say that it felt like I was mov-
> ing very, very fast in time and space. I was traveling through a tunnel. It didn't
> look like a tunnel, but when you're in a tunnel, all you see is blackness around
> you. If you move very fast you can feel the sides moving in on you whether
> there are sides there or not because of the darkness.[61]

As these examples indicate, modern descriptions of migration to the
other world suggest underground burrowing, weightless navigation through
space, hiking through the wilderness, and other disparate imagery. We have
seen a similar topographic jumble in medieval accounts: Germanic mountain
tunnels mingle with desert wastes, deep valleys, forest paths, volcanic craters,
and aerial pastures.

A significant difference, though, is the absence of the two paths motif in
modern accounts. Despite the diverse topographic imagery, modern near-
death literature assumes that there are no radical partings of the way. Medieval vision stories, on the other hand, divide otherworld traffic, for didactic
reasons, into broad and narrow, dark and light, descending and ascending
ways. Modern accounts tell us that despite the differences in individual experiences, all move in one direction from darkness to light, from death to
heaven. And just as Gregory the Great made moral capital of the two paths
theme, so interpreters of near-death visions find an edifying metaphor in the
notion of a single itinerary: "As Moody has implied, it seems to be the *same*
journey, with different people encountering different segments of what

appears to be a *single, common* path."[62] Here, as in medieval vision literature, the metaphor of the path takes on concrete meaning in the context of the otherworld journey; it may then be translated into metaphor again as an interpretive or didactic device. This conversion from metaphor to vision and back to metaphor—like an alchemical process—energizes what might otherwise be an inert figure of speech.

The researchers agree that passage from darkness to light is a nearly universal sign of transition to a new phase of near-death experience; but they disagree on the timetable. Moody assigns tunnel and drifting episodes to the moment of separation from the body; for Sabom and Ring, on the other hand, they mark the shift from local out-of-body experience (Sabom's "autoscopic NDE") to transcendent otherworld visions. This may surprise the reader who is trying to make the details fit a "single, common path."

Such discrepancies occur not because of incoherence in individual reports, but because Moody, Sabom, Ring, and others attempt to construct an overarching narrative by selecting typical features from a great number of differing accounts. In the interest of portraying near-death experience as in essence a unitary phenomenon, the researchers create a pattern out of the welter of various tunnels and paths, lights and presences, gardens and edifices. As Moody acknowledges, this is overorganizing; but apparently it is irresistible.[63] Since the otherworld journey remains fundamentally a narrative form, it is understandable that near-death researchers are not content to dissect the elements of the testimonies they collect without fusing them together again in a developmental sequence. That is the only way to represent the dramatic coherence of the individual account. A story, rather than a catalogue of assorted motifs, is what captures our imagination, today as in the Middle Ages.

The Light

Proceeding according to the logic of the story, then, rather than by an invariant timetable, we arrive at the experience of light. According to Kenneth Ring:

> The passage from the third to the fourth stage of the core experience is marked by one singular feature: the appearance of light. It is usually described as a brilliant golden light. This light, however, almost never hurts one's eyes but is, on the contrary, very restful, comforting and, apparently, of ineffable beauty. Some of our respondents told me they felt enveloped by this light, and virtually all who experienced it felt drawn to it.[64]

In some reports, light acts almost as a vehicle. One near-death experiencer—communicating her story through nationally televised packets of light—told of riding a "laser beam of light" that rushed her past planets and luminaries

at a tremendous speed.[65] For those who begin their journey in darkness, the
light may have an attractive power, pulling them toward its source:

> There was this panic, the panic of cardiac arrest. . . . Then I could feel myself
> going through this tunnel, being drawn through this tunnel. And there was
> this light at the end. God it was so bright! And as I neared it I could feel the
> warmth enveloping me. . . .[66]

> Finally I was sucked into the light source, not unlike one is swept up into a
> whirlpool. I became one with the light.[67]

> . . . I was going down a long black tunnel with a tremendous alive sort of light
> bursting in at the far end. I shot out of the tunnel into this light. I was in the
> light, I was *part* of it, and I knew everything—a most strange feeling.[68]

Near-death accounts suggest that journey to the light is assured by the
heliotropism of our nature; no obstacles can block the inevitable homecoming.
We have seen in medieval texts traces of the comparable Platonic and
Augustinian theme of the gravitation of the soul in the direction of its strongest
affinities.[69] It is a *leitmotif* of the *Paradiso*, as when Beatrice tells Dante,

> . . . thou shouldst no more wonder at thy ascent than at a stream falling from
> a mountain-height to its foot; it would be a wonder in thee if, freed from hindrance,
> thou hadst remained below, as on earth would be stillness in living
> flame.[70]

But the ordeals and tests that abound in traditional Christian vision literature
express a conviction that the soul is just as likely to be weighed down
by perversity and thwarted by malicious forces as to ascend, following its
original inclination, to God. Beatrice therefore warns Dante:

> It is true that, as a shape often does not accord with the art's intention because
> the material is deaf and unresponsive, so sometimes the creature, having the
> power, thus impelled, to turn aside another way, deviates from this course,
> and, as fire may be seen to fall from a cloud, so the primal impulse, diverted
> by false pleasure, is turned to the earth.[71]

Lacking this cautionary note, contemporary near-death narratives come close
to the Swedenborgian and spiritualist idea that inhabitants of the other world
travel by an effortless attraction toward higher realms.

Some near-death survivors speak of being suspended in space and watching
the light grow nearer and larger until it dispels the surrounding mist and
gloom. Though they arrive at the light in different ways, however, they use
similar words to describe its enthralling qualities. Clear, white, orange,
golden, or yellow in hue, the light is of a different order from normal daylight,
brighter yet more soothing.[72] In addition to seeing by virtue of this light, one
is caught up in it.[73] The light radiates wisdom and compassion; it floods the
mind, expanding awareness until one seems to comprehend everything in a
single gaze.

Speaking before a recent IANDS conference, a woman who nearly died in childbirth recalled her encounter with a bright white light in these words:

> It was a dynamic light, not like a spotlight. It was an incredible energy—a light you wouldn't believe. I almost floated in it. It was feeding my consciousness feelings of unconditional love, complete safety, and complete, total perfection. . . . It just *powed* into you. My consciousness was going out and getting larger and taking in more; I expanded and more and more came in. It was such rapture, such bliss. And then, and then, a piece of knowledge came in: it was that I was immortal, indestructible. I cannot be hurt, cannot be lost. We don't have anything to worry about. And that the world is perfect; everything that happens is part of a perfect plan. I don't understand this part now, but I still know it's true. . . . Later, when I was saying the Lord's prayer, and I got to the part that says "thine is the kingdom, and the power, and the glory," I thought that nothing could describe this experience any better. It was pure power and glory.[74]

A correspondent to *Anabiosis* who suffered brain damage from the failure of a heart pump that was keeping her alive during open-heart surgery, writes that she was bathed in a yellow light:

> It was in, around, and through everything. It is what halos are made of. It is God made visible. In, around, and through everything.[75]

A retired policeman who hemorrhaged after surgery was, like Salvius, ushered directly into the light:

> It was the most beautiful thing I have ever experienced! I never lost awareness; there was no blackness, no tunnel. It's impossible to describe. It truly can't be put into words. If one could put a definition on peace and love, or describe it, make it tangible, you might get pretty close. I didn't want to ever leave that brilliance![76]

Appearing on "Phil Donahue," he told of receiving messages from the light that "weren't messages because I just 'knew' everything."[77] Music and color seemed superfluous; "there was no need for anything more than the light."

In accounts of the light, contemporary testimony bears a striking resemblance to medieval narratives. Both medieval and modern descriptions of otherworld light blend visual qualities such as splendor, clarity, and transparency with sensory/emotional effects such as warmth and energy.[78] This mixture of imagery suggests the convergence of knowledge and love, an idea made explicit by many texts in both periods. The visionary may behold a light that is at once all-knowing and all-loving, and which fuses together his scattered thoughts and desires, uniting intelligence and will. By contemplating the whole of creation in this light, he becomes whole. In Gregory's *Dialogues* and Dante's *Paradiso* we have seen examples of this illuminated unifying vision. Comparison to modern near-death narratives shows this to be one of the few truly "core" experiences that cut across cultural and historical boundaries.

Accounts of the vision of light display what William James calls the "eternal unanimity" of mystical discourse:

> I became one with the light. As I became one with this omnipresent light, its knowledge became my knowledge. I was in a single instant what my life had been and what had been of meaning in my life. The superficial aspects of my life . . . were consumed in that . . . instant by the energy of the light. . . . In the same moment, the direction of the whole of mankind became evident to me.[79]

Still, in near-death narratives as in the devotional and mystical literature of the world, the encounter with ultimate reality comes in a variety of flavors. Near-death accounts have in common a sense of ecstatic participation in totality, but this takes forms that range from intimate conversations with God to general saturation in an atmosphere of intelligence and love. Some might say that the light was more than a person, because it was a surrounding presence; others might say that it was more than a surrounding presence, because it was also a person. They agree, at any rate, in making an effort to communicate what was for them the supreme manifestation of existence.

The testimony Moody collected portrays the light as a loving presence, perhaps without a human form, but possessing a "very definite personality."[80] As an all-purpose designation, Moody coins the term "being of light." Like the luminous men of biblical and visionary literature, the being of light is understood by some to be an angelic guardian or guide, occasionally performing the soul-extracting function of otherworld guides in traditional accounts. More often, however, the spirits of deceased relatives or friends serve as guides, while the luminous presence is an exalted cosmic figure, sometimes identified with God or Christ. Glossing his description of the light, the former policeman told an interviewer:

> I knew it was God. I knew . . . this is the hard part. . . . There is no doubt in my mind that it was God. God was me and I was God. I was part of the light and I was one with it. I was not separate. I am not saying that I am a supreme being. I was God, as you are, as everyone is.[81]

In George Ritchie's *Return from Tomorrow*, this encounter is explicitly Christian:

> The light which entered that room was Christ; I knew because a thought was put deep within me, "You are in the presence of the Son of God." I have called Him "light," but I could also have said "love," for that room was flooded, pierced, illuminated by the most total compassion I have ever felt. It was a presence so comforting, so joyous and all-satisfying, that I wanted to lose myself forever in the wonder of it.[82]

Similarly, after hearing doctors pronounce him dead, one of Moody's informants felt himself tumbling through a black passageway toward a brilliant glow which attracted him because it seemed to be Christ:

> For immediately, being a Christian, I had connected the light with Christ, who said, "I am the light of the world." I said to myself, "If this is it, if I am to die, then I know who waits for me at the end, there in that light."[83]

This report represents what Moody considers a Christian interpretation of an underlying universal experience:

> . . . . while the description of the being of light is utterly invariable, the identification of the being varies from individual to individual and seems to be largely a function of the religious background, training, or beliefs of the person involved. Thus, most of those who are Christians in training or belief identify the light as Christ and sometimes draw biblical parallels in support of their interpretation.[84]

The near-death testimony Moody presents has no harp-playing seraphs, no haloed martyrs holding their heads, no Christ emblazoned with a kingly *Chi-Rho*. Moody therefore reasons that most people have essentially the same vision, even though they may overlay it with different culturally inherited forms.

Karlis Osis and Erlendur Haraldsson bring the same approach to evaluating the differences between American and Indian deathbed visions of religious figures:

> If a patient sees a radiant man clad in white who induces in him an inexplicable experience of harmony and peace, he might *interpret* the apparition in various ways: as an angel, Jesus or God; or if he is a Hindu, Krishna, Shiva or Deva.[85]

Citing with approval Moody's notion of "figures of light," Osis and Haraldsson suggest that such a designation "might describe these entities much better than the names of deities assigned to them by our patients."[86]

Although this analysis has the advantage of smoothing down the rough edges of conflicting religious world-views, it disregards the testimony of those who feel that their encounter with a specific religious figure was a matter of direct intuition rather than mere labeling. The woman who told Kenneth Ring that Jesus appeared to her with a communion chalice would probably take offense at Osis and Haraldsson's suggestion that this was "embroidery."[87] In our consideration of medieval visions, moreover, we have seen that the line between immediate experience and interpretive construction is difficult to trace. Indeed, the being of light is no less an imaginative form than the monk Edmund's St. Nicholas decked out in his ceremonial insignia; the vagueness of this term suits it to those who might be embarrassed by lush religious symbolism. As such, the being of light is just as culturally specific as the saints and angels who populate the medieval Christian other world.

Judgment

The next step, as depicted by Moody, is a nonverbal colloquy between the being of light and the visionary:

> At first, when the light came, I wasn't sure what was happening, but then it asked, it kind of asked me if I was ready to die. It was like talking to a person, but a person wasn't there. The light's what was talking to me, but in a voice.[88]

Those Moody interviewed felt that their exchange with this being was immediate and direct and could be rendered only in the crudest fashion by spoken words. The being would ask something like, "Are you prepared to die?" or "What have you done with your life to show me?"[89] What was expected in return was not a specific answer, but a general self-scrutiny, putting one's whole life in question.

For readers acquainted with the history of Western eschatological literature, this questioning will strike a familiar note. Traditionally, the soul's ascent is interrupted by an interrogation that tests its doctrinal allegiance, ritual preparedness, moral standing, or esoteric training. The motif is strongest in Gnostic accounts of challenge by planetary guardians, in Semitic legends of harassment by aerial spirits, and in Muslim traditions concerning the questioning in the grave and at the gates of the heavens; softer echoes of this theme can be found, as we have seen, in early and medieval Christian visionary and eschatological writings. In today's upbeat near-death literature, however, which invariably depicts the universe as friendly to human interests, the questioning has been transformed from an ordeal into an affirmation. The being of light communicates, but never excommunicates. In Moody's words:

> The being, all seem to agree, does not direct the question to them to accuse or threaten them, for they still feel the total love and acceptance coming from the light, no matter what their answer may be. Rather, the point of the question seems to be to make them think about their lives, to draw them out.[90]

Kenneth Ring, whose account of the journey from darkness to light is somewhat out of phase with Moody's, describes a similar meeting with a "presence" that manifests all the traits of the being of light, except that it usually remains unseen. Ring's subjects undergo a similar gentle examination.

According to the reports gathered by Moody, Ring, and others, the examining spirit sometimes displays, as visual evidence, a record of one's past thoughts and deeds. No doubt this is a more elaborate form of the proverbial notion that a drowning man sees his life flash before his eyes. That some people on the brink of death seem to recall their past in an instant is amply documented in nineteenth-century memoirs and medical annals as well as recent near-death studies. DeQuincey describes a typical instance:

> I was once told by a near relative of mine that, having in her childhood fallen into a river, and being on the very verge of death but for the assistance which

reached her at the last critical moment, she saw in a moment her whole life, clothed in its forgotten incidents, arrayed before her as in a mirror, not successively, but simultaneously; and she had a faculty developed as suddenly for comprehending the whole and every part.[91]

Albert Heim, who found the panoramic life review quite common among survivors of nearly fatal falls, recounts his own experience when a gust of wind tossed him from an Alpine crag:

> ... I saw my whole past life take place in many images, as though on a stage at some distance from me. I saw myself as the chief character in the performance. Everything was transfigured as though by a heavenly light and everything was beautiful without grief, without anxiety, and without pain.[92]

Accident victims who suddenly face the prospect of imminent death more often report this visual replay of memories than do survivors of critical illness. In both cases, however, the events of a lifetime seem to be compressed into a rapid sequence or jumble of vivid pictures.[93] Noyes and Kletti quote the following report from a man who nearly drowned as a child:

> ... A series of events that had happened to me up to that point in my life literally flashed before me in a kaleidoscope, montage effect. They were going very fast like one of those strobe lights you see today, like a real fast flip of slides, instant takes, that sort of thing. They were all past events and highlights or impressionistic points. . . . There was a certain detachment as I watched all this. I had the sensation that I was on the outside looking in and it seemed that this reoccurence [sic] of my life was taking place in front of me and I was viewing it. I had a euphoric sense.[94]

Albert Heim compares it to "images from film sprung loose in a projector."[95] Others say that it is like looking through pictures in a family album or watching a movie or video replay.[96]

The boundaries of time melt down for this review, as events march past in reverse or normal chronological order, or appear as an undivided whole. The viewer is detached, as if watching a play, but so convincing is the impersonation of his past that he may feel he is reliving each scene. Especially childhood memories—the underside of a table seen from all fours, the smell of a pudding, the pinch of elastic on a Halloween mask, the distance from foot to bicycle training pedal, the contents of a school gym locker—all spill forth with every sensory detail and accompanying emotion reawakened.

It is easy to recognize an affinity between the panoramic life review and the various forms of encounter with deeds in medieval vision literature. Moody makes the point that judgment is portrayed through symbols that reflect the technology of the day.[97] For the traditional book or mirror of deeds, near-death visions provide plausible substitutes: a slide show, movie, or, for the more technically advanced, a hologram. One woman who revived from cardiac arrest tells of watching details of her life being noted down; in her case, the recording angel was a computer.[98]

The weighing of deeds occurs as well, if only in a metaphorical sense:

> I seemed to be weighing the "goods" and "bads" in life.... It seemed as
> though I was weighing life, thinking about what had happened and deciding
> whether or not it was worth continuing to live.[99]

The most important similarity, though, is that both medieval and modern narratives depict the review as an involuntary projection of inner contents
(thoughts, words, and past deeds) onto an external stage. The scene is presented from a third-person perspective, with the remembered self as actor
and the observing self as spectator. Albert Heim writes, "I acted out my life,
as though I were an actor on a stage upon which I looked down from practi-
cally the highest gallery in the theatre. Both hero and onlooker, I was as
though doubled."[100] So, too, in the medieval visions of Gunthelm and Thurkill, as in accounts by more recent near-death survivors, the reenactment of
memories becomes a theatrical exercise, the central play within the play of
the otherworld journey.

As a mode of judgment, however, the near-death life review differs
sharply from its medieval counterpart. In both cases, the judgment is, in a
sense, self-judgment; but for modern near-death subjects this almost never
carries with it a sense of sin or penalty. Though there may be pangs of regret
for misdeeds and missed opportunities, guilt, that anathema of humanistic
psychology, has no place in near-death reports. For some, the life review
serves up only consoling and cheering memories of halcyon childhood days.[101]
For others, it serves a psychoanalytic function, a therapeutic revisiting and
releasing of childhood traumas. The purpose is to understand one's life rather
than to react against it:

> It was like I got to see some good things I had done and some mistakes I had
> made, you know, and try to understand them. It was like: "Okay, here's why
> you had the accident. Here's why this happened. Because so and so and so."
> ... it all had meaning.[102]

Asked whether the scenes were positive or negative, the respondent con-
tinued: "They were *both*. But there was no *feeling* of guilt. It was all *all
right*." Another survivor interviewed by Ring comments, "I had the feeling
that it was complete comfort and even things I did wrong, on viewing them,
weren't wrong."[103]

For those who find certain episodes tedious or painful, these accounts
suggest, it may be possible to view selectively, skipping ahead to more pleasant scenes. As in psychoanalysis, however, the detached observer stance and
the reassuring presence of a nonjudgmental guide permit most subjects to
revive difficult memories without being wounded by them. Modern near-
death accounts thus project into the other world a vision of humane psychoanalytic or "client-centered" therapy. This is parallel to the way in which
Gregory the Great related his recipe for pastoral care (alternating doses of
fear and hope) to a divine plan for the cure of souls.[104]

Similarly, there is a connection between the earthly and the otherworldly penal code in both medieval and modern texts. While the medieval sinner is hauled before the divine tribunal and summarily punished, the modern sinner—or, rather, misfit—is rehabilitated. In an even more forgiving metaphor, contemporary visions substitute the notion of schooling for that of criminal process. The life review, according to some of those Moody interviewed, is "an educational effort on the part of the being of light," exchanging what Moody calls the "reward-punishment model" for "a vision which features not unilateral judgment, but rather cooperative development towards the ultimate end of self-realization."[105] Death is not a final reckoning in which accounts are closed; progress can continue even after death. As one of Moody's informants puts it, "No matter how old you are, don't stop learning. For this is a process, I gather, that goes on for eternity."[106] In this picture of unending self-development we see yet another mark of affinity to spiritualism, which was one of the first popular movements to discard the traditional eschatological principle that death sets a seal on one's character and to replace it with the prospect of continual schooling.[107]

A particularly expansive account of the life review occurs in *I Died Three Times in 1977*, in a passage that exemplifies all the features just mentioned, from the third-person viewpoint to the emphasis on learning, growth, self-judgment, and ultimate reassurance:

> And into this great peace that I had become there came the life of Phyllis parading past my view. Not as in a movie theatre, but rather as a reliving. . . . The reliving included not only the deeds committed by Phyllis since her birth in 1937 in Twin Falls, Idaho, but also a reliving of every thought ever thought and every word ever spoken PLUS the effect of every thought, word and deed upon everyone and anyone who had ever come within her sphere of influence whether she actually knew them or not PLUS the effect of her every thought, word and deed upon the weather, the air, the soil, plants and animals, the water, everything else within the creation we call Earth and the space Phyllis once occupied. . . . I had no idea a past-life review could be like this. I never before realized that we were responsible and accountable for EVERY SINGLE THING WE DID. That was overwhelming!
>
> It was me judging me, not some heavenly St. Peter. And my judgment was critical and stern. I was not satisfied with many, many things Phyllis had done, said or thought. There was a feeling of sadness and failure, yet a growing feeling of joy when the realization came that Phyllis had always done SOMETHING. She did many things unworthy and negative, but she did something. She tried. Much of what she did was constructive and positive. She learned and grew in her learning. This was satisfying. Phyllis was okay.[108]

"Falling into Heaven": Mystical States and Visions of the Whole

The experience of comprehensive knowledge, which some narratives associate with the encounter with light or the life review, is another aspect of the emphasis on learning. In *Reflections on Life After Life*, Moody quotes an interview that spells this out:

> This seems to have taken place after I had seen my life pass before me. It seemed that all of a sudden, all knowledge—of all that had started from the very beginning, that would go on without end—that for a second, I knew all the secrets of all ages, all the meaning of the universe, the stars, the moon—of everything.[109]

When Moody asked the interviewee if her taste of omniscience canceled the value of ordinary learning, she replied:

> No! You still want to seek knowledge even after you come back here. I'm still seeking knowledge. . . . It's not silly to try to get the answers here. I sort of felt that it was part of our purpose.

One person Moody interviewed said that he found himself in "libraries" and "institutions of higher learning." Another spoke of visiting a "school" where one could receive instruction on any topic simply by directing attention to it, "a place where the *place* is knowledge."[110]

Those who say they were shown "the big secret" often lament that, upon revival, the revelation is lost.[111] Like the medieval visionaries, they are permitted to keep their memories of the lesser sights of the other world, in order to bring a message to humanity; but they find it nearly impossible to retain a clear impression of that instant of direct, unmediated absorption in all of reality. If any vestige of the comprehensive vision remains, then it resists translation into waking thoughts.[112] Forgetfulness, which has as important a place as remembering in the mystical literature of the world, is a recurrent element in near-death reports.

Near-death experiencer Jayne Smith, speaking to an audience in Charlottesville, recounted an episode that illustrates this common principle. She recalled meeting four robed men who promised to answer her questions. To her first question—"Everything has been so beautiful and so perfect, what about my sins?"—the tallest of the men responded, "There are no sins, not in the way you think about them on earth. The only thing that has any meaning here is what you think. What is in your heart?" At this she was able to look into her heart and saw "only love" and she wondered how she could have forgotten that this was so. The second question— "Can you tell me what everything is all about?"—was answered in two or three short sentences, whose truth she immediately recognized. As in fairy tales, where the protagonist always gets three wishes or boons, Jayne followed these questions with a third: "Since I have to go back, can I take it all back?" The verdict she received respects the division we have seen between didactic and mystical messages: "You can take the answer to the first one back, the answer to the second you won't be able to remember."[113]

What we are seeing in these tales of knowledge and forgetting is a common motif of folklore and religious storytelling. According to a Talmudic and

Midrashic legend frequently retold in Hasidic circles, the child in the womb learns the Torah backward and forward and is shown the secrets of the universe, but just at birth an angel strikes it on the mouth to make it forget.[114] In what seems to be a variation on this theme, a Jewish acquaintance of mine told me of a vision she had while in labor. Just before her first child was delivered, she received a fleeting and instantly forgotten revelation of the whole universe. She was told that all new mothers are granted this all-embracing knowledge, so that its influence will guide them even though its specific content must be lost.

For some, a certain aura, half-phrase, or taste of the revelation remains. One near-death visionary who was told in "four words" what life is all about, describes his frustration in trying over the years to reconstruct the message: "The closest I can come and have any satisfaction with is 'In your own image.'"[115]

Stories of this kind may have a familiar ring even to those who have never before heard the idea dramatized so concretely. They evoke a sense of having forgotten truths we once knew in childhood or in the womb, or that we still know in a part of ourselves, in some inner Eden shut off from the rest. The idea that we have forgotten our essential nature runs through classical, Hellenistic, and Gnostic philosophy; Upanishadic, Buddhist, and Hindu scripture; Sufi poetry; and nearly every religious or speculative literature that speaks of the need to reawaken and recover lost self-knowledge.[116] Psychologists sympathetic to this teaching, such as William James, interpret it to mean that there are many realms of consciousness screened off from one another. Very little concrete information can be transferred from one realm to the other, for each one is darkness to the other, and to move between them requires a kind of death.[117]

Along with these mystical revelations which, as transpersonal psychologists like to say, are "state-bound" and therefore cannot be translated to mortal, waking consciousness, the visionary may bring back particular messages or commissions. Just as in the medieval narratives, these messages condense the overall didactic intent of the narrative and provide the rationale for the otherworld journey itself. Like Alberic, Tundal, and St. Paul of legend, Jayne Smith received secrets of the "third heaven" kind, which afterward she could not utter even to herself; but along with these mysteries came a message of the "second heaven" kind that she was, in a sense, charged with retelling.[118] The revelation that there is no sin and that inner intention is all that counts epitomized the moral lesson underlying her whole story.

Similarly, a young woman who came close to death by taking a drug overdose recounts in *Vital Signs* that while immersed in light she somehow received instruction: "I knew I wasn't alone. I knew I was not supposed to die. I knew I was not supposed to try and commit suicide again."[119] Reports of this kind from suicide attempters are often cited by researchers who wish to combat the notion that their work might encourage people to take their own lives.[120]

Otherworld Topography

Though they miss the tour of hell, modern near-death visionaries finish their journey just as medieval visitors do, with a glimpse of heaven that is cut short by return to the body. For Jayne Smith, the entry into paradise provided welcome relief from the annihilating ecstasies of immersion in the light. She stepped into a realm of more "subtle" illumination, a flowery meadow saturated with colors she had never seen before. Nearly every witness to this heavenly region speaks of colors in this way; one man describes them as the colors of Utopia, the perfect originals of which earthly hues are only a copy.[121] Along with verdant lawns, pure blue sky and lakes, and a mixed pallet of flowers and rainbows, the other world is ornamented with the colors of precious metals and jewels mined from the empyrean: "the world split . . . everything was silver. . .like diamonds and stars."[122]

Motifs of paradise topography are the most constant features of Western otherworld journey narration. It is no surprise, then, to find that near-death narratives recall the pastoral meadows, formal gardens, seraphic choirs, life-giving trees and fountains, spacious courts, golden gates, and shining walled cities of biblical and early Christian revelation.[123]

As in the medieval narratives, otherworld architecture combines spatial boundlessness with order and structure. We have seen this in descriptions of the tunnel; it is also true of heavenly buildings. Something like the Knight Owen's cloister without walls recurs in a long interview recorded by Kenneth Ring. A woman who barely survived heart failure (she was comatose for three days in her home before being discovered) tells Ring that she felt herself pulled through a funnel by a powerful wind, and was greeted by her mother who led her to a beautiful place with "marble all around." Asked if it was a building, she replies, "Yes, it was and yet it seemed to have no walls. And yet there was a lot of marble and music and people were walking by and working and doing things, and just smiling. . . . The closest thing I could compare it to is possibly a mausoleum. . . . It was *immensely* filled with light. . ."[124] Similarly, Angel de Milio told the audience of ABC's "The Last Word" that she found herself approaching a place that was "domed" in light.

Otherworld Demography

In near-death reports, as in medieval visions, the other world is inhabited by throngs of white-clad or etheric beings whose rank is lower than the being of light, but whose company seems just as welcome. Unlike the angelic or divine presence whose boundaries as an individual tend to blur into a bright cosmic mist, these spirits are recognizably human; most are deceased relatives or friends. Sabom quotes a typical account:

> I came to some place and there were all my relatives, my grandmother, my grandfather, my uncle who had recently committed suicide. They all came

toward me and greeted me. . . . My grandparents were dressed . . . all in white and they had a hood over their heads. . . . They all looked better than the last time I saw them . . . very, very happy . . . .[125]

The white robes no longer designate Cistercians, as they did in St. Patrick's Purgatory, but are standard issue for spirits; some, moreover, appear in familiar street clothes, as if to assure the newcomer that normal social life continues on the other side.

In agreement with spiritualist accounts, this encounter with departed loved ones is as naturalistic as possible, considering the circumstances. Aunt Lucy looks the same as ever, only younger and healthier. But scattered through near-death literature are anomalous apparitions of old-fashioned Catholic patron saints, mythological figures, and occult familiar spirits. A man who survived accidental electrocution told researchers at Evergreen State College that a centaur with the face of Jesus appeared in a chariot to conduct him through the clouds to the next world.[126] Elisabeth Kübler-Ross claims that in addition to the deceased family and friends who are sure to be present at death, there is a "vast army of thousands of guides," some assigned to watch over individuals, others dedicated to working against nuclear holocaust.[127] While psychologist Ronald Siegel classes near-death guide visions with imaginary playmates and hallucinated companions, Kübler-Ross reverses the argument, asserting that lonely children and stranded mountaineers who feel accompanied are actually sensing the presence of their guardian spirits. Not long ago, she dismayed many of her followers by playing tapes of "Willy," her own materialized spirit guide, performing a country-and-western rendition of "You Are My Sunshine," but after some unfortunate incidents, she has left behind this overt spiritualism.[128]

Family reception parties are common in the deathbed visions collected by Karlis Osis. Osis states that when spirits appear to the dying, they have a "take-away" function; joining the doctors and living family gathered around the hospital bed or beckoning from the other shore, they help their charge to disembark smoothly from the body. One of Moody's informants recalls that "multitudes" of departed relatives and friends were hovering around the ceiling of the delivery room where she lay after a critical episode that occurred in childbirth: "I felt that they had come to protect or to guide me. It was almost as if I were coming home, and they were there to greet or to welcome me."[129] As the next chapter will indicate, these welcoming spirits assume a different role when it comes time for the visionary to revive.

CHAPTER 8

Back to Life

Approaching the Point of No Return

KENNETH RING INDICATES that spirits of departed relatives are seen in the most advanced stage of near-death experience ("entering the light") rather than at its inception.[1] As we saw in the last chapter, however, family members often arrive to herald death; as psychopomps, they may also have the task of sending the visionary back to life. In the narrative quoted from Sabom in the previous chapter, these roles are compressed into a single incident; the family appears only to turn around and walk away, speaking words of dismissal: "my grandmother looked over her shoulder and she said, 'We'll see you later but not this time.'"[2] A recent Associated Press story describes a similar episode, in which a young stabbing victim who was "clinically dead" for five minutes testified that his dead brother forced him to return to life: "He put his hand on me, he pushed me away. He said 'We don't want you.' . . . [He] pushed me back on the (operating) table and said: 'You can't come here, there is no room.'"[3]

In medieval narratives as well, spiritual beings double as guide and gatekeeper, extracting the soul of the dying man and sending it back if it is destined to return. The most striking difference between medieval and modern versions, however, is that the medieval guide is an authority figure: Christ or the Virgin, a holy monk or an angel, a local parish patron or a widely renowned saint. The medieval other world mirrors the structure of the feudal society that lies beneath and supports it; given the importance of hierarchy and intercession in the medieval social, ecclesiastical, and cosmic scheme, it would be inappropriate for a friend or family member of equal status to conduct the soul on its journey, to shield it from perils, or to send it back to life. Hence, if the medieval visionary wins security through a feudal compact with his spiritual patron, the near-death subject finds reassurance in reunion with his family or in a direct bond (no intermediaries needed) with divinity or cosmos.

Nonetheless, there are parallels between medieval and modern depictions of that final encounter with God or guardian in which the visionary learns that it is time to return to life. Like Salvius, Drythelm, Adamnán, Tundal, and Edmund, many near-death subjects report being torn away from the enjoyment of heaven by a command to go back to the body. Even the wording is similar: "Go and do what you can and you will have another chance to return."[4] "You have to go back. There is something very important you have to complete."[5] "Go back, your work on earth has not been completed. Go back now."[6]

Just as medieval otherworld guides resemble the priestly figures who administer rites of dying and recovery, so in modern visions it is sometimes a physician, in hospital rather than ghostly or ecclesiastical whites, who blocks the way to death. Modern visionaries, too, are inclined to argue with the gatekeeper: "Why did you bring me back, Doctor? It was so beautiful!"[7] "Why did you bring me back to life when I was doing so well with God?"[8]

Often, however, the visionary feels inwardly impelled to revive. External commands may shade into internal feelings of obligation, and an encounter with gods or guides may take the form of a confrontation with oneself, as it did for Virginia Falce, whose heart stopped during a tonsillectomy:

> . . . as I was getting closer to the light, I was having an argument with myself. And I was saying, "Don't you think you should go back and take care of your children?" . . . I remember I said NO! I love my children. And I loved them up there. But it was a different kind of love. . . .
>
> Well, the argument inside my head continued. . . . I don't know how long it took, but all I know is now I was thinking, yes, I should go back. But the choice was mine. I knew I had to go back. It was a reluctant choice, honestly. And it was a logical choice, unemotional. OK, I have to go back and do my job. I didn't want to and there wasn't anything pulling me back. The minute I had accepted the logic, "I've got to go back and take care of them," I could feel myself come back.[9]

The line between outer and inner voices is especially difficult to trace in accounts which indicate that communication in the other world is telepathic.

Kenneth Ring finds that although relatives and friends may insist that the newcomer return and await a more timely call, the godlike presence often leaves it to the individual to choose for himself.[10] The decision to return, then, is part of the whole process of self-evaluation or judgment. The panoramic review may call to mind important ties to life—a child or invalid who needs care, a marriage worth working at, schooling to complete. Some who nearly succeeded at suicide report that they decided to return, or were sent back, in order to have a second chance at making a go of their lives. Family bonds and "unfinished business," rather than conviction of sin and desire to repent, are the reasons given for the decision or the command to return. In addition, some near-death subjects, like their medieval counterparts, feel they have been sent back for a special purpose, usually one that is closely related to the didactic intent of the narrative as a whole.[11]

Noyes and Kletti call attention to recurrent testimony that the visionary has received a mission from God.[12] As in the Middle Ages, these are "ordinary people" who, by virtue of their near-death experience, acquire a special role. Ring writes, "Potentially, then, those who have these experiences become 'prophets' to the rest of us who have fallen back to sleep or have never been awake."[13]

The general message that the visionary brings back is, as Moody puts it, "the importance of two things in life: learning to love other people and acquiring knowledge."[14] Just as important is the consoling discovery that life does continue after death, that we are not judged harshly by an external authority, and that our fondest hopes and ideals are realized in the afterlife. One of Ring's informants felt that she had to return to life in order to bring this message to her children: "I *have* to make them realize that death is not a frightening or a horrible end. *It is not. I know* it is not! It's just an extension or another beginning."[15]

In modern as well as medieval narratives, the journey ends just at the point where the visionary would have to exchange his temporary visa for permanent citizenship. A spirit or presence may be stationed at this border, or it may be marked only by what Ring calls the "decisional crisis." In some cases, as Moody indicates, the "point of no return" appears in concrete, visual form—a wall, fence, river, lake, mountain, door, gate, or curtain of mist.[16] We have encountered similar topographic images in medieval obstacle scenes, where, like the two paths motif, they represent a moment of unescapable testing and irrevocable choice. For the medieval visionary, the question to be settled is whether he will join the company of the elect or the damned. For the near-death subject, however, the critical juncture occurs when he must choose between turning back to the body or remaining with the blessed dead. Other symbols connected with judgment have been converted in the same way; as we have seen, the modern visionary may review his past or weigh the pros and cons of life in order to determine whether it is worthwhile to return. The approach to a border, then, is yet another instance of the way in which images of testing, judgment, and ordeal recur without the authoritarian or condemnatory significance they once had. Free from the shadow of doom as well as from random perils, the near-death subject nonetheless faces both roadblocks and crossroads.

Descriptions of the sensation of returning to the body resemble those in medieval accounts. Usually revival is instantaneous, following immediately upon the decision or command to return, "just like the snap of a finger."[17] Near-death experiencer Reinee Pasarow recalls "coinciding with the moment of that revelation, the light, the universe or God himself proclaimed IT IS NOT TIME, and that proclamation hurled me from this magnificent universe of love."[18]

Several witnesses characterize the return as an abrupt dissolve of the

otherworld scene followed by sudden, jolting reentry into normal consciousness or sleep. A neurological interpretation might relate this to the spasmodic
"jump" that sometimes occurs during the hypnagogic phase just as one is
falling asleep.[19] Theorists of out-of-body experience, however, prefer the
older, more dualistic explanation that the jolt is caused by an unbalanced or
imperfectly timed reunion between the body and the wandering spirit. In his
survey of popular and occultist lore concerning out-of-body travel, Benjamin
Walker notes the common belief that the soul ventures abroad even during
sleep and must be awakened gently to avoid disturbing its proper connection
to the body. The literature of "astral projection" is full of warnings about the
violent shock of sudden return to the body.[20]

In a few cases, the return is not only abrupt, but explosive. After being
told by her father that she must go back to complete "something very important," IANDS member Helen Nelson experienced a painful "rushing feeling"
in which "every limb, every bone in my body was being crushed from me,"
and she came to consciousness with "a lot of electrical energy ... like a
BANG!"[21] Other accounts resume the birth imagery associated with leaving
the body; they rush back through the darkness or tunnel at high speed.[22]
Reentry through the head may also suggest rebirth, as in the following report:

> Reluctantly I entered it through what seemed to be the natural door, the for-
> mer soft spot at the top of my head, at the same time asking myself, "Why
> must I return? Do I have to come back? Could I ever get the weak frame back
> into action again?"[23]

What makes this account especially intriguing is that the fontanelle (or "little
fountain") at the top of the head has been considered in many cultures to be
a link between the soul and the native world of spirit from which it emigrates
at birth and to which it may return at death. For the Hopi, its closure is a
sign of the spiritual obduracy that sets in as individuals or peoples age and
wander from their original aim. In Hindu texts, as in the *Bardo Thödol*, the
fontanelle is the "brahmanic aperture," the only auspicious place from which
to exit the body at death.[24]

The Visionary Transformed

Return to the body concludes the otherworld journey, but it is by no means
the end of the story. Just as in medieval vision literature, the structure of the
account is dictated by a didactic aim; conversion remains the central theme
of otherworld journey narration, and those who return from the dead are
expected to be indelibly marked. Talk-show host Greg Jackson must have had
this in mind when he prompted a near-death experiencer by saying, "It must
have just changed your life extraordinarily ...."[25] As eager as people are to
hear about the afterlife, they are equally attentive to testimony about the
transforming effects of the otherworld journey.

Contemporary narratives resemble their medieval counterparts in depicting two kinds of aftereffect. The outstanding feature is a conversion in values and way of life, but the visionary also exhibits certain peculiar symptoms, verifying that he has indeed journeyed to the other side. This is the physical and emotional "branding" that, in the Middle Ages, was the visionary's equivalent of the pilgrim's badge.

Several accounts describe a liminal period after recovery, during which the near-death subject, with one foot still in the other world, finds it excruciatingly difficult to adjust to normal life. As in medieval narratives, this is connected with reluctance to leave behind the blissful surroundings of the other world, and it is also one of the reasons for the visionary's initial reticence. Both elements are clearly present in the ardent testimony Joe Geraci gives during a videotaped interview:

> It was at least six months before I could even speak to my wife about it. It was such a beautiful, swelling feeling inside, that every time I tried to express it, I'd think I would just explode, you know, I would break down and cry. And she, for the longest time, couldn't figure out what was wrong with me. . . .
>
> The minute I came back [from clinical death], the pain returned immediately, and the fear . . . everything human came back. And I remember being very angry that they brought me back. And my wife ended up asking me why later: "You seemed angry. How come?" I just couldn't tell her.
>
> That was probably the most frustrating six months of my existence. After experiencing perfection . . . I didn't want to let it go. And it wasn't easy. After I recovered the second time and went home . . . everything just seemed to change. It was almost like I was starting my life all over. I was a baby. I hadn't made the mistakes I had made in my life. Things weren't messed up. . . . I can recall, in my attempt to hold on to this feeling, to hold on to this peace, that I began to bump into earthly things that of course aren't going to escape from you—you know they're there. My first frustrating experience was with the television. I couldn't watch television. There would be a cosmetic commercial. . . . I'd have to turn it off because it was something false, it was unnecessary, it was fake. It just didn't belong, it was insignificant. Any type of violence, even an old Western movie, I'd have to turn it off, because to me that was total ignorance; there was just no reason on earth to show people killing people. That was frustrating, especially when the family's sitting down trying to watch television and Dad gets up and turns it off. So I finally just learned to go to my room.[26]

Geraci eventually sought the advice of a close friend, a priest known in the neighborhood as Father Bob, who seemed to understand him even though he himself had never been near death:

> Perhaps the most important thing that he did for me was to help me to . . . accept life . . . that I was here for a reason. And it did help, you know. I'm back to watching television. I even like the boxing matches. I've come a long way! [laughter]

As Geraci's words suggest, there can be no better test of the visionary's "reaggregation" into society than his willingness to rejoin the family circle in front of the television set and to tolerate its acculturating influence. We have seen comparable situations in medieval literature, in which the visionary returns to life in a hypersensitive, raw, newborn state: Edmund weeps continually, Gottschalk has no taste for food or business affairs, Orm is speechless, Alberic fails to recognize his mother. In the medieval accounts as well, difficulties are resolved when the visionary accepts his new role—as monk or penitent—and, urged on by his spiritual advisers, finds a way to communicate his vision for the benefit of others.

The problems of adjustment are described in several issues of *Vital Signs*. P. M. H. Atwater devotes a column to the alienated feelings of those who return from death:

> You see the world around you through different eyes. How do you tell your loved ones that? Will they understand what you're saying? Will they be hurt? Threatened? Confused? Frightened? Who is the new you and how do you live again?[27]

Helen Nelson speaks of a mixture of exhilaration, fear, and loneliness, and an overpowering intensity of sensation: "I didn't just see the sun shining. I saw the sun actually burning!" She found it difficult to speak to people ("everyone seemed . . . alien . . ."), and, in turn, her children told her that she looked like another person. Her eyes seemed to have changed, and she projected a glow noticeable even to strangers:

> We would go out to the shopping center. I'd be walking and people would stop me, total strangers, and they'd say, "Who are you?" And I'd say, "Well, why?" And they'd say, "You have this big light around you." And I'd say, "Well I just had a very unusual experience. Maybe that's what it is!"[28]

Some report new-found psychic powers; according to the researchers, telepathy, precognitive insights, out-of-body sensations, and déjà vu episodes occur with unusual frequency to survivors of visionary near-death experience.[29] Apparently this is a mixed blessing; for Helen Nelson, the ability to see into the inner thoughts and feelings of other people tended to exaggerate rather than to overcome her sense of isolation. But for the readers of near-death literature, such reports of paranormal effects may, like the miracle stories of hagiography, help to validate the account.

Another common effect is that the near-death subject bears the imprint of vivid memories or recurrent "flashbacks" of the other world. Many say that their recall of the experience is not diminished by time and that this puts it in a different class from other memories.[30] Noyes and Kletti quote the testimony of a woman who, forty-seven years after an episode in which she nearly froze to death, can still hear "music, not of this world but from unseen stars."[31]

For some near-death subjects, even an imperfect recollection of the vision can act as a mental sanctuary ("sometimes when I have bad times I go back and I take strength from it"[32]) or as an inner standard against which to compare oneself ("I use the experience on a daily basis to gain perspective on my life"[33]). Like Salvius, who was fed for three days by the lingering fragrance of heaven, Helen Nelson speaks of occasionally recovering the knowledge she received as a "faint whiff of perfume," too subtle to define but strong enough to redirect her life.[34]

In the reports we are considering, the loneliness, alienation, and hyper-sensitivity that sometimes mark return from the other world are, in effect, signs of sanctification and as such cannot be equated simply with posttrau-matic depression.[35] However harrowing the liminal phase may be, it is redeemed by a set of positive changes that form the conversion theme of the narrative.

The near-death researchers—especially Kenneth Ring and Bruce Grey-son—have collected impressive evidence, both anecdotal and statistical, for the salutary effects of visionary near-death experience. As classified in *Life at Death*, the benefits include greater zest for life, less concern for material things, greater self-confidence, independence and sense of purpose, attraction to solitary and contemplative pursuits, delight in the natural world, tolerance, and compassion toward others.[36]

In their study of survivors of extreme danger, Noyes and Kletti found similar effects. Many of their subjects were left with a profound sense of serenity, humility, and wonder, and with a heightened awareness of death which, rather than depressing their spirits, enhanced the urgency and value of living.[37] Noyes and Kletti discovered that a close brush with death, even when it is not associated with visionary experience or with physical trauma, may nonetheless yield many of the same fruits; as summarized by Noyes, they are:

> (1) a reduced fear of death; (2) a sense of relative invulnerability; (3) a feeling of special importance or destiny; (4) a belief in having received the special favor of God or fate; and (5) a strengthened belief in continued existence.[38]

Thus, the mere fact of having escaped or having been rescued from imminent death can be revitalizing. Similarly, a sense of rebirth may come from endur-ing other kinds of crisis. Psychologists have often commented, for example, on the orienting, reintegrating, or initiatory potential of the passage through mental illness. For Noyes, as for Stanislav Grof, who likens near-death reports to psychedelic visions, rebirth is essentially the same experience regardless of its proximate cause.[39]

The near-death researchers freely acknowledge the affinity between near-death experience and other routes to spiritual resuscitation.[40] The sur-vivors themselves, however, usually insist on the difference between actual death and rebirth and its many psychological analogues or counterfeits. Their sense of renewal and loss of fear of death they attribute exclusively to the unique experience of dying and returning from death, or to specific revela-tions they received. One of Sabom's subjects comments:

> I think once you've penetrated the big secret just a bit like I did, it's enough to convince you, enough to convince me that I'm going to have no fear .... I don't think God wanted me to die ... if he wanted me, he would have kept

me . . . . He wanted me to get a peek into this big secret and shove me right back again.[41]

Sabom and Ring indicate that the loss of fear of death lasts longer and goes deeper in survivors who did have blissful visionary experiences. This suggests that while the charm of having escaped death may fade, a recollection of having glimpsed the afterlife can dissolve, perhaps permanently, the whole burden of mortal dread. The visionary, then, has a twofold consolation: having died he knows that death is not painful, and having crossed the threshold he knows "beyond a shadow of a doubt" that life will continue:

> If that is what death is like, then I'm not afraid to go. . . . If that's any way like the hereafter is, then I'm not afraid to go at all. I have absolutely no fear at all . . . I'm convinced. I think I had just a peek into it.[42]

Putting it even more positively, near-death experiencer Vita Ventra enthuses in "Prophetic Voices":

> Death is a beginning, Ken, it's beautiful. There's a light, it's love, it's the most beautiful . . . if you really love somebody, you've got to be happy for where they're going. It's an adventure and they're not alone. You see, we're afraid of somebody being alone. But they're not alone. . . . It's just as though you're being held in a cradle of love, and just being carried to the most beautiful, magical story God could ever create.

This total reassurance, rather than the blend of fear and hope favored by Gregory the Great, is the modern medicine of salvation. The therapeutic virtues of overcoming fear of death are praised in many near-death reports; for example, Geraldine De Vito has revealed on television and in the pages of *Vital Signs* that her joyful near-death vision later enabled her to cope with the death of her thirty-eight-year-old husband, to guide him throughout his illness and in his last moments, and to comfort the rest of the family. For De Vito, it seemed clear that this gift was the reason for her own encounter with death.[43] An Australian woman, writing to *Anabiosis*, speaks for many when she says, "I don't fear death now, *nor do I fear life*."[44] Here we have a decidedly optimistic rendering of the maxim found in "art of dying" manuals: "to learn to die is to learn to live."

In contemporary near-death testimony, as in Gregory's *Dialogues*, there is always a purpose behind the otherworld journey; death by accidental summons is disallowed.[45] The visionary may have a special task to complete; or, like Drythelm, he may be sent back to life with the realization that "from now on I must live not according to my old habits, but in a much different manner." In describing the visionary's fulfillment of his mission and the reordering of personality and values that accompanies it, the near-death account becomes a full-blown conversion narrative, departing from traditional Christian forms only by its absence of "conviction of sin" and its nonpartisan religiosity.

Perhaps closest in spirit to the Christian penitential otherworld vision story is the near-death testimony of suicide attempters. A young woman, now affiliated with IANDS, tells *Vital Signs* readers that it took a near-death vision, brought on by a deliberate overdose of antidepressants, to break a cycle of addiction and despair. She insists that the transforming aftereffect of the near- death journey is the real key to its significance:

> ... the part of my story that's important is not so much the experience. ...
> What matters is how my life changed as a result. ... Just prior to the experi-
> ence ... I did my usual thing and ended up in a psychiatric hospital for about
> a month. And now I'm working in one. I'm the helper instead of the one being
> helped.
> I don't drink or do drugs anymore. I just had my second year anniversary
> with AA. And I'm helping other people with their addictions and their feel-
> ings. And that's just amazing! If there's anything I didn't do, it was deal with
> my emotions. I didn't live in reality. I didn't accept life as it was. I didn't take
> responsibility for me. I was into blaming a lot of people. So it's almost like my
> whole philosophy of life has changed.
> ... Prior to the experience I didn't feel like I should be alive. After the
> experience I knew I was supposed to be alive. It was a vague feeling, but I
> knew.
> I believe the experience was given to me to help me get on the right road,
> to help me see I am valuable and I should be helping people. And that's what
> I'm doing through my AA involvement and through my job. I'm reaching out
> a lot more than I did. I was really self-centered, and I'm growing out of that.[46]

The conversion depicted by these contemporary visionaries is often of the sort William James associates with "healthy-mindedness."[47] Rather than repenting in dust and ashes or turning to monklike seclusion, the near-death survivor looks for ways to enjoy the fruits of normal life, to live for the present, to think positively, and to help others. The institutional form for conversion becomes service organizations—hospices, hospitals, crisis intervention groups, Alcoholics Anonymous—which still reflect the influence of the "healthy-minded" movements James described and, in the case of AA, helped to inspire.

What the Cistercian vision narratives did for monastic vocation, near-death narratives do for volunteer work. Unlike their Cistercian counterparts, however, contemporary vision narratives are designed not to enhance the prestige of particular organizations, but only to emphasize the value of love, learning, and service to others. Except in some conservative evangelical narratives (which depict near-death conversion polemically in "born-again" terms), there is little evidence of deliberate use of near-death testimony for propaganda purposes. In the near-death literature we are considering, there is no consensus for or against particular religious institutions. One of Sabom's informants, who became a churchgoer and teetotaler as a result of his experience, puts the emphasis on his nonsectarian volunteer work:

> ... I promised the good Lord that I was going to work for him the rest of my
> life and that's what I have been doing. I work for the Veterans Volunteer
> Service, where I can go around and visit patients and talk with them ...[48]

Ring, on the other hand, presents testimony from many people who lost interest in the institutional church insofar as they identified it with "ritual and trappings," denominational exclusiveness, or dogmatic and authoritarian religion.[49] Between those who are led to greater church involvement and those who find themselves growing away from the church, however, there seems to be little competition; all agree that what counts is inward spirituality rather than outward forms, and humanitarian rather than sectarian service.

In general, doctrinal considerations do not seem to be an important issue for the near-death testimony we are considering. An experience that "changed my whole life like a flip-flop" need not translate into a new set of beliefs.[50] Its main effect appears to be on the vitality and sincerity of belief. One of Sabom's informants reports, "I believed in Jesus Christ before [the NDE], but I didn't actually live it. I live it today."[51] A professed agnostic, on the other hand, tells Ring, "I find myself praying sometimes to [pause] an unknown Force."[52] Only in explicitly polemical Christian near-death narratives, such as Maurice Rawling's *Beyond Death's Door* and the account published by Jess E. Weiss called "I Was An Atheist—Until I Died," is there an effort to promote a specific doctrinal message.

In short, the conversion depicted by contemporary near-death literature coincides with and exemplifies its overall didactic message: that one should not fear death, that one should give up guilt and worries and live in the moment (the medieval *memento mori* translates today into "be here now"), and that the key to life is love, learning, and service. The one article of faith—and it is considered to be a matter for experience-based confidence rather than hypothetical or dogmatic credence—is that there is life after death. On that single platform, enthusiasts of near-death experience can raise an entire edifice of nonsectarian, healthy-minded religion. By apparently providing empirical vindication for religious hopes, near-death visions release the moral and emotional energy needed for transforming one's life. This is a benefit extended, perhaps in dilute form, from the visionaries themselves to the vast audience whom they reach through the popular media.

Just as the influence of the spiritualist movement spread far beyond the numbers represented in the rosters of various spiritualist organizations, so the near-death movement, if it can be called that, is diffused throughout society by television, popular books, magazines, and newspapers.[53] At the same time, people with a sustained interest in near-death studies are drawn toward IANDS. Through local chapters, newsletters, and informal correspondence, IANDS provides a community in which near-death experiencers can meet and share with others the fruits of their visionary conversion. Jayne Smith, whose ecstatic near-death vision was described earlier, told a conference in Charlottesville how her odyssey in search of religious fellowship finally led her to IANDS:

> When you've experienced total unconditional love, and then you are back in this world and can't find it anywhere, it leaves a kind of empty feeling. I was raised Episcopalian. Before my experience, religion and God seemed such a

long ago and far away thing; everything happened 2000 years ago. . . . But after my near-death experience, I couldn't wait to go back to church.

So I went to church and heard a sermon on smoking and drinking. I found it a terrible letdown. I went other times, but the sermons weren't on anything that matters. . . . I know God is about joy and I kept waiting for some minister to tap into love and joy and celebration, and to tell his congregation, "you are love." Because that's what we are, I'm dead sure [laughter.][54]

Smith tried a Unitarian church which she found "interesting, like a town meeting, but not spiritual." Finally she met a Presbyterian minister who, because he had once attempted suicide, seemed to be "on the same wavelength." For several years she read books on psychic experience, studied healing, and joined the Spiritual Frontiers Fellowship (founded in 1956 by the medium Arthur Ford and a group of Christian clergy and laymen). But not until *Life After Life* was published did she feel able to tell her family about the experience. Thanks to Raymond Moody, who "validated our experience for us," Smith found a way to communicate her vision in public, accompanying Kenneth Ring and other IANDS members on talk shows and at conferences, and drawing on her skills as an actress to reconstruct for others a revelation that has not grown stale or less vivid, she claims, after thirty years.

Similarly, Virginia Falce, self-described as "just a housewife" from a traditional Roman Catholic Italian background, found that, although she "came back a changed person," it took over twenty years, and a meeting with Kenneth Ring, for her to understand her experience fully. Her encounter with the near-death researchers helped Falce to find out what her mission might be:

I *knew* I had something to do . . . . After this hospital visit [because of a second heart attack] I was interviewed by Ken Ring and began talking about my earlier experience. I began working with terminally ill patients through a group called "Making Today Count." And I love it! They're not patients, they're my friends! And I'm always learning. . .[55]

Falce became an active member of IANDS, joining the radio, television, and college lecture circuit.

For Helen Nelson, as for Virginia Falce and Jayne Smith, Kenneth Ring was a major influence:

Then I met Ken Ring. It was like opening a dam. It just poured out of me. The relief, the understanding. It was astounding! Then slowly I found a balance. I started talking with people. I started working with Ken. I got a divorce. I started to change my life completely.[56]

Like Falce, she began to volunteer her services as a counselor for dying patients and as a lecturer, working in temporary shifts as a secretary in order to support herself: "I really live for my lectures."

Joe Geraci, whose verse eulogy to Falce appeared in *Vital Signs* when she died in 1982, is another near-death experiencer who, thanks to Kenneth Ring, found a part-time vocation with IANDS. A retired policeman, now public school administrator and poet, Geraci speaks with charm and humility (as in the interview quoted earlier) about his inexpressibly blissful immersion in eternal light and his difficulties with the normàl world upon return. Like Falce, Geraci found that his vision did not fit his expectations as a Roman Catholic; both he and Falce tell of shedding inherited doctrines over the years as they gradually came to appreciate the significance of their experience. IANDS and the near-death lecture circuit became, for these and other vision-aries, the best vehicle for the kind of public, nonsectarian "witnessing" that would be in tune with their mystical, open-minded, and pluralistic outlook.

The link between conversion and narration is similar to what we have seen in medieval return-from-death stories. By telling the story, the visionary may be fulfilling in part the mission that he or she has been given. As P. M. H. Atwater puts it, "all survivors are to some degree evangelists."[57] Com-municating the vision to others not only enacts an implicit or explicit decree from the other world, but also establishes the visionary in a new role in life and in community with others. The situation is similar, perhaps, to that of Black Elk, the Oglala Sioux holy man who was healed of disturbing afteref-fects only when he acted out his otherworld visions with the help of (and for the sake of) his community.[58] Because otherworld journey narration is a mutual venture that can create a bond between visionary and audience, con-temporary near-death visionaries prefer to "share" rather than "tell" or "describe" what befell them. Tracy Lovell remarks, "The more I share my experience, the more I get out of it. . . . Once I started sharing it with people like Ken and talking at classes, it helped me get a lot closer to people."[59] According to some testimony, the public narration of near-death reports has the potential to heal wounds and divisions, and to create a sense of commu-nity for humanity at large. Joe Geraci tells an interviewer:

> I believe love can be just as infectious as hate. It has to turn around. And to do that, people have to start somewhere. On a small scale, just me telling you about my experience, and someone reading what you're going to write. It mul-tiplies quickly. And I'm not the only one who has had this experience. There are thousands of us all around the world. Multiply my story by a thousand and you'll see how quickly it can grow! It can be done. In fact it has already started.[60]

The connection between conversion, narration, and recovery notwith-standing, contemporary narratives retain the motif of initial reticence. The near-death experiencer, like the medieval visionary, is depicted as modest, not interested in becoming a celebrity, and unsure of what reception his story will meet. Once again, this is partly a convention, designed to woo the sym-pathy of the reader. It is also more than a convention. Although contemporary near-death subjects are unlikely to be accused of vainglory, they often face disbelief and embarrassment. Family members or medical personnel effec-tively silence the visionary by suggesting, with expressions of sympathy or scorn, that his brain was addled by pain or drugs.[61] Some report that they stopped trying to tell others about their experience after their first attempts were rebuffed. Skepticism is not the only barrier to communication, however; one survivor told viewers of the ABC talk show "The Last Word" that doctors and nurses refused to discuss her near-death vision with her because, fearing a malpractice suit for botched surgery, they did not wish to take credit for ushering her, even temporarily, into the next world.[62]

Physicians, especially, seem constrained by their professional standards, their scientific training, their position of authority, or their chronic busyness, to ignore any revelations that do not have direct medical significance. Patients, in turn, may feel that the physician is uninterested and unapproachable. The researchers have found, therefore, that nurses are more likely to be aware of the near-death visions of their patients; often the doctor is the last one to know. One of Sabom's informants remarks, "I'll be damned if I share my feelings about death and dying with anyone who makes 2-minute U-turns at the foot of my bed."[63]

Some visionaries, anticipating ridicule or doubting their own sanity, keep silent from the beginning; and there are those who feel that they have been given a secret to protect. Neurologist Ernst Rodin, who views his own ecstatic near-death vision as the product of a "toxic psychosis," initially treated it with reverence: "I regarded the experience as sacred and matter to be discussed only with my wife."[64] Like St. Salvius, contemporary visionaries find that the potency of the experience can be dissipated by easy talk. Tracy Lovell explains, "I didn't talk about it for a year or more. I . . . felt it was a very personal thing. And I didn't want anybody to ruin it."[65]

Beyond these motivations for reticence, some feel that the otherworld vision cannot be rendered in words. Noyes and Kletti call attention to the recurrent use of "as if" expressions, and Ring, counting heads, discovered that 49 percent of his informants found their experience indescribable. Ineffability has been considered a standard feature of mystical experience ever since William James made it one of his "four marks," so it is no surprise to encounter it in these studies of near-death experience.[66]

The Visionary and the Interviewer

In order to bring the benefits of his message to the public, then, the near-death subject must, like the medieval visionary, move beyond feelings of modesty, reticence, ineffability, taboo, or resentment at being sent back to life. To conquer the initial resistance, an outside influence may be needed. This is where the near-death researcher enters the scene. Raymond Moody, Kenneth Ring, Michael Sabom, Bruce Greyson, and their colleagues play a role similar to that of the prior who convinced Edmund of Eynsham to relate his vision for the sake of the church. They accomplish this not by commanding obedience, of course, but by reassuring the visionary that he is not crazy and letting him know that there is a community for whom his revelations have meaning and value.

Often the researcher is the first to hear the story and as such performs a therapeutic function. Sabom notes that many patients who began by saying

"you won't believe this, but . . ." or "I've never told anyone about this, but
. . ." ended the session by expressing relief and gratitude.[67] We have seen that
interviews with Kenneth Ring had a similar effect for Jayne Smith, Helen
Nelson, Virginia Falce, and Tracy Lovell. Ring's relationship with his subjects grew into friendship, and his involvement became such that he began
to feel his house had turned into a "near-death hotel."[68]

Insofar as they seek to do an objective study, however, the researchers
must, at least in the first interview, present a sympathetic but bland exterior.
With varying success, they have attempted to avoid coaching their informants. Moody notes that he generally began with "as neutral a question as
possible." Yet, on a few occasions, when he feared overtaxing a patient, he
violated this rule:

> They were in a great deal of pain and yet obviously wanted very much to talk.
> I led them on a bit, I confess, because I wanted in a way to get the interviews
> over with as quickly as possible so that they would be more comfortable. In
> these cases, I asked them about whether certain elements of the composite
> near-death experience had been present in their experiences. However, if they
> did not recall them, they said so. This in a way gives me encouragement.[69]

Similarly, we have seen that Ring and Sabom, after listening to a free account
from their informants, pursued a line of questioning that drew explicitly on
imagery from *Life After Life*.

Moody acknowledges that any interview technique is "flawed scientifi-
cally since . . . questions convey information."[70] The "neutral question" is an
ideal that is difficult to realize in practice; given its therapeutic implications,
the encounter between the visionary and the interviewer can hardly be emotionally neutral. Under these charged conditions, the interviewer cannot help
but influence the way in which the visionary comes to terms with his experience. One reason for the rarity of negative near-death reports may be that
the interviewer—whose line of questioning is designed to be reassuring and
upbeat—is unlikely to elicit disturbing testimony.

This influence goes deeper than the use of unintentionally loaded questions. The most noncommittal line of questioning still falls short of providing
sterile laboratory conditions; the mere human presence of the interviewer
contaminates the data. Just as involuntary muscular movements can imper-
ceptibly guide a planchette to form sentences rather than gibberish, so the
interviewer can unwittingly steer the conversation by subliminal signals more
subtle than direct speech or overt body language. Our social existence is a
web of such mutual influencing, much of it below the threshold of conscious
communication; only this can account for the way in which infants learn, pet-
owners come to resemble their pets, and *Zeitgeist* leaks into even the most
hermetically sealed enclaves of tradition.

The potential for mutual influence is greatest for those who work out an
understanding of their near-death experience over a long period of time and
in a context of activity with IANDS. Moody, who currently is looking at near-
death experience as a "developmental crisis," finds it significant that people

do not, as he puts it, jump from the deathbed to the soapbox; rather, they come to appreciate the meaning of their experience only gradually.[71] Helen Nelson observes, "It has taken me 23 years to really understand this experience. It was real then. It is more real now."[72] Joe Geraci finds that his recollection, as well as his understanding, of the vision has grown from the time of the first interview through the years of communicating it to others.[73]

Some will say that the researchers' case is damaged decisively by this evidence for the collaborative character of the interview and the plastic nature of near-death testimony. The interview situation might be compared to the tacit collusion between subject and hypnotist.[74] And if anecdotal reports of strange phenomena—such as UFO sightings—are subject to distortion, then those that have a chance to grow and acquire new meaning under the aegis of emotionally interested researchers cannot, from the critics' point of view, be taken seriously; thus, all such accounts may be grouped under the label "notoriously unreliable."[75]

The next two chapters will consider this and other areas of dispute concerning the validity of near-death literature. I will present and comment on the arguments made by the main antagonists in the debate: the debunkers, who see near-death studies as another lost cause in the annals of psychical research or as a symptom of the spreading pestilence of superstition and pseudo-science, and the researchers, who are constantly refining their techniques in the hope of reaching those in the scientific and medical establishment who are not already dogmatically prejudiced against them.

PART IV

THE INTERPRETATION
OF NEAR-DEATH VISIONS

CHAPTER 9

Ecstatics and Statistics

IN OUR THEMATIC consideration of contemporary near-death literature, we have followed the visionary's itinerary from the deathbed to the other world and from revival to telling the story. We have seen that the near-death researcher participates in the visionary's efforts to create a coherent narrative. It then becomes the researcher's task to gather individual case histories into an organized body of data and to interpret those data to the public.

The researcher's influence thus extends beyond the interview. By doubling as author and authority, he helps to determine the final shape of near-death testimony. As author, he chooses which narratives to publish, in which order, and under which rubrics; as authority, he steps in to mediate between the reader and the data, offering statistical analysis and commentary and engaging in controversy over the scientific value of near-death reports. Popular accounts in the media reinforce this influence by presenting near-death experience as the "findings" of a few prominent researchers.

This pattern is comparable to the narrative layering of medieval visions, discussed in chapter 5. We have seen that the vision story is formed in an inner dialogue between the visionary and his culture and develops in the telling and retelling, until it finally comes into the hands of an author who shapes it further for didactic, polemic, or literary use.[1]

In collections of vision stories, from Gregory's *Dialogues*, to the *Book of Revelations* compiled by Peter of Cornwall, to *Life After Life*, the message conveyed by any single account is determined partly by the company it keeps. A clear contemporary instance of this is the way in which different researchers handle explicitly Christian near-death testimony. Michael Sabom, for example, tells of several patients whose near-death visions culminated in encounters with a figure whom they identified as Christ. Although none of his subjects converted in the sense of exchanging one ideology or church for another, some of the testimony he quotes has a "born-again" tone: " 'when I was in that tunnel and came out, I knew my life was given to Jesus Christ.' . . . 'the pastor said he had never seen anyone so anxious to come forward and accept Christ as I was.' . . . 'He made me through this experience to be able to completely put myself in the hands of the Lord and totally believe.' "[2] In Sabom's book, cases such as these are mixed in with other, more secular forms of near-death conversion, and, as we have seen, no doctrinal conclusions are drawn. When similar stories are cited in evangelical near-death literature, however, a very different picture emerges. Near-death testimony becomes evidence for the centrality of Christ and biblical fundamentalism and is used as an instrument in the assault on liberal near-death studies.

This shows how important it is to study the near-death narrative in its entirety, just as it is received by the public. To do so, we must look more closely at the role of the author as a presence in the narrative, and consider the part he plays in the debate concerning "proof" of life after death.

Credentials

In contemporary near-death studies, as in medieval vision literature, there are conventions that govern the roles of both the visionary and the author. The visionary, as we have seen, is portrayed as unwilling at first to be thrust into the public eye and unlikely to lie or exaggerate. If anything, Moody points out, near-death experiencers are more likely to suppress their unusual memories.[3] Perhaps the most appealing characteristic of near-death visionaries is their humility: "I am just a plain, ordinary citizen just about like any man you would meet on the street."[4] Given the "common man" quality of many near-death experiencers, their sudden elevation to a kind of prophetic status seems all the more extraordinary, and at the same time more convincing and relevant to the rest of humanity.

The author, in turn, wishes to be seen as a moderate and reasonable professional, rather than an impassioned metaphysician. He may state outright that he is no propagandist or charlatan; Moody writes, "I very much want to pursue a career in the teaching of psychiatry and the philosophy of medicine, and attempting to perpetrate a hoax would hardly be conducive to that aim."[5] For all his sympathy toward the paranormal, the researcher does not wish to be taken for an occultist or spiritualist; for all his dedication to science, he is too humane to become a Frankenstein or Faust.

Like Adam of Eynsham, the contemporary narrator frames his work with an introduction designed to win trust and a conclusion defending the validity of the visions. He begins by disarming skeptics with the confession that he, too, was a skeptic at first, and even now remains baffled by what he has to report.[6] He is modest, self-effacing, and able to keep things in perspective, thanks, in part, to his sense of humor. Raymond Moody's introduction to *Life at Death*, quoted on the back cover, praises Kenneth Ring for having a "fantastic sense of humor"; and Ring returns the compliment in *Vital Signs*, with an anecdote to illustrate Moody's love of innocent pranks.[7] A sense of humor is one trait that certainly would not have recommended a narrator to medieval readers; we have seen the observation made by Caesarius of Heisterbach and Jacques de Vitry that those who return from death never laugh again. Today, however, laughter is a sign of spiritual regeneration rather than of empty levity.[8] Thus, in both periods, the prefatory remarks put readers at ease about the narrator's motives and pave the way for acceptance of his findings. Conventions like these seem to surface spontaneously, however, rather than arising out of deliberate calculation; Sabom, Ring, Greyson, and their colleagues show every sign of sincerity.

In addition, the author wins his readers' confidence by placing openly before their scrutiny the procedures that were followed: the method of selecting subjects, the questions used in interviews, and the techniques of statistical analysis. If he is aware of any bias or emotional involvement that might affect his findings, he makes no secret of it.[9] At the same time, each project is an attempt to improve on its predecessors; the implication is that, as in other scientific disciplines, progress is being made toward more exact description and more adequate theoretical models.

Verification

Contemporary narratives, like some of their medieval counterparts, move from introductory remarks that establish the credentials of the researcher and his subjects to concluding arguments that seek to verify the content of the visions. Despite this structural similarity, however, today's "proofs" have different purposes from those encountered in medieval texts. Today, the author addresses real rather than straw skeptics; he must answer the doubts of those who feel that the authority of science prevents them from believing in life beyond death or a transcendent reality of any kind.

Although Moody, Ring, Sabom, and Greyson, unlike some parapsychologists, insist that they are not trying to prove survival of death, they do wish to persuade readers of the validity and importance of near-death visions. They wish to verify that something extraordinary, even paranormal, is taking place—yet not so extraordinary as to be beyond scientific or commonsense credence.[10] To that end, each researcher enumerates what he finds to be the most impressive or inexplicable features of near-death experience, restates the scientific objections that have been raised, marshalls counterarguments, and tentatively proposes an interpretive model or "'new paradigm" that might allow science to make room for this hitherto neglected body of data.

In the minds of many readers, and to the dismay of many critics, the researchers' conclusions give us license at least to look beyond the strictures of materialism. Some readers simply ignore the repeated disavowals of "proof" for life after death; a correspondent to *Vital Signs* exclaims, "what Dr. Ring and others on the IANDS staff are doing is tremendous! They are creating a new *science* for mankind. That science will eliminate our 'last enemy'—death."[11]

Paradoxically, the authors' caveats lend credibility to the more remarkable claims made by the visionaries themselves. Once reassured of the researchers' scientific objectivity, the reader may not feel bound to be quite so fastidious in drawing conclusions. Given the permission to take near-death narratives seriously, it is an easy step for many to embrace them as experiential evidence of life beyond death. This step is encouraged, of course, by the sensationalist books and articles that far outnumber the more moderate works of the near-death researchers.

In the next chapter I will treat the controversy between near-death researchers and their critics, and in the chapter following I will propose a way to interpret some of the disputed questions. First, it will be helpful to review the main grounds on which the researchers argue for the validity of near-death experience.

UNANIMITY

The researchers agree that the similarities of near-death reports are more striking than their differences and see this unanimity as a key to the validity of near-death experience. As Osis and Haraldsson put it: "if there is another mode of existence, we should expect all patients to see essentially the same thing ... regardless of whether they are men or women, Americans or Indians, college-educated or illiterate."[12] Speaking more cautiously, Moody observes, "if, as we have found to be the case, their independent reports agree quite well, we have the right to be impressed by that fact, even though it does not constitute proof."[13] And Ring, arguing against the idea that near-death experience is dreamlike, comments that it is unlikely that "at the moment of (apparent) death everyone should dream fragments of a common dream."[14]

INVARIANCE

What makes the apparent unanimity of near-death reports so impressive to the researchers is that it seems undisturbed by differences in cultural, medical, and demographic circumstances.[15] The evidence for this will be questioned below.

UNEXPECTED FEATURES

A corollary to the two points made above is the argument that near-death reports do not conform to individual or socially conditioned expectations. Osis and Haraldsson, among others, cite cases in which the content of the vision appears to conflict with the subject's professed desires, fears, or beliefs. Contending with the idea that near-death experience is just wish-fulfilling fantasy, Moody writes:

> First, consider the great similarity in content and progression we find among the descriptions, despite the fact that what is most generally reported is manifestly not what is commonly imagined, in our cultural milieu, to happen to the dead.[16]

Moody also stresses the nontraditional character of near-death visions:

> In fact, in all the reports I have gathered, not one person has painted the mythological picture of what lies hereafter. No one has described the cartoonist's heaven of pearly gates, golden streets, and winged, harp-playing angels, nor a hell of flames and demons with pitchforks.[17]

Osis and Haraldsson draw a similar conclusion from their comparative study of American and Indian deathbed visions.[18] In the chapters to come, I will return to the question of "mythology" in near-death visions.

PARANORMAL ELEMENTS

According to some investigators, the presence of verified paranormal episodes is the best evidence for the extraordinary character of near-death experience. If a patient can accurately describe the events of his resuscitation, then his account of another world may be accurate too. In addition to veridical out-of-body reports, researchers point to the life review, with its time-defying simultaneity and rare precognitive flashes, and to the appearance of appropriate otherworld figures: the child who sees a dead uncle instead of the living parent he might like to imagine, or the patient who is surprised by the spirit of someone he did not know was dead.[19]

On the other hand, paranormal events are occasionally invoked as an argument against the out-of-body hypothesis. Some critics of survival evidence use extrasensory perception to account for mediumistic or out-of-body reports that convey information unattainable by normal means. They would rather accept the notion of ESP, however unproven, than admit the possibility of survival of death. In answer to the ESP explanation, Sabom tries to link veridical out-of-body reports with the moment of apparent death and to see whether the perspective matches an ascended spirit's eye view; his approach is similar to that of Karlis Osis, who has made systematic studies of out-of-body reports in an effort to distinguish them from mere clairvoyance.

PROXIMITY TO DEATH

Although the researchers acknowledge that impressive near-death reports may come from subjects who were in little physical danger, they seem glad to find any evidence that a patient was declared "dead" or was unconscious at the time of his vision. As Bruce Greyson points out, it is difficult to assign a time to a remembered vision; nonetheless, researchers search for medical data to corroborate the visionary's subjective sense of having died, or to distinguish near-death experience from the broader range of "altered states of consciousness." The implications of this will be discussed below.

SUBJECTIVE QUALITY OF NEAR-DEATH EXPERIENCE

Reports of lucidity and painlessness suggest to some interpreters that the subject was disengaged, at least partly, from his afflicted flesh.[20] In addition, many investigators seem to believe, even if they do not say it explicitly, that near-death experience is evidence for a transcendent reality simply because it surpasses normal states of mind. Near-death reports convey an experience that is so profound, timeless, joyful, and revelatory as to seem self-endorsing; and some interpreters assume that for such a state of consciousness to occur there must be a special realm of existence that corresponds to it.

TRANSFORMING EFFECTS

If the joyful and mystical insights of near-death experience can carry over into life, then that is a kind of evidence of its lasting validity. Thus, some investigators follow the time-honored principle of judging a revelation by moral and spiritual effects. This provides double reinforcement: as transforming effects witness to the soundness of the vision, so conviction that the vision was true helps to sustain the transformation.

CONVERGENCE OF EVIDENCE

Osis maintains that while the case for survival of death cannot be made on the basis of a single "crucial experiment," it is supported by the convergence of many different kinds of experimental evidence: deathbed visions, out-of-body trials, mediumistic phenomena (particularly spontaneous, "drop in" communications and "cross correspondence" cases), crisis apparitions, voice phenomena, and reincarnation memories.[21] Similarly, some investigators consider the most telling argument for the extraordinary character of near-death experience to be the cumulative weight of the points made above and the inadequacy of any single "explanation" to account for all its features.[22] Critics argue, on the other hand, that the combination of different kinds of evidence is no stronger than its weakest link; this will be discussed in chapter 10.

In order to support the claims just outlined, researchers turn to the quantifying methods of social science. The studies done by Osis, Ring, Sabom, and Greyson are similar in their use of statistical analysis to counter some of the reductionist interpretations of near-death experience. Their figures show, among other things, that there is little correlation between the frequency or content of near-death visions and such factors as age, gender, medical condition, use of drugs or anesthetics, religious affiliation, or prior familiarity with near-death literature.

Quantitative analysis also brings to light features of near-death experience that would otherwise lie undetected in the mass of anecdotal testimony. For example, Greyson discovered through statistical surveys that, contrary to Moody's impression, those who attempt suicide seem just as likely as other people to report blissful near-death visions. Lest this appear to promote suicide, Greyson also has figures to prove that the effect of the experience is to discourage future self-destructive acts.[23] Ring's portrait of near-death experience as a progression through five stages similarly depends on the reduction of subjective reports to quantifiable data; from the tables in *Life at Death* we learn that 60 percent of his "core experiencers" described a sense of peace, 37 percent noticed detachment and separation from the body, 23 percent entered the darkness, 16 percent saw the light, while only 10 percent went so far as to enter the light. Without these statistics, things would not appear so orderly.

As in other quantifying studies in the social sciences, however, this orderliness may cloak a fundamental untidiness in the lived experiences that the statistics are supposed to represent. Estimates of the frequency of near-death experience provide a case in point. At one extreme, cardiologist Fred Schoonmaker projects that 60 percent of those who "die" from cardiac arrest will report an experience along the lines of *Life After Life*. This is based on an eighteen-year study of 2300 cardiac arrest survivors, 1400 of whom had near-death visions.[24] At the other extreme, there are cardiologists who claim never to have encountered this phenomenon, or who find its incidence negligible.[25] Clustered together in a somewhat more plausible middle range are Ring's estimate of 43 percent frequency (48 percent if self-referred subjects are included), Sabom's finding of 43 percent, and a recent Gallup Poll showing that of the 15 percent of Americans who believe that they have come close to dying, 34 percent recall being in an ecstatic or visionary state.[26]

As Greyson points out, these estimates are affected by the researchers' sampling methods and ways of defining near-death experience.[27] The rapport or lack of rapport between the investigator and his informants can also account for some of the variation. It is of little surprise that Schoonmaker came up with such a generous estimate; for he reports that 18 percent of those who initially told him they had no memories of what occurred while they were unconscious later produced near-death reports, "only after repeated invitations and reassurances."[28]

Even if a consensus on frequency could be reached, its significance is far from obvious. Strictly speaking, the frequency of near-death experience has little bearing on its validity. As William James pointed out, "if you wish to upset the law that all crows are black, you must not seek to show that no crows are; it is enough if you prove one single crow to be white."[29] In any case, those who doubt the intrinsic value of near-death reports will not be won over by evidence that they are common.

It is clear, however, that the readers of near-death literature find strength in numbers. Near-death testimony seems at once more relevant and more revelatory when accompanied by statistics to show that such ecstatic visions are occurring to many people from all walks of life. Charts and tables seem to lend a scientific imprimatur to what would otherwise be mere hearsay. The statistical arguments are therefore an important element in the appeal of near-death literature; yet this is so only because they come in conjunction with the stories. Were it not for the inspiring effect of the stories, the idea that one stands, say, a 40 percent chance of having a visionary experience would be cold comfort in the face of death.

Despite the discrepancies in estimates of frequency, most critics are willing to accept the premise that something like near-death experience actually can take place. They focus instead on discrediting the use of near-death testimony as evidence for survival of death, disallowing the visionary's claim to have been "dead" and demonstrating that near-death experience can be explained by natural causes. We have already seen that most of the responsible researchers concede that their data do not prove survival after death. The next chapter will consider the debate on the remaining two questions.

CHAPTER 10

Explanations and Counterexplanations

Were They Dead?

THE POPULAR APPEAL of return-from-death stories rests partly on the assumption that temporary absence of vital signs is equivalent to death. In deference to current medical opinion, however, Moody, Ring, Sabom, and Greyson point out that, by some definitions, none of the subjects they interviewed had actually died. Nonetheless, they do not wish to dismiss the testimony of those who speak from experience.

The matter is complicated because there is no consensus on the medical, let alone the philosophical, meaning of death. In the medical context, where clinical situations make it necessary to agree on a pragmatic definition, the question is decided by committee. In 1968, for example, a group at Harvard Medical School announced four criteria: "unreceptivity and unresponsivity, no movement or breathing, no reflexes, and flat electroencephalogram."[1] Doctors must rely on guidelines of this sort when they decide whether to give up resuscitation efforts or to remove organs for transplant.

Occasionally, however, patients are reported to have come back to life even after meeting the stringent requirements set by Harvard Medical School. Cardiologist Fred Schoonmaker claims to have interviewed fifty-five patients who recovered from "brain death" and had vivid memories of blissful visions. Since misdiagnosis, faulty EEG readings, or simple tampering with the data cannot be ruled out, this finding is unlikely to disturb the medical establishment. In any case, as techniques are refined for rescuing patients after brainwave cessation, the definition of death will change, the threshold will be pushed back, and some modern-day Lazaruses may find that, in medical terms, they no longer qualify.

An article in the British medical journal *Lancet* puts it succinctly:

> Only a deliberate use of obsolete definitions of death can enable one to claim
> that anybody has under clinical conditions returned to tell us what lies beyond
> death, for by working definition, periodically updated, death is just beyond the
> point from which anyone can return to tell us anything.[2]

Defining death as a permanent condition, or, as Hamlet would have it, "the undiscovered country from whose bourn no traveler returns," seems to dispose neatly of any sensational claims.

Stephen Vicchio, a philosophy professor who has written articles critical of near-death literature, amplifies this argument with a critique of the idea of a "moment of death."[3] Empirically speaking, he points out, there is no moment of death because cells deteriorate at different rates. Dying is a process, while death is only a concept. From a philosophical point of view, Vicchio warns us that to define the moment of death in more than provisional, approximate terms is to be guilty of what Alfred North Whitehead calls the "fallacy of misplaced concreteness." Similarly, life, according to Vicchio, is just "an abstraction used to label the sum of the metabolic activities by which an organism grows, reproduces, etc."

Yet there is something profoundly unsatisfying about yielding the privilege of defining life and death to ad hoc committees that must constantly adjust to the current state of medical technology. In any case, those who have had near-death visions usually are undaunted by medical and philosophical vetoes; they report simply that they *knew* they were dead: "I have no clinical proof I actually died. Yet when your life ends you don't need proof. You know. Professionals matter not and neither does anyone else's opinion."[4]

The researchers seem to be in a quandary as to how to give credit to this kind of testimony without appearing naive about the medical definition of death. At times they treat near-death experience as an "altered state of consciousness" not specific to death. Kenneth Ring, who blames the media for focusing attention on the claim of return from death, would like to see near-death experience "disassociated from the moment of dying." Ring, Moody, and Greyson agree that the sense of leaving the body and the exalted feelings and perceptions which characterize near-death reports can be found in other contexts as well: in the face of sudden danger (as Russell Noyes has shown); in drug experiences; in shamanic, yogic, devotional, or meditative practices; or in spontaneous mystical states.[5] Disassociating near-death reports from death may steal some of their fire as evidence for the afterlife, but it has the advantage of making them seem more humanly familiar, as part of a class of recognizable, if unusual, experiences.

On the other hand, the researchers are unwilling to relinquish the uniqueness of near-death experience. Although they class near-death experience with other routes to transcendence, they emphasize that, according to subjective reports, near-death experience is quite different from drug experience, hallucination, or dreaming. Michael Sabom still insists that physical proximity to death is crucial in that it sets near-death experience apart from other "altered states."[6] Moody and Ring see a "modest correlation" between the degree of closeness to irreversible death and the depth or completeness of the near-death experience.[7] As a result, researchers continue to comb medical charts for evidence of "clinical death" or unconsciousness and for data that might corroborate the patient's out-of-body view of the resuscitation efforts.

Models of Death

Discussion of the connection between near-death experience and death is muddled at times, by the researchers as well as their critics, because they mix two very different models of what happens at death: the medical view of death, which we have just considered, and the traditional idea that death occurs when the spirit leaves the body. Kübler-Ross, for example, offers standard medical definitions in her *Encyclopedia Britannica* article on "Death" but says elsewhere that death consists in the severing of the cord linking the immortal spirit to the physical body.[8] Moody, who is inclined to accept the definition of death as irreversible biological deterioration, also suggests that the "mechanism" for death may be "separation of the mind from the body."[9]

The problem is not that these models are necessarily incompatible, but that there is no consensus on how they might be related. The mysterious process by which the spirit disengages from the body (if one believes that such a thing occurs) need not follow the same timetable as the physiological events leading from cardiac failure to brainwave cessation and finally to "somatic" or "cellular" death. The connection between "death" on the medical model and "death" viewed as the spirit's exit from the body is therefore only approximate. The fact that both models might apply to the dead does not mean that they should be used interchangeably to interpret the near-death or return-from-death reports of the living.

If, as the imagery suggests, medical death and departure from the body are two distinct notions, then the relevance of some of the researchers' corroborating medical data is questionable. Followed to its logical conclusion, the dualistic model, like the "altered states" idea, removes the rationale for attempting to verify near-death experience on the basis of medical signs of death. We can choose instead to view near-death experience as part of the larger class of dissociative or out-of-body states. This would be consistent with a belief shared by many cultures that the spirit can leave the body in sleep, illness, and ecstasy, and that death is just a more lasting form of visionary travel.[10]

At the same time, if we observe the distinction between dualistic and medical models of death, then some of the critics' objections become irrelevant as well. Even if there is no physiological "moment of death," there may yet be a precise instant when the spirit severs its attachment to the body. If the visionary's claim to have died is based on an experience of this sort, shaped by a dualistic model, then medical data can neither vindicate nor discredit his claim.

Of course, we are not in a position to judge whether someone's impression of having died is founded on such an experience, or whether it derives from mistaking the symptoms, overhearing physicians declare the case hopeless, or relying on obsolete definitions of death. Insofar as this study primarily concerns the fictional landscapes of otherworld journey narratives, this presents no problem; but beyond this it is possible to grant a certain validity to individual reports. Though the patient labors under false assumptions, the influence of his real or imagined danger can expose him in an immediate way to the prospect of his death. Feeling oneself to be *in extremis* can trigger a profound imaginative rehearsal for death.

Hence, even though we grant that medical data can neither corroborate nor disprove subjective reports of near-death experience, and that transcendent or out-of-body visions occur in circumstances other than dying, we are not entitled to say that near-death experience has nothing to do with death. For those who have "been there," as well as for those who accept their testimony, near-death experience is a confrontation with death, the purpose of which is to decipher death. As such, it is said to be more lucid in quality and more transforming in effect than visions not linked with dying.

As long as we refrain from using medical data to corroborate this claim, no logic requires us to disallow it on medical grounds. Whether near-death experience occurs in the grip of death or only in the face of death, it may still constitute a revelatory encounter with death. By disassociating near-death reports from the medical view of death, we are able to connect them more closely to the human meaning of death, which is where their real interest lies.

In the next chapter I will return to this point and suggest that acknowledging the imaginative character of otherworld journey narration is essential if we are to respect the testimony of individuals who believe they have returned from death.

"Natural" Causes

Unless Occam's razor has dulled, the responsible investigator will search diligently for natural explanations for unusual phenomena. If near-death visions can be explained as hallucinations, following standard etiology, then there is no need to resort to more exotic interpretations. On this both the near-death researchers and their critics agree; the question under debate is whether any adequate natural explanations exist. While the skeptics propose an abundance of physiological, pharmacological, and psychological solutions to the puzzle, the researchers resolutely defend the unexplained status of near-death experience; for every explanation, they offer a counterexplanation.

The most common skeptical reaction is to dismiss near-death experience as the by-product of an overwrought or undernourished nervous system. Near-death visions are labeled hallucinatory on several grounds: (1) they occur under the influence of drugs, anesthetics, or stressful conditions that are known to trigger hallucination; (2) they display patterns of imagery similar to those found in hallucinations and dreams; (3) they fill psychological needs, mimic the symptoms of mental or emotional disorders, or reflect unconscious fantasies and drives.

DRUGS

It is undeniable that near-death experiences occur to patients under the influence of a wide range of medications, including tranquilizers, analgesics, anesthetics, insulin, steroids, psychoactive drugs, stimulants (such as adrenaline and amphetamine), and depressants (such as alcohol, barbiturates, and narcotics). Whether used for therapy, entertainment, or self-destruction, these drugs have the potential to bring on dissociative or visionary experience. Neurologist and psychopharmacologist Ronald K. Siegel, psychiatrist Nathan Schnaper, and psychologist James E. Alcock are among the critics who have called attention to the role of drugs in near-death visions.[11]

Yet one cannot build a coherent theory of near-death experience on a psychopharmacological basis; not all near-death subjects were under medication, and, in any case, the effects of different drugs vary endlessly. Since the critics, like the researchers, wish to find a comprehensive explanation for the recurrent features of near-death experience, they look to underlying physiological and psychological mechanisms as a source for visionary states.

OXYGEN DEPRIVATION

If near-death reports cannot be explained by drugs alone, there is good reason to consider other toxic conditions that may have hallucinogenic effects. No matter how lucid the subject feels, if he is physically on the point of death, then he is bound to suffer from some kind of metabolic disturbance, whether it be fever, exhaustion, trauma, infection, liver poisoning, uremia, or blood gas imbalance.[12] Any one of these conditions can be a potent source of delirium and delusion; but the critics most often cite oxygen deprivation— hypoxia or anoxia—as the cause of near-death experience. Psychiatrist Richard Blacher of the Tufts University School of Medicine writes, "I suggest that people who undergo these 'death experiences' are suffering from an hypoxic state, during which they try to deal psychologically with the anxieties provoked by the medical procedures and talk."[13]

This is the view expressed by Ernst A. Rodin, a neurologist who scrutinizes his own near-death experience in an article for the *Journal of Nervous and Mental Disease* ("The Reality of Death Experiences: A Personal Perspective"). Although he calls his near-death vision under surgery "one of the most intense and happiest moments of my life," he concludes in retrospect that it was a "toxic psychosis" induced by an oxygen-starved brain. To hypoxia he attributes his feelings of bliss and invulnerability, his mistaken belief that he was dead, and his sense of "the eternal present."

LIMBIC LOBE SYNDROME

Reduced supply of oxygen, which, according to Rodin, is the "final common pathway" of death, can in turn trigger seizure activity in the brain's limbic system, which includes the hippocampus, hypothalamus, amygdala, temporal lobe, and other structures associated with memory, mood, and emotion. Several neurologists and psychologists believe that limbic lobe agitation may be the physiological basis for near-death experience.

Daniel Carr, a neuropsychologist at Massachusetts General Hospital, argues that the very vividness of near-death visions is a sign that they are complex hallucinations with an origin in limbic lobe dysfunction. Although there is no clinical evidence linking near-death visions to this syndrome, subjective accounts of near-death experience include features that neurologists recognize as indications of limbic lobe hyperactivity. Carr cites the following symptoms: "depersonalization, involuntary memory recall, intense emotions such as euphoria, and auditory, visual, or kinetic hallucinations."[14]

Perhaps the most arresting similarity between near-death experience and limbic lobe seizure is the feature of panoramic recall. Sudden and unbidden revival of scenes stored in the memory is a symptom sometimes associated with the "aura" or premonitory sensations which precede seizure in temporal lobe epilepsy. The connection between panoramic memory and temporal lobe excitation was first demonstrated experimentally during the 1930s by Canadian neurosurgeon Wilder Penfield; when he electrically stimulated the temporal cortex of his epileptic patients, a few reported seeing their lives flash before them and reexperiencing long-forgotten incidents.[15] Noyes and Kletti cite this as evidence that temporal lobe activity is the physiological mechanism behind the life review and other features of near-death experience.

ENDORPHINS

Given that most near-death subjects are not epileptic, however, partisans of the limbic lobe theory have had to look for some aspect of the physiology of dying that might be responsible for agitating limbic lobe neurons. Rodin, as we have seen, proposes cerebral hypoxia. Carr, in a more extended and technical discussion, suggests that the trigger may be endogenous opioid peptides, such as endorphins and enkephalins, the morphinelike chemicals secreted by certain brain cells during extreme stress. Popularly known as the brain's natural painkillers, endorphins and their relatives bind to opiate receptors to block some of the worst effects of shock, infection, trauma, vigorous exercise, severe psychological distress, and other insults to the organism. In addition, Carr believes, they may release the neuronal inhibitors that normally restrain limbic lobe discharge, thus acting not only as endogenous opiates but also as "endogenous hallucinogens."[16] According to Carr this provides a clue to the "pathogenesis" of near-death visions.

Carr is not the first theorist to emphasize the role of endorphins in visionary and ecstatic experience, however. Since their discovery in the early 1970s, these helpful neurohormones have received a great deal of public attention, promoted as the explanation for "runner's high" and an assortment of other conditions in which analgesia and bliss suddenly supervene upon agony and effort. It is no wonder, then, that inquirers would search here for a clue to the mystery of near-death visions. Some investigators, including Carr and a group of near-death researchers at Evergreen State College, pursue the endorphin theory without drawing reductionist conclusions; but in the minds of the debunkers, the endogenous opiates are a neurochemical equivalent for and answer to grace.

SENSORY DEPRIVATION

The endorphin explanation remains controversial nonetheless. To be on safer ground and to provide a more general and inclusive account of the source of near-death visions, some investigators turn instead to the hallucinogenic effects of sensory deprivation and social isolation. In a review of *At the Hour of Death*, parapsychologist John Palmer, known for his skeptical studies of out-of-body reports, objects that Osis and Haraldsson did not give enough attention to the possibly deranging effect of being bedridden.[17] Perhaps the dying patient, restricted to his bed, in a sterile monotonous environment, cut off from other people, is comparable to the consciousness researcher who goes into experimental trance by immersing himself in a tank of warm water and epsom salts or strapping sliced ping-pong balls over his eyes. Perhaps he is like the polar explorer, mountain climber, desert wanderer, shipwrecked sailor, or long-distance trucker, whose mind compensates for loneliness and embellishes the blank landscape by supplying imaginary companions, consoling mirages, and diverting graphics.

Ronald Siegel makes the notion of sensory deprivation one of the bases for his reductionist critique of near-death studies. According to Siegel, all the various triggers for near-death visions amount to different forms of perceptual isolation. Combined with the boredom, confinement, and anxiety of a hospital sickbed are physiological factors, such as drugs, exhaustion, and toxic conditions (including those discussed above), each of which works to impede the brain's ability to receive and sort out external impressions. The result is that the central nervous system, while hyperaroused by stress, is starved for stimuli. Obeying a biological imperative—for unless it is fed it will die—the brain turns inward in search of substitutes for its sensory nourishment. It must make do with emergency rations, made from random blips in the visual cortex mixed with the stored goods of the memory. Birth recall, the life review, fantasies of heaven, and psychedelic landscapes are all products of this neural foraging.

On another analogy, which Siegel derives from the "perceptual-release" theory of hallucination propounded by Hughlings Jackson and L. J. West, the brain is like a man in a room looking out a window. As daylight ends, and the outer scene fades, the illuminated interior is reflected in the window. The man thinks he is looking at the outside world, but what he sees only mirrors his inner landscape.[18]

No matter which analogy is preferred, the result is the same. Siegel treats turning inward as a pathological state, and does not distinguish the experience of a trained contemplative from that of a paranoiac or a volunteer subject hallucinating spiderwebs in the laboratory.

FALSE SIGHT

Siegel derives his analysis of near-death experience from an elaborate theory of hallucination, based on the work of psychoneurologist Heinrich Klüver, who developed a taxonomy of mescaline visions, and on his own previous studies of the subjective reports of marijuana users. In his debunking articles on near-death experience, however, he presents no clinical evidence for drug or sensory deprivation effects. Rather, he draws on analogy: "the remarkable similarity of imagery in life after death experiences and imagery in hallucinatory experiences invites inquiry about common mechanisms of action." Whether the trigger is sensory deprivation, drugs, toxic conditions, or severe psychological stress, Siegel claims that the hallucinatory pattern remains the same. By arguing from analogy rather than cause, he is able to make a more sweeping—and less testable—dismissal of the validity of near-death visions.

Regardless of their source, Siegel maintains that hallucinations begin with simple forms of imagery (Klüver's "form constants"), which can be classed into four types according to geometric shape: lattice, cobweb, tunnel, and spiral. These geometric forms, and variations on them, combine in symmetrical patterns, often brilliantly colored. At the center of the visual field, the hallucinating subject may see a bright light, producing the impression of a tunnel, with images moving toward or away from the central point.[19] Any significance attributed to this imagery would be sheer geomancy; the forms are but the work of discharging optical neurons or of electrical disturbance in the visual cortex. Yet the vision soon progresses from such simple structures to a second stage, which Siegel calls complex imagery, in which the form constants provide a scaffolding for scenes rich in subjective meaning: flashbacks to childhood, fantasies built up from memory images, externalized wishes and fears.

Siegel dissects near-death visions along the same lines. The sense of going through a tunnel toward a bright light "is the result of stimulation of the central nervous system that mimics the effects of light on the retina" and is then embellished with psychological artifacts as the vision moves from the simple to the complex stage.[20] The bright majestic cities and strange edifices of the other world are no different from the architectural forms that Siegel's hallucinating subjects construct using the geometric constants as building blocks. Aerial perspectives and a sense of leaving the body are common in drugged states, according to Siegel. In short, although the standard hallucinatory features of memory flashback, imaginary companions, and sensations of travel may be more intense for the subject who believes he is dying, Siegel claims that they are not essentially different from drug experiences. There seems to be an equal share of mystical utterances in near-death and in drug testimony; such features as ineffability, a sense of merging with the surroundings, and heightened reality occur frequently in the reports of Siegel's laboratory visionaries.

Siegel thus turns the unanimity argument on its head. If near-death reports agree so well with one another, it is because they reflect "common structures in the human brain and nervous system, common biological experiences, and common reactions of the central nervous system to stimulation."[21] Siegel enhances his neurological explanation with psychological theories, and in a sweeping manner consigns belief in the afterlife to the history of human and animal folly:

> From early observations of animals burying their dead, through awareness of the seasonal cycles of nature, to recognition of inherited resemblances of the living and the dead, early *homo sapiens* developed the concept of life after death in an effort to explain these behaviors and their underlying feelings.[22]

If Siegel is right, then nature has constructed a fail-safe system to compel us to trick ourselves about death; our neurochemistry, our earliest experiences, our egoistic needs, our diverse cultures all work to reinforce this grand delusion. Fortunately, however, enlightenment is just around the corner; for we shall soon discover, Siegel asserts, that the visionary's heavenly Jerusalem is a product of his internal architecture:

> Through such research and hypotheses we have begun to understand the nature of hallucinations as stored images in the brain. Like a mirage that shows a magnificent city, the images of hallucinations are actually reflected images of real objects located elsewhere. The city is no less intriguing and no less worthy of study because it is not where we think it is. Further experiments will help to localize it.[23]

Siegel's work on hallucinations is no doubt quite solid, and does offer fascinating parallels to near-death visions. In lumping together different kinds of visionary and mystical experience, he helps us to recognize that there is no elite domain of human experience cut off from the rest. Having acknowledged this, however, we have only begun the work of understanding the significance of visionary experience. Truly each generation needs to discover in its own way that the heavenly city "is not where we think it is"; but to suggest that "further experiments will help to localize it" seems arrogant.

In addition to Siegel's ambitious explanation of the hallucinatory basis of near-death experience, there are several interpreters who link near-death visions to hypnagogic or hypnopompic reverie—a condition in which vivid forms and sounds, faces and scenes present themselves to the mind just as one is on the verge of sleeping or waking.[24] Hypnagogic and hypnopompic images, like near-death visions, are sharply defined and have an "out there" quality that distinguishes them from usual dream imagery. Here, perhaps, is a neuropsychological analogue for the classical and medieval notion that the gate of dreams is the gate of death.

As a neuropsychological basis for out-of-body reports, some theorists have proposed autoscopy (self-seeing), the rare condition of hallucinating one's double.[25] Otto Rank considered it a symptom of "narcissism," but recent studies show that it behaves like a neurological disorder, often occurring in association with epilepsy, temporal lobe irritation, brain trauma, alcoholism, or schizophrenia. Though it may have inspired some *Doppelgänger* legends, this disorder sheds little light on near-death reports. Those subject to autoscopic hallucination do not speak of leaving the body; rather, they remain in the body and see a phantomlike mirror image of themselves, often from the shoulders up.[26] In traditional folklore, moreover, the double is a haunting figure, a harbinger of death, rather than a consoling emblem of survival; nor do modern patients afflicted with autoscopy find it to be the pleasant experience that near-death reports portray.

Whatever the merits of the hypnopompic and autoscopic theories, they are but two more variations on the theme advanced by Ronald Siegel that near-death experience is a kind of short circuit in the central nervous system. However compelling this mode of explanation may be, it cannot account for near-death visions that are triggered merely by the expectation of death, nor can it interpret the symbolic content of visions, without drawing on psychological theories.

PSYCHOLOGY

Many critics look to psychology as the court of final appeal, the source of the most embracing and most effectively debunking verdict on near-death experience. This method of interpretation demands no knowledge of hypoxia, endorphins, entoptic fireworks, or Klüver's constants; it is enough to detect in near-death experience signs of the psyche's frantic effort to deny death. Although contemporary psychological treatments of this subject differ, all rest on the axiom that the mind will resort to any stratagem to push from view the prospect of its own annihilation; according to Freud, both logical paradox and ontological revulsion prevent us from facing the truth:

> Our own death is indeed unimaginable, and whenever we make the attempt to imagine it we can perceive that we really survive as spectators. Hence the psychoanalytic school could venture on the assertion that at bottom no one believes in his own death, or to put the same thing in another way, in the unconscious every one is convinced of his own immortality.[27]

The first psychologist to apply Freudian principles to the interpretation of near-death testimony was Freud's close friend, the Swiss pastor Oskar Pfister. In a convoluted but influential paper, Pfister turns Albert Heim's engaging account of the blissful visions of falling Alpinists into an illustration of the "casuistry" and atavism of mental processes in mortal danger.[28]

According to Pfister, the effect of extreme danger is to flood the awareness with "shock thoughts and fantasies" in which realistic observations are strangely mixed with meaningless reveries. This occurs, Pfister suggests, because the mind is protecting itself with what Freud calls a "stimulus barrier," allowing enough awareness of the threat to intensify and quicken response, but holding back the overwhelming realization of doom.[29] Hallucinations also provide a "counter-cathexis," a distraction from paralyzing pain and fear, and a comforting illusion of invulnerability and detachment. As hope of reaching safety fades, the balance between realistic and fantastic shifts. No longer yoked to the struggle for survival, mental processes are now entirely at the service of the "pleasure principle"; the mind comforts itself with memories and pseudo-memories, imagined glimpses of the future, and paradisical scenery.[30] If there is any sense of discomfort over past misdeeds, its purpose is only to gratify what Pfister considers a neurotic craving for absolution.

Pfister proceeds from this analysis to a dramatic interpretation of near-death visions, which owes more to his devotion to Freudian teachings than it does to direct consideration of the evidence. Like Freud, Pfister sees our inner world as a battleground where the conscious ego struggles to assert dominance over the dark and chaotic forces of the unconscious. Since the ego is not equipped to meet the threat of death, mortal danger leaves it helpless and humiliated before its ancient enemy. There follows regression to a childish and primitive mode of thought, under the sway of "maternal-like" powers, while consciousness "plays the role of a banished king subsisting only on scanty, unintelligible news from his former land; who having given up his kingship, must play a passive role while awaiting help from fortune." Pfister ingenuously compares this psychic situation to "the seizure of power by primary and primitive people, upon the collapse of proud cultures."

As these statements illustrate, Pfister's preoccupation with Freudian categories and the theatrical, military, political, royal, and mythic imagery in which they are expressed prevents him from letting the testimony speak for itself. In order to construct his Freudian allegory, he distorts some of the narrative facts, asserting, for example, that the reports of survivors of mortal danger are "affect-impoverished." Pfister's study has a quaint, dated ring today, but psychologists still consider him a pioneer for his insight that near-death visions serve a double function, simultaneously enhancing and inhibiting the subject's contact with reality. In this respect he anticipates the depersonalization theory of near-death experience.

Following Pfister's paper by thirty-seven years, psychiatrist R. C. A. Hunter published "On the Experience of Nearly Dying," a Freudian interpretation of near-death experience, in which he analyzed the clinical case history of a nurse under his care who nearly died of anaphylactic shock. In the course of her asphyxiated ecstasy, Hunter's patient had witnessed a vivid replay of childhood memories and a vision of the Taj Mahal.

Perhaps because professionals habitually see things through their own disciplines, Hunter argues that psychological rather than physiological conditions would account best for his patient's vision. Her narrative followed the same pattern that Pfister detected for accident victims: "the initial recognition of danger, a brief fear reaction, a denial of the threat, and the so-called 'review phenomenon.' . . ." The patient was reluctant to awaken, Hunter concludes, because she "was enjoying a markedly wish-fulfilling 'dream' or hypnopompic hallucination which was idiosyncratically appropriate to her affective response to her life situation and took into account the sudden threat to her life." To decode the specific images of the vision, one need only use the tools of dream analysis; in this case, Hunter detects the symbolization of family conflicts and, probing deeper, suggests that the pool and dome of the Taj Mahal represent "intrauterine and breast fantasies." Here, too, psychoanalytic conventions give the interpretation a parochial quality.

Pfister's and Hunter's studies provide in germ the guiding principles for subsequent psychological interpretation of near-death experience; the central idea is that the mind cannot accept its death and therefore imagines itself detached from the body, fantasizes immortality, and regresses to infantile and "oceanic" consolations.[31]

The most compelling elaboration of this thesis comes from psychiatrist Russell Noyes, Jr. Prompted by Albert Heim's article, Noyes collected over two hundred accounts by survivors of life-threatening danger. Like Ring and Sabom, Noyes set out to systematize this anecdotal material; the results of his surveys, done in collaboration with Roy Kletti and others, agree with Heim's informal conclusions as closely as the studies performed by Ring and Sabom match *Life After Life*. Unlike the Moody-inspired studies, however, the work of Noyes and his colleagues resists being construed (or misconstrued) as evidence for life after death. This is partly because Noyes couches his findings in psychological terms that sometimes verge on reductionism; in addition, however, he concentrates on the reports of accident victims who faced the prospect of death rather than on the more dramatic cases of revival from apparent death. Belief that death is imminent, Noyes tells us, is all that is needed to trigger the defensive mechanisms of brain and psyche which give rise to near-death experience.

Noyes's studies confirm Pfister's contention that life-threatening crises, unlike lesser dangers, rarely have an immobilizing effect. After a brief surge of fear, most victims react in obedience to the biological imperative to struggle for life. Faced with its ultimate challenge, the organism is not likely to dissipate its resources in pointless diversions; if near-death visions occur, they must have an adaptive function. Noyes agrees with Pfister and Hunter that near-death experience is a coping strategy but departs from his Freudian predecessors by suggesting that even the transcendent and otherworldly aspects of the experience have a positive contribution to make to psychic health.

In his interpretation of near-death experience, Noyes brings in both psychological analysis of subjective effects and neurophysiological studies of adaptation to extreme stress. On a physiological level, he explains, sudden danger sets off a central-nervous-system alarm that elicits "an adaptive neural mechanism combining heightened arousal with dissociation of consciousness from that arousal."[32] In support of this statement, Noyes cites the work of neurologists Roth and Harper showing that a similar combination of arousal and inhibition occurs in certain epileptic and "phobic anxiety-depersonalization" syndromes.

As Noyes describes it, the double response of hyperalertness and depersonalization is most evident in an initial phase of "resistance," in which subjects experience vivid, racing thoughts, narrowed focus of attention, expanded time, freedom from pain, calm, objectivity, and detachment from the body and its surroundings. The next phase is the life review, followed in some cases by a stage of transcendent or mystical experience. For Noyes, the value of near-death experience depends on whether these three stages have any adaptive features.

The benefits of the first phase are obvious. As Heim and Pfister observed, a peculiar combination of contrasting states enhances the efficiency of survival efforts; while arousal sharply increases mental voltage, detachment simultaneously insulates against shock. As an adaptive mechanism, this way of reacting to the threat of death is as normal as the "fight or flight" syndrome to which it is related.[33] Near-death experience might be a healthy response to danger, then, rather than a sign of dysfunction. Noyes acknowledges this but does not take it as far as he might; his studies suggest that there might be some situations in which the out-of-body experience is appropriate and others in which it is inappropriate and pathological. Although this does not tell us whether near-death visions convey objective truth, it should at least help to answer those who deem them unsound because of pathological origin.

The adaptive value of the later phases of near-death experience is less obvious. What purpose is served by the ecstatic sensations and otherworldly visitations that occur when resistance gives way to surrender? Noyes's response is mixed. Like Pfister and Hunter, he proposes that otherworld visions are wish-fulfilling but otherwise pointless fantasies which humor the ego's neurotic demand for survival. The life review is a "retreat from the future" impelled by nostalgia for a child's innocence of time and death.[34] In its developed form, the out-of-body experience is not only a helpful response to danger, but also a symptom of what Graham Reed calls "ego-splitting" in recoil from the unacceptable prospect of death. As such it is a rejection of truth rather than a route to profound realization.

On the other hand, Noyes remarks on the transformative effects of near-death experience and suggests that the life review, out-of-body journeys, and mystical states of the dying may permit them to achieve a new level of integration that surpasses rather than undoes the ego's life work. In Noyes and Kletti's words:

> the vastly alerted mind may be set to work upon final tasks. . . . the individual nearing death may accept the reality before him and, from a transcendent perspective, capture a glimpse of his life in harmony with the universe.[35]

Thus they hint at something more than merely transient adaptive value.

Unfortunately, Noyes and Kletti do not explain how a hallucinatory condition that is intrinsically regressive and delusionary could come to be the vehicle for such high attainment. This makes it easy for some critics to brush aside their tentative recognition of the spiritual significance of near-death experience and to use their findings to support a reductionist interpretation. James Alcock explains that the culminating vision Noyes describes is just a "peak experience," which does not warrant any "metaphysical claims."[36] Similarly, when Noyes and Kletti relate the life review to phenomena of reminiscence in the elderly and bereaved, Siegel and Alcock take this as evidence that the review is nothing but a mnemonic quirk.[37] Observations that shed light on the conditions of near-death experience are thus turned into ammunition for debunking.

The most extreme example of this reductionism can be found in the writings of astronomer and champion skeptic Carl Sagan. In "The Amniotic Universe," the final chapter of *Broca's Brain*, Sagan reduces Stanislav Grof's lush description of "perinatal symbolism" to a remarkably partisan unriddling of near-death experience. In the course of explaining near-death experience as state-dependent birth recall, Sagan makes short shrift of the entire history of religious conceptions of death and rebirth, paradise and the fall, penance and baptism, deities and demigods. This vast range of experience and lore might derive, Sagan suggests, from shadowy memories of the four perinatal estates of man: our Edenic intrauterine bliss, its disruption by seismic contractions, our delivery from darkness into light, and our postnatal swaddling.[38] Sagan concludes:

> Religion is fundamentally mystical, the gods inscrutable, the tenets appealing but unsound because, I suggest, blurred perceptions and vague premonitions are the best that the newborn infant can manage. . . . Religious doctrine is fundamentally clouded because not a single person has ever at birth had the skills of recollection and telling necessary to deliver a coherent account of the event.[39]

If I have used military analogies to describe some of the reductionist critiques of near-death experience, that is because Alcock and Sagan, at least, represent an organized group of debunkers known as the Committee for the Scientific Investigation of Claims of the Paranormal. Since its founding in 1976 by Carl Sagan, Martin Gardner, Isaac Asimov, and others, this committee has dedicated itself to attacking what Asimov calls "the vast Castle of Pseudo-science,"[40] by publishing criticism and lobbying against media coverage on such popular themes as UFOs, metal-bending psychics, Velikovsky, ancient astronauts, biorhythms, the Bermuda triangle, and so on. Near-death experience is just one of the disreputable subjects they have taken on, and their technique for disposing of it is the same as in all cases: they wield a devastating "nothing but."

One effect of their debunking campaigns is to polarize the opposition; fringe causes tend to cluster together, and their champions begin to speak a common language, even when they have little in common beyond the fact of being labeled fringe.[41] In the case of near-death studies, the researchers sometimes overlook the merits of contributions made by Noyes and his colleagues, simply because they have to defend their findings against reductionist use of those conclusions. Operating on the assumption that the validity of near-death experience depends on its immunity to medical and psychological explanation, they make themselves vulnerable to the "nothing but."

Counterarguments

In the previous chapter we considered the main grounds on which near-death researchers defend their findings, and in this chapter we have reviewed the explanatory theories offered by their critics. The debate continues, however, for the researchers are prepared to answer or anticipate skeptical interpretations by citing counterexamples or calling attention to features of near-death experience that remain irreducibly unexplained.

Their strategy is to fend off contending explanations one by one, tackling in turn depersonalization, autoscopy, wish-fulfillment, hypoxia, limbic lobe seizure, sensory isolation, endorphins, and so on. Each of these theories has its weak spots, which the researchers are quick to point out. But although they argue the specifics of each case, their general reasoning is usually the same; for every pathological condition presumed to cause near-death visions, one can find subjects who were demonstrably free of its influence; therefore no single psychological or physiological syndrome can account for near-death experience.

Along with statistics to support this argument, the researchers offer anecdotal evidence of the "white crow" variety. Michael Sabom tells of a patient whose out-of-body vision seems to falsify the oxygen-deprivation theory: while apparently unconscious, he watched his physician take a blood sample, which was then measured to show high oxygen and low carbon dioxide levels.[42] In Sabom's view, this recollection, corroborated by medical charts, conveniently dates the out-of-body experience and shows that even if hypoxia is a sine qua non for death, it is not a necessary condition for near-death experience.

Taking this argument a step further, the researchers cite statistics that show an inverse relationship between near-death experience and various pathological mind-altering conditions. Recollection, if not experience, of near-death visions seems to be hindered rather than promoted by the deranging or dampening effect of alcohol, anesthetics, and drugs. Survivors who report the most vivid, coherent, and purposeful visions, closest in detail to the "core" experience described in *Life After Life*, are precisely those whose faculties were clearest.[43] As Osis and Haraldsson put it, "medical factors which cripple communication with the external world also cut down phenomena related to an afterlife." And Kübler-Ross laments that overmedication is robbing terminal patients of the glimpse of heaven that is their deathright.[44] The researchers have neglected to reconcile this argument with their claim that near-death experience involves disengagement from the body's disordered or unconscious senses; a critic could maintain that these findings demonstrate the dependence of near-death experience on normal biological and psychological activity.

One advantage on the researchers' side, however, is that there can be no direct evidence linking a particular physical or psychological condition to near-death experience. The skeptics are ultimately forced to argue on the basis of analogy; and since likenesses are inexact, the researchers can always find ways in which near-death experience deviates from or surpasses the scope of its proposed analogues.

The counterarguments depend on subjective reports about near-death experience. Backed by the collective testimony of hundreds of subjects, researchers contrast the alert, blissful, lucid quality of near-death experience to the confusion, anxiety, and perceptual distortions that accompany such disorders as hypoxia, limbic lobe syndrome, autoscopy, depression, and schizophrenic hallucination. They point out that the visual and affective aspects of autoscopy bear little comparison to out-of-body experience; that temporal lobe stimulation induces a revival of memories that, unlike the near-death life review, feels "mechanical" and "forced"; that limbic lobe seizures bring with them strange smells and tastes, feelings of foreboding and random crowding of thoughts; that Beta-endorphin injections induce drowsiness along with analgesia; and so forth.[45]

In addition, against Siegel's sweeping comparison of near-death visions to the psychoneurology of hallucination, the researchers cite nearly unanimous testimony that near-death experience is subjectively different from dreaming or intoxication; that it is, as one of Sabom's subjects puts it, "realer than here."[46] Siegel rebuts this by saying that "hallucinations can occur in states in which consciousness is 'clear'"; in his view, the heightened sense of reality is no more than a gauge of the depth of delusion:

> During the peak hallucinatory period the subjects frequently described themselves as having become part of the imagery. At such times they stopped using similes in their reports and asserted that the images were real. This point marked the transition from pseudohallucination to true hallucination.[47]

In response to Noyes, the researchers press a point he already concedes: near-death experience, with its expansive quality and transforming effects, scarcely resembles the shrunken, lifeless world of depersonalization. Perhaps it is only from our normal, middling vantage point that the two extremes of disintegration and higher integration appear, by a coincidence of opposites, to look the same.

In considering the way near-death visions seem to surpass ordinary modes of experience, the researchers shift from the defensive to the offensive, bringing forward those bits of evidence, either spiritual or paranormal, that naturalistic explanations must inevitably overlook. Near-death experience is marked, they tell us, not only by clear thinking, but by a hyperlucidity for which neither pathological nor normal mental functioning can account. Osis describes patients who light up just before death, their acuity and well-being suddenly lifted above even the level of sound health, by a vision that brings both this world and the next into focus. Rather than the bizarre cartoon figures, strangers, or living personalities who populate hallucinations, they see deceased relatives or religious guides bearing a timely invitation to death.[48] Upon return to life, they may accurately describe relatives whom they had encountered for the first time in their visions. Such reports, along with the veridical out-of-body descriptions and paranormal evidence discussed above, not only challenge the adequacy of pharmacological and pathological explanations; they strain the capacity of the materialist world-view itself. The evidence for these anomalies, however, is never decisive enough to persuade those who are not already predisposed to accept them.

Finally, the researchers insist on the unanimity, cross-demographic invariance, and nonmythological character of near-death reports, features that suggest to them that near-death visions are not products of wishful thinking or cultural determination. If wish-fulfillment dictated the content of the visions, Ring argues, they would be idiosyncratic, ruled by the anarchy of individual whims. Instead, he finds "*consistent patterning* of the core experience across different people."[49] The other investigators concur.

On this point the statistics seem, at first glance, unequivocal. Age, sex, race, geographic location, education, occupation, religious upbringing, church attendance, prior knowledge of near-death studies, all have negligible effect on the likelihood of near-death visions.[50] Suicide victims seeking annihilation, fundamentalists who expect to see God on the operating table, atheists, agnostics, and *carpe diem* advocates find equal representation in the ranks of near-death experiencers. And their answers to survey questions show that, for all the religious implications of near-death experience, a person's beliefs about God, life after death, and heaven and hell do not determine the content of his vision.

This conclusion is based on responses to before-and-after questionnaires about religious convictions and attitudes toward death. But there are reasons to be wary of these findings. In the first place, before-and-after questions are likely to elicit testimonials about the weakness of faith before and its vitality and sophistication after near-death experience; we have seen that the interview contributes in this way to the formation of a conversion narrative.

Secondly, the questions require respondents to organize the flux of their experience into quantifiable units of belief. Near-death investigators borrow this technique from the polltakers who periodically test our nation's religious-ness by tabulating the number of adherents to particular doctrines and insti-tutions. The critics do not object to this technique, perhaps because they share the assumption that religiousness can be measured in this way; but it can be misleading. Standardized questionnaires cannot possibly probe deeply enough to test the undercurrents and eddies of belief, doubt, trust, defiance, fear, hope, and fancy that form a religious sensibility; they cannot detect the "subconscious incubation" that might explain how a Protestant agnostic could wake up one day as a New Age mystic.[51] Nor can they, as Greyson points out, do justice to our ambivalence about death.[52] A more general prob-lem with this method is that it perpetuates the modern error of identifying religiousness with conceptual adherence to a static set of beliefs.[53]

The statistics reveal that near-death visions can diverge from professed (and hence possibly superficial) expectations and beliefs—but the same can be said of dreams. Divergence from conscious wishes may signal obedience to unconscious or subliminal drives. Moody acknowledges this with respect to atheists:

> "Atheism" may be, in some cases, just verbal behavior masking personal feel-ings that may be very different, perhaps even deeply religious . . . it would be almost impossible to determine the degree of prior religious belief in these cases, since everyone in our society is at least exposed to religious concepts.[54]

By the same logic, it should be no surprise that people with a traditional religious upbringing may also encounter an afterlife quite different from the one they profess to expect. If contemporary near-death visions are nearly devoid of hells, pearly gates, and angelic choirs, that may tell us only that these images no longer exert as deeply formative an influence as they have in the past; their power is diluted by forces of modernity and pluralism that affect even those who deliberately attempt to hold to tradition. Considered in the light of our comparison of medieval and modern accounts, this point becomes more obvious. Either humanity has just recently learned how to have near-death visions that are free of cultural and mythological influence, or (far more likely) the current crop of visions conveys what is, in effect, a new *mythos*.

Sympathetic interpreters of near-death experience tend to resist the lat-ter view because of two widely held assumptions: that myth is equivalent to fiction or falsehood, and that if the mind could separate itself from the body it would instantly drop the burden of its era's dogmas, fables, and prejudices. We have seen similar assumptions underlying medieval evaluation of vision-ary experience; in their current form, these ideas are hangovers from the eigh-teenth- and nineteenth-century rationalism that colored the thought of the early spiritualists and psychical researchers as much as that of their skeptical critics.

These ideas are baldly stated in the introduction to *The Principles of Nature*, the proto-spiritualist work dictated from trance by Andrew Jackson

Davis. Here the editors extol Davis's death-mimicking clairvoyant raptures in a passage that falls somewhere between a restatement of Pauline visionary eschatology and an Enlightenment manifesto:

> His mind is now entirely freed from the sphere of the body and, consequently, from all preconceived ideas, from all theological isms, and from all influences of education and local circumstances, and all his impressions are received from the interior or spiritual world. . . . He is thus elevated above all the narrow, local, and sectarian prejudices that pervade the earth. His philosophy is only that which is involved in the laws and principles which control the Universe and mankind unerringly, and his theology is only that which is written on the wide-spread scroll of the heavens, in which every star is a word, and every constellation a sentence.[55]

The editors would indeed be embarrassed if Davis's Swedenborgian cosmology and progressive spirituality could be shown to bear traces of his culture. But a few generations later, the cultural influence is easy to spot.

Similarly, Moody tells us that near-death reports do not convey a "mythological picture" of the afterlife, and Ring, Sabom, Osis, and Grosso agree that, aside from a retrospective "filtering" or interpreting role, traditional religious conceptions play no part in the otherworld drama.[56] The argument for this, unfortunately, is circular: the features that seem to recur most often are labeled "core"; when their recurrence is tested again and confirmed, this is proclaimed as evidence for the cross-cultural invariance of the essential aspects of near-death experience. Similarities to traditional eschatological literature are interpreted as a sign of the persistence of the core experience; on the other hand, differences are supposed to show that modern narratives, unlike their traditional counterparts, provide a direct transcript of what happens at death, uncontaminated by religious presuppositions or church censorship.[57] Thus, Michael Grosso contrasts the horrific afterlife scenarios of traditional visions to the "empirical picture" which he finds more "humane."[58]

The case for the universal and nonmythological character of near-death experience rests, at least in part, on selective treatment of the evidence. Osis and Haraldsson emphasize the absence of hells and devils in American deathbed scenes and the neglect of Vedic cosmology and reincarnation in Indian visions. Similarities on this score are less remarkable, however, when we consider that India is by no means cut off from Western or progressive developments and that many of the nurses from whom they collected their Indian reports were Christian. But the authors do not elaborate on the possible cultural reasons for similarities between American and Indian visions, nor do they give much weight to differences that emerge in their study. In the Indian survey, for example, they found more "no consent" deaths and negative feelings, more religious figures, and, except in brain-impaired patients, few female figures. Also, as one might expect, they found no visions of Krishna or Shiva in America; but they dispose of this difference in the same way as the

other researchers do, by attributing it to culturally influenced ways of interpreting or labeling an essentially similar encounter with a figure of light.[59]

In short, the universality and nonmythological character of near-death
testimony is a matter of perspective. Between those whose attention is captured by the discrepancies among different visions and those who are dazzled
by their similarities, there is a temperamental distance, unlikely to be bridged
by logical arbitration. Such unanimity as is found, moreover, might be considered an artifact of the interview technique, a product of summary generalizations that mask underlying differences, or a sign of conformity to unacknowledged cultural patterns. We have seen, moreover, that the critics stand
ready to attribute the consistency of near-death reports to common features
of neural wiring, as Siegel would have it; common mechanisms of dying, as
Rodin holds; common reminiscences of birth, as we learn from Grof; or common psychological response to the threat of death. Unless these naturalistic
explanations can first be ruled out, the unanimity claim will not help the near-
death cause. Of the researchers, only Greyson fully acknowledges this
problem.[60]

The debate does not stop here, but to treat every specific point of contention in detail is beyond the scope of the present study. We have seen
enough, in any case, to guess that the final outcome will be a draw.

On one side, the skeptics lose credit for disregarding experiential facts
and for treating as cause what is at best analogy. Compounding this error, the
genetic fallacy rules much of the debunking of near-death testimony. On the
other side, the researchers, who score heavily against the claim that any single
naturalistic explanation suffices, usually overlook the possibility that the various explanations taken together might constitute a comprehensive theory.
With the exception of Greyson, Kevin Drab, and one or two others, the
researchers treat near-death experience as a unitary, coherent phenomenon,
and reject on that basis any explanation that does not cover all of its facets in
each of its instances. James Alcock points out correctly, however, that it is
more plausible to view near-death experience as a composite of different
experiences capable of being interpreted separately.[61]

Thus, the debunkers are easy to fend off one at a time; but if they gang
up, as Alcock recommends, then any feature of near-death experience that is
not finished off by endorphins can be dispatched by temporal lobe seizure,
depersonalization, state-dependent birth recall, and so forth. Knock down
these explanations and others, gloved and ready, will soon appear in their
place. The only aspect of near-death experience that cannot be matched with
a theoretical antagonist is its paranormal component. This is a moot point,
however; there have not been enough documented cases to impress those
who are inclined on principle to doubt, and skeptics who might ordinarily
reject the notion of extrasensory powers are willing to invoke it temporarily
as a lesser evil to explain away veridical out-of-body reports.

The problem, then, is not a lack of explanations, but an overabundance;
and, no doubt, more explanations are yet to come. If a comprehensive theory

of near-death experience does not exist, it is only because it is so difficult to hold in mind simultaneously, let alone to synthesize, all of the medical, psychological, philosophical, historical, social, literary, and logical factors that would have to be included. In the view of the debunkers, this is just a practical difficulty, which in time and through the cooperative efforts of scientists will be overcome. On the day that occurs, they suggest, the pretensions of near-death literature will finally be exploded, and we will have to tell those who report visionary experiences that they were beguiled by mechanisms which are so well understood as to leave no room for their sense of revelation.

Neurologist Ernst Rodin applies this merciless logic to himself, as we have seen, when he dismisses his own ecstatic near-death experience as a toxic psychosis. Moreover, he is dismayed to think that in his final moments he will once again be captivated by the same neural chimera: "despite my current awareness that these visions and beliefs will be utterly false, I know that I will accept them as full truth when the time comes." He considers this an "unsolvable dilemma."[62]

Kenneth Ring and a few other researchers suggest that the answer to Rodin's dilemma is to adopt a new, more generous paradigm for scientific inquiry, one that will take account of the paranormal and transformative features of near-death experience.[63] Time-traveling tachyons, Karl Pribram's holographic model of consciousness, non-Euclidean geometry and topology, Hiroshi Motoyama's "paraphysics," the uncertainty principle, and observer-legislated reality in the realm of quantum physics are among the notions proposed to make sense of near-death experience.[64]

Of course, the application of these scientific or quasi-scientific models to inner experience raises as many questions as it answers; and the pursuit of a new paradigm seems premature at a stage when there is still mileage left in the old one. It was not Thomas Kuhn's view that we can hop from one paradigm to the next at will. The attempt to do so, which has long been a convention of psychical research, serves only to confirm the fringe status to which the debunkers would relegate near-death literature. Moreover, it may only be a matter of time before a new paradigm—if it has merit—will become the established view, and will either appear irrelevant or be used by reductionist interpreters to explain away whatever is being touted as a paranormal or spiritual phenomenon. It is instructive to compare the current interest in new paradigms (or in new phenomena that have been spotted, in hazy outline, on the far horizons of science) to the enthusiasm that the early spiritualists and psychical researchers expressed for electricity and magnetism. They were disappointed in their expectation that these mysterious powers would force science to recognize psychic phenomena; perhaps history will repeat itself.

It is not Newtonian physics that leads Rodin to reject the evidence of his vision and thus to deprive himself of its possible benefits; it is simply the old attitude of reductionism, which has dogged religious thought since the dawn of skepticism—well before Newton or Bacon—and has hardly become more sophisticated in its latest forms. If there is a way out of the impasse in which Rodin finds himself, that way was shown by William James, in *The Varieties of Religious Experience* and in his life work.

In the *Varieties*, James uses psychological and medical observations to shed light on the nature of religious melancholy and joy, conversion, and mystical states, and shows that these subjective phenomena inhabit those same realms of human experience, where the sublime coexists with the spurious. When it comes to questions of truth or value, however, James refuses to yield the privilege of interpretation to doctrinaire skeptics. Against "medical materialists" and dogmatists of every stripe, he insists that an experience should not be evaluated on the basis of its origin; he proposes, instead, these general criteria: "immediate luminousness . . . philosophical reasonableness, and moral helpfulness." Speaking in more traditional terms, he urges us to decide the validity of subjective religious phenomena solely on the basis of their "fruits for life."

We can easily imagine how James, if he were alive today, would approach the problem of interpreting near-death testimony. He would find the naturalistic theories of interest to the extent that they fill in connections, correlating visions of the other world with structures and events "on the hither side"; but he would not allow the pursuit of explanations to rob individuals of their "right to believe" in what they experienced.[65]

After all, not only extraordinary visions but also normal states of consciousness are linked with electrical and chemical events in the brain, hormonal tides in the body, inherited drives, and cultural coercion. Yet we do not apply reductionist vetoes to our ordinary experience. Love can be explained in terms of neurochemical and social mechanisms, ranging from the influence of advertising to the lure of pheromones; but scarcely anyone suggests that knowledge of these mechanisms should prohibit people from believing that they are in love and rearranging their lives accordingly. And though lovers and visionaries are prone to delusion, the only fair method for "testing the spirits" is to apply the pragmatic criteria that James recommends.

Clearly, we need to find a middle path between the extremes of dismissing near-death testimony as "nothing but" and embracing it as "proof." Moody and his colleagues try to tread such a path and are on the whole more successful at it than their critics. Greyson, especially, has begun to mediate between the opposing camps, by providing a balanced appraisal of the merits of psychological theories of near-death experience. Yet, paradoxically, the researchers play into the debunkers' hands by assuming that the validity of near-death experience stands or falls on our ability to discriminate it from dream, hallucination, intoxication, or indoctrination; to link it with medical signs of death; and to corroborate its paranormal elements. In staking their claim on the unexplained status of near-death experience, the researchers put their material at the mercy of scientific progress; on these terms, if an explanation should be found, then near-death literature would lose its power to elicit a sense of wonder, or to hint at the possibility of freedom from ordinary, habitual modes of experience.

There is an alternative to this religion of the gaps, however. It lies in the recognition that the "explained" phenomena of nature and human experience are no less hospitable to spiritual interpretation than the assortment of oddities that have thus far—but perhaps only temporarily—eluded science. Even if it is possible to account for every feature of near-death experience under every condition in which it occurs, the task of interpretation remains unfinished. The next chapter will consider whether our comparative study has yielded any insights that might contribute to this task.

CHAPTER 11

Evaluating Near-Death Testimony

Experiential Claims

ONE CONCLUSION to which the present study leads is that the West has seen no steady progress from literal to literary use of the otherworld journey motif. The line between fiction and confession is necessarily blurry, but contemporary near-death reports—like their medieval predecessors—at least claim to represent actual experience. In this final chapter we will consider whether it is possible to take this claim seriously without being naive.

Some might feel inclined to disregard the question, as do the social and literary historians who concern themselves only with the cultural transmission of otherworld journey imagery. For if we take visionary accounts at face value, as a factual description of what happens after death, we run the risk of enclosing ourselves in a shrunken utopia, cut off from the scientific and historical awareness that is our culture's special gift. Theologians, as much as other intellectuals, might wish to ignore experiential claims in order to avoid having to weigh testimony that either conflicts with accepted religious and scientific principles or brings the mysteries of life, death, and the hereafter embarrassingly close. It is safer to treat the otherworld journey solely as a metaphor or literary motif that illustrates a psychological or moral truth. In this way, we render it harmless; we attenuate the visionary virus until it is so weak that it produces immunity instead of contagion.

This approach fails to account, however, for what makes the other world such a powerful symbol. We have seen that the otherworld journey motif remains potent only as long as it retains at least a hint of correspondence to a sensed, dreamed, or imagined reality. An image like the review of deeds continues to have some vitality because we imagine ourselves undergoing such an experience, we visualize this experience as taking place in another world, and we sense that the image has further possibilities as yet unexplored. By contrast, an expression like "The road to hell is paved with good intentions," which we recognize as exclusively metaphorical, seems trite. It has become a dead circuit, no longer connected to real or imagined experience. The experiential dimension must therefore be considered if we are to understand the whole range of otherworld journey imagery—from its vestiges in our ordinary discourse to the more overt forms found in near-death literature.

It is, moreover, unfair to the individuals who report near-death experience to discount their claims in advance. The current controversy surrounding the rights and needs of the dying—and the fact that many people are turning to books like *Life After Life* for guidance or consolation—puts us under an obligation to assess near-death literature in an informed and sympathetic way.

It is a good sign, then, that some religious thinkers have taken an interest in interpreting near-death literature. Before I make suggestions of my own, it will be useful to consider the main currents of theological opinion on the subject.

When *Life After Life* appeared, it provoked widely varying reactions. In *Reflections on Life After Life*, Moody remarks that there were some among the clergy who accused him of selling "cheap grace," while others thanked him for producing a book that was such an asset to their pastoral work with the dying and bereaved. This pattern of response continues as public awareness of near-death experience grows. The loudest reaction against *Life After Life* and its successors comes from conservative Christians who see these books as a Satanic trick, designed to lull us into a false sense of security about the future life, to lure us into occult practices such as astral projection, to beguile us into accepting the advances of demons disguised as departed spirits, and to sell us a secular (but fundamentally diabolic) bill of goods about salvation without Christ. At the same time, as we noted above, there has been a proliferation of "born again" versions of near-death experience—complete with recollections of hell which, according to Maurice Rawlings, are "repressed" by the Life After Lifers.

On the other side, Moody reports that Christian clergy often tell him that *Life After Life* has strengthened their faith in the traditional Church teachings which it is their office to represent. It gave one minister the confidence to affirm at a funeral that the woman he eulogized had gone to join her deceased husband with Christ: "I wasn't speaking figuratively or symbolically; I meant it. This gave them comfort...."[1] Near-death testimonials play a similar role in the pages of *Guideposts, Soul Searcher, Spiritual Frontiers*, and other magazines of Christian or Christian/spiritualist inspiration.

Among professional Christian theologians, the idea that near-death testimony might make a case for life after death has received critical attention, both favorable and dissenting. A few mavericks—notably John Hick and Paul Badham—suggest that clinical and parapsychological evidence might provide just the empirical elixir we need to invigorate our culture's withered eschatological imagination. Nonetheless, neither of these theologians relies on empirical arguments alone. In *Death and Eternal Life,* Hick combines the evidence from mediumship and parapsychology with scientific, philosophical and moral grounds for conceiving the future life on an evolutionary model. Badham's view is that near-death experiences and other psychic phenomena, although they provide no guarantee of immortality, can at least disarm naturalistic objections and make room for a faith founded on the experience of relationship to God.[2]

In general, however, academic circles have not seen much theological debate over the implications of near-death research. The predominant trend has been to ignore or repudiate efforts to find evidence for existence after death. One reason for this is that many Christian thinkers believe that the idea of personal survival has been rendered obsolete by recent scientific, philosophical, and linguistic discoveries. Beyond this standard and widespread skepticism, however, several generations of liberal and neo-orthodox theologians have warned against preoccupation with the hereafter. It is a narcissistic distraction from the ethical and social mission of the church, they argue, and it is moreover both childish and arrogant to expect more from rational or empirical proofs than from biblical promises. A Lutheran pastor writes, "If life after death could be empirically verified 'beyond a shadow of a doubt,' then there would seem to be little need for faith."[3]

For some religious critics, the most serious flaw in near-death literature is its portrait of death as a pleasant, gentle transition. Converging streams of Freudian, existentialist, and neo-orthodox thought, along with modern biblical scholarship, have produced a strong sentiment among theologians that it is essential to the Christian message to affirm the reality and sting of death.[4] Ever since Oscar Cullmann drew (perhaps overdrew) the distinction between the resurrection faith of Christianity and the Greek philosophical idea of natural immortality, this contrast has been a recurrent theme, even a rallying cry, of theological writing.[5] Stephen Vicchio speaks for many when he complains that "the empty tomb for Kübler-Ross and Moody is superfluous if not redundant. There is no need for Easter if we are immortal."[6]

Those who pit Cullmann against Kübler-Ross and her ilk are heirs to a long tradition of Christian polemic against the opponent—pagan or straw man—who would ground our hopes in knowledge rather than faith, in nature rather than sacred history, in the soul's intrinsic purity rather than God's willingness to cleanse it. Pragmatically speaking, however, the real issue in these debates is whether the alternative views make a difference in religious life; do they breed complacency or catalyze conversion? The answer to this question cannot be decided solely on biblical, doctrinal, or philosophical grounds. A great deal depends on social climate and personal temperament; as I shall suggest below, the history of religion tells us that similar eschatological conceptions may serve, under different circumstances, either to awaken efforts to merit an afterlife or to make such efforts redundant by feeding people pie-in-the-sky consolations.

In the current atmosphere of skepticism and cultural fragmentation, fears and doubts about survival of death can be just as morally and spiritually paralyzing as a monolithic faith in its certainty. Those who testify to the transforming effect of near-death experience often say that their conviction that death is not the end gave them the freedom and energy to change their way of life. On the other hand, when the quest for immortality is isolated from other religious concerns, as in psychical research, it can become something tawdry, egoistic, and this-worldly. So, too, medieval Christian vision literature runs the gamut from profound to mechanical understanding of penance, purgatory, and conversion. Perhaps the doctrine itself is not at fault, but only its abuse; the present danger is not that people will become convinced of immortality, but that the whole subject will be trivialized by a narrow focus on the case for or against survival.

Clearly, a new approach is needed; to make near-death testimony an arena for restaging old philosophical or theological battles will not suffice. It appears to be impossible, in any case, to determine objectively whether near-death reports are accurate or inaccurate depictions of the future life. It might therefore be more fruitful for theologians to consider near-death visions as works of the religious imagination, whose function is to communicate meaning through symbolic forms rather than to copy external facts. This is the aspect of near-death literature that I have attempted to highlight.

Double Vision

The purpose of comparing medieval and modern vision narratives has been to benefit from the stereoscopic effect, the depth perception, which the juxtaposition of two separate perspectives can provide. It will be helpful, then, to review the results of this comparison before proceeding to generalize about the religious implications of otherworld journey narration.

In broad terms, the similarities we found were as follows: both medieval and modern narratives depict the death and revival of individuals whose experience is held up as an example of what we can expect in our own final moments. The manner of death—departure of the spirit from the body—is described in frankly dualistic terms, the separated spirit looking down upon its former dwelling place with indifference or contempt.

After leaving the body, the visionary finds himself in a liminal condition, hovering just overhead and watching the scene of crisis in a mood of detachment. The beginning of the otherworld journey proper is signaled by the advent of a guide and by motifs of visionary topography and travel such as paths, valleys, and tunnels. The guide, who is the narrator's alter ego, escorts the visionary from place to place, pushing the story forward and interpreting the inner significance of otherworld scenes; he thus calls attention to the symbolic character of the other world, and to the need for spiritual instruction in this life and the next.

In the pivotal episode of both medieval and modern journeys, the visionary confronts himself by means of various graphic representations. He meets his thoughts, words, and deeds; learns the weight of his soul; or reviews his life in a book, play, or movie—and in such fashion brings judgment upon himself.

Although medieval hell and purgatory scenes find scarcely any counterparts in the near-death testimony collected by Moody and his colleagues, motifs of paradise topography are much the same in both periods: shining edifices, gardens, meadows, heavenly cities, and so forth. In addition, the ultimate experience of contemplative vision, though treated only rarely and briefly by medieval otherworld journey narratives (for reasons discussed in chapter 5), is consistently described as a comprehensive vision of the whole, in which cognitive and affective powers fuse. It is a moment when the dramatic action of the otherworld journey seems to be suspended and unmediated awareness floods in; but an instant later the play resumes, a message is formulated, and the visionary feels compelled, against his desires, to return to life.

Upon revival, the visionary is physically and spiritually changed. Reticent and overwhelmed at first, he is eventually persuaded to communicate his discoveries and share his mission with others. Once an ordinary *vir quidam*, average guy, or "just a housewife," the visionary takes on a prophetic role, teaching by word and by the example of a transformed life.

We also saw that in both periods the otherworld journey narrative evolves through the visionary's conversation with others, and that the narrator shapes the account to conform to the conventions of the genre in which it will appear, whether sermon, allegory, chronicle, Christian polemic, contemporary best-seller, tabloid testimonial, statistical study, or television talk show. In all these different formats, the vision story retains its didactic aim: the other world is not described to satisfy theoretical curiosity, but to serve as a goad toward transformation.

There is bound to be disagreement over whether these recurrent motifs—guides, paths, barriers, encounters with deeds, and so forth—constitute a universal lexicon or whether they provide only the syntactic structure of the otherworld vision. Many of the areas of similarity appear to be formal rather than substantial; for when we fill in the picture, supplying the emotional content and the culturally specific features that make up a concrete vision, we discover significant divergences.

Thus, despite the structural resemblance between descriptions of the soul's exit from the body, we find that medieval visions exemplify the two deaths theme, while modern visions portray only the comforting prospect of a good death. So, too, although the guide is essential in both periods as a narrative expedient, didactic instrument, guardian of the threshold, and psychopomp, his character and relation to the visionary are understood quite differently. In medieval visions, the guide stands for hierarchical and feudal authority; in modern visions, he represents benevolent parental acceptance. His role appears to be shaped by cultural presuppositions about social and family structure, judicial process, education, and pastoral or psychological cure of souls.

The most glaring difference is the prominence in medieval accounts of obstacles and tests, purificatory torments, and outright doom. Aside from continuing the hellfire traditions of early Christian apocalyptic, medieval narratives serve as vehicles for the consolidation of Catholic teachings on purgatory and penance. In modern accounts, on the other hand, a sense of inevitable progress softens the rigors of final reckoning; the review of deeds is transformed from an ordeal into an educational experience; and the only serious obstacle is the barrier marking the point of no return. These narratives are shaped throughout by optimistic, democratic, "healthy-minded" principles that transparently reflect a contemporary ideology and mood.

The contrast to medieval accounts is sharpened when we set near-death narratives against the background of nineteenth- and twentieth-century spiritualism and its intellectual offshoot, the psychical research movement. The spiritualist other world, like that of near-death literature, is a social utopia, mirroring the progressive causes with which many spiritualists and psychical researchers have been connected: prison, insane asylum, and school reform; abolition; feminism; socialism; Christian perfectionism; and other high-minded liberal concerns have been validated by mediumistic and clairvoyant descriptions of the ideal conditions of the spirit world.[7]

Although ours is a less fertile period for generating utopian schemes, near-death literature expresses and provides otherworld validation for similar progressivist ideas. It is no wonder, then, that it provokes the ire of conservative religious thinkers, whose objections to current near-death studies echo earlier reactions against spiritualism.[8]

In its otherworld cosmology, as well, near-death literature is as close to spiritualism as it is distant from medieval visions. Medieval vision narratives, as we saw, are the outcome of a long history of development and suppression of cosmological schemes for the soul's journey to God; they retain vestiges, sometimes sublimated or confused, of older conceptions of the planetary spheres as places of interrogation and punishment. Naturally, this idiom is completely foreign to modern accounts; near-death literature reflects instead a short history of attempts to reconcile the spirit world with the world of Faraday, Maxwell, Darwin, and Einstein. Though less inclined than spiritualism to localize the other world in the outer atmosphere, modern narratives make similar use of scientific vocabulary—energy, magnetism, vibrations, dimensions, evolution—now supplemented by terms drawn from relativity theory, quantum mechanics, and holography to update the imaginative cosmology.

In focusing on the reports of those who return from death, however, modern accounts are closer to their medieval counterparts than to spiritualist literature. The return-from-death story, unlike mediumistic accounts of the afterlife, conforms to the pattern of a conversion narrative. Rather than mapping the spirit world in great detail, the return-from-death story emphasizes the visionary's special task, the message he is charged to bring back to humanity, and the transformation of his way of life.

On the other hand, medieval and modern narratives differ considerably in their understanding of the *nature* of the visionary's message, commission, and conversion. Moral rehabilitation is too vague a goal for medieval visions; they are concerned, as we have seen, to promote particular penitential and monastic institutions. Modern narratives, however, advocate the renunciation of worries and fears and conversion to a life of love, learning, and service; this is an individualistic, anti-institutional, humanistic ideal, of which churches, hospices, and other service organizations may be the incidental beneficiaries. Considered closely, then, the differences between medieval and modern accounts of return-from-death conversion are as impressive as the similarities.

These comparative observations force us to conclude that the visionaries of our own age are no more free of cultural influence than those of less pluralistic eras. We have seen that the otherworld journey story—which comprises every level of the experience to which we have access, as well as every layer of narrative reconstruction—is through and through a work of the socially conditioned religious imagination; it is formed in conversation with society, even if it takes place in the solitude of the deathbed and in the private chamber of inner experience.

Once we recognize this, we can no longer insist that *Life After Life*, Gregory's *Dialogues*, or any other work of visionary eschatology paints a true picture of what occurs at the extreme border of life. If we wish to avoid the self-defeating extremes of shallow relativism and naive affirmation, then our only recourse is to focus on the imaginative and symbolic character of otherworld visions.

The remainder of this chapter will consider whether this approach can yield a fuller understanding of near-death literature and of visionary and religious testimony in general. I should explain at the outset, however, that I am not attempting to provide a systematic theory of near-death visions. Such a theory would require the collaborative efforts of many different interpreters. Perhaps the solution to the puzzle of near-death experience will always remain in the distance, drawing us along by receding as we approach it. What I offer here is not a conclusion designed to close the book on the subject, but a set of suggestions and thought experiments intended to point out promising directions for further inquiry.

Although this discussion is preliminary and open-ended, it is guided by certain assumptions about the symbolic character of religious discourse; in case these assumptions are not by now apparent, I will make them explicit.

In speaking of *symbolism*, I have in mind a definition that the reader may not share but may be willing to grant for the purpose of discussion. According to most dictionaries, a symbol is an image or object that represents something beyond itself. To this minimal definition I would add—following the view expressed in various ways by Samuel Taylor Coleridge, Paul Tillich, Ernst Cassirer, Suzanne Langer, and Paul Ricoeur, among others—that a symbol participates in the reality that it represents. It does not copy or fully contain that reality, but it does communicate some of its power. Unlike a metaphor, it cannot adequately be translated into conceptual terms.

By *religious imagination*, I understand the capacity to create or to appreciate religious symbols. In this book, we have caught a glimpse of some of the features of the religious imagination. We have seen that it works not only with universal patterns—such as death and birth—but also with culturally specific and idiosyncratic material, and that it can fuse the universal and the particular into a seamless narrative whole.

Connected to this understanding of symbol and religious imagination is an assumption about the nature of religious discourse and of theology. *Theology*, as I understand it, is a discipline of critical reflection on religious experience and religious language. As such, no matter how objective or systematic it becomes, it cannot escape the fundamental limitations that apply to religious discourse in general.

To put it bluntly, I do not believe that any of our notions of God, the soul, or the other world are likely to be true in the ordinary sense of the word. One reason for this is human weakness: we are too thick-headed, twisted, or frightened to see clearly. Another reason, which perhaps brings less discredit, is that we have no mode of expression that combines the virtues of analytic and symbolic thought: our concepts are too abstract and one-dimensional, while our images and symbols are too concrete; we sense that both modes of understanding are necessary, yet they seem incompatible. For this and other reasons that have been adduced by countless philosophers and religious thinkers, there is no sensory, imaginative, or intellectual form capable of fully expressing the transcendent. We can intuit and be forever changed by a higher reality, but we cannot apprehend or describe it in the direct and unequivocal manner with which we seem to know the objects of ordinary experience. Such understanding as we do receive of the transcendent comes to us through symbols, and it is through symbols that we communicate this understanding to one another.

Thus, although theology involves analytic thought, its fundamental material is symbol. Its task is to assess the health of our symbols; for when one judges a symbol, one cannot say whether it is true or false, but only whether it is vital or weak. When a contemporary theologian announces, for example, that God is dead or that God is not only Father but also Mother, he or she is not describing the facts per se, but is evaluating the potency of our culture's images for God—their capacity to evoke a sense of relationship to the transcendent.

To say that theology is a diagnostic discipline is also to say that its method is pragmatic. In evaluating religious ideas and images, theology deals with ranges of experience that cannot be verified—which even overflow our normal categories of thought. One need not abandon the idea that there is an ultimate truth in order to recognize that for now, at least, pragmatic criteria must be used. If we have no direct sensory or conceptual access to the reality for which we aim, then we must judge those images and ideas valid that serve a remedial function, healing the intellect and the will. In this sense, all theology is pastoral theology, for its proper task is not to describe the truth but to promote and assist the quest for truth.

I suggest, therefore, that a pragmatic method and a sensitivity to symbol must go hand in hand if we wish to give a fair hearing to the claims of near-death literature. If we fully recognize the symbolic nature of near-death testimony (and accept the limits that imposes on us), then in the end we will be able to accord it a value and a validity that would not otherwise be possible; this in turn will yield further insight into the visionary, imaginative, and therapeutic aspects of religious thought in general.

Corporeal Imagery

The advantage of paying close attention to the way in which otherworld visions reflect imaginative modes of thought becomes evident when we look at visionary accounts of the soul's exit from the body. We have seen that near-death reports, like their medieval predecessors, presume an old-fashioned dualism that most contemporary philosophers and theologians find inadequate to deal with the complexities of mind–body interaction. For some, this makes it difficult to take near-death visions seriously. A philosophy professor told me that although he was fascinated by near-death studies, he would hate to have to give up his hard-won sophistication and go back to thinking of the soul as "housed in the body like an oyster in a shell."[9] He could not decide whether to heed his philosophical training or the empirical data of out-of-body experience; one or the other would have to go.

Fortunately, however, a third alternative becomes available if we enact what I have called the Copernican revolution of regarding the other world as the domain of imagination and interpret its features accordingly. Without requiring adherence to any particular school of philosophical or psychological idealism, this revolution or change in perspective allows us to reclaim a whole range of imagery and experiential testimony that we might otherwise have to reject on theoretical grounds. Not only dualism and somatomorphism but also personification imagery, theatrical and cosmological symbolism, and externalization of deeds can be understood and valued as imaginative forms rather than descriptive models. They provide coherent patterns for dramatizing inner experience, yet they entail no particular metaphysics. They have a logic of their own, but if we try to grasp them in theoretical terms, we lay hold of nothing but confusion; and, like other category errors, this can lead to unwarranted skepticism.

· Several vexing issues are clarified, then, if we view otherworld visions as artifacts of the imagination; most important, it should silence those critics who invoke the "fallacy of misplaced concreteness" or similar vetoes against the claims of near-death literature. If the other world is the inner world projected on the stage of the imagined cosmos, then here, if anywhere, is the place where concrete and graphic, embodied and animated principles belong. When we think theoretically, we must guard against spatializing and hypostatizing our ideas; perhaps we could not think creatively at all, however, if we lacked the capacity to imagine, though only subliminally, a realm in which our ideas can act. For this reason, I have suggested that many symbolic and even metaphorical expressions contain latent reference to another world.

The concrete imagery of near-death visions is dictated not only by their imaginative character but also by their narrative quality. The otherworld journey, as we have seen, is at its very roots a story. In order to fulfill its narrative purpose of engaging interest and its didactic purpose of impelling the audience from ideology to action, it must portray the afterlife as an active realm, and the soul as a protagonist whose experiences epitomize and interpret those of earthly life. If the soul must take on the shape of the body for that purpose, then so be it; if near-death visions had to conform to the requirements of abstract philosophical theology they would make dull stories indeed.

In the context of religious storytelling, then, it is not necessarily progress when, in deference to subtler understandings of spiritual perfection, we pluck off the limbs, erase the features, and shave our image of the soul into a bald, symmetrical bit of geometry, incapable of motion or life. The same is true of images of the divine; attempts to picture God as transcending time, space, and gender may end by making God appear unsubstantial, neuter, and inert. In either case, the religious imagination is at work; the question is whether it works vigorously, harnessed and disciplined by spiritual practice, or whether it works lamely, hindered by misplaced theoretical scruples.

Perhaps there is no need to forgo speaking of the divine or the self in ways that feed the imagination. This is the view William Blake endorses when he urges us to imagine God as a person rather than a metaphysical principle:

> God Appears & God is Light
> To those poor Souls who dwell in Night,
> But does a Human Form Display
> To those who Dwell in Realms of day.[10]

Blake's attitude is a welcome antidote to the intellectualism that has prisoned academic theology; but his insistence on anthropomorphism is misguided. The point is to give up dull abstractions, not to espouse one form of imagery over another. Even the most vivid images for God and the soul can lose potency with time. Corporeal imagery can become tyrannical, as St. Augustine discovered during the long period in which he struggled to free himself from a childishly materialist understanding of God, good, and evil; sometimes what is most needed is a fresh gust of iconoclasm, a healthy disdain for imaginative forms. When an archetype degenerates into a stereotype, then the laws of religious imagination no longer bind us to it, but call on us to register the changes that a new situation demands. At its best, theology is the art of detecting and serving these changing needs of religious symbol systems; thus, it proceeds in a rhythm of creation and destruction rather than a progressive conquest of truth.

If we view theology in this way, as an essentially therapeutic rather than theoretic discipline, it is easier to come to terms with religious change while maintaining respect for tradition. Religious teaching is an art, an activity, and an interaction with others; doctrine is only its by-product. A gifted religious teacher is not only able to transmit a tradition but also to read the historical and personal situation and respond appropriately, discerning spontaneously what is required. Similarly, the modes of speculative and systematic religious thought that we call theology succeed when they are attuned to the needs of their times. What is needed is not the pursuit of superficial "relevance" for its own sake, but a balance between preservation and innovation. Theology should maintain links to the authoritative sources and stored wisdom of the past, while remaining flexible enough to alter doctrinal formulas for the sake of progress or reformation in religious life. Such flexibility is only possible if we acknowledge that theology, like the primary acts of religious teaching and inquiry which are its material, has to do not with truth-telling but with truth-seeking.

This is especially true of eschatological doctrines; within every major tradition they vary greatly not only in ideological content but also in the extent to which they permit the imagination to visualize a concrete other world. If we recognize that religious teaching is a therapeutic art, then we can see the value of teachings which are evasive on the subject of an afterlife—from Jesus' parabolic sayings about the Kingdom of God to Thoreau's insistence on "one world at a time"—yet we can appreciate the elaborate depictions of heaven and hell that from a Christian legacy in sermon, scholastic *sententia*, and cathedral stone. We can acknowledge that the Buddha, as "Supreme Physician," correctly diagnosed the condition of his hearers when he refused to satisfy their curiosity about the destiny of saints after death, and when he maintained silence on the other leading metaphysical issues of his day; yet we can also see the *dharma* reflected in the Pure Land sects, which promise rebirth in a lush celestial paradise.

Gregory the Great, whose voice has been so prominent in the Christian literature of the other world, speaks directly to this point:

> The medicine that lessens one disease adds force to another; and the bread that enhances the life of the strong destroys that of little ones. Therefore the speech of teachers should be shaped according to the condition of the hearers.[11]

In short, when we sit in judgment on traditional or newly coined conceptions of God, the soul, or immortality we should consider the context in which they appear, rather than measure them against a narrow intellectualist standard.

The Question of Interpretation

The present study has demonstrated the need to take into account the imaginative, narrative, didactic, and therapeutic character of eschatological visionary literature; at the same time it has yielded a guiding principle for the interpretation of religious discourse in general. This approach not only helps us to come to terms with the varied religious expressions of our own culture, but also contributes to our effort to understand other traditions. Recognizing the imaginative character of religious utterances does not entail renouncing our faith in an ultimate and objective truth, but it does allow us to stop pitting one set of beliefs against another. It means that the hope for reconciliation does not depend on our ability to identify areas of conceptual agreement or to dissolve apparent differences among the world's religions into a vague consensus. Moreover, it enhances historical self-awareness to learn that, as the study of near-death narratives makes plain, we are not cut off from our myth-making past. Like our ancestors, and like people of other cultures today, we come into contact with reality in ways that are shaped by language, social structure, geography, and weather, along with the particular forces that differentiate us from our neighbors. If we can appreciate this in ourselves, we can appreciate it in others. We need not strip the temples and unclothe the gods in order to discover affinities between different religious world-views.

Yet the benefits of this outlook can be ours only if we are willing to renounce the notion that some original and essential religious experience can be discriminated from subsequent layers of cultural shaping. This is the error in method against which theologian Gordon Kaufman warns:

> Our "religious experience," whatever this turns out to be, is never a raw, pre-conceptual, pre-linguistic experience, the undialectical foundation on which theology can be built. It (like all the rest of experience) is always a construction or composite, heavily dependent for its form and qualities on the learned terms and concepts which give it particular flavor and shape.[12]

In a sense, this observation can serve to protect the integrity of experiential testimony. If we heed Kaufman's rejection of the notion of raw experience, then we will not make the assumption that the visionary who sees Christ or Krishna is only "labeling" an underlying experience which can be described more accurately and directly as encounter with a "being of light" or the "higher self." As I have suggested, such modern expressions may seem more palatable, but they are no less culturally determined or mythically cultivated.

For Kaufman, the fact that we have no access to uncultivated religious experience means that theology should be seen as an act of deliberate imaginative construction, finding its materials in reflection on our language and social experience rather than private oracles. The advantage of this position is that it calls on religious thinkers to acknowledge and take responsibility for their own reflective and creative work in framing ideas of the universe and of God. Its disadvantage is primarily practical: if we follow Kaufman's suggestion that theology should be related to but not rooted in individual religious experience, then we run the risk of widening the gap between the amateur theologian who examines his own experience in the search for truths and the professional who knows better.

Indeed, it is already the case that academic theologians tend to avoid questions of inner experience rather than risk privatism, subjectivism, or the transgression of Kantian boundaries; yet this is happening at a time when—to judge by the success of *Life After Life* and other books about individual spiritual experience—the wider public is hungry for theoretical and practical guidance in precisely this area.[13] Just as scholars are becoming more sophisticated about the social character of religion, the social context for religion is growing increasingly individualistic. For many people, personal experience seems to be the only available arena for religious discovery and the only guide for choosing among the dizzying array of competing world-views and paths. Under the pressures of secularism and pluralism, religion has become more than ever a matter of "what the individual does with his own solitariness."[14] There has never been a period in which undue skepticism about religious experience could be more damaging.

All of this bears on the problem of interpreting otherworld visions. If we wish to maintain a middle path between reductionism and naiveté, then we must mediate between the impersonalism of social theories that stress the coerciveness of language and culture at the expense of individual experience and the exaggerated individualism of earlier interpreters like William James and Henri Bergson, who disregard the social side of religion in favor of its private dimension and its solitary "geniuses."[15] Since debates are often muddled by unacknowledged differences in usage, it will clarify our task to discriminate three ways in which the terms *social* and *individual* can apply to religious experience:

1. Religious experience is invariably social in that religious life and thought are shaped by linguistic and social forces; for this reason, Clifford Geertz describes religion as a "cultural system."

2. Religious traditions reflect and promote social order and, in many cultures, tend to value the group over the individual. In archaic societies, according to Mircea Eliade, religious experience is profoundly collective—the individual feels his identity securely only when merged with the community, reenacting the mythical acts, of its foundation, purging himself of idiosyncrasy. Many of the historical religious traditions also have a communal focus; the Hebrew Bible is the story of a people's response to God's acts, not the diary of a solitary seeker. Yet the extent to which religious experience is communal depends on the degree and quality of social cohesion in a given group. The social character of religious experience, in this sense, is a variable rather than a constant. It can therefore, as Wilfred Cantwell Smith argues, be misleading to generalize about the fundamental significance of religious community on the basis of a particular situation.[16] To make archaic religion the standard is no more reasonable than to suppose, as James did, that the sepa-

ration between personal and institutional religion which characterized his own intellectual milieu should stand for all time and apply to all forms of religious experience.

3. Religious experience is invariably individual in that, as Smith says, "to be religious is an ultimately personal act." No matter how communal their society may be, human beings are essentially alone in the experience of life and death and in the encounter with transcendent values. This is as constant as the fact of social conditioning (number 1 above) and is not altered by changing conditions of social structure. Individual experience may not be the locus of authority, but it is the touchstone for authenticity; in this context, the opposite of "individual" is not "social," but "insincere."

In interpreting contemporary near-death literature, therefore, we can say without contradiction that it records the genuine and irreducibly personal experiences of individuals (number 3), that it is nonetheless a product of the social religious imagination (number 1), and that one sign of its social character is its individualistic message (number 2). If we keep these three rudimentary distinctions in mind, then our awareness of the cultural shaping of near-death testimony need not lead to relativism or skepticism. The antireductionist principle of judging religious experience by its fruits rather than its origins applies as well to current sociological insights as it does to the "medical materialism" against which William James battled.

Having cleared the way by defending near-death testimony against the new reductionisms of social science, we are free to apply pragmatic criteria toward interpreting the content of near-death visions. As I have suggested, a pragmatic method is ideally suited for dealing with testimony that cannot be verified in other ways. If there is validity to religious accounts of life or death, it is not because they provide a direct transcript of the truth, but only because they act as a lure toward truth, by leading people out of anxious, mechanical, or vicious patterns of thought and behavior. As long as our religious ideas and images perform this leading function, and do not falsify our experience along the way, then we can say, with James, that they are "true in so far forth."[17]

We can use this pragmatic approach without necessarily embracing James's pragmatic theory of truth. We should not adopt James's pragmatic method, however, without stretching it to include attention to the workings of the religious imagination and the cultural forces that shape it. What James calls the "cash value" of a religious conception depends on the state of the economy in which it is circulated, and cannot be measured against any universal or timeless rate of exchange. With this in mind, I have criticized theological interpretations of near-death literature that do not take into account its particular implications for our culture.

We cannot return to James, then, but we can combine a Jamesian respect for the validity of individual religious experience with a greater sensitivity to the cultural shaping of that experience. We can expand his pragmatic method by incorporating into it an appreciation of the symbolic and therapeutic character of religious discourse. Having done so, we can turn to

the task of interpreting near-death visions with a renewed sense of the right-
ness of treating them as socially conditioned, imaginative, and yet nonetheless
real and revelatory experiences.

This is the approach that allows us to respect the visionary's claim that
he experienced death, even if he did not meet medical criteria. As the previous chapter points out, it is enough to know that the shock of extreme danger or expected death opened him to a discovery of what death means to him
at the core of his being. When he stepped onto the stage of the other world—
which is the inner world, turned inside out—he confronted his own deeply
held image and presentiment of death, perhaps just as he will at the time of
his actual death. Thus we can say, in the fullest possible sense, that the visionary "met his death."

Indeed, it is no coincidence that the ordinary expression "he met his
death" is compatible with the testimony of near-death visionaries. Here is one
instance in which our language preserves a vestige of otherworld journey
imagery in a saying that, though commonplace, nonetheless retains a vital
charge. Dormant in our everyday speech, this expression has the potential to
spring into a full-blown imaginative or visionary experience; its potency is a
sign that the traditional and folkloric view of death as a symbolic encounter
still has authority for us. If we recognize this, then the testimony of near-
death visionaries will begin to seem less foreign. On the basis of this common
ground of imaginative experience, we have reason to accord some validity to
the visionary's claims. Certainly this is a more fruitful and more humane
approach than the application of external medical tests.

The same logic applies to the conviction of having survived death.
Though it proves nothing about our own prospects for life beyond the grave,
we are entitled to accept an individual's report that he experienced something in himself that surpasses death. Given the immense practical significance of this claim, it would be foolish to deny it solely because of scientific
opinions. Science can hardly have the last word on a subject about which it
has so little to say; and the transforming effects of near-death experience
speak for themselves.

So the benefits of reading visionary testimony as a work of the imagination keep accumulating; and if we move on to consider the near-death vision
as a narrative whole, its immunity to reductionist criticism becomes even
greater. We have seen that arguments against the validity of visionary experience depend on analyzing it into component parts. The critics of near-death
research remind us that near-death experience is a composite and that its
individual elements may be "explained" by distribution to various physical,
psychological, and social facts.

Yet it is our prerogative as imaginative beings to form meaningful
wholes out of the elements of sensation, perception, language, memory, and
so forth, which we are given. Imagination, which Coleridge calls the power
"to shape into one," fuses these bits of experience into a dramatic sequence,
aimed toward a destination, and therefore not reducible to their origin or

cause. In acts of telling and retelling, near-death experience takes shape as a unified and unifying whole. Once this narrative integrity is achieved, no amount of analytical dissection can destroy it.

This immunity is lost, however, the moment we begin to try to verify near-death experience by isolating veridical elements, ruling out pathological causes, or breaking it down into statistics. Paradoxically, the very method that permits us to respect visionary testimony prohibits us from using it to make a case for survival. To this extent, we must frustrate the truth claims of near-death literature.

In every respect, our defense of near-death reports depends on treating them as symbolic expressions that can never be translated into direct observations or exact concepts. This will disappoint those who wish to have their doubts about life after death resolved. It has positive religious implications as well, however, for it requires us to give up our insistence on objective verification (which has been the source of so much grief throughout history) and in its place to cultivate an appreciation of symbol. Instead of regretting the fact that religious experience is symbolic rather than descriptive, we might rejoice that the truth empties itself into our human language and cultural forms. To attempt to strip away those forms in the belief that they merely embellish, veil, or obstruct the truth is, in effect, a revival of the Docetist heresy.

Even if we grant that near-death visions convey something real, there is no reliable way to formulate what that something is. We cannot take a consensus of the visionaries, their visions are too culturally specific. We cannot crack their symbolic code; and we know before we start that every explanation or interpretation, however thoughtful, will leave the essential mystery untouched. As the remainder of this chapter will suggest, we can appropriate the messages of near-death literature only in an indirect fashion; and yet that may prove to be no insignificant thing.

Another World to Live In

The narrative integrity of near-death visions derives not merely from the fact that a story is told but, more importantly, from the fact that the story has an aim. What seems at first glance to be a visionary travelogue describing for the curious the sights of an exotic supernatural realm turns out to be the story of a conversion experience; and, as we have seen, its main purpose is to communicate to others the new insights gained by the convert.

Otherworld vision stories resemble conversion narratives in two respects. Most obviously, they trace the protagonist's recovery from a condition of sin, melancholy, malaise—or from death itself, which is the fundamental reference point and emblem for all states of despair. Although modern near-death narratives give us deliverance without conviction of sin, they nonetheless follow the conversion pattern, often beginning with an allusion to the protagonist's long-standing enslavement to fear of death, and ending, as the medieval narratives do, with an account of his regenerated way of life. The death-first pattern of contemporary reports thus serves a function parallel to that of the hell-first pattern of medieval narratives.

The second, and more intriguing, similarity between conversion experience and near-death visions is the way in which inner transformation colors perceptions of the outer world. Not only do otherworld visions resemble conversion, but, in this respect, conversion narratives resemble otherworld visions. William James suggests as much in his discussion of conversion, when he points out that a sudden sense of inward illumination can spill over into the landscape, saturating it with beauty, light, newness, vitality, and harmony. James's prime example for this is Jonathan Edwards's account of his own conversion experience, in which the face of nature seemed to change, and the voice of thunder was transformed from a dreadful summons into a sweet invitation.[18] James also cites several anonymous witnesses who entered the "state of assurance" under the auspices of evangelical revival; the following narrative, taken from E. D. Starbuck, is representative:

> It was like entering another world, a new state of existence. Natural objects were glorified, my spiritual vision was so clarified that I saw beauty in every material object in the universe, the woods were vocal with heavenly music; my soul exulted in the love of God, and I wanted everybody to share in my joy.

For a secular variation on the same theme, we can turn to Gustav Fechner, a philosopher whom James admired, who attained to his "daylight view" of the panpsychic intelligence of plants and planets after emerging from a period of painful seclusion:

> I still remember well what an impression it made upon me when, after suffering for some years from an ailment which affected my sight, I stepped out for the first time from my darkened chamber and into the garden with no bandage upon my eyes. It seemed to me like a glimpse beyond the boundary of human experience. Every flower beamed upon me with a peculiar clarity, as though into the outer light it was casting a light of its own. To me the whole garden seemed transfigured, as though it were not I but nature that had just arisen. And I thought: So nothing is needed but to open the eyes afresh, and with that old nature is made young again.[19]

In this passage there converges an entire spectrum of literal and metaphoric conversion and otherworld journey motifs. A comparable account by Alphonse Ratisbonne, also quoted by James, likens a sudden conversion experience to emerging "from a sepulchre, from an abyss of darkness," and finding that "in an instant the bandage had fallen from my eyes."[20] But the special charm of Fechner's account is that these age-old symbols of awakening and renewed sight—exit from a darkened chamber, having a covering drop from the eyes, entering a luminous garden—take on literal form. The same may be said of near-death narratives; here the literal sense comes to rest on the passage from death into life, from the darkened chamber of the body and its lidded vision to the lucid garden which, as Fechner puts it, "lies beyond the wall of this world."

William James holds that the principle by which a conversion experience transfigures the landscape can also operate in reverse, in a melancholic refiguring of the world which strips it of value, interest, and hence of visual allure; and we have seen that this is the chief feature of what psychologists now call depersonalization, the condition that resembles and yet is the very antithesis of visionary near-death experience. According to James, this is more than a psychological principle; he maintains that our exalted or depressed states, assisted by our ideals, beliefs, doubts, and philosophic opinions, positively shape the character of the world. Not conversion only, but all meaningful experience has the power to endow the environment with reality and value, just as pathological, disordered, or lethargic states of mind correspondingly denature it.[21]

Considered in this way, the otherworld vision seems less bizarre; though exceptional, it is part of the normal range of religious and, in the sense just mentioned, even of ordinary experience. As a special form of conversion experience, in which the landscape is transfigured as a corollary of subjective transformation, the visionary journey dramatizes the way imagination contributes to our perception of the world. To use a Blakean analogy, imagination plays the demiurge and—aided by the visionary's exalted mood—creates a new world to dwell in, or restores the natural world according to its Edenic exemplar.

If this is true, it still does not mean that we can decode the features of otherworld topography by tracing them to particular states or objects of mind. Such attempts usually betray dogmatic assumptions; thus Freudian Géza Róheim sees phallic imagery in the architecture of the other world, while neurologist Ronald Siegel relates it to optic and mnemonic structures, and Swedenborg proposes an elaborate system of correspondences in which houses and cities are thoughts, animals and birds are affections, gardens are ordered ideas, and so forth.[22] If we are inclined to adopt a Jungian approach, or to apply the teachings of the *Tibetan Book of the Dead* (which counsels the deceased to recognize his afterlife visions as a projection of the mind's own radiance), we must realize that our impartiality is at risk. Nor does the "intentional" character of otherworld visions call for any particular brand of philosophical idealism or endorse any special school of phenomenology; to enter these intellectual frameworks requires a large added step.

Without committing ourselves to such a step, the main conclusion we can draw, is that the other world—in its literal or metaphoric forms—plays a significant role in our imaginative appropriation of moral and religious ideals. George Santayana, though no friend of literal eschatologies, implies this in his famous definition of religion:

> Any attempt to speak without speaking any particular language is not more hopeless than the attempt to have a religion that shall be no religion in particular.... Thus every living and healthy religion has a marked idiosyncrasy; its power consists in its special and surprising message and in the bias which

that revelation gives to life. The vistas it opens and the mysteries it propounds are another world to live in; and another world to live in—whether we expect ever to pass wholly over into it or not—is what we mean by having a religion.[23]

Like Fechner's story, this passage brings together metaphorical and literal senses. Santayana seems to suggest that myth, ritual, conversion, moral improvement, and other aspects of religious life are intimately related to a primitive—and perhaps consciously repudiated—understanding of the other world as an actual place. For those of use who have abandoned thinking about other worlds, this produces a shock of recognition, demonstrating that our metaphorical ways of having "another world to live in" exert their power on the imagination only because we continue, at least subliminally, to visualize a literal other world. It is better to acknowledge this, and look for its possible benefits, than to ignore it and be unconsciously determined by it. The chief virtue of our tendency to conceive of another world may be that it provides a sense of orientation in *this* world, through which we would otherwise wander without direction.

Orientation

In the vision literature we have considered, conversion motifs merge with pilgrimage motifs because the journey to the next world is actually a guide for pilgrimage through life. The maps of death and afterlife that these accounts contain are meant to help us get our bearings, right now, in relation to the cosmos in which we dwell, or wish to dwell.

Biologists Peter and Jean Medawar have expressed this:

> Only human beings guide their behaviour by a knowledge of what happened before they were born and a preconception of what may happen after they are dead: thus only human beings find their way by a light that illumines more than the patch of ground they stand on.[24]

Comparative study of religion shows that *homo religiosus* has never found it sufficient to orient himself solely in terms of his place in local history, in the rat race, in private concerns that devour his energy. The imaginative cosmologies and eschatologies of different cultures testify to our human need to find a place to occupy in a wider universe.

This has not always been formulated in terms of life after death. Even the contemplation of death, unadorned by images of the beyond, can have this orienting effect insofar as it makes us place ourselves, with greater urgency and purpose, in the midst of life; and a sense of the mystery of existence, of infinite presence or surrounding emptiness, can have the same value as a graphic depiction of the steps to paradise and hell. Buddhist evocations of the inexhaustibly productive void are as well suited as Dante's *Divine Comedy* to meet the need for orientation. The question they address is not necessarily "What was I before I was born, and what will I be when I die?"

but rather "Where am I now in relation to the north, south, east, and west of the cosmos, the yesterday and tomorrow of history, the higher and lower ranks of being?" And the answer to this question can legitimately take many different forms, as long as it succeeds to some degree in correlating our position in the social order with our position in the cosmic order. Thus I have suggested that otherworld journey narration is most likely to become prominent at times when a culture develops, or encounters through contact with other cultures, new perspectives on the social and natural universe which—until assimilated by the religious imagination—give rise to "cognitive dissonance" and spiritual dislocation.

It is the religious imagination that turns map into cosmos and cosmos into home; in visionary literature this is accomplished by sending scouts to visit the farther reaches and return with eyewitness accounts that imaginatively appropriate the current world-picture. Without such reports of actual experience, we seem to live in an unevaluated and desacralized universe.

If the otherworld journey is a way for the religious imagination to digest a culturally fashioned cosmology, then it is not surprising that these narratives, today as in the past, raise questions of a scientific order. The narrators who attempt to provide verification, according to the investigative canons of their day, are only extending this original impulse to link cosmology with imaginative experience. Although they may never achieve a profound synthesis of scientific and religious world-views, they are at least making an effort in that direction, unlike those religious thinkers who are so disenchanted by the failed alliances of the past that they look for religion only in those areas—such as ethics—that do not overlap with the domain of science.

Fortunately, these are not the only options. A third possibility, as Gordon Allport tells us, is the "ceaseless struggle to assimilate the scientific frame of thought within an expanded religious frame."[25] The intent of this book has been to point the theological interpretation of near-death experience in this direction; acknowledging scientific and historical contributions without succumbing to positivism, taking experiential claims seriously, and yet posing the question of verification on a deeper level.

Otherworld journey narratives orient us in two ways: as works of visionary topography they provide an updated, culturally sanctioned picture of the cosmos, and as works of moral and spiritual instruction they call on us to inhabit this cosmos, by overcoming the fear or forgetfulness that makes us as insensible to life as to death. All this is the action of the religious imagination, that power that makes our ideas and ideals come to life and act on us. Although most of us do not seek visions (nor are we advised to do so by the visionary literature we have considered), we can at least respect the testimony of vision literature as an extreme instance of the legitimate imaginative means through which one can instill a religious sense of the cosmos.

It is one thing to acknowledge in general terms the orienting value of otherworld visions; it is quite another to decide whether their specific content might be relevant to our own view of life and death. In order to understand the conditions, both cultural and natural, that shape near-death experience, we have assumed the role of spectators and cannot easily divest ourselves of that role. In comparing medieval and modern visions, we seem to have stepped outside our own cultural context and may feel at a loss as to how to step back into it and make judgments. Such incapacity for wholehearted participation is the intellectual's occupational disease; among scholars engaged in the comparative study of religion it can produce a sense of nostalgia for days of innocence or for some idealized form of archaic or traditional religiosity.

When we try to evaluate near-death experience, we may feel stymied by our own sophistication. We have gotten beyond reductionism to the extent that we can say of near-death visions, as William James says of mysticism, that they "usually are, and have the right to be, absolutely authoritative over the individuals to whom they come"; but we find ourselves effectively collared by the corollary that these revelations cannot legislate to— perhaps cannot even be shared with—the general public. As a result, those individuals whose understanding has been shaped by an overwhelming visionary experience seem to be isolated from the rest of us who are trying to make sense of things without the aid of direct revelation.

To some extent, this quarantine is necessary. At this stage I see no justification for treating contemporary near-death testimony as the foundation for a new eschatology or religious movement. Near-death literature is at its best when it is modest and anecdotal; pressed into service as philosophy or prophecy, it sounds insipid. There is no match here for the revelatory literature of the great religious traditions; and it seems unlikely that a Gregory the Great or a Dante will emerge to shape near-death testimony into a religiously sophisticated or artistically ordered statement. Neither could the medieval visions we considered stand on their own; they thrived insofar as they exemplified a wider tradition.

In the end, a revelation is binding only if it binds. On a personal scale, it must organize life into a meaningful whole, without excluding other experiences. On a social scale, it must create or serve a community; and on this score near-death testimony breaks down into private testaments which, despite their common features, have not mustered the collective energy to produce a coherent world-view. Those who experience near-death visions, as well as those who are affected by hearing them, still face the problem of finding a community and a context in which to search again for and apply the insights they have received.

In our fragmented religious situation, the otherworld journey narrative has lost some of its orienting power. It can remind us of the need for orientation, the need to have a consecrated cosmos as the setting for a spiritual journey, but it cannot provide the means or material to accomplish this. We are thrown back on our own devices, our own partial and provisional solutions.

Under these circumstances, the most significant contribution made by near-death literature today may be that it puts in experiential terms questions about life and death which are so urgent as to call not for answers but for vital response. The moment of death—whether it is an imminent prospect or just an idea—still has a salutary shock value; it can make what James would call "live options" out of metaphysical notions that might otherwise seem remote, abstract, or obsolete.

If near-death literature is to have any prophetic value or evidential weight, it will be because it communicates insights capable of being verified—not in medical charts, but in our own experience. We may find no difficulty in respecting the testimony of those whose lives have been transformed by a near-death vision, but we can verify their discoveries only if, in some sense, we experience them for ourselves. The same can be said of other forms of religious testimony; for, unlike the generalizable truths of science, religious truths are true only insofar as religious people make them their own.

In this respect, there is no great distance between those who have experienced near-death visions and those who have only read of them. The visionary—who must continually struggle to understand and not to betray his or her original vision—is in the same boat with the rest of us. All of us need to work at verifying our beliefs, whether they derive from personal experience or from venerated hearsay. A conviction that life surpasses death, however intensely felt, will eventually lose its vitality and become a mere fossil record, as alien as any borrowed doctrine, unless it is tested and rediscovered in daily life.

This study has demonstrated a fundamental kinship between otherworld visions and the more common forms of imaginative experience. Whether we fall into the "experiencer" or the "nonexperiencer" category on a near-death survey, we are all, in a sense, otherworld travelers. Otherworld visions are products of the same imaginative power that is active in our ordinary ways of visualizing death; our tendency to portray ideas in concrete, embodied, and dramatic forms; the capacity of our inner states to transfigure our perception of outer landscapes; our need to internalize the cultural map of the physical universe; and our drive to experience that universe as a moral and spiritual cosmos in which we belong and have a purpose.

Whatever the study of near-death visions might reveal about the experience of death, it teaches us just as much about ourselves as image-making and image-bound beings. To admit this is no concession to the debunkers; on the contrary, by recognizing the imaginative character of otherworld visions, we move beyond the merely defensive posture of arguing against reductionism. Within the limits here discussed we are able to grant the validity of near-death testimony as one way in which the religious imagination mediates the search for ultimate truth.

Appendix

Chronological Table for Medieval Christian Otherworld Journey Literature

Included here are dates (some approximate) for the vision narratives, people, and historical events discussed; this is not intended to be a complete chronology.

c. 445	Traditional date for founding of St. Patrick's Purgatory
480–543	St. Benedict
c. 484/486–578	St. Brendan
540(?)–604	St. Gregory the Great
575	Gregory of Tours writes book 4 of the *History of the Franks* (the Vision of Sunniulf)
590	Gregory of Tours writes book 7 of the *History of the Franks* (the Vision of Salvius)
584	Death of St. Salvius of Albi
	Plague in Rome (the setting for several vision stories in the *Dialogues* of Gregory the Great)
593–594	Gregory the Great writes the *Dialogues*
633	Date for the vision of St. Fursa, according to Bede
648–650	Death of St. Fursa
673–735	The Venerable Bede
c. 675–695	Valerio of Bierzo fl. (author of the visions of Maximus, Baldarius, and Bonellus)
March 25, 678 or 679	Date reported for the Vision of Barontus of Longorus
696	Date for the Vision of Drythelm of Melrose, according to Bede
699	Date for the Vision of Drythelm, according to Roger of Wendover

206

704	Death of Adamnán of Iona
716	St. Boniface, letter to Abbess Eadburga (the Vision of the Monk of Wenlock)
731	Bede completes the *History of the English Church* (visions of Fursa, Drythelm)
early 9th century	The Vision of Rotcharius
	The Vision of a Poor Woman
801–865	St. Ansgar of Bremen
806–882	Hincmar of Rheims (supposed author of the Vision of Bernoldus)
824	The Vision of Wetti (falls ill October 30, tells vision November 3, dies November 4)
	Heito records the Vision of Wetti
827	Walahfrid Strabo puts the Vision of Wetti into verse
835	The Vision of Raduin
835–861	Prudentius of Troyes (the Vision of an English Priest)
late 9th century	The Vision of Ansgar, in *Vita Sancti Anskarii*, by Rimbertus and others
c. 885	Date for the Vision of Charles the Fat (d. 888), according to Hariulf and William of Malmesbury
early 10th century	The Vision of Adamnán (second part)
	The Vision of Laisrén
	The Voyage of Brendan (Latin narrative based on eighth-century legend)
941	Date for the Vision of an English Man, according to Vincent of Beauvais (the Vision of Drythelm)
late 10th century	The Vision of Ansellus Scholasticus, a monk of Rheims (written in verse by order of St. Odo of Fleury)
	Aelfric of Eynsham, Anglo-Saxon homilies (fl. c. 1000)
11th century	The Vision of Heriger (poetic satire of otherworld visions)
	The Vision of Adamnán (first part)
	Cluny, institution of commemoration of the dead on November 2
1010–1070	Otloh of St. Emmeran (*Book of Visions*)
1098–1179	Hildegard of Bingen
late 11th century	Vision of St. Paul, Redaction 4
	Vision of Leofric, Earl of Mercia (d. 1057)
12th century	*Debate between the Body and the Soul* (Royal manuscript)
c. 1100	Alberic of Settefrati born; has otherworld vision at age of 10; enters Monte Cassino under abbacy of Gerard (1111–1123); tells vision to Guido, the first author of the Vision of Alberic
November 1125	Date reported for the Vision of Orm (d. 1126)

c. 1126	Sigar of Newbald writes the Vision of Orm
1127–1137	Abbot Senioretto of Monte Cassino persuades Alberic to restore the distorted account of his vision, with the help of Peter the Deacon
1130	Augustinian canons regular receive jurisdiction over St. Patrick's Purgatory (cave on Saints' Island)
1136	Cistercian monastery at Melrose founded
1140–1200	St. Hugh, Bishop of Lincoln
1146	Date for the Vision of the Boy William, according to Vincent of Beauvais
February/March 1149	Date for Tundal's vision, according to author Marcus, an Irish monk from Cashel
1153	Date for the Vision of the Knight Owen (St. Patrick's Purgatory), according to H. of Sawtry
1160	Date for the Vision of the Monk of Melrose, according to Helinand de Froidmont (based on the Vision of Drythelm)
1161	Date for the Vision of a Cistercian Novice, according to Helinand (the Vision of Gunthelm)
c. 1170–1240	Caesarius of Heisterbach (*Dialogue on Miracles*)
after 1180	German verse version of the Vision of Tundal, by Alber
1180/1183	Jocelyn of Furness describes St. Patrick's Purgatory (on a mountain in Connaught)
1186	Translation of relics of St. Patrick to Down
1186/1187	Giraldus Cambrensis, *Topography of Ireland*, describes St. Patrick's Purgatory as a bipartite island on a lake in Ulster
1186–1190	Period during which H. of Sawtry composed the *Treatise on the Purgatory of Saint Patrick*, according to St. John D. Seymour
1190	Date for the Vision of Gottschalk
1196	Date for the Vision of Edmund, the Monk of Eynsham ("dies" on Good Friday, revives on Easter)
1197	Adam of Eynsham (Edmund's brother) writes the Vision of the Monk of Eynsham
12th–13th centuries	Conrad of Eberbach, *Exordium magnum Cisterciense*
early 13th century	*Draumkvaede* (Vision of Olav Asteson)
	Debate between the Body and the Soul (the Vision of Fulbert)
	Raoul de Houdenc, *Songe d'enfer*
1200–1206	Peter of Cornwall, prior of the Augustinian house of Holy Trinity, Aldgate, compiles the *Book of Visions*, including visions of the Cistercian monks at Stratford Langthorne
October 1206	(All Soul's Week) Date for Thurkill's vision, according to Ralph of Coggeshall and Roger of Wendover

1208–1215	Period during which H. of Sawtry composed the *Treatise*, according to F. W. Locke
1215	Fourth Lateran Council
1248	Pilgrimage of Godalh to St. Patrick's Purgatory
1254	Letter of Pope Innocent IV on purgatory
1228/1230–1298	Jacobus de Voragine *(The Golden Legend)*
1258–1263	St. Thomas Aquinas writes *Summa contra gentiles*
1264	Death of Vincent of Beauvais
1265–1321	Dante Alighieri
1274	Second Council of Lyons
late 13th century	*Disputation between the Body and the Soul*
	Hildebrand of Himmerod, *Libellus de contemplatione*
1300	Dante dates the beginning of his descent, 6 P.M. on Good Friday; begins ascent of Purgatory 6 A.M. on Easter
1353	Pilgrimage of George, Knight of Hungary, to St. Patrick's Purgatory
1355/1358	Guillaume Deguileville, *Le Pèlerinage de l'âme*
1358	Pilgrimage of Louis de Sur to St. Patrick's Purgatory
c. 1369/1385	William Langland, *Piers Plowman*
1397	Pilgrimage of Raymond de Perelhos to St. Patrick's Purgatory
15th century	The Vision of Lazarus
1406	Pilgrimage of William Staunton (or Stranton) to St. Patrick's Purgatory
1411	Pilgrimage of Antonio Mannini and Laurence Rathold of Pasztho to St. Patrick's Purgatory
1494	Pilgrimage of monk of Eymstadt to St. Patrick's Purgatory
1497	Pope Alexander VI closes the cave of St. Patrick's Purgatory
1503	Pope Pius III reopens St. Patrick's Purgatory

Notes

For works that are cited only in the notes, I have supplied full bibliographic information. Works included in the bibliography are cited in brief form here.

Introduction

1. Discussed in *Shamanism: Archaic Techniques of Ecstasy*, tr. Willard Trask (New York, 1964).

2. This famous phrase originates with Plotinus, *Ennead* 6, 9:11.

3. See the works by d'Ancona, Becker, Dana, and Dods cited in the bibliography; on the case for Islamic sources, see Asín Palacios, Cerulli, Muñoz y Sendino, and the critical discussion by Theodore Silverstein, "Dante and the Legend of the Mi'raj."

4. ABC, January 6, 1983.

5. Gregory of Tours, *Historia Francorum libri decem*, ed. Rudolf Buchner, vol. 2, bk. 7, pp. 88–94. I have given a free translation here. For a more literal translation, see the discussion of this vision in chapter 3.

6. *Vision und Visionsliteratur im Mittelalters;* see also the earlier, brief article, "Die *Visionen* des Mittelalters." I am grateful to Bernard McGinn for calling my attention to these works.

7. "The Sentiment of Rationality" can be found in *The Will to Believe and Other Essays in Popular Philosophy*, ed. Frederick H. Burkhardt et al. (Cambridge, Mass., and London, 1979), pp. 70–76.

Chapter 1

1. See André Leroi-Gourhan, *Les religions de la préhistoire* (Paris, 1964); and Johannes Maringer, *The Gods of Prehistoric Man*, tr. Mary Ilford (New York, 1960).

2. On the interpretation of the Paleolithic burial sites discussed below, see Leroi-Gourhan, pp. 37–64; and Maringer, pp. 14–37, 74–89.

3. The use of ethnographic parallels to interpret prehistoric archeological findings is still controversial. In his Ingersoll Lecture at Harvard Divinity School, Wilfred Cantwell Smith cautioned against reading a doctrine of immortality into the evidence for Paleolithic funeral practices. (I am grateful to him for sending me the typescript of this lecture, dated June 15, 1966.) The present discussion is meant as food for thought, rather than as an argument for ethnographic analogy.

4. "Every soul shall taste of death" (Qur'an, Sura 21:35). "What man can live and never see death?" (Ps. 89:48). "For the born, there is no such thing as not dying" (Samyutta Nikaya 2; ed. L. Feer, Pali Text Society, 1884–98).

5. Samuel Johnson: "Depend on it, Sir, when a man knows he is to be hanged in a fortnight, it concentrates his mind wonderfully." In James Boswell's *Life of Johnson*, ed. R. W. Chapman (3rd ed.; Oxford, 1953), 19 September 1777, p. 849.

6. See Henri Breuil, *Four Hundred Centuries of Cave Art*, tr. Mary E. Boyle (Montignac, 1952), along with the works by Leroi-Gourhan and Maringer.

7. See Horst Kirchner, "Ein archäologischer Beitrag zur Urgeschichte des Schamanismus," *Anthropos* 47 (1952): 244–86; and Mircea Eliade, *Shamanism*, pp. 481, 502–4.

8. Art historian Andreas Lommel has gone so far as to declare that the shamanic experience of taking flight from the body, exploring inner worlds, and visualizing the abstract forms of living things is responsible for the very beginnings of artistic representation. *Shamanism: The Beginnings of Art*, tr. Michael Bullock (New York and Toronto, 1967), p. 147.

9. "Nostalgia for Paradise," in *Myths, Dreams, and Mysteries*, tr. Philip Mairet (New York and Evanston, Ill., 1960), p. 61.

10. Eliade, *Shamanism*, pp. 45–53, 135–39.

11. See Knud Rasmussen, *Intellectual Culture of the Igulik Eskimos*, in *Report of the Fifth Thule Expedition, 1921–24*, vol. 7, no. 1 (Copenhagen, 1929), pp. 124 ff.

12. Eliade, *Shamanism*, pp. 262, 275.

13. *Structure and History in Greek Mythology and Ritual* (Berkeley and Los Angeles, 1969), pp. 88–98.

14. John G. Neihardt, *Black Elk Speaks* (New York, 1959). For a revealing glimpse of the Christian influences on Black Elk's memoirs, see Raymond J. DeMallie, *The Sixth Grandfather* (Lincoln, Neb., and London, 1984).

15. My introduction to this subject comes from Jane Smith, who has written and taught on many aspects of Islamic eschatology and conceptions of the afterlife in the world's religious traditions. On rites of passage, the founding investigator is Arnold van Gennep; see especially *The Rites of Passage*, tr. Monika B. Vizedom and Gabrielle L. Caffee (Chicago, 1960), chap. 6, "Initiation Rites," and chap. 8, "Funerals." Van Gennep maintains that some otherworld journey narratives are "only the oral residue of rites of initiation," p. 92, *n.* 1. Victor Turner has applied van Gennep's theory of ritual process to pilgrimage, and relates this to funeral practices and conceptions of the afterlife in his article "Death and the Dead in the Pilgrimage Process" (in *Religious Encounters with Death*, ed. Frank E. Reynolds and Earle H. Waugh pp. 24–39). On apocalyptic movements and texts, see the works by Paul Hanson, George MacRae, Bernard McGinn, and Geo Widengren mentioned below; see also Alan F. Segal's discerning reappraisal of the heavenly ascent pattern in Hellenistic religion ("Heavenly Ascent in Hellenistic Judaism, Early Christianity,

and Their Environment," in *Aufstieg und Niedergang der römischen Welt*, ed. Wolfgang Haase [Berlin and New York, 1980] 2, 23.2, pp. 1333–94). The most comprehensive general study of Western vision literature is by Ernst Benz, *Die Vision: Erfahrungsformen und Bilderwelt*. See also the engaging book by Wendy Doniger O'Flaherty, *Dreams, Illusion, and Other Realities* (Chicago and London, 1984), a study of Indian and Western dream-journeys and transformations which interweaves mythic tales and epistemological theories.

16. Inanna is called Ishtar in Akkadian. See Samuel N. Kramer's translations of the Sumerian and Akkadian versions in *Ancient Near Eastern Texts Relating to the Old Testament*, ed. James B. Pritchard (3rd ed., Princeton, 1969).

17. *The Treasures of Darkness: A History of Mesopotamian Religion* (New Haven and London, 1976), pp. 62–63.

18. Tablet VII (iv), tr. E. A. Speiser in *Ancient Near Eastern Texts*.

19. Tablet X (iii), tr. Speiser.

20. Ps. 6:4–5. See also Ps. 30:9, 88:5–6, 115:17, Eccles. 3:20–21, 9:4–10, Isa. 14:9–17, 38:18.

21. Alexander Heidel points out that biblical passages that speak of Sheol as a narrow, silent house of gloom, are referring, at least metaphorically, to the grave; this imagery can coexist with hope for a brighter postmortem existence for the righteous. *The Gilgamesh Epic and Old Testament Parallels* (Chicago and London, 1946), pp. 173–91.

22. See S. G. F. Brandon, *The Judgment of the Dead*, pp. 6–48; H. Frankfort, *Ancient Egyptian Religion* (New York, 1961), pp. 88–123.

23. See Thorkild Jacobsen, in *Before Philosophy: The Intellectual Adventure of Ancient Man*, ed. H. Frankfort et al. (Baltimore, 1949), pp. 137–40. Gilgamesh is said to have lived close to the time of Khufu (Cheops), for whom the great pyramid at Giza was built.

24. F. L. Griffith, ed. and tr., *Stories of the High Priests of Memphis* (Oxford, 1900), pp. 44–50.

25. *Odyssey* 11, lines 486–91; cf. Eccles. 9:4, "a living dog is better than a dead lion." There are significant differences as well: Hades, though underground, is not described as a "pit"—a common designation for Sheol. Sheol, in contrast to Hades and Arallu, has no ruling god. Arallu is dusty, but Hades and Sheol have marshes and rivers.

26. Paul Foucart, *Les Mystères d'Eleusis* (Paris, 1914), pp. 392 ff.

27. See George E. Mylonas, *Eleusis and the Eleusinian Mysteries* (Princeton, 1961), pp. 118, 264–68.

28. H. G. Evelyn-White, tr., *Hesiod, the Homeric Hymns, and Homerica* (Cambridge, Mass., 1936), lines 480–82. This hymn is thought to date from the seventh century B.C.

29. Quoted by Mylonas, *Eleusis*, p. 264.

30. W. K. C. Guthrie, tr., *Orpheus and Greek Religion* (2nd ed.; London, 1952), pp. 172–73. The convention has been to call these tablets (which appear to date from the fourth to second century B.C.) "Orphic" or "Orphic-Pythagorean"; but our knowledge of the makeup of these esoteric brotherhoods is too scanty to justify treating this as an exact historical designation.

31. *Phaedo* 64, 67, 69cd, 107cd.

32. *Soma equals sema; Kratylos* 400c; *Gorgias* 493–94. Plato's predecessor, Parmenides, presents his quest for knowledge in the guise of a chariot ride to the heavenly realm of a wise goddess.

33. *Gorgias* 523–27; *Phaedo* 112–14.

34. *Phaedo* 114d.

35. *Phaedo* 108.

36. Plutarch, "Concerning the Face Which Appears in the Orb of the Moon" (*Moralia* 920–45), "On the Delays of the Divine Vengeance" (*Moralia* 548–68), "The Sign of Socrates" (*Moralia* 575–98). In "The Divine Vengeance" and "The Sign of Socrates," Plutarch relates two return-from-death tales whose influence on medieval Christian vision literature will be discussed below. On the syncretic forms of astral mysticism at work in these narratives, see Franz Cumont, *After Life in Roman Paganism* (New Haven, 1922).

37. Aeneas and his father, in touring Elysium, pass through "the wide fields of air" (bk. 6, line 887). Later Roman commentators, ignoring the geographic inconsistency, took this as a reference to the Stoic tradition, followed by Plutarch, that places the Elysian fields on the moon. See R. G. Austin, *Aeneidos liber sextus* (Oxford, 1977), Commentary, pp. 272–73. If Alan Segal is right that "the journey up and the journey down are structurally equivalent" in that both patterns serve to mediate between upper and lower worlds, between gods and humans, between life and death, then perhaps such inconsistencies can be forgiven ("Heavenly Ascent," p. 1339).

38. "Heavenly Ascent." Segal's structuralist interpretation of Hellenistic ascent motifs provides a sound alternative to the theories of Reitzenstein and Bousset (the "History of Religions" school), who attempted to derive a vast array of Hellenistic soteriological and cosmological speculations from a Persian astral redeemer myth.

39. The following discussion is indebted to the presentation of Gnostic thought by Hans Jonas, *The Gnostic Religion: The Message of the Alien God and the Beginnings of Christianity* (2nd ed.; Boston, 1963), and Kurt Rudolph, *Gnosis: The Nature and History of Gnosticism*, tr. Robert McLachlan Wilson et al. (Edinburgh and San Francisco, 1983).

40. ". . . easy is the descent to Avernus: night and day the door of gloomy Dis stands open; but to recall thy steps and pass out to the upper air, this is the task, this the toil." *Aeneid* 6, 124–49, tr. H. Rushton Fairclough (London, 1916), p. 514.

41. Epiphanius, quoting a Gnostic Gospel of Philip, cited by Hans Jonas, p. 168. See also the Hermetic treatise known as *Poimandres*, tr. Robert M. Grant, *Gnosticism: A Source Book of Heretical Writings from the Early Christian Period* (New York, 1961), p. 217.

42. See Kurt Rudolph, *Gnosis*, pp. 277–82, and George MacRae, "Apocalyptic Eschatology in Gnosticism," in *Apocalypticism in the Mediterranean World and the Near East*, ed. David Hellholm (Tübingen, 1983), pp. 317–19. This collection of essays faithfully represents the range of current scholarship on apocalyptic literature and movements. Also recommended are the essays in *Visionaries and Their Apocalypses*, ed. Paul Hanson (Philadelphia, 1983); and the introductory work by George W. E. Nickelsburg, *Jewish Literature between the Bible and the Mishnah* (Philadelphia, 1981).

43. On the relationship between eschatology and apocalyptic, see Paul Hanson's introduction to *Visionaries and Their Apocalypses*, p. 12. In the same volume, see Klaus Koch, "What Is Apocalyptic? An Attempt at a Preliminary Definition," pp. 16–37, and John J. Collins, "Apocalyptic Eschatology as Transcendence of Death," pp. 61–84.

44. 4 Ezra 5:4–5, tr. B. M. Metzger, in *Old Testament Pseudepigrapha*, ed. James H. Charlesworth, vol. 1, p. 532.

45. 4 Ezra 7:30–31.

46. See S. H. Hooke, *Middle Eastern Mythology* (Harmondsworth, Eng., 1963), pp. 161–64.

47. 1 En. 14:2, 8–10, tr. Michael A. Knibb, *The Ethiopic Book of Enoch* (Oxford, 1979), vol. 2, pp. 95, 97–98.

48. 1 En. 14–19, 21–25.

49. 1 En. 37–71.

50. *Visions of the End*, p. 15. The classical or formative period of Jewish apocalyptic is usually dated from 200 B.C. to A.D. 100. The fourth century marks the end of apocalypses as a genre in Christian writing, but, as McGinn shows, apocalyptic themes continue to appear in a variety of literary settings throughout the Middle Ages.

51. For an introduction to Merkabah literature, see Gershom G. Scholem, *Major Trends in Jewish Mysticism* (3rd rev. ed.; New York, 1954), pp. 40–79. For a more detailed historical account, see Scholem's *Jewish Gnosticism, Merkabah Mysticism and Talmudic Tradition* (New York, 1965). See also Ithamar Gruenwald, *Apocalyptic and Merkabah Mysticism* (Leiden, 1980); and D. J. Halperin, *The Merkabah in Rabbinic Literature* (New Haven, 1980). In his introduction to 3 Enoch (in *The Old Testament Pseudepigrapha*, ed. Charlesworth, pp. 223–54), P. Alexander concisely presents current scholarship on the evolution of Merkabah traditions, showing how much remains unexplained about the historical interaction of Merkabah mysticism, Gnosticism, and apocalypticism.

52. See Scholem, *Major Trends*, pp. 244–86.

53. See Moses Gaster, tr., the Revelation of Moses, in "Hebrew Visions of Hell and Paradise," *Studies and Texts in Folklore, Magic, Medieval Romance, Hebrew Apocrypha, and Samaritan Archaeology* (London, 1925–28; repr. ed., Jerusalem and New York, 1971), vol. 1, pp. 125–43.

54. Tr. and ed. Dan Ben-Amos and Jerome R. Mintz (Bloomington, Ind., 1970), p. 4.

55. Treated by Howard Rollin Patch, *The Other World*, pp. 27–79.

56. See also the article on "Descent into Hades (Ethnic)" in Hastings's *Encyclopedia of Religion and Ethics*.

57. Martin Haug and E. W. West, ed. and tr., *The Book of Arda Viraf* (Bombay and London, 1872). This work was composed late enough to be influenced by Jewish and Christian apocryphal literature. On Zoroastrian eschatology, see R. C. Zaehner, *The Dawn and Twilight of Zoroastrianism* (London, 1961); Mary Boyce, *Zoroastrians: Their Religious Beliefs and Practices* (London, 1979) and *A History of Zoroastrianism* (Leiden, 1975), vol. 1; and J. Pavry, *The Zoroastrian Doctrine of a Future Life from Death to Individual Judgment* (New York, 1926).

58. Traditions concerning the Prophet's ascension have been linked to brief indications in the Qur'an, Sura 17:1, 81:19–25, 53:1–18. The oldest connected account occurs in the biography by Ibn Ishaq (d. A.D. 727), tr. A. Guillaume, *The Life of Muhammad* (Lahore, Karachi, and Dacca, 1955), pp. 181–87. One of the most popular renditions comes from al-Ghaiti (d. A.D. 1574), tr. Arthur Jeffery, *A Reader on Islam* (The Hague, 1962), pp. 621–39. See the articles on *Mi'radj* and *Isra'* in the *Shorter Encyclopedia of Islam*. Tor Andrae discusses the ascension in his masterful study of Muhammad as a figure of legend, *Die Person Muhammeds in Lehre und Glauben seiner Gemeinde* (Stockholm, 1918), pp. 39–85. I would like to thank Wil-

liam A. Graham, Jr., for pointing this out to me and giving me his own (unpublished) translation.

59. See B. Schrieke, "Die Himmelsreise Muhammeds," *Der Islam* 6 (1916): 1–30; and J. R. Porter, "Muhammad's Journey to Heaven," in *The Journey to the Other World*, ed. H. R. Ellis Davidson, pp. 1–26.

60. Parallels have been noted to the ascent narratives in 2 Enoch, 2 Baruch, the Ascension of Isaiah, and elsewhere in Judeo-Christian apocalyptic literature; other scholars, in turn, have investigated the influence of mi'raj narratives on medieval Christian visions, Dante included. In addition, the Zoroastrian Book of Arda Viraz plays a part in several different attempts to reconstruct the transmission of otherworld journey motifs in later Muslim and Christian works. Of course, there is a natural tendency for experts to emphasize the region or period with which they are most familiar; thus, biblical scholars focus on the Semitic background of apocalypses and otherworld journeys, Iranologists such as Widengren and Bousset trace the visionary journey and many other eschatological themes back to Persia, and classicists such as A. Dieterich derive visits to hell from the Greek *nekyia*. Fortunately, it is not necessary for our purposes to untangle the web of historical influences; for an introduction to some of the problems involved, however, see James Barr, "The Question of Religious Influence: The Case of Zoroastrianism, Judaism, and Christianity," *Journal of the American Academy of Religion* 53 (June 1985): 201–35.

61. Geo Widengren, the historian of Iranian religion, maintains that these legends follow a pattern—the ascent of a divine messenger, the giving of a heavenly book—which has its roots in ancient Near Eastern myths of sacral kingship, which surfaced in Judeo-Christian and Zoroastrian depictions of prophetic consecration, and which emerged in Manichaean and Shi'ite literature as a way of validating claims for the esoteric transmission of religious authority. See *The Ascension of the Apostle and the Heavenly Book* (Uppsala, 1950) and *Muhammad, the Apostle of God, and His Ascension* (Uppsala, 1955).

62. Guillaume, *The Life of Muhammad*, p. 185.

63. *The Precious Pearl*, attributed to al-Ghazali, tr. Jane Idleman Smith (Missoula, Mont., 1979). See also Jane Idleman Smith and Yvonne Yazbeck Haddad, *The Islamic Understanding of Death and Resurrection* (Albany, 1981) p. 39; and Ragnar Eklund, *Life between Death and Resurrection according to Islam* (Uppsala, 1941).

64. See Annemarie Schimmel, *Mystical Dimensions of Islam* (Chapel Hill, N.C., 1975), pp. 148, 218–20; and Tor Andrae, *Die Person Muhammeds*, pp. 79–85.

65. See Reynold A. Nicholson, *Rumi, Poet and Mystic* (London, 1950), pp. 52–53, 102, 103, 131, 186.

66. Tr. S. Radhakrishnan, *The Principal Upanishads* (London, 1953), pp. 593–648.

67. Chuang Tzu, chap. 21, quoted by Max Kaltenmark, *Lao Tzu and Taoism*, tr. Roger Greaves (Stanford, 1969), p. 65.

68. Ibid., p. 117. See also Edward H. Schafer, "A Trip to the Moon," *Parabola* 8 (October 1983): 68–81.

69. See Edward Conze, ed., *Buddhist Scriptures* (Harmondsworth, Eng., 1959), pt. 3, "Other Worlds and Future Times," pp. 221–36.

70. The Mahavastu, tr. J. J. Jones, in *Sacred Books of the Buddhists* (London, 1949), no. 16, p. 6.

71. Kenneth K. S. Ch'en, *Buddhism in China* (Princeton, 1964), pp. 282–83, 288.

72. The descent of Izanagi and Izanami appears in the oldest written chron-

icle of Japan, known as Kojiki 1:7, 9. Tr. Basil Hall Chamberlain, "Ko-ji-ki, or Records of Ancient Matters," *Transactions of the Asiatic Society of Japan* 10 (1882), Supplement. On the shamanic visionary journey in Japan, see Carmen Blacker, *The Catalpa Bow: A Study of Shamanistic Practices in Japan* (London, 1975), pp. 186–234.

 73. *The Tibetan Book of the Dead*, available in translations by W. Y. Evans-Wentz (London, Oxford, and New York, 1960) and by Francesca Fremantle and Chögyam Trungpa (Boulder, Colo., and London, 1975). See also Lati Rinbochay and Jeffrey Hopkins, *Death, Intermediate State and Rebirth in Tibetan Buddhism* (London and Valois, N.Y., 1979).

Chapter 2

 1. St. Augustine, *Tractatus in Johannem* 98, *PL* 35:1885. Theodore Silverstein has meticulously traced the history of the Vision of St. Paul and its influence on otherworld vision literature in the West; see especially his *Visio Sancti Pauli: The History of the Apocalypse in Latin Together with Nine Texts*. For the long Latin version I have followed the edition by M. R. James in *Apocrypha anecdota*, vol. 1; this text is available in English translation (by Andrew Rutherfurd) in *The Ante-Nicene Fathers*, vol. 9. For the medieval Latin redactions, I have consulted the texts edited by Silverstein and by Herman Brandes. An English translation of Redaction 4 (early twelfth century) is included as an appendix in my dissertation.

 2. This combines the bottomless pit of Rev. 9 and 20 with the scroll "sealed with seven seals" of Rev. 5.

 3. Redaction 4, paraphrasing *Aeneid* 6:616–27. See Silverstein, pp. 65–66.

 4. *Visio Sancti Pauli*, p. 3.

 5. My translations from this work are based on the Latin edition by Umberto Moricca. An English version, translated by Odo John Zimmerman, is available in the Fathers of the Church series.

 6. *Dialogues* 4:37.

 7. Ibid.

 8. Evidence for the universality of lore concerning death by mistaken identity can be found in Stith Thompson's *Motif Index*, vol. 3, F0–F199. In our own day, the story has come to life on the screen in "Here Comes Mr. Jordan" and "Heaven Can Wait."

 9. Stephen who died and revived, not Stephen the blacksmith.

 10. *Dialogues* 4:38.

 11. *Dialogues* 4:43.

 12. On Gregory's eschatology, see Milton M. Gatch, "The Fourth Dialogue of Gregory the Great: Some Problems of Interpretation."

 13. I am using the dual-language edition by Bertram Colgrave and R. A. B. Mynors, but supplying my own translations of the Latin text.

 14. *Bede's Ecclesiastical History*, ed. Colgrave and Mynors, p. 488.

 15. Ibid., p. 488.

 16. In the *Dialogues*; quoted by Benedicta Ward, "Miracles and History," in *Famulus Christi*, ed. Gerald Bonner (London, 1976), pp. 70–76.

 17. See St. John D. Seymour, *Irish Visions of the Other World* and "The Eschatology of the Early Irish Church." On Anglo-Saxon eschatology, see Milton M. Gatch, *Preaching and Theology in Anglo-Saxon England: Aelfric and Wulfstan*

(Toronto and Buffalo, 1977). On the difference between a purgatorial state and purgatory as a place, see Jacques Le Goff, *The Birth of Purgatory*.

18. See *The Birth of Purgatory*, p. 228.

19. In *Tours of Hell*, Martha Himmelfarb points out that studies of apocalyptic literature early in this century were flawed by the assumption that the chronology of known texts is equivalent to the history of a literary tradition; Himmelfarb maintains that this fallacy helped to support a habitual overemphasis on classical precedents for the motif of visits to hell.

20. During the Middle Ages, the Purgatory was situated on the largest of the islands in Lough Derg (Saints' Island); its present, and possibly original, location is on the smaller Station Island. On the history of Lough Derg, see the works by Ludwig Bieler, Shane Leslie, Daniel O'Connor, and St. John D. Seymour cited in the bibliography. On the legend of St. Patrick's Purgatory as a literary tradition, see George Philip Krapp, Henry Leigh Douglas Ward, and C. M. van der Zanden. My article on "St. Patrick's Purgatory: Pilgrimage Motifs in a Medieval Otherworld Vision" (*Journal of the History of Ideas* 46 [Oct.–Dec. 1985]: 467–85) provides a longer and more fully documented version of the present discussion.

21. *Image and Pilgrimage in Christian Culture*, p. 131. The Turners devote an engaging chapter of this book to the modern pilgrimage to Lough Derg.

22. Almost nothing is known about the author; later writers, following a sheer guess made by Matthew of Paris, expand the "H." to "Henricus." The date of the *Treatise* is still in doubt. F. W. Locke argues that it was composed between 1208 and 1215 ("A New Date for the Composition of the *Tractatus de Purgatorio Sancti Patricii*"). St. John D. Seymour, Marianne Mörner, and others believe that the treatise was composed after 1186, the year in which the relics of St. Patrick were formally translated to Downpatrick, but before the thirteenth century. The question of dates is discussed in my article on "St. Patrick's Purgatory."

23. Accounts of this pilgrimage site appear as homage to St. Patrick in the chronicles of Roger of Wendover, the *Golden Legend* of Jacobus de Voragine, the *Early South English Legendary*, and the *Catalogue of Saints* of Peter de Natalibus.

24. References to the Purgatory in *exempla* books of the thirteenth through fifteenth centuries are mentioned in my article on "St. Patrick's Purgatory."

25. On the pilgrimage from the thirteenth through the fifteenth centuries, see Ludovico Frati, "Il Purgatorio di S. Patrizio secondo Stefano di Bourbon e Umberto di Roma" and "Tradizioni storiche del Purgatorio di San Patrizio"; Hippolytus Delehaye, "La pèlerinage de Laurent de Pasztho au Purgatoire de S. Patrice"; and J. P. Mahaffy, "Two Early Tours in Ireland."

26. *Hamlet*, I, 5, ll.146–38.

27. Leslie, *St. Patrick's Purgatory*, p. 1.

28. Unless otherwise noted, my discussion and translation of passages from the *Treatise* are based on the oldest extant version, which was edited by C. M. van der Zanden from a manuscript in the library of the University of Utrecht. This edition will hereafter be designated as "Utrecht." Other Latin and vernacular versions of the *Treatise* are listed under "The Purgatory of St. Patrick" in the bibliography.

29. Utrecht, p. 23.

30. This phrase occurs in the version given by Roger of Wendover, *Flores historiarum*, ed. H. O. Coxe, vol. 2, p. 257.

31. On pilgrimage as an assigned juridical or ecclesiastical punishment, see Jonathan Sumption, *Pilgrimage: An Image of Mediaeval Religion*.

32. Utrecht, p. 9.

32. Utrecht, p. 9.

33. For dragons, cf. the Vision of Adamnán and medieval versions of the Vision of St. Paul, discussed by Silverstein, *Visio Sancti Pauli*, p. 66. Graded immersion is an especially common motif, occurring in the Apocalypse of Peter, the long Latin version of the Vision of St. Paul, and the visions of Sunniulf, the Monk of Wenlock, Charles the Fat, and Alberic. Boiling cauldrons occur in the Vision of the Boy William. The *Treatise* differs from many of these earlier accounts, however, in that it makes no attempt to correlate the level of immersion to the degree or kind of sin; but it is interesting to note that a sixteenth-century description of pilgrimage to Lough Derg includes a penitential exercise of graded immersion in the lake (see J. P. Mahaffy, "Two Early Tours," p. 12). The wheel appears in the Apocalypse of Peter, the Sibylline Oracles, and Redaction 4 of the Vision of St. Paul.

34. H. R. Patch notes the frequent repetition of negative phrases in descriptions of paradise, *The Other World*, p. 322.

35. Le Goff writes, "In Purgatory, a liturgical chain was forged binding the dead to the living." *The Birth of Purgatory*, p. 153.

36. Utrecht, p. 22.

37. Utrecht, p. 23.

38. See Ernest J. Becker, *A Contribution to the Comparative Study of Medieval Visions of Heaven and Hell*, p. 92; and Elizabeth Willson, *The Middle English Legends of Visits to the Other World*, p. 25. Caesarius of Heisterbach describes a Cistercian funeral during which one of the onlookers had a vision of white-clad men carrying the soul to heaven as white monks carried the body in procession to the grave (*Dialogue on Miracles* 11:8).

39. Discussed in chapter 5.

40. This eschatological use of the pilgrimage motif was carried on by the Anglo-Saxon homilists. See Gatch, *Preaching and Theology in Anglo-Saxon England*, pp. 66, 104.

41. See R. W. Southern, *The Making of the Middle Ages* (London, 1953), p. 222.

42. Utrecht, p. 21.

43. See J. A. Herbert, *Catalogue of Romances*, vol. 3, 596; F. C. Tubach, *Index exemplorum*, nos. 3213, 3215, 3232, 3234, 3660, 3898, 4001, 4523, 4544; Jonathan Sumption, *Pilgrimage*, p. 296; and Le Goff, *The Birth of Purgatory*, pp. 82, 177–81, 243, 269, 277, 293–94.

44. "Death and the Dead in the Pilgrimage Process," in Reynolds and Waugh, *Religious Encounters with Death*, p. 35.

45. Tr. Seymour in *St. Patrick's Purgatory*, p. 58.

46. "Veneranda dies," sermon (incorrectly attributed to Pope Calixtus II) for the vigil of December 30, c. A.D. 1125, in *Liber S. Jacobi, Codex Calixtinus*, ed. Walter Muir Whitehill (Santiago de Compostela, 1944), vol. 1, bk. 1, chap. 17, p. 157.

47. Cf. Antonio Mannini in L. Frati, "Il Purgatorio di S. Patrizio," p. 158; Louis de Sur in ibid., pp. 74–75; Raymond de Perelhos in O'Sullivan-Beare, *Historiae Compendium*, p. 24; Laurence Rathold de Pasztho, ed. Delehaye, p. 50; George Crissaphan in Seymour, *St. Patrick's Purgatory*, p. 28; William Staunton in Krapp, p. 59; and Shane Leslie, *Saint Patrick's Purgatory: A Record from History and Literature*, pp. 51–61.

48. "Veneranda dies," p. 152.

49. Daniel O'Connor, *Saint Patrick's Purgatory: Lough Derg*, p. 105.

Chapter 3

1. Drythelm, Fursa, Barontus, the Monk of Wenlock, and Wetti are absent for one night; Thespesius and Gunthelm for three days; and Alberic for nine days.

2. *Visio Baronti*, ed. W. Levison, p. 380 (reading "spem" as "spm," an abbreviation for "spiritum"). In other contexts, *anima* is the animating principle, while *spiritus* is reserved for speaking of the higher powers of the soul.

3. Ibid.

4. On the history of Christian attitudes toward death, see the works of Ariès, Boase, Gatch, and Huizinga cited in the bibliography, and the essays in *La mort au moyen âge*.

5. Discussed by Louise Dudley, *The Egyptian Elements in the Legend of the Body and Soul*; M. R. James, *The Testament of Abraham*, pp. 1–76; and Th. Batiouchkof, "Le Débat de l'Ame et du Corps," *Romania* 20 (1891): 1–55, 513–78. An assortment of Coptic and Syriac Christian narratives on the two deaths and the soul's experience in the other world can be found in the massive work by Violet MacDermot, *The Cult of the Seer in the Ancient* Middle East (Berkeley and Los Angeles, 1971).

6. The motif appears in a weaker form in the Greek and Latin versions; *Visio Sancti Pauli*, p. 24. For Islamic parallels, see Jane Idleman Smith and Yvonne Yazbeck Haddad, *The Islamic Understanding of Death and Resurrection* (Albany, 1981), pp. 37–39. Al-Ghazali reports that "the good soul slips out like the jetting of water from a water-skin, but the profligate's spirit squeaks out like a skewer from wet wool," *The Precious Pearl*, tr. Jane Idleman Smith (Missoula, Mont. 1979), p. 22.

7. The Testament of Abraham appears to have been originally written in Greek by a Jewish author living in Egypt c. A.D. 100; in its present form, however, it shows signs of Christian influence. This is the story as told by the longer of the two Greek recensions; both versions are available in English translations by E. P. Sanders in *The Old Testament Pseudepigrapha*, ed. Charlesworth, and by M. E. Stone. See discussion of this text by M. R. James, in his introduction to the Greek edition, and G. W. Nickelsburg, Jr., *Jewish Literature between the Bible and the Mishnah* (Philadelphia, 1983), pp. 248–53. The Life of Adam and Eve, the Death of Moses, and the History of Joseph the Carpenter also contain episodes of refusal to die; see Samuel E. Loewenstamm, "The Death of Moses" and "The Testament of Abraham and the Texts concerning Moses' Death," in *Studies on the Testament of Abraham*, ed. G. W. Nickelsburg, Jr. (Missoula, Mont., 1976), pp. 185–225.

8. Margaret Miles finds evidence of an incarnational spirituality, however, even in patristic authors and ascetic figures who have traditionally been viewed as violently dualistic and hostile to the body's claims: *Fullness of Life: Historical Foundations for a New Asceticism* (Philadelphia, 1981).

9. *PL* 73:1012. Book 4 of Gregory's *Dialogues* reports several instances of good deaths accompanied by music.

10. Aelfric, *Homilies*, ed. Thorpe, vol. 2, pp. 460–66; Jacques de Vitry, *Exempla*, ed. Crane, no. 132, p. 59. See also Seymour, "The Bringing Forth of the Soul in Irish Literature," p. 19.

11. Sermon 69 of *Sermones ad Fratres in Eremo*, *PL* 40:1355–57. Another Latin version is edited by Th. Batiouchkof in *Romania* 20 (1891): 576–78.

12. Letter 10, ed. Reinhold Rau, p. 42.

13. *Dialogue on Miracles*, 4:39.

14. See Eleanor Kellogg Henningham, *An Early Latin Debate of the Body*

and Soul. On popular religious aspects of the Middle English poems, see Robert W. Ackerman, "The Debate of the Body and Soul and Parochial Christianity," *Speculum* 37 (1962):541–65.

15. *The Departing Soul's Address to the Body,* tr. S. W. Singer, pp. 5–6.

16. Ibid., p. 17.

17. *The Debate between the Body and the Soul,* tr. F. J. Child, pp. 17–18. See Thomas Wright, ed., in *The Latin Poems Commonly Attributed to Walter Mapes* (London, 1841), p. 335.

18. "Soul and Body," tr. R. K. Gordon in *Anglo-Saxon Poetry* (New York, 1962), pp. 282–83.

19. *The Departing Soul's Address,* tr. S. W. Singer, p. 1.

20. *Dialogue on Miracles,* 11:1. Augustine similarly describes death as "bitter to the senses and contrary to nature," *City of God* 13:6.

21. Ed. Comper, p. 6.

22. *Visio Baronti,* p. 380.

23. Ibid.

24. Ibid., p. 392.

25. Irenaeus, *Adversus haereses,* bk. 2, chap. 34; Augustine, *De Genesi ad litteram,* bk. 10, chaps. 24, 39; Tertullian, *De anima,* chaps. 3, 7.

26. Tr. W. A. Craigie, chap. 14, p. 223.

27. Quoted by Dudley, *Egyptian Elements,* p. 125. As Dudley points out, this particular soul is green from the stain of avarice. Thespesius sees souls tinted various colors according to their passions who become clear through expiation and punishment. On the association of colors with sins, see Bloomfield, *The Seven Deadly Sins,* and Silverstein, *Visio Sancti Pauli,* pp. 74–75.

28. For souls as birds (a more common motif in Celtic and Islamic lore), see Thespesius; Gregory, *Dialogues* 4:11; and Barontus. On the fiery ball, see Gregory, *Dialogues* 2:35, 4:7.

29. *Dialogue on Miracles,* 1:32.

30. Ibid., 4:39. These descriptions of the soul as a sphere may reflect a classical belief that the sphere is the perfect form, the proper shape for souls as for the divine essence. Cf. Parmenides, Fragment 8:43; and Boethius, *The Consolation of Philosophy* 3:12.

31. In using the term "Copernican revolution," I am putting Kant's famous metaphor for critical philosophy to an application that he would not have been likely to anticipate or endorse. But the expression is useful for portraying any radical reversal of perspective in which an object or power that once appeared to be peripheral comes to be seen as a central force around which everything else must orbit.

32. The phrase is Coleridge's, taken out of context. Coleridge had in mind the refusal of mechanistic philosophers to acknowledge any realities that cannot be represented by a clear and distinct mental image, but he would be the last one to turn the advocacy of spiritual philosophy into a veto on the exercise of imagination.

33. See Stephen D. Crites, "The Narrative Quality of Experience," *Journal of the American Academy of Religion* 39 (September 1971): 291–311, and "Angels We Have Heard," in *Religion as Story,* ed. James B. Wiggins (New York, 1975), pp. 23–64; Richard R. Niebuhr, *Experiential Religion* (New York, 1972); Amos Wilder, *Theopoetic: Theology and the Religious Imagination* (Philadelphia, 1976).

34. *Dialogue on Miracles,* 7:43.

35. See Bloomfield, *The Seven Deadly Sins,* pp. 18, 23; Franz Cumont, *The*

After Life in Roman Paganism (New Haven, 1922), pp. 106–7; Plato, *Gorgias* 523C–E; and the the hymn attributed to Zarathustra (Yasna 51:13, tr. Duchesne-Guillemin) to the effect that the soul will be stripped naked when it reaches the otherworld bridge.

36. Cf. Zoroastrian traditions on the three-day period during which the soul hovers over the body (R. C. Zaehner, *The Dawn and Twilight of Zoroastrianism*, pp. 302–21). For Islamic parallels, see Smith and Haddad, p. 50.

37. On the role of the guide in tour apocalypses, see Martha Himmelfarb, *Tours of Hell.*

38. Ed. Colgrave and Mynors, p. 488. See also the visions of Laisrén, Wetti, the Boy William, and Tundal.

39. Cf. the Vision of Tundal.

40. This pattern (perhaps originally derived from apocalyptic narratives, such as the Apocalypse of Peter) occurs in the visions of Gunthelm, Orm, the Boy William, the Monk of Eynsham, and Tundal. On the question-and-answer format in tour apocalypses, see Himmelfarb, *Tours of Hell.*

41. *Bede's Ecclesiastical History*, ed. Colgrave and Mynors, p. 490; the Vision of St. Paul has a similar exchange.

42. Kuno Meyer, ed., pp. 118–19.

43. David Traill, *Walahfrid Strabo's Visio Wettini.* Rotcharius and the Poor Woman, whose visions antedate and seem to have influenced that of Wetti, also see Charlemagne in torment.

44. H. E. Salter, *Eynsham Cartulary*, vol. 2, pp. 275–76, 344.

45. On the progression from *genius* to patron saint in late antique Christianity, see Peter Brown, *The Cult of the Saints* (Chicago, 1981), chap. 3, "The Invisible Companion," pp. 50 68.

46. See discussion by Traill, *Visio Wettini.* Cf. the *Shepherd* of Hermas, Mandatum 6: "Two guardian spirits *(Genii)* abide with man: one a [spirit] of righteousness, and one of iniquity."

47. Cf. the Vision of Tundal: "Ever since your birth, I have been with you always and everywhere, and you never have heeded my counsel," ed. Wagner, p. 11. This scene also calls to mind the Vision of St. Paul, in which souls are rebuked or applauded by their guardian angels and animating spirits.

48. *Visio Baronti*, p. 386.

49. As in the visions of Barontus, Fursa, the monk of Wenlock, and Laisrén.

50. *Bede's Ecclesiastical History*, ed. Colgrave and Mynors, p. 490.

51. Ed. Wagner, p. 34.

52. Gregory describes Benedict's ascension in *Dialogues* 2:27; for the vision of a ship, see *Dialogues* 4:36. On the ship as funereal symbol, see H. R. Ellis Davidson, "The Ship of the Dead," in *The Journey to the Other World*, pp. 73–89.

53. This is a common theme in the eschatological lore of many traditions; cf. the Bhagavad Gita 7:30, 8:5, 12:8.

54. The Vision of Wetti [Heito], ed. Dümmler, chap. 6, p. 269. The *via amoena* may be considered a subset of the *loca amoena*, identified by Ernst Robert Curtius as one of the *topoi* of medieval rhetoric, in *European Literature and the Latin Middle Ages*, tr. Willard Trask (New York, 1953), pp. 195–200.

55. "Ibant obscuri sola sub nocte per umbram . . ." *Aeneid* 6:268.

56. *Bede's Ecclesiastical History*, Colgrave and Mynors, p. 490. Cf. the Vision of the Monk of Eynsham, ed. Salter, chap. 15, p. 304.

57. Matt. 7:13, 14. The idea goes back to Prov. 2, 8:20, 16, where the "right way" and "path of the just" is contrasted to the "dark way" and "path to death"; cf. Jer. 21:8. M. R. James quotes a Latin fragment of the early Christian *Didache*, in which the theme is taken up with reference to guardian sprits: "In the world there are two paths, of life and of death, of light and of darkness. In these paths are stationed two Angels, one of righteousness, the other of iniquity" (*The Testament of Abraham*, p. 14). For classical parallels, such as the Pythagorean "Y," to which Plato (*Gorgias* 524a), Cicero (*De re publica* 6:12), and Vergil (*Aeneid* 6:540) allude, see Cumont, *The After Life*, p. 76. In Egyptian mortuary literature, an intriguing precedent is the Book of the Two Ways in the Coffin Texts. The Upanishads and later Hindu scriptures speak of a path of light leading from the fire of cremation, sacrifice or yogic austerities to reunion with *brahman*, the ultimate, and a path of darkness, passing from the smoke of the cremation fire to the moon, before returning to life on earth (Chandogya Upanishad 4:15, 5:10; Bhagavad Gita 8:24–27; for the "narrow path," see Brhad-aranyaka Upanishad 4:4).

58. *Dialogue on Miracles*, 4:53. Cf. the Vision of Gottschalk.

59. H. R. Patch summarizes the methods of approach to the other world, pointing out the classical, biblical, Celtic, and Germanic sources for topographic imagery.

60. See Silverstein, *Visio Sancti Pauli*, pp. 115–16, n. 77. Gregory refers to this idea in book 4 of the *Dialogues*, but identifies the lower infernal with hell and the upper infernal with earth. After the twelfth century, however, Augustine's discussion of the two levels of hell was taken as an endorsement of the doctrine of purgatory.

61. *The Birth of Purgatory*, p. 4; see pp. 154–65, 225–26, and elsewhere. Le Goff, drawing on the work of Georges Duby and, less directly, Georges Dumézil, offers a structuralist interpretation of the historical records of belief in purgatory. Some historians feel that Le Goff attaches exaggerated importance to the late appearance (after 1170) of the word *purgatorium* as a substantive, thereby underestimating indications of a localized image of purgatory in earlier documents that do not happen to use this term; see R. W. Southern's review, "Between Heaven and Hell," *Times Literary Supplement* (June 18, 1982): 651–52.

62. *Dialogue on Miracles*, 12:38.

63. Gregory of Tours, *History of the Franks*, ed. Buchner, vol. 2, bk. 7, pp. 90–92.

64. *Bede's Ecclesiastical History*, ed. Colgrave and Mynors, p. 270.

65. Ed. Cancellieri, p. 148.

66. Ibid., p. 162.

67. See St. John D. Seymour, *Irish Visions*, p. 152. The same pattern occurs in accounts of Muhammad's heavenly journey.

68. See Bloomfield, *The Seven Deadly Sins*.

69. *The Book of the Secrets of Enoch* (Oxford, 1896), pp. xxxix, xlii.

70. In this and other respects, Irish vision literature differs from that of England and the Continent because of the greater influence of apocryphal literature on Irish monastic spirituality. In particular, a fragmentary Priscillianist apocryphon has been identified as the source of heavenly punishments in Irish vision literature. See Dom Donatien de Bruyne, "Fragments retrouvés d'apocryphes Priscillianistes," *Revue Bénédictine* (July 1907): 318–35; M. R. James, "Irish Apocrypha"; and St. John D. Seymour, "Notes on Apocrypha in Ireland."

Chapter 4

1. *The Judgment of the Dead*, p. 146.

2. S. T. Coleridge, *Biographia Literaria*, ed. J. Shawcross (London, 1907), vol. 1, chap. 10, p. 107, chap. 13, p. 249.

3. Discussed herein in chapter 3. See George W. E. Nickelsburg, Jr., "Eschatology in the Testament of Abraham: A Study of the Judgment Scene in the Two Recensions," in *Studies on the Testament of Abraham* (Missoula, Mont., 1976), pp. 23–64.

4. This episode is the source for Thurkill's Adam, who weeps in one eye and laughs in the other. M. R. James points out, in an introduction to his edition of the Greek text, that the Testament of Abraham was read at St. Alban's Abbey during the time in which the Vision of Thurkill was composed there. The image of Adam alternately laughing on the right side and weeping on the left as he sits in judgment also occurs in a version of the mi'raj legend. See A. Jeffery, ed., *Islam: Muhammad and His Religion* (Indianapolis, Ind., 1958), p. 40.

5. Fiery river: the Sibylline Oracles and the visions of St. Paul, Ezra, Adamnán, Alberic, and Owen. Fetid river: Gregory's account of the vision of the soldier in Rome. Knives: the Vision of Gottschalk. Locked gate: the visions of Barontus, Adamnán, and Edmund of Eynsham. High wall: visions in the Drythelm line; also the Carolingian Vision of the Poor Woman. Mountain: the visions of St. Paul, Charles the Fat, Laisrén, Wetti, and Owen.

6. Quoted by St. John D. Seymour, *Irish Visions*, p. 56.

7. For biblical references to testing or refining by fire, see Ps. 11:7; Ps. 66:10–12; Ezek. 22:18–22; 1 Cor. 3:12–15; 1 Pet. 1:7; Rev. 3:18.

8. R. C. Zaehner, *The Dawn and Twilight of Zoroastrianism* (London, 1961), p. 318. Mary Boyce, *Zoroastrians* (London, 1979), pp. 26–28. The idea that only the wicked will feel pain is put forth by the Pahlavi (Middle Persian) text called the *Bundahishn*, tr. E. W. West, in *Sacred Books of the East*, vol. 5, Pahlavi Texts, part 1 (Oxford, 1880).

9. Gregory, *Dialogues* 4:45.

10. *Bede's Ecclesiastical History*, ed. Colgrave and Mynors, p. 272. The first sentence echoes Isa. 43:2, which is not explicitly eschatological; rather, it compares the Babylonian exile to a purificatory trial by fire.

11. Ed. A. T. Quiller-Couch, ed., *The Oxford Book of English Verse, 1250–1900* (Oxford, 1901), no. 381. This poem is believed to be based in part on the early-thirteenth-century Norse vision ballad, *Draumkvaede*.

12. See Franz Cumont, *After Life in Roman Paganism* (New Haven, 1922), p. 185.

13. In this case, falsehood, covetousness, discord, and lack of concern for the weak. Cf. the Vision of St. Paul, Redaction 3, and Augustine, *Ennarratio in Psalmum* 57, PL 36:688, mentioned by Silverstein, *Visio Sancti Pauli*, p. 74.

14. *Dialogues* 4:41.

15. *Summa contra Gentiles*, chap. 90.

16. *Dialogues* 4:41.

17. See Le Goff, *The Birth of Purgatory*; and Seymour, *Irish Visions*, p. 55.

18. "Bridge" in *Hastings' Encyclopedia of Religion and Ethics*, 1953 ed., vol. 2, pp. 848–57. This discussion is indebted to Knight's survey. Since writing this section on bridges, I have found a lucid treatment of the subject by Peter Dinzelbacher

and Harald Kleinschmidt, "Seelenbrücke und Brückenbau im mittelalterlichen England," *Numen* 31 (1984): 242–87.

19. This is an arch game, known in Germany as "Golden Bridge" and in France as "Heaven and Hell," in which a victim is captured and interrogated. The prisoner may be asked to choose between heaven and hell, or to demonstrate in some way his allegiance with the angels or the demons. See William Wells Newell, *Games and Songs of American Children* (New York and London, 1884; rev. ed., 1902), pp. 204–11. Many arch games seem to be related, as Alice Bertha Gomme shows, to the practice of consecrating a new city or house through ritual sacrifice. *The Traditional Games of England, Scotland, and Ireland*, 2 vols. (London, 1894–98). Just as the bridge sacrifice is a specialized form of foundation sacrifice, so is the bridge game a subset of the general category of arch games. Its special otherworld significance is revealed by an "old rhyme" quoted by G. G. King: "On all souls' night on London bridge,/ The quick and dead together walk,/ The quick and dead together talk" (*The Way of St. James*, vol. 3, p. 271). But "London Bridge" is only one of many traditional games that are based on otherworld journey lore. In hop-scotch, for example, the player hops while kicking a stone through ten or so divisions of a labyrinth (in Australian versions) or tomb-shaped ground plan whose last three sections are known in Italy as Inferno, Purgatorio, and Paradiso. The transmission of otherworld journey motifs through games would make a fascinating study in itself.

20. See King, *The Way of St. James*, vol. 1, pp. 100–101.

21. See Jacobus de Voragine, *The Golden Legend*, St. James; King, *The Way of St. James*, vol. 1, pp. 82–84; vol. 3, p. 541.

22. Yasna 51:13, Duchesne-Guillemin.

23. Described in the Pahlavi text *Dastan-i Menok-i Krat*, tr. Zaehner, *Dawn and Twilight*, pp. 302–5.

24. Yasna 46:11.

25. In Zoroastrian tradition, fire is a supreme symbol of Ahura Mazda and a sacrament linking heaven and earth. Zoroastrian dualism prohibits the presence of such a venerated element in the realm of punishment. Therefore, although fire appears in a cathartic capacity in the Zoroastrian apocalypse, the Zoroastrian hell is cold and gloomy. A similar line of thought is evident in Christian vision narratives that describe the fire of doom as smoky, giving heat but not light.

26. Matt. 13:30; Gregory, *Dialogues* 4:36. Also cited in the Vision of Barontus, p. 391.

27. *Dialogues* 4:38; based on Matt. 7:14.

28. Gregory of Tours, *History of the Franks*, ed. Buchner, 4:33, p. 240.

29. From a Latin *Visio Esdrae* found in a twelfth-century manuscript first edited by Adolfo Mussafia and more recently by Otto Wahl, in *Apocalypsis Esdrae, Apocalypsis Sedrach, Visio Beati Esdrae* (Leiden, 1977), pp. 54–55. The bridge episode is a medieval interpolation into this Latin version of what was originally a Greek apocalypse. Peter Dinzelbacher demonstrates the influence of the *Visio Esdrae* on the Vision of Alberic in "Die Vision Alberichs und die Esdras-Apokryphe," *Studien und Mitteilungen zur Geschichte des Benediktiner-Ordens und seiner Zweige* 87 (1976): 435–42.

30. Some rather heavy-handed attempts have been made to derive the medieval Christian test-bridge, along with other features of the otherworld landscape, from Islamic sources; but recent investigation of apocalyptic literature suggests that Christian influence on Islamic otherworld imagery is equally likely. See the works of

Miguel Asín Palacios and Enrico Cerulli. For criticism of their arguments, see Silverstein, "The Vision of St. Paul: New Links and Patterns in the Western Tradition" and "Dante and the Legend of the *Mi'raj*: the Problem of Islamic Influence on the Christian Literature of the Otherworld." Also on this subject are the works by Olschki and Muñoz y Sendino cited in the bibliography.

31. H. R. Patch's term in *The Other World*, p. 323.

32. This episode, with its threefold division of souls, appears in the latter part of the Vision, designated Adamnán II by Seymour and dated to the tenth century or earlier. The fourfold division is an Anglo-Saxon tradition, based on a statement by St. Augustine; it occurs in the visions of Drythelm and the monk of Wenlock, the first section of the Vision of Adamnán (usually considered later than Adamnán II), and the Vision of Tundal, which appears to depend on Adamnán. See Seymour, *Irish Visions*, p. 31. Le Goff views the threefold classification as an anticipation of the tripartite division of the other world (*The Birth of Purgatory*, pp. 220–21), but the threefold classification also has more ancient roots; cf. the psychostasy scene in the longer Greek version of the Testament of Abraham, a text which, according to Seymour, was available in the Irish church ("Notes on Apocrypha in Ireland," pp. 109–10).

33. Floating planks perform the same function in the late-twelfth-century Vision of Gottschalk.

34. Letter 10, ed. Reinhold Rau, *Briefe des Bonifatius* (available in English tr. by Ephraim Emerton).

35. "Hoc autem insinuante Apostolo, purgatorii nomen habere cognovi." *Visio Alberici*, ed. Cancellieri, chap. 17, pp. 168–70. Alberic's vision was recorded in 1117, several decades earlier than the date Jacques Le Goff assigns to the "birth" of purgatory as a place. Le Goff claims, however, that the term *purgatorii* in the text implies *fluminis purgatorii*, so that this does not qualify as a use of *purgatorium* as a substantive (*The Birth of Purgatory*, p. 397, n. 17).

36. Rom. 7:24, paraphrased to fit the occasion: the narrative substitutes *de itinere mortis* for *de corpore mortis*.

37. Seymour, *Irish Visions*, p. 128. Cf. the Vision of Thurkill on the postmortem consequences of unjust tithing.

38. The Vision of St. Paul, ed. M. R. James, sect. 14, p. 17.

39. Biblical references to the book of life: Exod. 32:32–3, Deut. 7:10, Luke 10:20, Phil. 4:3, Rev. 20:12, 15.

40. Colgrave and Mynors point out that this echoes the triumphant claim of the evil spirits in Irish and Old English apocrypha concerning the exit of the soul. *Bede's Ecclesiastical History*, chap. 13, p. 500, *n*. 1.

41. *Visio Baronti*, p. 386.

42. The Vision of Alberic, ed. Cancellieri, chap. 18, p. 170.

43. Ibid., pp. 170–74. Jacques de Vitry tells of a similar occurrence among the living: a certain man who wished to make confession found himself weeping so copiously that he could not speak and had to write his sins down for the priest to read. The priest realized that the man's sins were forgiven, however, when the paper on which they were recorded turned out to be blank. *Exempla*, ed. T. F. Crane, no. 301, p. 126. Cf. the ninth-century Vision of an English Priest, described by Prudentius of Troyes, in which the prayers of angels wipe out the record of sins.

44. Deut. 5:27; also Job 31:6; Prov. 16:2, 20:23, 21:2; Ps. 62:10, En. 41:1, 61:8; and 4 Ezra 34. See S. G. F. Brandon, *The Judgment of the Dead*, on the psychostasy in ancient Egyptian and classical iconography of judgment. The image of the balance

is first known to occur in Egyptian mortuary literature. It is prominent as well in Iranian and Islamic depictions of the afterlife and recurs in Jewish rabbinic literature.

45. For a vivid example, see the cathedral of Autun. Brandon notes that artistic treatments of the subject betray a certain confusion about what gets weighed—a soul against another soul or against a demon, a chalice against a lamb, and so forth— but in the vision narratives, the soul is usually weighed against its evil deeds, or else its good deeds are weighed against its sins. For illustrations of the weighing of souls in medieval cathedrals, see Alfred Maury, *Croyances et légendes du Moyen Age* (Paris, 1896; new ed., Geneva, 1974), p. 174, and Brandon, *The Judgment of the Dead*, pp. 231–33.

46. On the possible influence of the longer Greek text of the Testament of Abraham on this scene, see Seymour, "Notes on Apocrypha in Ireland," p. 109.

47. *Dialogue on Miracles* 8:77.

48. *Paul and Palestinian Judaism* (Philadelphia, 1977), pp. 33–59, 125–47, 366–74.

49. *Visio Baronti*, p. 388. Similarly, Gregory tells of a monk in his monastery who was warned in a dream to prepare for a long journey. When the monk expressed his fear that he did not have the fare, he was told, "if your sins are what concern you, they are forgiven" (*Dialogues* 4:49).

50. St. Boniface, *Briefe des Bonifatius*, ed. Rau, p. 32. Note that these are sins of which the monk was previously unaware, rather than conscious guilt feelings.

51. This is a fairly standard list of sins proper to monastic life, but only three of them (*cupiditas, vana gloria,* and *torpor et desidia*) have a place among the cardinal sins. See Bloomfield, *The Seven Deadly Sins*, p. 347, note 103.

52. This is similar to the judgment scene in the Vision of St. Paul, except that the witness in this case is still alive. Cf. Wisd. 4:6, 4:20, 5:1.

53. The Vision of Gunthelm also shows sinners acting out their crimes. On the use of types to represent the vices, see Bloomfield, *The Seven Deadly Sins*, p. 165.

54. Guerrino il Meschino and George, Knight of Hungary. The cardinal sins are presented according to the SALIGIA list of Henry of Ostia (see Bloomfield, *The Seven Deadly Sins*, pp. 73, 86–87).

Chapter 5

1. *Dialogue on Miracles*, 5:44.

2. The narratives mentioned here belong to what I have called the Drythelm line, in which the hell-first pattern is prominent. The Vision of Gunthelm is an exception, as Thomas Wright notes in *St. Patrick's Purgatory*, p. 39 n.

3. Gregory of Tours, *History of the Franks*, 7:1.

4. Ibid.

5. *Bede's Ecclesiastical History*, ed. Colgrave and Mynors, bk. 4, chap. 12, p. 494.

6. *Dialogues* 4:37, p. 286.

7. *Speculum historiale*, A.D. 1126, chap. 85.

8. *PL* 87:433.

9. Tr. C. S. Boswell, *An Irish Precursor of Dante*, p. 44.

10. Ed. Salter, *Visio monachi de Eynsham*, vol. 2, p. 292.

11. Ed. Wagner, *Visio Tnugdali*, p. 55.

12. Drythelm and Thurkill also comment that reentry into the body takes place in an instant.

13. The Vision of Gottschalk, ed. G. W. Leibniz, *Scriptores Rerum Brunsvicensium*, vol. 1, p. 875.

14. Compare this to the well-known passage in *Aeneid* 6, quoted in chapter 1 herein.

15. *Ecclesiastical History*, p. 488.

16. *Dialogues* 4:37.

17. *Chronica monasterii Casinensis*, ed. W. Wattenbach, in *Monumenta Germaniae Historica, Scriptores*, vol. 7, bk. 4, chap. 66, p. 794. Aelfric, too, seems to have noticed the resemblance between Bede's account of Drythelm's vision and Gregory's narrative, for immediately after retelling the Drythelm story, the homilist presents an anecdote derived from *Dialogues* 4:38, combined with elements from the same chapter in which Gregory's account of the hermit Peter occurs (*The Homilies of Aelfric*, ed. Thorpe, pp. 348–57).

18. *Western Society and the Church in the Middle Ages* (Harmondsworth, 1970), p. 257. On Cistercians and purgatory, see Jacques Le Goff.

19. *Dialogue on Miracles*, 1:5, 32, 34; 12:23. Similar anecdotes appear in the *Exordium magnum Cisterciense* by Conrad of Eberbach (discussed by Dinzelbacher, *Vision und Visionsliteratur*, pp. 217–22) and the *Book of Revelations* compiled by Peter of Cornwall in the early thirteenth century (discussed by Holdsworth, "Visions and Visionaries," pp. 146–52).

20. In the *Chronicon*, *PL* 221: 1059–60. Bede's formula for the transformation of the visionary recurs almost word for word in Helinand's account.

21. *Dialogue on Miracles*, 1:32.

22. Quoted by David Rothe in Thomas Messingham, *Tractatus de purgatorio Sancti Patricii*, *PL* 180:981.

23. The Vision of Gottschalk, ed. Leibniz, p. 875. In addition, he loses his appetite and most of his property.

24. *Ecclesiastical History*, p. 274.

25. Ed. Ludovico Frati, "Il Purgatorio di S. Patrizio," p. 161.

26. The Vision of Alberic, ed. Cancellieri, chap. 47, p. 204.

27. *Ecclesiastical History*, p. 488.

28. Ed. Reinhold Rau, *Briefe des Bonifatius*, pp. 40, 42.

29. David Traill, *Walahfrid Strabo's Visio Wettini*, p. 15. There are some classical precedents, however, particularly in Lucian's satirical visits to the other world.

30. Gregory of Tours, *History of the Franks*, ed. Buchner, p. 92.

31. Tundal even repeats the warning about the "secret words which it is not granted to man to utter." Ed. Wagner, p. 52. The Vision of St. Paul observes this admonition to the extent that it is silent about what Paul saw in the third heaven, revealing only the lesser secrets of the second and first heavens.

32. *Dialogue on Miracles*, 12:55.

33. *Visio Wettini*, ed. Traill, p. 201, lines 672–77.

34. Roger of Wendover, *Flores historiarum*, ed. Coxe, vol. 3, p. 209.

35. Thurkill's itinerary is retraced by H. L. D. Ward in "The Vision of Thurkill, Probably by Ralph of Coggeshall," and P. G. Schmidt, "The Vision of Thurkill."

36. Ed. Salter, p. 369.

37. *Tractatus de purgatorio sancti Patricii*, ed. van der Zanden, pp. 4–5.

38. Traill, *Visio Wettini*, pp. 75, 85, 87, 187.

39. Adam of Eynsham, H. of Sawtry, and Ralph of Coggeshall appear to be modeling their prefaces on the remarks Gregory makes in *Dialogues* 4:43.

40. The Vision of the Monk of Eynsham, ed. Salter, p. 286. Cf. Guido's prologue to the Vision of Alberic, ed. Inguanez, p. 86.

41. Ed. Inguanez, p. 83.

42. *Visio Thurkilli*, ed. Schmidt, p. 3.

43. Montague Rhodes James and Claude Jenkins, *A Descriptive Catalogue of the Manuscripts in Lambeth Palace Library* (Cambridge, 1930–32), p. 77 (Lambeth MS. 51, folio 32v). See also C. J. Holdsworth, "Eleven Visions Connected with the Cistercian Monastery of Stratford Langthorne."

44. The Vision of the Monk of Eynsham, ed. Salter, p. 370.

45. Cf. Gregory, *Dialogues* 4:32; and Bede, *Ecclesiastical History*, chaps. 13–14.

46. Alberic and Tundal both hear angels repeating Augustine's opinion that "no one is free from sin, not even a child who has lived only one day on earth" (*Confessions* 1:7).

47. Luke 22:71. Echoed in the visions of Salvius and Thurkill. See also the visions of the monk of Wenlock and Edmund of Eynsham.

48. See discussion of modern "proofs" below, chapters 9 and 10. See Gregory, *Dialogues* 4:12, 14, 18, 27; and the visions of the Monk of Wenlock and Wetti. Many of these powers are common to hagiographic literature in general.

49. *Visio Thurkilli*, ed. Schmidt, p. 4.

50. "The Vision of Thurkill," pp. 50–64.

51. See Hugh Farmer's discussion of the Vision of Orm, which is also the experience of an illiterate visionary recorded by a lettered cleric. Farmer points out the probable influence of local church art motifs such as the mouth of hell, but attributes the scriptural and liturgical phrases, and the borrowings from Bede's Vision of Drythelm, to the priest who recorded the boy's vision ("The Vision of Orm," p. 74).

52. "The Vision of Thurkill," ed. H. L. D. Ward, p. 439.

53. Discussed by Schmidt, "The Vision of Thurkill."

54. Holdsworth, "Visions and Visionaries in the Middle Ages," p. 149.

55. The Vision of Alberic, ed. Cancellieri, p. 132. Alberic claims to be restoring the original narrative by adding details omitted by Guido of Montecassino, the first narrator, and by subtracting elements invented by a subsequent redactor.

56. The Vision of the Monk of Eynsham, ed. Salter, p. 344; see Salter's introduction, pp. 257–83.

57. The visions of Alberic (prefatory letter, ed. Inguanez, pp. 83–84) and Thurkill (ed. Schmidt, p. 37) borrow the words of Rev. 22:19 to call down God's wrath on those who would add to or subtract from their report.

58. Quoted by M. R. James and Claude Jenkins, "A Descriptive Catalogue."

59. Ed. Salter, p. 370.

60. *St. Anselm's Proslogion*, ed. and tr. M. J. Charlesworth (Oxford, 1965).

61. "If I find your heart prepared by love, then it is no trouble at all to furnish proofs." *Dialogues* 4:6.

62. "Miracles and History," in *Famulus Christi*, ed. Gerald Bonner (London, 1976), pp. 70–76.

63. *Dialogues* 4:50.

64. Ibid., 4:32, 27.

65. Ibid. 4:38.

66. Ed. van der Zanden, p. 6.

67. "corporaliter, sed [non] in re." Ed. Delehaye, "La Pèlerinage de Laurent de Pasztho," p. 54. See Seymour, *St. Patrick's Purgatory*, pp. 66–67, 69.

68. *Dialogues* 2:35.

69. *Paradiso* 22, tr. Sinclair, pp. 322–23. Cf. the visions of Paul, the monk of Wenlock, and Fursa; Dante may be influenced here by Cicero's Dream of Scipio.

70. Ibid., 33, pp. 482–83. On the vision of the whole, see David N. Bell, "The Vision of the World and of the Archetypes in the Latin Spirituality of the Middle Ages," *Archives d'histoire doctrinale et littéraire du moyen âge* 44 (1977): 7–31.

71. Valerio of Bierzo, *PL* 87:436.

72. The Vision of Alberic, ed. Inguanez, p. 99.

73. See, for example, Gregory's *Homilia in Ezechielem* 5, *PL* 76:989–90.

74. For a detailed survey of the historical development of attitudes toward the imagination in the West, see Murray Wright Bundy, *The Theory of Imagination in Classical and Mediaeval Thought* (Urbana, Ill., 1927). See also Bloomfield, "The Problem of Imaginatif," in *Piers Plowman as a Fourteenth-Century Apocalypse* (New Brunswick, N.J., 1961), pp. 170–74; and Winthrop Wetherbee, " 'Imagination' and 'Genius,' in Medieval Poetry," *Medievalia et Humanistica* (1976): 45–64.

75. Hugh of St. Victor, *De unione corporis et spiritus*, *PL* 177:288. Cf. Augustine, *Confessions*, 13:14.

76. *Folewer* 26, quoted by Randolph Quirk, "Vis Imaginativa," *Journal of English and Germanic Philology* 13 (1914): 81–83.

77. Richard of St. Victor makes a point of this in *Benjamin minor*, *PL* 196, chaps. 17–21.

78. Ibid., chap. 6, cols. 5C–6A.

79. *De discretione animae spiritus et mentis*, ed. N. Häring, *Medieval Studies* 22 (1960): sect. 43, p. 183.

80. The Carmelite mystics of the sixteenth century carried this idea to the point of actively discouraging visionary experience. St. John of the Cross insists on the necessity of sensory, imaginative, and even spiritual deprivation as a prelude to the contact or "union of resemblance" with God, in which the whole hierarchy of being and knowing is surpassed.

81. *De Genesi ad litteram*.

82. See *Inferno* 2, tr. Sinclair, pp. 34–35; *Purgatorio* 1, tr. Sinclair, pp. 18–19.

83. *Paradiso* 33, tr. Sinclair, pp. 480–81, 484–85.

84. *The Love of Learning and the Desire for God*, tr. Catharine Misrahi (rev. ed.; New York, 1974), chap. 4, pp. 65–86.

85. See the frequently reprinted article by Clifford Geertz, "Religion as a Cultural System," in *The Interpretation of Cultures* (New York, 1973), pp. 87–125.

Chapter 6

1. *Globe* (April 8, 1980): 11. Similar articles appear often in the pages of the *National Enquirer* and its imitators; see bibliography below for some examples.

2. Near-death experience has been a topic on such national talk shows and "magazine" format shows as "Phil Donahue," "Merv Griffin," "Good Morning

America," "Nightline," "CBS Morning News," "The Today Show," "NBC Today," "The David Susskind Show," "That's Incredible," "20/20," "PM Magazine," "The Last Word," "The Sandy Freeman Show," "In Search Of," "You Asked For It," as well as on regular network news programs and countless local news and feature shows. In the United Kingdom, near-death experience has been publicized almost as widely; the BBC documentary "At the Hour of Death" (in the Everyman series, March 1982) dealt sympathetically with the subject. Many of these programs have featured near-death reports on several occasions. In addition, near-death anecdotes, as well as more serious treatments of the subject, continue to appear in nearly every major magazine and newspaper in the country, including the *New York Times*, *Washington Post, Philadelphia Inquirer, Boston Globe, San Francisco Chronicle, Baltimore Sun, Los Angeles Times, Hartford Courant*, and, among magazines, *Glamour, Cosmopolitan, People, McCall's, Newsweek, Time, Good Housekeeping, U.S. News and World Report, Science Digest*, and *Reader's Digest*. Reports and critiques of near-death research can often be found in medical, psychological, and psychiatric journals.

3. For example, the films *Resurrection* (Universal Pictures, 1980) and *Beyond and Back* (Sunn Classic Pictures, 1977), and the novel by Richard Matheson, *What Dreams May Come* (New York, 1978).

4. David Brudnoy, "Nightscene," WNEV, Boston, March 11, 1980.

5. See Mircea Eliade, "Cultural Fashions and History of Religions," in *Occultism, Witchcraft, and Cultural Fashions: Essays in Comparative Religion* (Chicago, 1976), pp. 1–17, in which he argues that a study of popular intellectual trends (such as the success of the French magazine *Planète*) "reveals something of Western man's dissatisfactions, drives and nostalgias" (p. 3).

6. Discussed in chapter 3 above.

7. Ed. Davis W. Clark (New York, 1852). See also John Myers, *Voices from the Edge of Eternity* (Old Tappan, N.Y., 1976); Edward H. Clarke, *Visions: A Study of False Sight* (Boston, 1878), written from his deathbed.

8. *The Journal of the American Society for Psychical Research* 1 (1907): 45–55 and 12 (1918): 585–646. The American Society for Psychical Research was founded in 1884.

9. See *At the Hour of Death*, pp. 1–8. Osis made remarks to this effect during a talk given at Harvard Divinity School on April 17, 1980. Ian Stevenson is Carlson Professor of Psychiatry and director of the Division of Parapsychology at the University of Virginia Medical Center.

10. Russell Noyes, Jr., "The Art of Dying," pp. 432–46.

11. "Notizen über den Tod durch Absturz," tr. Russell Noyes, Jr., and Roy Kletti, in "The Experience of Dying from Falls."

12. "Schocken und Shockphantasien bei höchster Todesgefahr," tr. Roy Kletti and Russell Noyes, Jr., in "Mental States in Mortal Danger."

13. *Life After Life*, p. 5; see also pp. 181–82.

14. "Commentary on 'The Reality of Death Experiences: A Personal Perspective' by Ernst Rodin," *The Journal of Nervous and Mental Disease* 168 (May 1980): 265.

15. See "Yale Conference a Success," *Vital Signs* (June 1982): 2; and Kenneth Ring, "Paranormal and Other Non-ordinary Aspects of Near-Death Experiences: Implications for a New Paradigm," p. 33.

16. Moody dedicates *Life After Life* to George Ritchie. (*Reflections on Life After Life* is dedicated to Elisabeth Kübler-Ross.)

17. The idea of the other world as an invisible realm coexisting with our own world is a popular motif of modern fantasy and science fiction. See, for example, H. G. Wells's "The Plattner Story." Rather than situate the other world in the normal space of the outer atmosphere or the planets, where its existence can be disputed by the evidence of space flights and astronomical observation, the new imaginative cosmology speaks of alternate dimensions or inner space.

18. By now, Moody says that he has spoken to over a thousand people who report near-death experience.

19. Moody, *Life After Life*, pp. 21–22.

20. See, for example, John Weldon and Zola Levitt, *Is There Life after Death?* and Tal Brooke, *The Other Side of Death: Does Death Seal Your Destiny?* Note the allusion to 2 Cor. 11:14.

21. *Vital Signs* (June 1982): 6.

22. Moody was referring to Kenneth Ring, *Life at Death: A Scientific Investigation of the Near-Death Experience*, and Michael B. Sabom, *Recollections of Death: A Medical Investigation*.

23. Ring, "Paranormal Aspects," p. 33. Ring mentions that he already knew about Noyes's work.

24. Ring, *Life at Death*, p. 17.

25. Ibid.

26. See F. W. H. Myers's *Fragments of Inner Life: An Autobiographical Sketch* (London, 1961); and Frank Miller Turner, *Between Science and Religion: The Reaction to Naturalism in Late Victorian England* (New Haven, 1974).

27. Ring, *Life at Death*, p. 17.

28. Ibid., p. 265.

29. Ibid., pp. 266–68.

30. Cf. Charles A. Garfield, "More Grist for the Mill: Additional Near-Death Research Findings and Discussion," *Anabiosis* [newsletter] 1 (May 1979): 5–7.

31. Ring, *Life at Death*, pp. 188–89.

32. See Ring, *Life at Death*, p. 39. To evaluate their findings, Ring and two assistants rated each taped interview with reference to a "weighted core experience index," based on Moody's list of recurrent elements. They assigned scores to represent the strength of each component in a subject's report, preferring conservative estimates to more generous ones (p. 33). Out of the 102 subjects they interviewed, who had been close to death 104 times, 49 (or 48 percent) reported at least some of the elements of the "core experience," and 26 percent had what Ring and his staff judged to be an especially deep experience.

33. Ring, *Life at Death*, pp. 102–3.

34. A videotape of Kenneth Ring interviewing several near-death subjects has the title "Prophetic Voices." Ring seems to consider near-death testimony prophetic not only because it carries a message for others, but also because it occasionally includes a glimpse into the future. See "Paranormal Aspects" and *Heading toward Omega*.

35. See Sabom, *Recollections of Death*, pp. 181–85.

36. Ibid., p. 3.

37. The study described in *Recollections of Death* lasted from May 1976 to March 1981, but Sabom continues to investigate near-death experience in Atlanta hospitals.

38. This gives a frequency of 43 percent, close to Ring's estimate. But since some patients have more than one near-death crisis, the figure reduces, as Sabom

indicates, to a 27 percent chance that a given near-death crisis will yield any remarkable experiences.

39. Sabom, *Recollections of Death*, p. 9.

40. Sabom lists these as: subjective sense of being dead, predominant emotional content (peace, fear, painlessness, lack of emotion, etc.), sense of bodily separation, observation of physical objects and events, dark region or void, life review, a
light, entering a transcendental environment, encountering others, return (pp. 10–
11).

41. In 19 percent of his reports, these two kinds of near-death experience are
combined (see pp. 52–54). Sabom's use of the term *autoscopic* is not meant to suggest
the disorder known to psychologists as autoscopic hallucination (discussed in chapter
10 below).

42. Sabom, *Recollections of Death*, p. 83; see also p. 7.

43. Ibid., see pp. 173–74, 181–83. For a generalist's survey of neurological
findings as they bear on the mind–body problem, see Gordon Rattray Taylor, *The
Natural History of the Mind* (New York, 1979).

44. *Vital Signs* (September 1981): 12.

45. Ibid.

46. Gerald F. Solfvin, Review of *At the Hour of Death*, *The Journal of the
American Society for Psychical Research* 72 (1978): 375.

47. See *Vital Signs* for current information on IANDS. In 1982, Kenneth
Ring went on sabbatical and Bruce Greyson took over as president. Nancy Evans
Bush is now the full-time executive director, Greyson heads the Research Division
and edits *Anabiosis*, and the newly elected president is John Alexander, a lieutenant
colonel who works in Washington for the U.S. Army Human Technologies Task
Force.

Chapter 7

1. See Osis and Haraldsson, *At the Hour of Death*, p. 3; and Marcia Seligson,
"Elisabeth Kubler-Ross," p. 78. Negative near-death experiences are mentioned (as
a rare occurrence) in Margot Grey, *Return from Death*, and George Gallup, Jr.,
Adventures in Immortality.

2. Osis and Haraldsson, *At the Hour of Death*, p. 2. In India, but not in
America, Osis and Haraldsson found a few "bad deaths" and instances of refusal to
die accompanied by terrifying visions.

3. Ibid., p. 3. See also William F. Barrett, *Deathbed Visions*.

4. Elizabeth Kemf, "E. Kübler-Ross: 'There Is No Death,' " p. 52. Similarly,
near-death investigator Michael Grosso goes so far as to say, "being born into this
world is painful and dying out of it seems to be pleasant" ("Toward an Explanation
of Near-Death Phenomena," p. 19). See also Osis and Haraldsson, *At the Hour of
Death*, p. 131.

5. Cf. P. M. H. Atwater, *I Died Three Times in 1977*; and Emily Thomas,
Anabiosis (November 1980): 5.

6. Kemf, "E. Kübler-Ross," p. 50.

7. *The Principles of Nature, Her Divine Revelation, and a Voice to Mankind* (Boston, n.d.), p. 645.

8. Ibid., p. 646.

9. "The Art of Dying," pp. 432–37, 439–40.

10. See "A Meliorist View of Disease and Dying," *Journal of Medical Phi-*

losophy 1 (1976): 212; and "On Natural Death," in *The Medusa and the Snail* (Toronto, 1980), pp. 83–86, where Thomas writes, "Pain is useful for avoidance, for getting away when there's time to get away, but when it is end game, and no way back, pain is likely to be turned off, and the mechanisms for this are wonderfully precise and quick. If I had to design an ecosystem in which creatures had to live off each other and dying was an indispensable part of living, I could not think of a better way to manage." See also G. E. Burch et al., "What Death Is Like," pp. 438–39.

11. Atwater, *I Died Three Times*, p. 13. Cf. *Life After Life*, p. 97.

12. Atwater, *I Died Three Times*, p. 19. Atwater does not provide clear medical details about the cause of her near-death crisis. For other expressions of joy or painlessness at death, see *Vital Signs* (June 1981): 6; (September 1981): 5; (December 1981): 3. See also Kenneth Ring, *Life at Death*, p. 35, Bruce Greyson and Ian Stevenson, "The Phenomenology of Near-Death Experiences," p. 1195; and John Audette, "*Between Life and Death*: A Book Review," *Anabiosis* (February 1981): 11. F. W. H. Myers makes a point of this in *Human Personality and Its Survival of Bodily Death* (New York, 1903), p. 212. For dissenting voices, see Charles Garfield, "More Grist for the Mill," p. 6; and Nathan Schnaper, "Comments Germane to the Paper Entitled 'The Reality of Death Experiences,' by Ernst Rodin," *The Journal of Nervous and Mental Disease* 168 (May 1980): 269.

13. Reinee Pasarow, "A Personal Account of an NDE," *Vital Signs* 1 (December 1981): 11, 14.

14. Moody, *Life After Life*, pp. 40–41.

15. Ibid., p. 40.

16. Sabom, *Recollections of Death*, p. 21. Cf. James H. Lindley, Sethyn Bryan, and Bob Conley, "Near-Death Experiences in a Pacific Northwest American Population: The Evergreen Study," p. 115; and Ring, "Paranormal Aspects," p. 11. Compare to medieval expressions of disdain for the lifeless body, discussed herein in chapter 3.

17. Moody, *Life After Life*, p. 54.

18. For a good facsimile reproduction of a fifteenth-century block-book, see W. Harry Rylands, ed., *The Ars Moriendi* (London, 1881).

19. See Ring, *Life at Death*, p. 80, Moody, *Life After Life*, pp. 76–79.

20. See the articles by Noyes and Kletti on depersonalization, cited in the bibliography.

21. "Depersonalization in the Face of Life-Threatening Danger: An Interpretation," p. 111.

22. Moody, *Life After Life*, p. 91.

23. Ron Rosenbaum, "Turn On, Tune In, Drop Dead," p. 33.

24. "Phenomenology," p. 1194. Perhaps this is related to the sensation, reported by some of Ring's informants, that the physical body is weightless (*Life at Death*, pp. 96–97).

25. Moody, *Life After Life*, pp. 46–50.

26. Seligson, "Elisabeth Kubler-Ross," p. 86.

27. See Ronald K. Siegel, "The Psychology of Life after Death," p. 96. See also N. Lukianowicz, "Autoscopic Phenomena."

28. Moody, *Life After Life*, pp. 46–50, 102; and Ring, *Life at Death*, p. 225.

29. P. M. H. Atwater, *Vital Signs* (September 1981): 13.

30. See Seligson, "Elisabeth Kubler-Ross," p. 92; and Moody, *Life After Life*, p. 49.

31. See Robert Darnton, *Mesmerism and the End of the Enlightenment in*

France (Cambridge, 1968); and R. Laurence Moore, *In Search of White Crows: Spiritualism, Parapsychology and American Culture.*

32. James Lowell Moore, ed., *Introduction to the Writings of Andrew Jackson Davis* (Boston, 1930), pp. 34–42.

33. Mark Woodhouse uses this term to propose a philosophical basis for near-death testimony in "Near-Death Experiences and the Mind-Body Problem," pp. 59, 63.

34. See D. Scott Rogo, *Mind Beyond the Body: The Mystery of ESP Projection*, pp. 351–52; and Ring, *Life at Death*, pp. 52, 224–25. In surveys of out-of-body experience, Robert Crookall found that most of his informants felt they were in a second body connected by a cord to the first. But in a more recent study, conducted by Celia Green, 80 percent of the subjects were "asomatic" rather than "parasomatic." See Janet Lee Mitchell, *Out-of-Body Experiences: A Handbook*, pp. 45, 813.

35. Seligson, "Elisabeth Kubler-Ross," p. 86. The idea of a tenuous connection between the body and its finer spirit replica is not confined to occultism, however. See Benjamin Walker, *Beyond the Body*, pp. 56–58, on classical and other parallels. The Western notion that the connecting strand is silver is related to Eccles. 12:6: "before the silver cord is snapped, or the golden bowl broken, or the pitcher is broken at the fountain, or the wheel broken at the cistern, and the dust returns to the earth as it was, and the spirit returns to God who gave it."

36. On departure through the head, see Moody, *Life After Life*, p. 47; and *Anabiosis* (February 1981): 7. Medieval visionaries are often depicted as exiting through the mouth, though the Irish visionary Laisrén goes out through the crown of the head. Departure through the head is the rule according to the folklore and religious traditions of many cultures, as well as in modern spiritualist and occultist accounts (see Walker, *Beyond the Body*, pp. 47–68). On hovering, see Ring, *Life at Death*, pp. 223, 35, 46–49, 71; and "Paranormal Aspects," p. 35. See also *Anabiosis* (February 1981): 7, 9; *Vital Signs* (June 1981): 6; (March 1982): 11; (June 1982): 11; and Moody, *Life After Life*, p. 36.

37. "Phenomenology," p. 1195. On warmth, see also Moody, *Life After Life*, p. 51. The idea that unusual sounds, such as cracking and humming, accompany the initial stages of travel out of the body is common in spiritualist and Theosophical literature (see Walker, *Beyond the Body*, p. 67).

38. Moody, *Life After Life*, p. 51; Ring, *Life at Death*, pp. 91–98, 41, 44, 59; and Greyson and Stevenson, "Phenomenology." For an exception to this, see the testimony of Helen Nelson in *Vital Signs* (September 1981): 6. There have been similar findings in recent studies of out-of-body experience reports. Janet Mitchell notes that vision and hearing are the most frequently mentioned, followed at a distance by touch, temperature, smell, and taste, in that order. She also finds expressions of lightness and completeness in out-of-body reports (*Out-of-Body Experience*, p. 45).

39. Moody, *Life After Life*, p. 45; Ring, *Life at Death*, pp. 96–97.

40. This occurred for 79 percent of the visionaries studied by Greyson and Stevenson ("Phenomenology," p. 1195).

41. Billy Pilgrim in *Slaughterhouse Five*. See Ring, *Life at Death*, pp. 96–98.

42. "Depersonalization in the Face of Life-Threatening Danger: A Description," pp. 19–27.

43. Ring, *Life at Death*, pp. 96–98; *Anabiosis* (February 1981): 9; *Vital Signs* (December 1981): 3.

44. For the Friar Felix story, see T. F. Crane, *Mediaeval Sermon-Books and Stories* (Philadelphia, 1883), p. 75.

45. R. C. A. Hunter, p. 86. The patient went on to a panoramic review of her life and a vision of the Taj Mahal, which Hunter decodes along Freudian lines. Discussed in chapter 10 below.

46. Heim, "The Experience of Dying from Falls," p. 46.

47. Swedenborg taught this. Among the spiritualists, this doctrine gave rise to mediumistic "rescue circles" (see Walker, *Beyond the Body*, p. 183).

48. *Vital Signs* (December 1981): 14. Cf. Ring, *Life at Death*, pp. 91–94.

49. Moody, *Life After Life*, pp. 37–38, 53–54; Ring, *Life at Death*, p. 98; Sabom, *Recollections of Death*, pp. 32–33.

50. Sabom, *Recollections of Death*, pp. 16, 165–66; Moody, *Life After Life*, pp. 84–85; Ring, *Life At Death*, pp. 83, 91–92; Lindley et al., "Near-Death Experiences," p. 122; Osis and Haraldsson, *At the Hour of Death*, pp. 52, 56–59.

51. Osis and Haraldsson, *At the Hour of Death*, pp. 153, 163.

52. Ring, *Life at Death*, p. 289, n. 3.

53. This is also a common motif in occult and spiritualist literature on "astral travel" (see Walker, *Beyond the Body*, p. 71).

54. Moody, *Life After Life*, pp. 33, 77.

55. Carl Sagan, "The Amniotic Universe," in *Broca's Brain*, pp. 301–7. Stanislav Grof is the originator of the birth recall theory of near-death experience (see *The Human Encounter with Death*, p. 154, n.); chapter 10 will discuss this theory.

56. See Stanislav and Christina Grof, *Beyond Death: The Gates of Consciousness*.

57. Moody, *Life After Life*, pp. 30–34; Ring, *Life at Death*, p. 36.

58. Ring, *Life at Death*, pp. 53–55. Greyson and Stevenson attribute the tunnel experience to 31 percent of their reports ("Phenomenology," p. 1194), but George Gallup, Jr., notices it in only 3 percent of the cases he surveyed.

59. "More Grist for the Mill."

60. May 1979, p. 3.

61. Sabom, *Recollections of Death*, p. 41. Cf. Moody, *Life After Life*, p. 62. The tunnel perspective can also be an optical effect. One near-death experiencer describes it as similar to glaucoma, *Anabiosis* (August 1980): 7. Ronald K. Siegel theorizes that the whole experience is a hallucination triggered by the impression of a point of light in the center of the visual field (see discussion of his views in chapter 10).

62. Ring, *Life at Death*, p. 66.

63. Moody, *Life After Life*, pp. 23–25. Ring notes that organizing near-death experience into stages does not do justice to its atemporal quality; but he defends this approach as a "narrative convenience" (*Life at Death*, p. 190).

64. Ring, *Life at Death*, p. 56. Cf. Sabom, *Recollections of Death*, pp. 43–44.

65. Angel de Milio, "The Last Word," ABC, January 6, 1983.

66. Helen Nelson, *Vital Signs* (September 1981): 5.

67. Reinee Pasarow, *Vital Signs* (December 1981): 11.

68. Quoted by Kevin J. Drab, "The Tunnel Experience: Reality or Hallucination?" p. 126.

69. Examples of this motif that were formative for medieval writers can be found in Augustine's *Confessions*, book 13, chap. 9.

70. *Paradiso*, canto 1, lines 136–40, tr. Sinclair, p. 24.

71. Ibid., lines 127–35.

72. See Tracy Lovell, *Vital Signs* (March 1982): 11; Maria Castedo, *Anabiosis* (February 1981): 7; and Moody, *Life After Life*, p. 58. See also Sabom, *Recollections of Death*, p. 43 (orange light); *Anabiosis* (May 1979): 3 (golden light); ibid. (February 1981): 9 (yellow light).

73. Helen Nelson, *Vital Signs* (September 1981): 5; Joe Geraci, *Vital Signs* (December 1981): 3; Sabom, *Recollections of Death*, p. 44.

74. Jayne Smith, IANDS conference in Charlottesville, October 16, 1982.

75. Betty Preston, *Anabiosis* (February 1981): 9.

76. Joe Geraci, *Vital Signs* (December 1981): 3.

77. NBC, July 13, 1981.

78. See Ring, *Life at Death*, p. 59.

79. *Vital Signs* (December 1981): 11.

80. Moody, *Life After Life*, pp. 59, 101–7.

81. Joe Geraci, *Vital Signs* (December 1981): 12.

82. In Jess E. Weiss, ed., *The Vestibule*, p. 76.

83. Moody, *Life After Life*, p. 62.

84. Ibid., p. 59. Cf. Ring, *Life at Death*, p. 57.

85. Osis and Haraldsson, *At the Hour of Death*, p. 37. (I assume that "Devi" is intended here, rather than "Deva.")

86. Ibid.; see also pp. 152, 154.

87. Ibid., p. 154. See Ring, *Life at Death*, pp. 59–60.

88. Moody, *Life After Life*, p. 64.

89. Ibid., p. 60.

90. Ibid., pp. 61–62.

91. Thomas DeQuincey, *Confessions of an English Opium-Eater*, quoted by Russell Noyes, Jr., "Dying and Mystical Consciousness," p. 30.

92. Heim, "The Experience of Dying from Falls," p. 50.

93. See Ring, "Paranormal Aspects," p. 40.

94. "Panoramic Memory: A Response to the Threat of Death," p. 184.

95. In a letter to Oskar Pfister, quoted by Noyes in "Dying and Mystical Consciousness," p. 30.

96. Noyes and Kletti, "Panoramic Memory," p. 184; Moody, *Life After Life*, p. 70; Ring, "Paranormal Aspects," p. 41, and *Life at Death*, pp. 71, 116–17.

97. *Reflections on Life After Life*, p. 38.

98. Betty Preston, *Anabiosis* (February 1981): 9.

99. Noyes and Kletti, "Panoramic Memory," p. 187.

100. In a letter to Oskar Pfister, quoted in "Shock Thoughts and Fantasies," p. 9.

101. Noyes, "The Experience of Dying," p. 178.

102. Ring, *Life at Death*, p. 73.

103. Ibid., p. 173.

104. *Moralia* 5: 32, *PL* 175: 710.

105. Moody, *Life After Life*, pp. 65, 98.

106. Moody, *Reflections on Life After Life*, p. 93.

107. See George Lawton, *The Drama of Life After Death*. Connected with the imagery of learning and growth is the pervasive use, in both spiritualist and near-death literature, of the idea of evolution, presented in a pre-Darwinian or high-minded sense that takes the sting out of Darwin's theory.

108. Atwater, *I Died Three Times*, p. 22.

109. Moody, *Reflections on Life After Life*, p. 10.

110. Ibid., pp. 13–14.

111. See Sabom, *Recollections of Death*, p. 186.

112. See Rick Bradshaw, *Anabiosis* (August 1979): 11.

113. IANDS conference, Charlottesville, October 16, 1982.

114. Babylonian Talmud, tractate Niddah; Midrash Tanhuma, Peduke 3. See Louis Ginzberg, *The Legends of the Jews*, tr. Henrietta Szold (Philadelphia, 1909), vol. 1, pp. 53–59; vol. 5, n. 19–20; Martin Buber, *Tales of the Hasidim*, tr. Olga Marx (New York, 1961), vol. 1, p. 144. A comparable Hindu account of forgetfulness at birth can be found in the Garbhopanishad (the Upanishad of the Womb or Fetus), mentioned by P. T. Raju in his foreword to *Death and Eastern Thought*, ed. Frederick H. Holck (Nashville and New York, 1974), p. 17.

115. Lindley et al., "Near-Death Experiences," pp. 116–17.

116. See Mircea Eliade, "Mythologies of Sleep and Forgetting," *Parabola* 7 (January 1982): 14–19.

117. See Ronald Fischer, "I Can't Remember What I Said Last Night . . . But It Must Have Been Good," in *Understanding Mysticism*, ed. Richard Woods (Garden City, N.Y., 1980), pp. 92–93; Charles Tart, "States of Consciousness and State-Specific Sciences," *Science* 176 (June 1972): 1203–18; and Kevin J. Drab, "Unresolved Problems in the Study of Near-Death Experiences: Some Suggestions for Research and Theory," *Anabiosis* 1 (July 1981): 35–37. Drab argues that near-death experience may be a composite of "discrete asc's" (Charles Tart's term), and that this would account for the suddenness of transitions from one stage to the next.

118. In another popular context, that of UFO lore, St. Paul's three heavens seem to have resurfaced as three kinds of "close encounter" (terminology coined by astronomer and UFO investigator J. Allen Hynek). As dramatized by the immensely successful movie *Close Encounters of the Third Kind*, the third kind of UFO encounter involves far more than a "take me to your leader" exchange; it is direct contact with an ineffable, wholly other reality, and as such has a transforming effect.

119. *Vital Signs* (March 1982): 12.

120. This was the subject of Bruce Greyson's presentation at the October 1982 conference in Charlottesville.

121. Ring, *Life at Death*, pp. 58–59.

122. Sabom, *Recollections of Death*, p. 46.

123. For examples, see Sabom, *Recollections of Death*, pp. 44–46; Ring, *Life at Death*, pp. 60–66; Moody, *Reflections on Life After Life*, pp. 15–18; Osis and Haraldsson, *At the Hour of Death*, pp. 160–82; Noyes and Kletti, "Depersonalization in the Face of Life-Threatening Danger: An Interpretation," p. 111. In *Return from Tomorrow*, George Ritchie describes "a city . . . constructed out of light."

124. Ring, *Life at Death*, pp. 63–65.

125. Sabom, *Recollections of Death*, p. 48.

126. Lindley et al., "Near-Death Experiences," p. 116.

127. Seligson, "Elisabeth Kubler-Ross," p. 74.

128. See ibid., p. 102; Ann Nietzke, "The Miracle of Kubler-Ross," *Cosmopolitan* (February 1980): 211; and Philip Zaleski, "Elisabeth Kubler-Ross."

129. Moody, *Life After Life*, pp. 55–56.

Chapter 8

1. Kenneth Ring, *Life at Death*, p. 60.

2. *Recollections of Death*, p. 48.

3. "Dead kin 'pushed' brother back to life."

4. Dowling R. Kennedy, *Anabiosis* [newsletter] (February 1981): 8.

5. *Vital Signs* (September 1981): 6.

6. *Life After Life*, p. 76.

7. Osis and Haraldsson, *At the Hour of Death*, p. 4.

8. Maria Castedo, *Anabiosis* (February 1981): 7. Cf. Ring, *Life at Death*, pp. 60–61. (Ring says that reluctance to return from death is more common among those who reach the final stage of "entering the light.")

9. *Vital Signs* (June 1981): 6.

10. Ring, *Life at Death*, pp. 67–81. Ring also notes that people encounter either a spirit or a presence, but not both. Similarly, Osis finds that the dying see religious figures only when a "professional" is needed, there being no sympathetic friends or kinfolk on hand (Osis and Haraldsson, *At the Hour of Death*, p. 197). But the testimony presented by Moody and Sabom does not support such a strict division of labor (see Sabom, *Recollections of Death*, pp. 49–50).

11. *Vital Signs* (June 1982): 3; Ring, *Life at Death*, p. 92; Moody, *Life After Life*, p. 80.

12. Noyes, "Attitude Change Following Near-Death Experiences," p. 236; Noyes and Kletti, "Depersonalization in the Face of Life-Threatening Danger: An Interpretation," p. 112. Ring, *Life at Death*, pp. 66, 72, 149, and "Paranormal Aspects," p. 42.

13. Ring, *Life at Death*, p. 255; *Heading toward Omega* is devoted to this theme.

14. Moody, *Life After Life*, p. 65.

15. Ring, *Life at Death*, p. 66. Perhaps related to this is Elisabeth Kübler-Ross's account of how she returned from a deliberately induced out-of-body excursion with the phrase "Shanti Nilaya" on her lips (this was to be the name of her hospice-estate; see Nietzke, "The Miracle of Kubler-Ross," p. 209) and with the conviction that she had been chosen to "carry the message" of immortality to mankind.

16. Moody, *Life After Life*, p. 73. Greyson and Stevenson say that over half of their sample reported a border of some kind ("Phenomenology," p. 1194). Ring, however, finds no visual imagery of this sort (*Life at Death*, pp. 99–100).

17. Sabom, *Recollections of Death*, p. 35.

18. *Vital Signs* (December 1981): 14.

19. On the relation between near-death experience and hypnagogic sleep, see chapter 10 herein.

20. Walker, *Beyond the Body*, pp. 76–77; Janet Mitchell, *Out-of-Body Experience*, p. 13.

21. *Vital Signs* (September 1981): 6.

22. See Virginia Falce, *Vital Signs* (June 1981): 6; and Reinee Pasarow, *Vital Signs* (December 1981): 14. Tom Sawyer, describing his experience in a videotaped interview with Kenneth Ring ("Prophetic Voices"), gives a similar account.

23. Julia Phillips Ruopp, "The Window of Heaven," in *The Vestibule*, ed. Jess E. Weiss, p. 53.

24. See Sir John Woodroffe, Foreword, *The Tibetan Book of the Dead*, ed. W. Y. Evans-Wentz (London, 1927), p. lxx.

25. ABC, "The Last Word," January 6, 1983.

26. "Prophetic Voices."

27. *Vital Signs* (June 1981): 7.

28. *Vital Signs* (September 1981): 6, 14.

29. Ring, "Precognitive and Prophetic Visions in Near- Death Experiences," p. 49; Sabom, *Recollections of Death*, pp. 116–23; Atwater, *Vital Signs* (June 1982): 8; Lovell, *Vital Signs* (March 1982): 12. According to Karlis Osis, the situation is similar for veterans of out-of-body travel (see Janet Mitchell, *Out-of-Body Experience*, p. 68).

30. See Greyson and Stevenson, "Phenomenology," p. 1195; Ring, *Life at Death*, p. 138; Sabom, *Recollections of Death*, p. 125; Geraci, *Vital Signs* (December 1981): 3; Lovell, *Vital Signs* (March 1982): 12.

31. Noyes and Kletti, "Depersonalization in the Face of Life-Threatening Danger: An Interpretation," p. 105.

32. Falce, *Vital Signs* (June 1981): 6.

33. Lovell, *Anabiosis* (August 1980): 8.

34. *Vital Signs* (September 1981): 6.

35. On the emotional disorders that sometimes follow major surgery, critical illness, and, especially, resuscitation from cardiac arrest, see R. G. Druss and D. S. Kornfeld, "The Survivors of Cardiac Arrest"; M. Dobson, "Attitudes and Long Term Adjustment of Patients Surviving Cardiac Arrest"; D. M. Dlin, "Survivors of Cardiac Arrest"; "The Experience of Dying"; Thomas P. Hackett, "The Lazarus Complex Revisited" (Hackett points out, however, that many patients have a positive, even elated, response).

36. *Life at Death*, pp. 141–58; Sabom, *Recollections of Death*, pp. 129–32; Moody, *Life After Life*, pp. 89–92; Greyson and Stevenson, "Phenomenology," p. 1195; Greyson, "Toward a Psychological Explanation of Near-Death Experience: A Response to Dr. Grosso's Paper," *Anabiosis* 1 (December 1981): 90–93.

37. Noyes and Kletti, "Depersonalization in the Face of Life-Threatening Danger: An Interpretation," pp. 111–12.

38. "Attitude Change," p. 235.

39. Noyes, "The Encounter with Life-Threatening Danger: Its Nature and Impact," p. 30. Charles Garfield agrees ("More Grist for the Mill," p. 5).

40. See Greyson, "Toward a Psychological Explanation," pp. 90–93.

41. Sabom, *Recollections of Death*, p. 186.

42. Quoted by Ring, *Life at Death*, p. 177; see also Moody, *Life After Life*, pp. 94–96; Sabom, *Recollections of Death*, pp. 60–61, 125, 212–13; Maria Castedo, *Anabiosis* (February 1981): 7, 9; Emily Thomas, *Anabiosis* (November 1980): 5.

43. "Portrait of an NDEr: Gerry De Vito," *Vital Signs* (June 1982): 11–12.

44. Carolyn Edgar, *Anabiosis* (February 1981): 9.

45. Osis and Haraldsson did find some "mistaken" identity cases in India, however. Often, it was a matter of "bureaucratic" mixup, as Osis points out; in one case, another man of the same name was said to have died at the moment the patient revived (*At the Hour of Death*, pp. 152–53).

46. Lovell, *Vital Signs* (March 1982): 12.

47. See Lectures 4 and 5, "The Religion of Healthy-Mindedness," in *The Varieties of Religious Experience*. Although James's discussion may give the impres-

sion that spiritual rebirth is the special province of the "sick soul," the material we are considering fits both his rubrics of "conversion" and "healthy-mindedness." James does not insist that "healthy-mindedness" must always be a "once-born" religion.

48. Sabom, *Recollections of Death*, pp. 130–31; cf. p. 132. Cathi Elms, *Anabiosis* (November 1980): 5.

49. Ring, *Life at Death*, pp. 162–66. Cf. Atwater: "most leave the church forever, more concerned with spiritual development than dogma or ritual or rules." *Vital Signs* (September 1981): 13. The study done at Evergreen State College supports Ring's view that the effect of near-death experience is an increase in spirituality rather than in conventional religiosity (Lindley et al., "Near-Death Experiences," pp. 118–19).

50. Sabom, *Recollections of Death*, p. 126. Sabom comments, "no change in the basic type of religious belief occurred—that is, no agnostic became a believer, no Protestant a Catholic, no Catholic a Jew," p. 129, *n*.

51. Ibid., p. 130.

52. Ring, *Life at Death*, p. 163.

53. On the demographics of the spiritualist movement in the nineteenth and early twentieth centuries, see George Lawton, *The Drama of Life After Death*; R. Laurence Moore, *In Search of White Crows*; and Geoffrey K. Nelson, *Spiritualism and Society*.

54. IANDS conference, October 1982.

55. *Vital Signs* (June 1981): 7. See also *Vital Signs* (December 1982): 2.

56. *Vital Signs* (September 1981): 14.

57. *Vital Signs* (September 1981): 13.

58. After witnessing the destruction of his people and the apparent failure of his vision, Black Elk derived some consolation from tellling his story to the human race as a whole, through the pen of John G. Neihardt (*Black Elk Speaks* [Lincoln, Neb., 1961]).

59. *Vital Signs* (March 1982): 12.

60. *Vital Signs* (December 1981): 12.

61. See Sabom, *Recollections of Death*, pp. 133–36, and Moody, *Life After Life*, pp. 86–87.

62. Angel De Milio, January 6, 1983.

63. Sabom, *Recollections of Death*, p. 141; see also pp. 133–36. Moody commented on this at the IANDS conference in Charlottesville, October 1982. See Osis and Haraldsson, *At the Hour of Death*, pp. 14, 67–68 (which notes that this was less pronounced in India); and Garfield, "More Grist for the Mill," p. 5.

64. *Anabiosis* (February 1981): 15.

65. *Vital Signs* (March 1982): 11.

66. James, "Mysticism," in *The Varieties of Religious Experience*; Noyes and Kletti, "Panoramic Memory," pp. 188–89; Ring, *Life at Death*, pp. 84–87, 70; see also Moody, *Life After Life*, pp. 25–26. On the other hand, Osis and Haraldsson indicate that only three of their cases had this feature; for this reason, they maintain that the paranormal deathbed vision differs from mystical and drug experiences.

67. Sabom, *Recollections of Death*, pp. 10–11, 136–37, 157.

68. Remark made at the IANDS conference in Charlottesville, October 1982.

69. Moody, *Reflections on Life After Life*, pp. 131–32.

70. Ibid., p. 129.

71. Comments made at IANDS conference in Charlottesville, October 1982.

72. *Anabiosis* (May 1979): 4.

73. *Vital Signs* (December 1981): 3.

74. James E. Alcock, a psychologist at York University, dismisses reincarnation evidence retrieved from hypnotic regression because of this aspect of hypnosis ("Psychology and Near-Death Experience," p. 165).

75. As Carl Sagan put it, "many of the belief systems at the edge or fringe of science are not subject to crisp experimentation. They are anecdotal, depending entirely on the validity of eyewitnesses who, in general, are notoriously unreliable" (*Broca's Brain*, p. 63). Cf. James E. Alcock, "Pseudo-Science and the Soul," pp. 68, 71.

Chapter 9

1. This is not an invariant pattern, of course. I have pointed out that many vision narratives arc deliberate concoctions that bear no direct connection to any individual's visionary experience. They may, nonetheless, convey an authentic message for the audience to whom they are addressed.

2. Sabom, *Recollections of Death*, pp. 130–31.

3. Moody, *Life After Life*, p. 139.

4. Jack D. Vance, *Anabiosis* (November 1979): 5. See also Virginia Falce, *Anabiosis* (May 1979): 4; and *Vital Signs* (December 1982): 2.

5. Moody, *Life After Life*, p. 131.

6. See Kenneth Ring, "Commentary on 'The Reality of Death Experiences: A Personal Perspective' by Ernst A. Rodin," *The Journal of Nervous and Mental Disease* 168 (May 1980): 274; and Moody, *Life After Life*, p. 6. At the IANDS conference in Charlottesville in October 1982, Bruce Greyson remarked, "we were devout atheists. We started out to prove this guy [Moody] was off his rocker or making it up." On initial skepticism among the early psychical researchers, see R. Laurence Moore, *In Search of White Crows*, p. 20.

7. June 1982, p. 6.

8. Some reports even attribute this quality to the being of light: "it was a fun person to be with! And it had a sense of humor, too—definitely." Moody, *Life After Life*, p. 64.

9. See, for example, Moody, *Life After Life*, p. 183.

10. See Ring, "Paranormal Aspects," p. 34.

11. December 1982, p. 13.

12. Osis and Haraldsson, *At the Hour of Death*, p. 59.

13. Moody, *Reflections on Life After Life*, p. 133.

14. Ring, *Life at Death*, p. 82.

15. See Osis and Haraldsson, *At the Hour of Death*, pp. 48, 94, 173–74; Ring, "Commentary on Rodin," p. 273; and Michael Grosso, "Toward an Explanation of Near-Death Phenomena," p. 6.

16. Moody, *Life After Life*, p. 175; see also pp. 140–41. It would be interesting to hear Moody comment on the *Tibetan Book of the Dead* (which he cites as a parallel to near-death reports); in that work, the assumption is that one's expectations and inner makeup will partly determine the content of after-death visions.

17. Ibid., p. 97.

18. Osis and Haraldsson, *At the Hour of Death*, pp. 17, 190–91; see also Grosso, "Toward an Explanation," pp. 14–15.

19. See Grosso, "Toward an Explanation"; Michael Sabom, "Commentary on 'The Reality of Death Experiences' by Ernst Rodin," *The Journal of Nervous and Mental Disease* 168 (May 1980): 266; Ian Stevenson, "Commentary," ibid., pp. 271–272; Osis and Haraldsson, *At the Hour of Death*, pp. 29, 56, 62–67; Ring, "Paranormal Aspects," p. 34, and *Life at Death*, p. 208. Elisabeth Kübler-Ross often speaks of such incidents, and they are a prominent feature of the survival evidence of the early psychical researchers. Osis and Haraldsson claim that there is a correlation between appropriate apparitions and "otherworldly feelings" (pp. 78, 80) and between the frequency of otherworld visions and the patients' closeness to death (p. 111). They also find it impressive that patients had visions and presentiments of death which, though they conflicted with medical prognosis, were ultimately proven right (pp. 87–88, 132).

20. Ring, "Paranormal Aspects," p. 47; Osis and Haraldsson, *At the Hour of Death*, pp. 129–31, 187; Grosso, "Toward an Explanation," pp. 8–9.

21. Osis and Haraldsson, *At the Hour of Death*, p. 11; comments made in talk by Osis at Harvard Divinity School, April 1980.

22. Grosso, "Toward an Explanation," p. 10.

23. Summarizing his project at an IANDS conference in Charlottesville, Greyson identified the reasons most often cited for this therapeutic result. In descending order of frequency, they are: a sense of having merged with the whole, "decathexis" from problems, belief that life is precious and meaningful, a more vivid sense of the reality of life, enhanced self-esteem (because death is not the end, or because one was deemed worthy of rescue), among others.

24. *Anabiosis* (May 1979): 1.

25. Stephen Vicchio, "Near-Death Experiences: A Critical Review of the Literature and Some Questions for Further Study," *Essence* 5 (1981): 79, citing the studies of Dobson and of Druss and Kornfeld.

26. Ring, *Life at Death*, pp. 191–92; Sabom, *Recollections of Death*, pp. 56–57 (because this figure comes from people who had more than one brush with death, Sabom notes that it translates into a 27 percent frequency per near-death crisis); George Gallup, Jr., *Adventures in Immortality*.

27. "Toward a Psychological Explanation."

28. *Anabiosis* (May 1979): 1.

29. "What Psychical Research Has Accomplished" (1897), quoted by R. Laurence Moore as the maxim of the psychical research movement and the epigraph for his book, *In Search of White Crows*.

Chapter 10

1. Quoted by Stephen Vicchio, "Near-Death Experiences," p. 59.

2. "The Experience of Dying," p. 1348.

3. In "Near-Death Experiences," "Near-Death Experiences: Some Logical Problems and Questions for Further Study," and "Against Hope of Raising the Dead: Contra Moody and Kübler-Ross," Vicchio draws on arguments made by Robert Morison, "Death: Process or Event?" in P. Steinfels and R. M. Veatch, ed., *Death Inside Out* (New York, 1975), pp. 63–70. Ernst A. Rodin makes similar points in "The Reality of Death Experiences: A Personal Perspective," p. 261.

4. P. M. H. Atwater, *Vital Signs* (June 1981): 4.

5. These remarks were made at the IANDS conference in Charlottesville, October 1982.

6. "Commentary on Rodin," p. 266; and *Recollections of Death*, p. 163.

7. IANDS conference in Charlottesville, October 1982. At the same session, Moody and Greyson suggested that near-death experience differs from other "altered states" because it so often comes unexpected and unsought, and because it occurs in a context of confronting "ultimate loss" (Moody's expression).

8. Marcia Seligson interview, p. 86.

9. Moody, *Life After Life*, pp. 150, 151.

10. See Stith Thompson, "Otherworld Journeys" in *Motif-Index of Folk-Literature*, vol. 3, F0–F199; Dean Sheils, "A Cross-Cultural Study of Beliefs in Out of the Body Experiences, Waking and Sleeping," pp. 697–741; Jane I. Smith, "The Understanding of *nafs* and *ruh* in Contemporary Muslim Considerations of the Nature of Sleep and Death," *Muslim World* 49 (1979): 151–62.

11. Siegel points out that nitrous oxide, ether, and ketamine not only trigger hallucination, but also permit sensory awareness, allowing patients to hear conversations during their apparent unconsciousness. See "The Psychology of Life after Death," pp. 922–23.

12. Nathan Schnaper mentions some of these conditions in his partial list of the etiologies for near-death experience. "Commentary," *The Journal of Nervous and Mental Disease* 168 (May 1980): 269.

13. "To Sleep, Perchance to Dream . . . ," p. 2291.

14. "Pathophysiology of Stress-Induced Limbic Lobe Dysfunction: A Hypothesis for NDEs," pp. 76–78.

15. Wilder Penfield, *The Mystery of the Mind: A Critical Study of Consciousness and the Human Brain* (Princeton, 1975).

16. Carr points out that in the agony and stress of critical illness or injury, the limbic system, which has the highest concentration of opiate receptors, must be flooded with endorphins and enkephalins.

17. *The Journal of the American Society for Psychical Research* 72 (1978): 394.

18. Siegel, "The Psychology of Life after Death," pp. 926–27.

19. "Hallucinations," p. 134. Siegel finds recurrence of the form constants in the reports of subjects who were trained to use "a standard descriptive code"; the untrained subjects were less successful in reducing their impressions to such consistent patterns.

20. Siegel, "The Psychology of Life after Death," p. 923.

21. Ibid., p. 927.

22. Ibid.

23. Siegel, "Hallucinations," p. 140.

24. See James E. Alcock, "Psychology and Near-Death Experience," pp. 162–63; Vicchio "Near-Death Experiences," p. 79; Schnaper, "Commentary," p. 269; John Palmer, "The Out-of-Body Experience: A Psychological Theory," p. 19–22. On these conditions in general, see Graham Reed, *The Psychology of Anomalous Experience: A Cognitive Approach* (London, 1972); and Gordon Rattray Taylor, *The Natural History of the Mind* (New York, 1979), pp. 215–30.

25. See Alcock, "Psychology and Near-Death Experience"; Janet Mitchell, *Out-of-Body Experience*, pp. 65–67. On autoscopy in general, see N. Lukianowicz, "Autoscopic Phenomena"; Otto Rank, *The Double* (Chapel Hill, 1971). Michael

Sabom and Celia Green use the term "autoscopic" to describe the first stage of an out-of-body experience, rather than to refer to a neuropsychological syndrome.

26. Moody raises this and other objections to the autoscopy theory, *Life After Life*, pp. 166–69.

27. Sigmund Freud, "Thoughts for the Times on War and Death" (1915), in *Collected Papers*, authorized translation under supervision of Joan Riviere (London and New York, 1959), vol. 4, pp. 304–5. Goethe anticipated this: "It is entirely impossible for a thinking being to think of its own nonexistence...." (quoted by Paul Edwards, "My Death," *The Encyclopedia of Philosophy*, vol. 5–6, p. 416).

28. "Shock Thoughts and Fantasies in Extreme Mortal Danger." Pfister found his material in Heim's report to the Swiss Alpine Clubs (discussed above) and in direct correspondence with Heim; he also interviewed an acquaintance who had narrowly escaped death on a battlefield.

29. Freud develops the idea of the stimulus barrier in *Beyond the Pleasure Principle*.

30. Pfister, "Shock Thoughts," p. 15. Pfister classifies these as historical, topographic, and metaphysical ideas.

31. See Jan Ehrenwald, "Out of Body Experience and Denial of Death," p. 229.

32. "The Encounter with Life-Threatening Danger," p. 27.

33. Noyes and Kletti, "Depersonalization in the Face of Life-Threatening Danger: An Interpretation," p. 106.

34. "The Experience of Dying," p. 179.

35. Noyes and Kletti, "Depersonalization in the Face of Life-Threatening Danger: An Interpretation," p. 113.

36. Alcock, "Psychology and Near-Death Experience," p. 169. "Peak experience" is Abraham Maslow's term.

37. "Panoramic Memory," pp. 191–92. See Alcock, "Pseudo-Science and the Soul," p. 69. Siegel and Alcock also suggest that misleading habits of memory are responsible in part for the out-of-body experience. When we recollect a scene, we often visualize ourselves from outside as part of the scene; the remembering self thus distances itself from the remembered self and constructs an imaginative out-of-body experience ("Hallucinations," p. 136; "Psychology and Near-Death Experience," p. 162).

38. These are Grof's four stages of perinatal symbolism.

39. *Broca's Brain*, pp. 309–10.

40. Introduction to James Randi, *Flim-Flam: The Truth about Unicorns, Parapsychology and Other Delusions* (New York, 1980), p. xi.

41. This has been demonstrated by historical and sociological studies of the psychical research movement and its contemporary heirs. According to Molly Noonan, this was the principle which partly governed·the selection of topics studied by the Society for Psychical Research and the American Society for Psychical Research in the early days; *Science and the Psychical Research Movement* (Ph.D. dissertation, University of Pennsylvania, 1977).

42. Sabom, *Recollections of Death*, p. 178.

43. Osis and Haraldsson, *At the Hour of Death*, pp. 28–30, 188; Moody, *Life After Life*, pp. 156–62; Sabom, *Recollections of Death*, pp. 168–71; Ring, *Life at Death*, pp. 210–12; Greyson and Stevenson, "Phenomenology," p. 1196.

44. Foreword to Grof and Halifax, *The Human Encounter with Death*, p. vii.

45. See Michael Grosso, "Toward an Explanation," p. 14; Sabom, *Recollections of Death*, pp. 172–74, 213.

46. *Recollections of Death*, p. 16. Cf. Ring, *Life at Death*, p. 83; and Lindley et al., p. 122.

47. Siegel, "Hallucinations," p. 136; "The Psychology of Life after Death," p. 922.

48. Osis and Haraldsson, *At the Hour of Death*, pp. 28–29.

49. Ring, *Life at Death*, pp. 208–9.

50. Greyson and Stevenson, "Phenomenology," p. 1195; Ring, *Life at Death*, p. 136; and Ring, "Religiousness and Near-Death Experiences: An Empirical Study," presentation to the 87th Annual Convention of the American Psychological Association (September 1979).

51. "Subconscious incubation" is William James's phrase, in the lecture on "Conversion," *The Varieties of Religious Experience*.

52. "Toward a Psychological Explanation," p. 98.

53. See Wilfred Cantwell Smith, *The Meaning and End of Religion* (new ed., San Francisco, 1978), and *Faith and Belief* (Princeton, 1979).

54. Moody, *Reflections on Life After Life*, p. 85.

55. Andrew Jackson Davis, *The Principles of Nature* (Boston, n.d.), p. xvii.

56. Moody, *Life After Life*, p. 97; Ring, *Life at Death*, pp. 201–2; Ring, "Commentary on Rodin," p. 273; Sabom, "The Near-Death Experience: Clinical and Religious Implications," presentation to the 87th Annual Convention of the American Psychological Association; Osis and Haraldsson, *At the Hour of Death*, pp. 190–91; Grosso, "Toward an Explanation," p. 6.

57. As Ring suggested in his paper on "Religiousness and Near-Death Experiences." See abstract in *Anabiosis* 1 (August 1979): 3.

58. "Toward an Explanation," p. 15.

59. Cf. Moody, *Life After Life*, p. 59; Ring, *Life at Death*, pp. 243–44; Grosso, "Toward an Explanation," p. 6.

60. "Toward a Psychological Explanation," p. 90.

61. "Pseudo-Science and the Soul," pp. 72–73, and "Psychology and Near-Death Experience," p. 156.

62. "The Reality of Death Experiences," p. 262.

63. Ring, *Life at Death*, pp. 187, 219–20, 251; "Paranormal Aspects," pp. 43, 45–48; and "Precognitive and Prophetic Visions in Near-Death Experiences," pp. 62–63. See also G. O. Gabbard and S. W. Twemlow, *Vital Signs* (March 1982): 10; G. O. Gabbard and Michael Sabom, *Vital Signs* (December 1981): 1; Mark Woodhouse, "Near-Death Experiences and the Mind-Body Problem," p. 57.

64. See Ring, *Life at Death*, pp. 220, 237, 247; and "Paranormal Aspects," p. 47; Stephen E. Braude, "The Holographic Analysis of Near-Death Experiences: The Perpetuation of Some Deep Mistakes," *Essence* 5 (1981): 53–63; F. Gordon Greene, "A Glimpse Behind the Life Review."

65. See "Conclusions" in *The Varieties of Religious Experience*; and "The Will to Believe," in *The Will to Believe and Other Essays in Popular Philosophy*, ed. Frederick H. Burkhardt et al. (Cambridge, Mass., and London, 1979), pp. 13–33.

Chapter 11

1. Moody, *Reflections on Life After Life*, p. 54.

2. "Death-bed Visions and Christian Hope." See also Paul and Linda Badham, *Immortality or Extinction?*

3. Robert Herhold, "Kübler-Ross and Life after Death," p. 363. See also J. D. Ousley, Letter to the Editor on "Death-bed Visions and Christian Hope," by Paul Badham, *Theology* 84 (January 1981): 44. In response to Herhold's argument, however, James W. Woelfel points out that it represents the fideistic stance of "vigorously biblical Protestant theologians"; Catholics, he maintains, still consider immortality demonstrable by reason, even if it is won only by faith. "Life After Death: Faith or Knowledge?" (Readers' Response), *The Christian Century* 93 (July 7–14, 1976): 632–34.

4. See, for example, Paul Tillich in *The Meaning of Death*, ed. Herman Feifel (New York, 1959), p. 30.

5. "Immortality of the Soul or Resurrection of the Dead?" in *Immortality and Resurrection*, ed. Krister Stendahl (New York, 1965), pp. 9–53.

6. "Against Raising Hope of Raising the Dead: Contra Moody and Kübler-Ross," p. 65. Herhold makes the same remark in "Kübler-Ross and Life after Death."

7. Discussed by R. Laurence Moore, George Lawton, Geoffrey K. Nelson, and Frank Miller Turner.

8. See R. Laurence Moore, "Spiritualism and the Complaint of Christian Orthodoxy," *In Search of White Crows*, pp. 40–69.

9. He probably had in mind Plato's remark in *Phaedrus* 250c.

10. From "Auguries of Innocence." William Blake, *Complete Writings*, ed. Geoffrey Keynes (London, 1971), p. 434. Here, with characteristic poetic polemics, Blake anticipates the Romantic tradition in literature and theology that sought to elevate the prestige of imagination, making it almost an organ for the perception of higher truths. Elsewhere he chides the Greek philosophers for conceiving of God "as abstracted or distinct from the Imaginative World," and contrasts this to the way Jesus, Abraham, and David "consider'd God as a Man in the Spiritual or Imaginative Vision" (Annotation to Berkeley's "Siris," *Complete Writings*, p. 774). Coleridge, whose distinction between Imagination and Fancy resembles Blake's distinction between Imagination and Memory, provides a more balanced and philosophically astute defense of the imagination, in such writings as *The Statesman's Manual* and the *Biographia literaria*.

11. *Regula pastoralis liber*, ed. H. R. Bramley (Oxford and London, 1874), part 3, prologue, p. 128.

12. *An Essay on Theological Method* (Missoula, Mont., 1975), p. 6.

13. Theological discomfort with experiential claims has a long history, but in its current forms it reflects the influence of such diverse thinkers as Hume, Kant, Feuerbach, Marx, Freud, and Barth. In setting boundaries on the theoretical and practical use of reason, Kant established that God—as Absolute—cannot be an object of possible experience. Many theologians have since felt compelled to characterize religious experience as categorically different from all other kinds of experience and hence not recognizably empirical, or even to condemn interest in religious experience as a self-centered, idolatrous fixation that substitutes for pure faith. A pragmatic view of religious experience has the potential to release us from some of these vetoes; as William James points out, the God of religious experience is a

More rather than a categorically transcendent All. Perhaps God is willing to descend from the status of "wholly other" in order to become available to human experience.

14. Alfred North Whitehead, *Religion in the Making* (New York, 1926; reprint ed., New York, 1960), p. 16. On the other hand, the fast-growing conservative and evangelical Christian communities constitute a significant exception to, and reaction against, this trend.

15. See James, *The Varieties of Religious Experience;* and Bergson, *The Two Sources of Morality and Religion,* tr. R. A. Audra and C. Brereton (New York, 1935). The sociological approach to cognitive religious claims reflects the influence of Marx, Weber, and especially Durkheim, who insists that the reality expressed by religious symbols is primarily a social one and, as such, cannot be understood by introspection.

16. Wilfred Cantwell Smith, *The Meaning and End of Religion* (new ed., San Francisco, 1978), p. 177.

17. *Pragmatism,* ed. Fredson Bowers and Ignas K. Skrupskelis (Cambridge, Mass., 1975), pp. 98–103.

18. *A Personal Narrative,* quoted by James in Lecture 10, "Conversion," *The Varieties of Religious Experience.*

19. *The Soul Life of Plants,* Conclusion, tr. Walter Lowrie in *Religion of a Scientist* (New York, 1946), p. 211.

20. Lecture 10, "Conversion," *The Varieties of Religious Experience.*

21. In putting forward this view, James occupies a theoretical position somewhere between the practical idealism of the optimistic Mind Cure philosophies he describes and criticizes in the *Varieties* and the more complex doctrines of intentionality that have become the specialty of modern schools of phenomenological inquiry. The details of his position cannot be covered here; I have only extracted the general insights that are relevant to interpretation of near-death testimony and are compatible with many different philosophical systems.

22. Géza Róheim, *Animism, Magic, and the Divine King* (London, 1930).

23. From *Reason in Religion,* quoted by Clifford Geertz as an introductory maxim to "Religion as a Cultural System"; in *The Interpretation of Cultures* (New York, 1973), p. 87.

24. *The Life Science* (London, 1977), quoted by Karl R. Popper and John C. Eccles in the frontispiece to *The Self and Its Brain* (New York, 1977).

25. *The Individual and His Religion* (New York, 1950), p. 132.

Bibliography

Medieval Christian Vision Literature: Primary Sources

This is a selected list of primary texts pertaining to medieval visions of the other world; it includes printed editions of works discussed or cited, along with English translations, if available.

Adamnán, the Vision of. Edited by Ernst Windisch. *Irische Texte*, vol. 1. Leipzig, 1880.

———. Translated by C. S. Boswell in *An Irish Precursor of Dante*. London, 1908; reprint ed., New York, 1972.

Aelfric. *Homilies*. In *The Homilies of the Anglo-Saxon Church*, vol. 2. Edited by Benjamin Thorpe. London, 1846.

Alberic, the Vision of. *Bibliotheca Casinensis* 5, 1, pp. 191–206. Montecassino, 1894.

———. Edited in Latin and translated into Italian by Francesco Cancellieri. *Osservazioni intorno alla questione promossa dal Vannozzi dal Mazzochi dal Bottari especialmente dal P. Abate D. Giuseppe Giustino di Costanzo sopra l'originalità della Divina Commedia di Dante, appoggiata alla storia della Visione del Monaco Casinese Alberic*. Rome, 1814.

———. "La Visione di Alberico." Introduction by Antonio Mirra. Text edited by Mauro Inguanez. *Miscellanea Cassinense* 11 (1932): 33–103.

Ansgar, Saint, the Vision of. In *Vita Sancti Anskarii a Rimberto et alio discipulo Anskarii conscripta*. Edited by C. F. Dahlmann. *Monumenta Germaniae Historica*, Scriptores 2, pp. 690–91. Hanover, 1829.

Atkinson, R., ed. and tr. *The Passions and Homilies from Leabhar Breac*. Royal Irish Academy. Dublin, 1887. [Homily 36, pp. 507ff., "On the Soul's Exit from the Body."]

Baldarius, the Vision of. See Valerio of Bierzo.

Barontus, the Vision of. *De SS. Baronto et Desiderio eremetis.* In *Acta Sanctorum* 3, 16 March, pp. 567–74. Edited by J. Bollandus et al. 1643 et seq.

———. *Visio Baronti Monachi Longoretensis.* In *Monumenta Germaniae Historica,* Scriptores Rerum Merovingicarum, vol. 5, pp. 368–94 and table 1. Hanover and Leipzig, 1910.

Bede's Ecclesiastical History of the English People. Edited and translated by Bertram Colgrave and R. A. B. Mynors. Oxford, 1969.

Bernoldus, the Vision of. Attributed to Hincmar of Rheims. *PL* 125, cols. 1115–19.

———. In *Monumenta Germaniae historica: Poetae Latini aevi Carolini.* Edited by E. Dümmler et al. Vol. 2, pp. 268ff. Berlin, 1881.

The Blickling Homilies. Edited by R. Morris. The Early English Text Society Original Series 58 (1874), 63 (1876), and 73 (1880); reprinted as 1 vol. London, New York, Toronto, 1967.

Bonellus, the Vision of. See Valerio of Bierzo.

Boniface, St. *Briefe des Bonifatius, Willibalds Leben des Bonifatius.* Edited in Latin and German by Reinhold Rau (after M. Tangl, P. H. Külb, W. Levison). Darmstadt, 1968.

———. *The Letters of St. Boniface.* Translated by Ephraim Emerton. New York, 1940.

Bran, the Voyage of. *The Voyage of Bran Son of Febal to the Land of the Living.* Edited and translated by Kuno Meyer. With an Essay upon the Irish Vision of the Happy Otherworld and the Celtic Doctrine of Rebirth (by Alfred Nutt). 2 vols. London, 1895 (vol. 1) and 1897 (vol. 2).

Brendan, St., the Voyage of. *Navigatio Sancti Brendani Abbatis.* Edited by C. Selmer. Publications in Mediaeval Studies 16. Notre Dame, Ind., 1959.

———. *The Voyage of Brendan: Journey to the Promised Land.* Translated by John J. O'Meara. Atlantic Highlands, N.J., 1976.

Caesarius of Heisterbach. *The Dialogue on Miracles.* Translated by H. von E. Scott and C. C. Swinton Bland. 2 vols. London, 1929.

———. *Dialogus miraculorum.* Edited by Joseph Strange. 2 vols. Cologne, Bonn, and Brussels, 1851.

Charles the Fat, the Vision of. See Hariulf, William of Malmesbury.

Charlesworth, James H., ed. *The Old Testament Pseudepigrapha.* 2 vols. Garden City, N.Y., 1983.

Comper, Frances M. M., ed. *The Book of the Craft of Dying and Other Early English Tracts concerning Death.* London, 1917; reprint ed., New York, 1977.

Conrad of Eberbach. *Exordium magnum Cisterciense.* Edited by Bruno Grieser. Rome, 1961.

Crane, Thomas, ed. *Mediaeval Sermon-Books and Stories.* Philadelphia, 1883.

Dante Alighieri. *La Divina Commedia.* Edited by C. H. Grandgent and Charles S. Singleton. 3 vols. Cambridge, Mass., 1972.

Dante Alighieri. *The Divine Comedy.* Edited and translated by John D. Sinclair. 3 vols. Oxford, 1939; reprint ed., New York, 1961.

The Debate between the Body and the Soul. (The Vision of Fulbert.) Edited by F. J. Child. Cambridge, 1888.

———. *Zur Visio Fulberti.* Edited by Herman Brandes. Potsdam, 1897.

Delehaye, Hippolytus, ed. "La Pèlerinage de Laurent de Pasztho au Purgatoire de S. Patrice." *Analecta Bollandiana* 27 (1908): 35–60.

The Departing Soul's Address to the Body. Translated by S. W. Singer. London, 1845.

Draumkvaede: A Norwegian Visionary Poem from the Middle Ages. Edited by Knut Liestøl. Studia Norvegica 3. Oslo, 1946.

Drythelm, the Vision of. See Aelfric, Bede, Helinand de Froidmont, Otloh of St. Emmeran, Roger of Wendover.

An English Priest, the Vision of. See Prudentius of Troyes.

Eynsham, the Vision of the Monk of. *The Revelation to the Monk of Evesham.* Edited by Edward Arber. London, 1869.

———. *The Revelation to the Monk of Evesham Abbey.* Translated by Valerian Paget. New York, 1909.

———. See Roger of Wendover.

———. *Visio monachi de Eynsham.* Edited by M. Huber in *Romanische Forschungen* 16 (1904): 641–733.

———. *Visio monachi de Eynsham.* Edited by H. E. Salter. In *Eynsham Cartulary,* vol. 2, pp. 257–371. Oxford Historical Society, vol. 51. Oxford, 1908.

———. *Visio monachi de Eynsham.* Edited by H. Thurston. *Analecta Bollandiana* 22, pp. 225–319. Paris and Brussels, 1903.

Frati, Ludovico, ed. "Il Purgatorio di S. Patrizio secondo Stefano di Bourbon e Umberto di Roma." *Giornale Storico della Letteratura Italiana* 8 (1886): 140–79.

———. "Tradizioni Storiche del Purgatorio di San Patrizio." *Giornale Storico della Letteratura Italiana* 17 (1981): 46–79.

Fursa, the Vision of. *Acta Sanctorum Bollandiana.* (16 January): 36b–41b.

———. See Aelfric, Bede.

———. *Vita virtutesque Fursei Abbatis Latiniacensis.* Edited by B. Krusch. *Monumenta Germaniae Historica,* Scriptores Rerum Merovingicarum 4, pp. 423–51. Hanover and Leipzig, 1902.

Gottschalk, the Vision of. Edited by G. W. Leibniz. *Scriptores Rerum Brunsvicensium.* Vol. 1, pp. 870–75. Hanover, 1707.

———. Edited by R. Usener. *Quellensammlung für schleswig-holsteinisch-lauenburgische Geschichte* 4 (1875): 75ff.

Gregory the Great. *Dialogi.* Edited by Umberto Moricca. Rome, 1924.

———. *Dialogues.* Translated by Odo John Zimmerman. New York, 1959.

Gregory of Tours. *Historiae Francorum libri decem.* Edited by Rudolf Buchner. Berlin, 1957.

———. *History of the Franks.* 2 vols. Translated by O. M. Dalton. Oxford, 1927.

Gunthelm, the Vision of. Edited by Giles Constable in "The Vision of a Cistercian Novice." *Studia Anselmiana* 40 (1956): 96–98.

———. Edited by Giles Constable in "The Vision of Gunthelm and Other *Visiones* Attributed to Peter the Venerable." *Revue Bénédictine* 66 (1956): 105–113.

———. See Helinand de Froidmont, Vincent of Beauvais.

Hammerich, L. L., ed. *Visiones Georgii.* Copenhagen, 1931.

Hariulf. *Chronicon Centulense ou Chronique de l'Abbaye de Saint-Riquier.* Translated into French by the Marquis Le Ver. Edited by Ernest Prarond. Memoires de la Société d'Emulation d'Abbeville, 3. Abbeville, 1899.

———. *Chronique de l'Abbaye de Saint-Riquier.* Edited by Ferdinand Lot. Paris, 1894.

Helinand de Froidmont. *Chronicon.* PL 212 [The Vision of Tundal, cols. 1038–55; the Vision of a Monk of Melrose, cols. 1059–60; the Vision of Gunthelm, cols. 1060–63].

Heningham, Eleanor Kellog. *An Early Latin Debate of the Body and Soul.* Menasha, Wis., 1939.

Holdsworth, C. J., ed. "Eleven Visions Connected with the Cistercian Monastery of Stratford Langthorne." *Cîteaux: Commentarii Cistercienses* 13 (1962): 185–204.

Jacobus de Voragine. *The Golden Legend.* Edited by Theodor Graese. Dresden, Leipzig, 1846.

Jacques de Vitry. *The Exempla; or Illustrative Stories from the "Sermones vulgares" of Jacques de Vitry.* Edited by T. F. Crane. Folklore Society Publications 26. London, 1890.

James, Montague Rhodes, ed. *The Testament of Abraham.* Cambridge, 1892.

James, Montague Rhodes, and Claude Jenkins. *A Descriptive Catalogue of the Manuscripts in the Lambeth Palace Library.* Cambridge, 1930–1932. [Lambeth Ms. 51, Peter of Cornwall, *Liber revelationum*, pp. 71–85.]

Jeanroy, A., and A. Vignaux. *Voyage au purgatoire de S. Patrice; Visions de Tindal et de S. Paul; textes languedociens du quinzième siècle.* Toulouse, 1903; reprint ed., New York, 1971.

Julian of Norwich, St. *A Book of Showings to the Anchoress Julian of Norwich.* Edited by Edmund Colledge and James Walsh. 2 vols. Toronto, 1978.

Krapp, G. P. *The Legend of Saint Patrick's Purgatory, Its Later Literary History.* Baltimore, 1900. [The Vision of William Staunton, pp. 54–77.]

Laisrén, the Vision of. Edited and translated by Kuno Meyer. *Otia Merseiana* 1 (1899): 113–19.

Lazarus, the Vision of. See Voigt, Max.

Leofric, the Vision of. Edited by A. S. Napier in "An Old English Vision of Leofric, Earl of Mercia." *Transactions of the Philological Society* 1907–1910, ii (London, 1909): 180–87.

Leslie, Shane, ed. *Saint Patrick's Purgatory: A Record from History and Literature.* London, 1932.

Mahaffy, J. P. "Two Early Tours in Ireland." *Hermathena* 18 (1914): 1–16.

Maximus, the Vision of. See Valerio of Bierzo.

"The Monk's Dream." Translated by Theodore Martin. *Erlanger Beiträge zur englischen Philologie* 1 (1889): 200–209.

Mörner, Marianne, ed. *Le Purgatoire de Saint Patrice par Berol.* Lund, 1917.

Odericus Vitalis. *The Ecclesiastical History.* Edited and translated by Marjorie Chibnall. Oxford, 1973. [Vol. 4, chap. 17: the Vision of Walkelin, pp. 236–50.]

Orm, the Vision of. Edited by H. Farmer. *Analecta Bollandiana* 75 (1957): 72–82.

O'Sullivan-Beare, Philip. "De purgatorio divi Patritii." In *Historiae Catholicae Iberniae compendium*, vol. 1, bk. 2. Dublin, 1850.

———. *Patritiana Decas.* Madrid, 1629. [Book 9: the Vision of Tundal, the Purgatory of Saint Patrick.]

Otloh of St. Emmeran. *Liber visionum.* PL 146, cols. 341–88. [Vision of Drythelm, cols. 380ff.]

Paul, St., the Vision of. Long Latin version. Edited by M. R. James in *Apocrypha Anecdota*, vol. 1. Texts and Studies II, 3, pp. 11–42. Cambridge, 1895.

———. Long Latin version. Translated by Andrew Rutherfurd. In *The Ante-Nicene Fathers*, vol. 9, pp. 149–66. Edited by Allan Menzies. 5th ed. New York, 1912.

———. Redaction 1, Vienna Fragment, Redaction 4. Edited by Herman Brandes in *Visio Sancti Pauli; ein Beiträg zur Visionsliteratur mit einem deutschen und zwei lateinischen Texten*. Gesellschaft für deutsche Philologie. Festschrift 5. Halle, 1885.

———. See Silverstein, Theodore.

Peter, the Apocalypse of. Translated by Andrew Rutherfurd. In *The Ante-Nicene Fathers*, vol. 9, pp. 141–47. Edited by Allan Menzies. 5th ed. New York, 1912.

Peter of Cornwall. *Book of Revelations*. See James, Montague Rhodes.

Peter the Deacon. *Chronica monasterii Casinensis*. Edited by W. Wattenbach. *Monumenta Germaniae Historica, Scriptores* vol. 7. Hanover, 1846; reprint ed., Stuttgart and New York, 1963. [Book 4, chap. 66, pp. 793–94, Peter the Deacon on the Vision of Alberic.]

The Phoenix. Edited by N. F. Blake. Manchester, 1964.

Plutarch. "On the Delays of the Divine Vengeance." *Moralia* 548–68. Translated by Phillip H. De Lacy and Benedict Einarson. Cambridge, Mass., and London, 1959. [The Vision of Thespesius, 563B–568.]

———. "On the Sign of Socrates." *Moralia* 575–98. Translated by Phillip H. De Lacy and Benedict Einarson. Cambridge, Mass., and London, 1959. [The Vision of Timarchus, 589–92.]

A Poor Woman, the Vision of. *Visio cuiusdam pauperculae mulieris*. Edited by Wilhelm Wattenbach and Wilhelm Levison in *Deutschlands Geschichtsquellen im Mittelalter*, 5. Bd. 1, pp. 260–61. Berlin, 1885. Reprint edition by Heinz Löwe in *DGQM Vorzeit und Karolinger* 3, pp. 317–18. Weimar, 1957.

Prudentius of Troyes. *Annales Bertiniani*. In *Monumenta Germaniae Historica*. Scriptores rerum Germanicarum 1. Hanover, 1883. ["Visio cuiusdam religiosi praesbiteri de terra Anglorum," p. 433.]

The Purgatory of St. Patrick. See Delehaye, Hippolytus; Frati, Ludovico; Hammerich, L. L.; Jeanroy, A.; Krapp, G. P.; Leslie, Shane; Mahaffy, J. P.; Mörner, Marianne; O'Sullivan-Beare, Philip; Seymour, St. John D.; Warnke, K.

———. *Tractatus de purgatorio sancti Patricii*. Edited by C. M. van der Zanden. *Etude sur le purgatoire de Saint Patrice, accompagnée du texte latin d'Utrecht et du texte anglo-normand de Cambridge*. Amsterdam, 1927.

———. *Tractatus de purgatorio sancti Patricii*. Edited by E. Mall. "Zur Geschichte der Legende vom Purgatorium des heil. Patricius." *Romanische Forschungen* 6 (1881): 139–97.

———. *Tractatus de purgatorio sancti Patricii*. Edited by Thomas Messingham (from H. of Sawtry, David Rothe, Matthew Paris, and others). In *Florilegium Insulae Sanctorum*. Paris, 1624. Reprinted in *PL* 180, cols. 973–1004.

Raduin, the Vision of. Edited by O. Holder-Egger in *Neues Archiv der Gesellschaft für ältere deutsche Geschichtskunde* 11 (1886): 262–63.

Roger of Wendover. *Chronica, sive Flores historiarum*. Edited by Henry O. Coxe. 3 vols. London, 1841. [Vol. 1: A.D. 699, the Vision of Drythelm, pp. 190–95. Vol. 2: A.D. 1153, the Vision of the Knight Owen (St. Patrick's Purgatory). Vol. 3: A.D. 1196, the Vision of the Monk of Eynsham, pp. 97–117; A.D. 1206, the Vision of Thurkill, pp. 190–209.]

———. *Flowers of History*. Translated by J. A. Giles. 2 vols. London, 1849.

Rotcharius, the Vision of. Edited by W. Wattenbach. In *Anzeiger für Kunde der deutschen Vorzeit*, Neue Folge, 22 (1875): 72–74.

Salvius, the Vision of. See Gregory of Tours.

Savigny, the Visions of a Monk of. Edited by E. P. Sauvage. In *Analecta Bollandiana* 2 (1883): 505-8.

Silverstein, Theodore. *Visio Sancti Pauli; The History of the Apocalypse in Latin together with nine texts.* London, 1935.

"The Soul's Address to the Body." In *The Vercelli Book* and *The Exeter Book.* Edited by George Philip Krapp and Elliott van Kirk Dobbie. *The Anglo Saxon Poetic Records.* New York, 1932, 1936.

Stone, M. E., ed. *The Testament of Abraham: The Greek Recensions.* Missoula, Mont., 1972.

Sunniulf, the Vision of. See Gregory of Tours.

Thespesius, the Vision of. See Plutarch.

Thurkill, the Vision of. See Roger of Wendover.

——. *Visio Thurkilli relatore, ut videtur, Radulpho de Coggeshall.* Edited by Paul Gerhard Schmidt. Leipzig, 1978.

——. "The Vision of Thurkill, Probably by Ralph of Coggeshall, Printed from a Ms. in the British Museum." Edited by H. L. D. Ward. *The Journal of the British Archaeological Association* 31 (1875): 420-59.

Timarchus, the Vision of. See Plutarch.

Tubach, Frederic C. *Index exemplorum: A Handbook of Medieval Religious Tales.* F. F. Communications, vol. 86, no. 204. Helsinki, 1969.

Tundal, the Vision of. Edited by H. Spilling in *Die Visio Tnugdali; Eigenart und Stellung in der mittelalterlichen Visionsliteratur bis zum Ende des 12. Jahrhunderts.* Munich, 1975.

——. See Helinand de Froidmont and Vincent of Beauvais.

——. *Versions Inédites de la Vision de Tondale.* Edited by V.-H. Friedel and Kuno Meyer. Paris, 1899.

——. *Visio Tnugdali: The German and Dutch Translations and Their Circulation in the Later Middle Ages.* Edited by Nigel F. Palmer. Munich and Zurich, 1982.

——. *Visio Tnugdali lateinisch und altdeutsch.* Edited by Albrecht Wagner. Erlangen, 1882.

——. *La Vision de Tondale, textes français, anglo-normand, et irlandais.* Edited by V.-H. Friedel and Kuno Meyer. Paris, 1907.

——. *The Visions of Tundale.* Edited by W. B. D. D. Turnbull. Edinburgh, 1843.

Valerio of Bierzo. *Sancti Valerii Abbatis opuscula. PL* 87 [The Vision of Maximus, cols. 431-33; the Vision of Bonellus, cols. 433-35; the Vision of Baldarius, cols. 435-36.]

Vincent of Beauvais. *Bibliotheca mundi seu Speculi maioris.* Vol. 2: *Speculum morale* [The Vision of an English Novice, p. 739]. Vol. 4: *Speculum historiale* [The Purgatory of St. Patrick, 789; the Vision of an English Man, 941; the Vision of the Boy William, 1146; the Vision of Tundal, 1127-33; the Vision of a Cistercian Novice, 1187]. Douay, 1624.

Voigt, Max. *Beiträge zur Geschichte der Visionenliteratur im Mittelalter.* Leipzig, 1924; reprint ed., New York, 1967. [The Vision of Lazarus, pp. 8-13; the Vision of Louis of France, pp. 226-45.]

Walkelin, the Vision of. See Odericus Vitalis.

Warnke, K., ed. *Das Buch vom Espurgatoire S. Patrice der Marie de France und seine Quelle.* Halle/Saale, 1938.

Wetti, the Vision of [Heito]. *Visio Guetini. PL* 105, cols. 771-80.

————. [Heito and Walahfrid Strabo]. Edited by Ernst Dümmler. *Monumenta Germaniae Historica*, Poetarum latinorum medii aevi, vol. 2, pp. 267–334. Berlin, 1884; reprint ed., Munich, 1978.

————. [Walahfrid Strabo]. *Walahfrid Strabo's Visio Wettini: Text, Translation and Commentary*. By David A. Traill. Bern and Frankfort/M, 1974.

William of Malmesbury. *De rebus gestis Anglorum*. Vol. 1. London, 1887. [The Vision of Charles the Fat.]

————. *William of Malmesbury's Chronicle*. Translated by John Sharpe. Edited and revised by J. A. Giles. London, 1847. [The Vision of Charles the Fat, pp. 102–5.]

William Staunton, the Vision of. See Krapp, G. P.

Medieval Christian Vision Literature:
Secondary Sources

Ariès, Philippe. *The Hour of Our Death*. Translated by Helen Weaver. New York, 1981.

———— *Western Attitudes toward Death: From the Middle Ages to the Present*. Translated by Patricia M. Ranum. Baltimore and London, 1974.

Asín Palacios, Miguel. *La escatologia Musulmana en la Divina Comedia*. Madrid, 1919. Reprinted as *Dante y el Islam*. Madrid, 1927.

————. *La escatologia Musulmana en la Divina Comedia: seguida de la historía y crítica de una polémica*. 2nd ed. Madrid and Granada, 1943.

Becker, Ernest J. *A Contribution to the Comparative Study of the Medieval Visions of Heaven and Hell*. Baltimore, 1899.

Benz, Ernst. *Die Vision: Erfahrungsformen und Bilderwelt*. Stuttgart, 1969.

Bieler, Ludwig. "Topography of Lough Dearg." *The Irish Ecclesiastical Record*, March 1, 1960.

Bloomfield, Morton W. *The Seven Deadly Sins*. East Lansing, Mich., 1952.

Boase, Thomas Sherrer Ross. *Death in the Middle Ages: Mortality, Judgment, Remembrance*. New York, 1972.

Bousset, Wilhelm. "Die Himmelsreise der Seele." *Archiv für Religionswissenschaft* 3–4 (Göttingen, 1900–1901): 136–69, 229–73.

Brandon, S. G. F. *The Judgment of the Dead*. New York, 1967.

Carey, John. "The Location of the Otherworld in Irish Tradition." *EIGSE: A Journal of Irish Studies* 19 (1982): 36–43.

Carozzi, Claude. "Structure et fonction de la Vision de Tnugdal." In *Faire Croire*, pp. 223–34. Rome, 1981.

Cerulli, Enrico. *Il "Libro della Scala" e la questione delle fonti arabo-spagnole della Divina Commedia*. Vatican City, 1949.

Dana, H. W. L. "Medieval Visions of the Other World." Ph.D. dissertation, Harvard University, 1910.

D'Ancona, Alessandro. *Scritti Danteschi*. Florence, 1974. Reprint ed., Florence, 1912–13.

Davidson, H. R. Ellis, ed. *The Journey to the Other World*. Cambridge and Totowa, N.J., 1975.

Dieterich, A. *Nekyia: Beiträge zur Erklärung der neuentdeckten Petrusapokalypse*. 2nd ed. Leipzig and Berlin, 1913.

Dinzelbacher, Peter. "Die Vision Alberichs und die Esdras-Apokryphe." *Studien und Mitteilungen zur Geschichte des Benediktiner-Ordens* 87 (1976): 435–42.

———.*Vision und Visionsliteratur im Mittelalters*. Stuttgart, 1981.

———. "Die Visionen des Mittelalters." *Zeitschrift für Religions- und Geistesgeschichte* 30 (1978): 116–18.

———. "Zur Entstehung von *Draumkvoede*." *Skandinavistik* 10 (1980): 89–96.

Dinzelbacher, Peter, and Harald Kleinschmidt. "Seelenbrücke und Brückenbau im mittelalterlichen England." *Numen* 31 (1984): 242–87.

Dods, Marcus. *Forerunners of Dante: An Account of Some of the More Important Visions of the Unseen World, from the Earliest Times*. Edinburgh, 1903.

Dudley, Louise. *The Egyptian Elements in the Legend of the Body and Soul*. Baltimore, 1911.

Ellis, Hilda R. *The Road to Hel: A Study of the Conception of the Dead in Old Norse Literature*. Cambridge, 1943.

———. *See* Davidson, H. R. Ellis.

Félice, Philippe de. *L'Autre monde: mythes et légendes: le purgatoire de saint Patrice*. Paris, 1906.

Fritzsche, C. "Die lateinischen Visionen des Mittelalters bis zur Mitte des 12. Jahrhunderts." *Romanische Forschungen* 2 (1886): 247–79; 3 (1887): 337–69.

Gatch, Milton M. *Death: Meaning and Mortality in Christian Thought and Contemporary Culture*. New York, 1969.

———. "The Fourth Dialogue of Gregory the Great: Some Problems of Interpretation," in *Studia Patristica* 10, part 1, pp. 77–83. Edited by F. L. Cross. Berlin, 1970.

. "Some Theological Reflections on Death from the Early Church through the Reformation." In *Perspectives on Death*, pp. 99–136. Edited by Liston O. Mills. Nashville and New York, 1969.

Gatto, G. "Le voyage au paradis: la christianisation des traditions folkloriques au Moyen Age." *Annales E.S.C.* (1979): 929–42.

Gurevic, Aaron J. "Au Moyen Age: Conscience individuelle et image de l'au-delà." *Annales E.S.C.* 37 (1982): 255–75.

Himmelfarb, Martha. *Tours of Hell: An Apocalyptic Form in Jewish and Christian Literature*. Philadelphia, 1983.

Holdsworth, C. J. "Visions and Visionaries in the Middle Ages." *History* 48 (1963): 141–53.

Huizinga, J. *The Waning of the Middle Ages*. Translated and adapted by the author and F. Hopman. New York, 1949; reprint ed., Garden City, N.Y., 1954.

James, M. R. "Irish Apocrypha." *Journal of Theological Studies* 20 (1918): 9–16.

King, Georgiana Goddard. "The Vision of Thurkill and Saint James of Compostela." *The Romanic Review* 10 (1919): 38–47.

———. *The Way of St. James*. 3 vols. New York and London, 1920.

Kohler, Kaufmann. *Heaven and Hell in Comparative Religion*. New York, 1923.

Krapp, George Philip. *The Legend of Saint Patrick's Purgatory: Its Later Literary History*. Baltimore, 1900.

Kroll, Jerome, and Bernard Bachrach. "Visions and Psychopathology in the Middle Ages." *The Journal of Nervous and Mental Disease* 170 (1982): 41–49.

Le Don, Gérard. "Structure et significations de l'imagerie médiévale de l'enfer." *Cahiers de civilisation médiévale* 22 (1979): 363–72.

Le Goff, Jacques. *The Birth of Purgatory.* Translated by Arthur Goldhammer. Chicago, 1984.

———. *La naissance du purgatoire.* Paris, 1981.

Leslie, Shane. *Saint Patrick's Purgatory.* London, 1932.

Locke, F. W. "A New Date for the Composition of the *Tractatus de Purgatorio Sancti Patricii.*" *Speculum* 40 (1965): 641–46.

McGinn, Bernard. *Visions of the End: Apocalyptic Traditions in the Middle Ages.* New York, 1979.

McNamara, Martin. *The Apocrypha in the Irish Church.* Dublin, 1975.

La mort au moyen âge. Colloque de l'Association des historiens médiévistes français, Strasbourg, June 1975. 2 vols. Strasbourg, 1977.

Muñoz y Sendino, José. *La Escala de Mahoma.* Madrid, 1949.

O'Connor, Daniel. *St. Patrick's Purgatory, Lough Derg.* Dublin, 1879. Rev. ed., Dublin, London, and New York, 1895. 2nd rev. ed., Dublin, 1910.

O'Connor, Sister Mary Catherine. *The Art of Dying Well: The Development of the Ars moriendi.* New York, 1942.

Olschki, Leonardo. "Mohammedan Eschatology and Dante's Other World." *Comparative Literature* 3 (1951): 1–17.

Owen, Douglas D. R. *The Vision of Hell.* Edinburgh, 1970.

Patch, Howard Rollin. *The Other World according to Descriptions in Medieval Literature.* Cambridge, 1950; reprint ed., New York, 1970.

Peters, E. "Zur Geschichte der lateinischen Visionslegenden." *Romanische Forschungen* 8 (1893): 361–64.

Petersen, J. M. *The Dialogues of Gregory the Great in Their Late Antique Cultural Background.* Leiden, 1984.

Reynolds, Frank E., and Earle H. Waugh, ed. *Religious Encounters with Death.* University Park, Pa., 1977.

Schmidt, P. G. "The Vision of Thurkill." *Journal of the Warburg and Courtauld Institutes* 41 (1978): 50–64.

Le sentiment de la mort au moyen âge. Etudes presentées au cinquième colloque de l'Institut d'études médiévales de l'Université de Montréal. Published under direction of Claude Sutto. Montreal, 1979.

Seymour, St. John D. "The Bringing Forth of the Soul in Irish Literature." *Journal of Theological Studies* 22 (1920): 16–20.

———. "The Eschatology of the Early Irish Church." *Zeitschrift für celtische Philologie* 14 (1923): 179–211.

———. *Irish Visions of the Other World.* London, 1930; New York and Toronto, 1930.

———. "Notes on Apocrypha in Ireland." *Proceedings of the Royal Irish Academy* 37c (1926): 107–16.

———. *St. Patrick's Purgatory: A Medieval Pilgrimage in Ireland.* Dundalk, 1918.

———. "The Seven Heavens in Irish Literature." *Zeitschrift für celtische Philologie* 14 (1923): 18–30.

———. "Studies in the Vision of Tundal." *Proceedings of the Royal Irish Academy* 37c (1926): 87–106.

———. "The Vision of Adamnan." *Proceedings of the Royal Irish Academy* 37c (1927): 304–12.

Silverstein, Theodore. "Dante and the Legend of the Mi'raj: The Problem of Islamic Influence on the Christian Literature of the Otherworld." *Journal of Near Eastern Studies* 11 (1952): 89–110, 187–97.

———. "Did Dante Know the Vision of Saint Paul?" *(Harvard) Studies and Notes in Philology and Literature* 19 (1937): 231–47.

———. *Visio Sancti Pauli: The History of the Apocalypse in Latin together with Nine Texts.* London, 1935.

———. "The *Vision of Leofric* and Gregory's *Dialogues.*" *Review of English Studies* 9 (April 1933): 186–88.

———. "The Vision of St. Paul: New Links and Patterns in the Western Tradition." *Archives d'histoire doctrinale et littéraire du moyen âge* 26 (1959): 199–248.

Spilling, Herrad. *Die Visio Tnugdali: Eigenart und Stellung in der mittelalterlichen Visionsliteratur bis zum Ende des 12. Jahrhunderts.* Munich, 1975.

Sumption, Jonathan. *Pilgrimage: An Image of Mediaeval Religion.* Totowa, N.J., 1975.

Thompson, Stith. *Otherworld Journeys.* In *Motif-Index of Folk-Literature,* vol. 3, F0–F199. Helsinki and Bloomington, Ind., 1934.

Turner, Victor and Edith. *Image and Pilgrimage in Christian Culture.* New York, 1978.

Van Os, Arnold Barel. *Religious Visions. The Development of the Eschatological Elements in Mediaeval English Religious Literature.* Amsterdam, 1932.

Wagner, Albrecht. *Ausgabe der Visio Tnugdali.* Erlangen, 1882.

Ward, Henry Leigh Douglas. *Catalogue of Romances in the Department of Manuscripts of the British Museum.* Vol. 2. London, 1893.

Willson, Elizabeth. *The Middle English Legends of Visits to the Other World and Their Relation to the Metrical Romances.* Chicago, 1917.

Wright, Thomas. *St. Patrick's Purgatory: An Essay on the Legends of Purgatory, Hell and Paradise Current during the Middle Ages.* London, 1844.

Near-Death Experience: Contemporary Works

Abell, George O., and Barry Singer, eds. *Science and the Paranormal: Probing the Existence of the Supernatural.* New York, 1981.

Alcock, James E. "Pseudo-Science and the Soul." *Essence: Issues in the Study of Ageing, Dying and Death* 5 (1981): 65–76.

———. "Psychology and Near-Death Experiences." In *Paranormal Borderlands of Science,* ed. Kendrick Frazier, pp. 153–69. Buffalo, 1981.

Anabiosis. A regular digest of news for the membership of the Association for the Scientific Study of Near-Death Phenomena. Vol. 1, no. 1 (May 1979) to Vol. 2, no. 3 (February 1981). [Replaced by *Vital Signs.*]

Anabiosis: The Journal for Near-Death Studies. Published semiannually by the International Association for Near-Death Studies. Vol. 1, no. 1 (July 1981) et seq.

Atwater, P. M. H. "Coming Back" [column]. *Vital Signs* 1 (June 1981) et seq.

———. *I Died Three Times in 1977.* Dayton, Va., 1980.

Audette, John. "Visions of Knowledge in NDEs." *Vital Signs* 1 (March 1982): 5–6.

Axelrod, Benjamin. "Pastoral Implications of 'Life after Life.'" *Soul Searcher: Quarterly Journal of Christian Psychic Research* 1, 3 (Spring 1978): 11–14.

Badham, Paul. "Death-bed Visions and Christian Hope." *Theology* 83 (July 1980): 269–75.

Badham, Paul and Linda. *Immortality or Extinction?* Totowa, N.J., 1982.

Barrett, William F. *Deathbed Visions.* London, 1926.

Berman, Alan L. "Belief in Afterlife, Religion, Religiosity and Life-Threatening Experiences." *Omega: Journal of Death and Dying* 5 (1974): 127–35.

Beyond and Back. Directed by James L. Conway. Screenplay by Stephen Lord. Sunn Classic Pictures, 1977.

Blacher, Richard S. "To Sleep, Perchance to Dream . . ." *The Journal of the American Medical Association* 242, 21 (November 23, 1979): 2291.

Blackmore, Susan J. *Beyond the Body: An Investigation of Out-of-the-Body Experiences*. London, 1982.

Blincow, N. "Exciting New Evidence That There Is Life after Death." *National Enquirer* (November 6, 1979): 1.

Bozzano, E. "Apparitions of Deceased Persons at Death-Beds." *The Annals of Psychical Science* 5 (1906): 67–100.

———. *Phenomènes psychiques au moment de la mort*. Paris, 1923.

Braude, Stephen E. "The Holographic Analysis of Near-Death Experiences: The Perpetuation of Some Deep Mistakes." *Essence* 5 (1981): 53–64.

Breecher, Maury. "For Them, Life Is Better after Near-Death Experience." *Boston Globe* (June 14, 1982): 25–26.

Breig, James. "Hell: Still a Burning Question?" *U.S. Catholic* (November 1977): 6–10.

Brickhouse, Richard. "Near-Death Experiences: Medical or Miracle?" *The Daily Progress*. Charlottesville, Va. (October 24, 1982): F1, F3.

Brody, Eugene B. "Research in Reincarnation and Editorial Responsibility: An Editiorial." *The Journal of Nervous and Mental Disease* 165 (September 1977): 151.

Brooke, Tal. *The Other Side of Death: Does Death Seal Your Destiny?* Wheaton, Ill., 1979.

Burch, G. E., et al. "What Death Is Like." *American Heart Journal* 76, 3 (1968): 438–39.

Butler, R. N. "The Life Review: An Interpretation of Reminiscence in the Aged." *Psychiatry* 26, 1 (1963): 65–76.

Carr, Daniel. "Pathophysiology of Stress-Induced Limbic Lobe Dysfunction: A Hypothesis for NDEs." *Anabiosis* 2 (June 1982): 75–90.

Cherry, Laurence B. "What Is It Like to Die?" *Glamour* (July 1981): 180ff.

Clark, Davis W., ed. *Death-bed Scenes: or Dying with and without Religion: Designed to Illustrate the Truth and Power of Christianity*. New York, 1852.

Comer, N. L., L. Madow, and J. L. Dixon. "Observations of Sensory Deprivation in a Life-Threatening Situation." *American Journal of Psychiatry* 124 (1967): 169.

"The Conversion of Kübler-Ross: from Thanatology to Seances and Sex." *Time* (November 12, 1979): 81.

Crichton, Ian. *The Art of Dying*. Chapter 9: "Glimpses into the Unknown," pp. 155–63. London, 1976.

Crookall, Robert. *Out-of-Body Experiences: A Fourth Analysis*. New Hyde Park, N.Y., 1970.

Currie, Ian. *You Cannot Die*. Agincourt, Ontario, and New York, 1978.

Davis, Marietta. *Scenes beyond the Grave: Visions of Marietta Davis*. Edited by Gordon Lindsay. Dallas, 1978. Originally published in 1856.

"Dead Kin 'Pushed' Brother Back to Life." Associated Press, *Boston Globe* (December 24, 1981). [Followed by *New York Daily News* photograph on December 25, 1981.]

"Death Trips: Hints of Immortality." *Human Behavior* 8 (May 1979): 48.

"Deathbed Visions: Worldwide Reports from Those at Death's Door." *Human Behavior* 7 (April 1978): 27.

Delacour, Jean-Baptiste. *Aus dem Jenseits Zurück*. Düsseldorf and Vienna, 1973.

———. *Glimpses of the Beyond*. Translated by E. B. Garside. New York, 1974.

"Denver Cardiologist Discloses Findings after 18 Years of Near-Death Research" [Fred Schoonmaker]. *Anabiosis* 1 (May 1979): 1–2.

Dlin, D. M. "Survivors of Cardiac Arrest." *Psychosomatic Medicine* 14 (1974): 61–67.

Dobson, M. "Attitudes and Long Term Adjustment of Patients Surviving Cardiac Arrest." *British Medical Journal* 3 (1971): 207–12.

"Dr. Elisabeth Kübler-Ross, who pioneered movement for candid counseling of dying people and their families, has moved into spiritualism." *New York Times* (September 17, 1979): 2, p. 10, col. 1.

"Dr. George Ritchie describes experiences during 9 minute period when doctors had pronounced him dead." *Washington Post* (June 3, 1977): 2, col. 1.

"Doctor Says Death Is 'Pleasant.'" *Hartford Courant* (March 30, 1975): 9, col. 1.

Drab, Kevin J. "Researcher Suggests Broader Classification for Near-Death Phenomena." *Anabiosis* 2 (November 1980): 6.

———. "The Tunnel Experience: Reality or Hallucination?" *Anabiosis* 1 (December 1981): 126–53.

———. "Unresolved Problems in the Study of Near-Death Experiences: Some Suggestions for Research and Theory." *Anabiosis* 1 (July 1981): 27–43.

Druss, R. G., and D. S. Kornfeld. "The Survivors of Cardiac Arrest." *Journal of the American Medical Association* 201 (1967): 291–96.

Eastman, Margaret. "The Evidence for Out-of-the-Body Experiences." *Proceedings, Society for Psychical Research* 53 (December 1962): 287–309.

Ebon, Martin. *The Evidence for Life after Death*. New York, 1977.

Eby, Richard E. *Caught Up into Paradise: A Physician's Amazing Account*. Old Tappan, N.J., 1971.

Ehrenwald, Jan. "Out-of-the-Body Experience and the Denial of Death." *The Journal of Nervous and Mental Disease* 159 (October 1974): 227–33.

"The Experience of Dying." *Lancet* (June 24, 1978): 1347–48.

Falce, Virginia. "Personal Reflections on Near-Death Experiences." *Anabiosis* 1 (May 1979): 4.

Flynn, Charles P. "Meanings and Implications of NDEr Transformations: Some Preliminary Findings and Implications." *Anabiosis* 2 (June 1982): 3–14.

Ford, Marvin. *On the Other Side*. Plainfield, N.J., 1978.

Gabbard, G. O., S. W. Twemlow, and F. C. Jones. "Do Near-Death Experiences Occur Only Near Death?" *The Journal of Nervous and Mental Disease* 169 (1981): 374–77.

Gallup, George, Jr., with William Proctor. *Adventures in Immortality: A Look beyond the Threshold of Death*. New York, 1982.

Garfield, Charles A. "Consciousness Alteration and Fear of Death." *Journal of Transpersonal Psychology* 7 (1975): 147–75.

———. "More Grist for the Mill: Additional Near-Death Research Findings and Discussion." *Anabiosis* 1 (May 1979): 5–7.

Gill, Derek. *Quest: The Life of Elisabeth Kübler-Ross.* New York, 1980.

Goleman, Daniel. "Back from the Brink." *Psychology Today* (April 1977): 56–60.

———. " 'The Child Will Always Be There. Real Love Doesn't Die.' " [Interview with Elisabeth Kübler-Ross.] *Psychology Today* (September 1976): 48–52.

———. "We Are Breaking the Silence about Death." [Profile of Elisabeth Kübler-Ross.] *Psychology Today* (September 1976): 44–47, 103.

Goulet, Yvonne. "Will People Throw Parties in Heaven?" *U.S. Catholic* 44 (April 1979): 6–10.

Green, Celia E. *Out-of-the-Body Experiences.* Oxford, 1968; New York, 1973.

Green, J. Timothy, and Penelope Friedman. "Near-Death Experiences in a Southern California Population." *Anabiosis* 3 (June 1983): 77–96.

Greene, F. Gordon. "A Glimpse behind the Life Review." *Journal of Religion and Psychical Research* 4 (April 1981): 113–30.

———. "Multiple Mind/Body Perspectives and the Out-of-Body Experience." *Anabiosis* 3 (June 1983): 39–62.

Grey, Margot. *Return from Death.* London, Boston, and Henley, 1985.

Greyson, Bruce. "Near-Death Experiences and Attempted Suicide." *Suicide and Life-Threatening Behavior* 11 (1981): 10–16.

———. "Toward a Psychological Explanation of Near-Death Experiences: A Response to Dr. Grosso's Paper." *Anabiosis* 1 (December 1981): 88–103.

Greyson, Bruce, and Charles P. Flynn, eds. *The Near-Death Experience: Problems, Prospects, Perspectives.* Springfield, Ill., 1984.

Greyson, Bruce, and Ian Stevenson. "The Phenomenology of Near-Death Experiences." *American Journal of Psychiatry* 137, 10 (October 1980): 1193–96.

Grof, Stanislav and Christina. *Beyond Death: The Gates of Consciousness.* New York, 1980.

Grof, Stanislav, and Joan Halifax. *The Human Encounter with Death.* New York, Toronto, and Vancouver, 1977.

Grosso, Michael. "Jung, Parapsychology, and the Near-Death Experience: Toward a Transpersonal Paradigm." *Anabiosis* 3 (June 1983): 3–38.

———. "Toward an Explanation of Near-Death Phenomena." *The Journal of the American Society for Psychical Research* 75 (1981): 37–60.

Hackett, Thomas P. "The Lazarus Complex Revisited." *Annals of Internal Medicine* 76 (January 1972): 135–37.

Heaney, John J. "Beyond Death." *Thought: Fordham University Quarterly* 50 (1975): 35–55.

Heim, Albert. "Notizen über den Tod durch Absturz." *Jahrbuch des schweizer alpen Club* 27 (1892): 327–37. [Translated by Noyes and Kletti, "The Experience of Dying from Falls."]

Herhold, Robert M. "Kübler-Ross and Life after Death." *The Christian Century* 93 (April 14, 1976): 363–64.

Heywood, Rosalind. "Attitudes to Death in the Light of Dreams and Other 'Out-of-the-Body' Experience." In *Man's Concern with Death*, by Arnold Toynbee et al., pp. 185–219. London, 1968; New York, 1969.

Hick, John. *Death and Eternal Life.* London, 1976.

Hill, J. Arthur. *Spiritualism: Its History, Phenomena and Doctrine.* New York, 1919.

Hobson, Douglas P. " 'Perithan Experience': Naming the Beyond." *Perspectives in Biology and Medicine* 21 (Summer 1978): 626–28.

Holck, Frederick H. "Life Revisited (Parallels in Death Experiences)." *Omega* 9 (1978–79): 1–11.

Hunter, R. C. A. "On the Experience of Nearly Dying." *American Journal of Psychiatry* 124, 1 (July 1967): 84–88.

Hynson, Lawrence M. "Belief in Life after Death and Societal Integration." *Omega* 9 (1978–79): 13–18.

Hyslop, James H. "Visions of the Dying." *The Journal of the American Society for Psychical Research* 1 (1907): 45–55.

———. "Visions of the Dying." *The Journal of the American Society for Psychical Research* 12 (1918): 585–646.

"In Search of Life after Death." Pyramid Film Producers, Santa Monica, Calif., 1976.

Ingber, Dina. "Visions of an Afterlife." *Science Digest* (January/February 1981): 95–97, 142.

Jackovich, Karen G. "Sex, Visitors from the Grave, Psychic Healing: Kübler-Ross Is a Public Storm Center Again." *People* (October 29, 1979): 28–30.

James, William. *The Varieties of Religious Experience.* The Gifford Lectures on Natural Religion, Edinburgh, 1901–1902. Cambridge, Mass., and London, 1985.

Jung, Carl G. *Memories, Dreams, Reflections.* Edited by Aniela Jaffe. Translated by Richard Winston and Clara Winston. New York, 1965.

Kalish, Richard A., ed. *Death and Dying. Views from Many Cultures.* Perspectives on Death and Dying Series 1. Farmingdale, N.Y., 1980.

———. *Death, Dying and Transcendence.* Perspectives on Death and Dying Series 3. Farmingdale, N.Y., 1980.

Kastenbaum, Robert, ed. *Between Life and Death.* N.Y., 1979.

———. *Is There Life after Death?* London, Melbourne, and Johannesburg, 1984.

Kellison, Catherine. "My out-of-body experience." *Cosmopolitan* 185 (December 1978). 182ff.

Kemf, Elizabeth. "E. Kübler-Ross: 'There Is No Death.'" *East West Journal* (March 1978): 50–53.

Klass, Dennis, and Audrey Gordon. "Varieties of Transcending Experience at Death: A Videotape Based Study." *Omega* 9 (1978–79): 19–36.

Kletti, Roy. See Noyes, Russell, Jr.

Koestler, Arthur. "Cosmic Consciousness: An alternative vision of life after death that substitutes concepts from physics and philosophy for the idea of personal immortality in heaven and hell." *Psychology Today* (April 1977): 52–54, 104.

Krishnan, V. "Near-Death Experiences: Reassessment Urged." *Parapsychology Review* 12, 4 (1981): 10–11.

Kron, Joan. "The Out-of-Body Trip: What a Way to Go!" *New York Magazine* 10 (December 27, 1976/January 3, 1977): 66–72.

Kronish, L. "Elisabeth Kubler-Ross: Messenger of Love." *Yoga Journal* (November 1976): 18–20.

Kübler-Ross, Elisabeth. *Death: The Final Stage of Growth.* Englewood Cliffs, N.J., 1975.

———. *On Death and Dying.* New York, 1969; new ed., New York, 1975.

———. *Questions and Answers on Death and Dying.* New York, 1974.

———. *To Live until We Say Good-bye.* Englewood Cliffs, N.J., 1978.

Kuhn, Harold B. "Out-of-Body Experiences: Misplaced Euphoria." *Christianity Today* 25 (March 13, 1981): 78ff.

Kurlychek, Robert T. "Assessment of Attitudes toward Death and Dying: A Critical Review of Some Available Methods." *Omega* 9 (1978–79): 37–47.

Lawton, George. *The Drama of Life After Death: A Study of the Spiritualist Religion*. New York, 1932.

Lief, Harold I. "Commentary on Dr. Ian Stevenson's 'The Evidence of Man's Survival after Death.'" *The Journal of Nervous and Mental Disease* 165 (September 1977): 171–73.

"Life in Heaven: Incredible New Eyewitness Accounts by 12 Who Came Back from the Dead." *Globe* (April 8, 1980): 11.

Lindley, James H., Sethyn Bryan, and Bob Conley. "Near-Death Experiences in a Pacific Northwest American Population: The Evergreen Study." *Anabiosis* 1 (December 1981): 104–25.

Lorimer, David. *Survival? Body, Mind and Death in the Light of Psychic Experience*. London, 1984.

Lukianowicz, N. "Autoscopic Phenomena." *American Medical Association Archives of Neurology and Psychiatry* 80 (August 1958): 199–220.

Lundahl, Craig R., ed. *A Collection of Near-Death Research Readings*. Chicago, 1982.

Lundahl, Craig R., and Harold A. Widdison. "The Mormon Explanation of Near-Death Experiences." *Anabiosis* 3 (June 1983): 97–106.

Malz, Betty. *My Glimpse of Eternity*. New York, 1977.

Mandel, Bill. "Death: Indescribably Wonderful Experience." *Philadelphia Inquirer* (March 23, 1975): 1D.

Marsh, Michael. "Beyond Death: The Rebirth of Immortality." *Hastings Center Report* 7 (October 1977): 40–42.

Matson, Archie. *Afterlife: Reports from the Threshold of Death*. Originally published as *The Waiting World*. New York, 1975.

Meek, George W. *After We Die, What Then?* Franklin, N.C., 1980.

Mitchell, Janet Lee. *Out-of-Body Experiences: A Handbook*. Jefferson, N.C., and London, 1981.

Monroe, Robert. *Journeys Out of the Body*. New York, 1971; 2nd ed., New York, 1977.

Moody, Raymond A., Jr. "City of Light, Realm of Shadow." *Reader's Digest* 111 (July 1977): 151–54. [Excerpts from *Reflections on Life After Life*.]

———. "Clinical Aspects of Near-Death Experiences." Abstract of presentation to the 87th Annual Convention of the American Psychological Association (September 1979). *Anabiosis* 1 (August 1979): 5–7.

———. "Is There Life After Death?" *Saturday Evening Post* 249, 4 (May/June 1977): 66–67, 82–85.

———. "Life After Life." Condensed in *Reader's Digest* 110 (January 1977): 193–215.

———. *Life After Life*. Atlanta, 1975; New York and Harrisburg, Pa., 1976.

———. "Reactions to 'Life After Life.'" In "Critics Corner," *Theology Today* 35 (July 1978): 192–95.

———. *Reflections on Life After Life*. Atlanta and Harrisburg, Pa., 1977; New York, 1978.

Moore, R. Laurence. *In Search of White Crows: Spiritualism, Parapsychology and American Culture*. New York, 1977.

Myers, F. W. H. *Human Personality and Its Survival of Bodily Death*. Edited by Richard Hodgson and Alice Johnson. 2 vols. New York, 1903; reprint ed., New York, 1961.

"Near-death experience in children: a first report." *Brain/Mind Bulletin* 9 (December 12, 1983): 1–2.

"Near-death experiences follow clearcut pattern." *Brain/Mind Bulletin* 5 (September 1, 1980): 1–2.

Nelson, Geoffrey K. *Spiritualism and Society.* London and New York, 1969.

"New Evidence of Life After Death." *National Enquirer* 52 (June 20, 1978): 1.

Nietzke, Ann. "The Miracle of Kubler-Ross." *Cosmopolitan* (February 1980): 206ff.

Noyes, Russell, Jr. "The Art of Dying." *Perspectives in Biology and Medicine* (Spring 1971): 432–46.

———. "Attitude Change Following Near-Death Experiences." *Psychiatry* 43 (August 1980): 234–42.

———. "Dying and Mystical Consciousness." *Journal of Thanatology* (January/February 1971): 25–41.

———. "The Encounter with Life-Threatening Danger: Its Nature and Impact." *Essence* 5 (1981): 21–32.

———. "The Experience of Dying." *Psychiatry* 35 (1972): 174–83.

———. "Near-Death Experiences: Their Interpretation and Significance." In *Between Life and Death.* Edited by Robert Kastenbaum (New York, 1979), chap. 6, pp. 73–88.

Noyes, Russell, Jr., and Roy Kletti. "Depersonalization in Response to Life-Threatening Danger." *Comprehensive Psychiatry* 18 (July/August 1977): 375–84.

———. "Depersonalization in the Face of Life-Threatening Danger: A Description." *Psychiatry* 39 (1976): 19–27.

———. "Depersonalization in the Face of Life-Threatening Danger: An Interpretation." *Omega* 7 (1976): 103–14.

———. "The Experience of Dying from Falls." In *Death, Dying and Transcendence.* Edited by Richard A. Kalish (Farmingdale, N.Y., 1980) , chap. 13, pp. 129–36.

———. "The Experience of Dying from Falls." *Omega* 2 (1972): 45–52. [Includes translation of "Remarks on Fatal Falls" by Albert Heim.]

———. "Panoramic Memory: A Response to the Threat of Death." *Omega* 8 (1977): 181–94.

Noyes, Russell, Jr., and Donald J. Slymen. "The Subjective Response to Life-Threatening Danger." *Omega* 9 (1978–79): 313–21.

Oakes, Annalee. "The Lazarus Syndrome: Caring For Patients Who've 'Returned from the Dead.'" *RN* (June 1978): 53–64.

O'Roark, Mary Ann. "Life after Death: The Growing Evidence." *McCall's* (March 1981): 24ff.

Osis, Karlis. *Deathbed Observations by Physicians and Nurses.* Parapsychological Monographs. New York, 1961.

Osis, Karlis, and Erlendur Haraldsson. *At the Hour of Death.* New York, 1977.

———. "Deathbed Observations by Physicians and Nurses: A Cross-Cultural Survey." *The Journal of the American Society for Psychical Research* 71 (July 1977): 237–59.

Ousley, J. D. "Possible Evidence for Life after Death." *Anglican Theological Review* 60 (July 1978): 259–77.

Palmer, John. "The Out-of-Body Experience: A Psychological Theory." *Parapsychology Review* 9 (1978): 19–22.

————. "Some Recent Trends in Survival Research." *Parapsychology Review* 6 (May–June 1975): 15–17.

Panati, Charles. "Is There Life After Death?" *Family Circle* 89 (November 1976): 78, 84, 90.

"The Peace of Near-Death." *Human Behavior* 5 (July 1976): 71.

Pfister, Oskar. "Shock Thoughts and Fantasies in Extreme Mortal Danger." Translated by Roy Kletti and Russell Noyes, Jr. in "Mental States in Mortal Danger." *Essence* 5 (1981): 5–20.

————. "Shocken und Shockphantasien bei höchster Todesgefahr." *Zeitschrift für Psychoanalyse* 16 (1930): 430–55.

Prophetic Voices. Videotape produced by WGBY-TV (Springfield, Mass.) and Dr. Andrew Silver. [Kenneth Ring interviews near-death experiencers.]

Rawlings, Maurice. *Before Death Comes*. Nashville, 1980.

————. *Beyond Death's Door*. Nashville, 1978; New York, 1979.

Richards, Jerald. "Raymond Moody, Near-Death Experiences and Life after Death." *Essence* 5 (1981): 199–217.

Richardson, Glenn E. "The Life-After-Death Phenomenon." *The Journal of School Health* 49 (October 1979): 451–53.

Ring, Kenneth. "Further Studies of Near-Death Experiences." *Theta* 7 (1979): 1–3.

————. *Heading toward Omega: In Search of the Meaning of the Near-Death Experience*. New York, 1984.

————. *Life at Death: A Scientific Investigation of the Near-Death Experience*. New York, 1980.

————. "Near-Death Studies: A New Area of Consciousness Research." Storrs, Conn., 1982.

————. "Paranormal and Other Non-Ordinary Aspects of Near-Death Experiences: Implications for a New Paradigm." *Essence* 5 (1981): 33–52.

————. "Precognitive and Prophetic Visions in Near-Death Experiences." *Anabiosis* 2 (June 1982): 47–74.

Ritchie, George G., Jr. *Return from Tomorrow*. With Elizabeth Sherrill. Lincoln, Va., 1977; Waco, Tex., and Carmel, N.Y, 1978; Old Tappan, N.Y., 1981.

Rodin, Ernst A. "The Reality of Death Experiences: A Personal Perspective." *The Journal of Nervous and Mental Disease* 168 (May 1980): 259–63.

————. "The Reality of Death Experiences: A Reply to Commentaries." *Anabiosis* 2 (February 1981): 15–16.

Rogo, D. Scott., ed. *Mind beyond the Body: The Mystery of ESP Projection*. New York and Harmondsworth, 1978.

————. "Parapsychology—Its Contributions to the Study of Death." *Omega* 5 (1974): 99–113.

————. "Research on Deathbed Experiences: Some Contemporary and Historical Perspectives." *Journal of the Academy of Religion and Psychical Research* 2 (1979): 37–49.

Rose, Seraphim. *The Soul after Death: Contemporary "After-Death" Experiences in the Light of Orthodox Teaching on the Afterlife*. Platina, Calif., 1980.

Rosen, David H. "Suicide Survivors: A Follow-Up Study of Persons Who Survived Jumping from the Golden Gate and San Francisco–Oakland Bay Bridges." *Western Journal of Medicine* 122 (1975): 289–94.

Rosenbaum, Ron. "Turn On, Tune In, Drop Dead." *Harper's* (July 1982): 32–43.

Sabom, Michael B. "The Near-Death Experience: Myth or Reality? A Methodological Approach." *Anabiosis* 1 (July 1981): 44–56.

———. *Recollections of Death: A Medical Investigation.* New York, 1982.

———. "Recollections of Death." *Omni* (February 1982): 59–60, 103–9.

Sabom, Michael B., and S. Kreutziger. "The Experience of Near Death." *Death Education* 1 (1977): 195–203.

———. "Near-Death Experiences." *The Journal of the Florida Medical Association* 64, 9 (September 1977): 648–50.

———. "Near-Death Experiences." *New England Journal of Medicine* 297, 19 (1977): 1071.

———. "Physicians Evaluate the Near-Death Experience." *Theta* 6 (1978): 1–6.

Sagan, Carl. *Broca's Brain: Reflections on the Romance of Science.* New York, 1979.

Seliger, Susan. "Dying to Talk about Life After Death." *U.S. Catholic* 42 (March 1977): 18–21.

Seligson, Marcia. "Elisabeth Kubler-Ross" [Interview]. *Playboy* 28 (May 1981): 69–106.

Sheils, Dean. "A Cross-Cultural Study of Beliefs in Out of the Body Experiences, Waking and Sleeping." *Journal of the Society for Psychical Research* 49 (1978): 697–741.

Siegel, Ronald K. "Accounting for 'Afterlife' Experiences." *Psychology Today* (January 1981): 65–75.

———. "Hallucinations." *Scientific American* 237 (October 1977): 132–40.

———. "The Psychology of Life after Death." *American Psychologist* 35 (1980): 911–31.

Smith, Jayne. ". . . Caught Up into Paradise." *Vital Signs* 3 (June 1983): 7, 10.

Snell, David. "How It Feels to Die." *Life* (May 26, 1967): 38–47.

Solow, Victor. "I Died at 10:52 A.M." *Reader's Digest* (October 1974): 178.

Spiritual Frontiers. [Quarterly journal of the Spiritual Frontiers Fellowship; regular column, "At the Brink of Death," relates personal testimony of near-death experience.]

Springer, Rebecca. *Within the Gates.* Dallas, 1971.

Stevenson, Ian. *Cases of the Reincarnation Type.* 3 vols. Charlottesville, Va., 1975–.

———. "Some Implications of Parapsychological Research into the Evidence of Man's Survival after Death." *The Journal of Nervous and Mental Disease* 165 (September 1977): 152–70.

———. "Some Implications of Parapsychological Research on Survival after Death." *Proceedings of the American Society for Psychical Research* 28 (1969): 18–35.

———. *Twenty Cases Suggestive of Reincarnation.* 2nd rev. ed. Charlottesville, Va., 1974.

Stevenson, Ian, and Bruce Greyson. "Near-Death Experiences: Relevance to the Question of Survival after Death." *The Journal of the American Medical Association* 242, 3 (July 20, 1979): 265–67.

Swihart, Phillip J. *The Edge of Death.* Downers Grove, Ill., 1978.

Tart, Charles T. "States of Consciousness and State-Specific Sciences." *Science* 176 (June 1972): 1203–18.

Thomas, L. Eugene, Pamela E. Cooper, and David J. Suscovich. "Incidence of Near-Death and Intense Spiritual Experiences in an Intergenerational Sample: An Interpretation." *Omega* 13 (1982–83): 35–42.

Toobert, Saul. "Do We 'Live' after Death?" *Contemporary Psychology* 22 (1977): 213–14.

Toynbee, Arnold et al. *Life after Death*. London, 1976.

———. *Man's Concern with Death*. London, 1968.

Ullman, Montague. "Discussion of Dr. Stevenson's Paper: 'The Evidence of Man's Survival after Death.'" *The Journal of Nervous and Mental Disease* 165 (September 1977): 174–75.

Urfer, Billy O. *Beyond Tomorrow*. Heber Springs, Ark., 1980.

Vaisrub, Samuel. "Afterthoughts on Afterlife." *Archives of Internal Medicine* 137 (February 1977): 150.

Vicchio, Stephen J. "Against Raising Hope of Raising the Dead: Contra Moody and Kübler-Ross." *Essence* 3 (1979): 51–67.

———. "Moody, Suicide and Survival: A Critical Appraisal." *Essence* 4 (1980): 69–77.

———. "Near-Death Experiences: A Critical Review of the Literature and Some Questions for Further Study." *Essence* 5 (1981): 77–89.

———. "Near-Death Experiences: Some Logical Problems and Questions for Further Study." *Anabiosis* 1 (July 1981): 66–87.

Vital Signs. A Quarterly Digest of News for the Membership of the International Association for Near-Death Studies, Inc. Vol. 1, no. 1 (June 1981) et seq. Replaces *Anabiosis* [newsletter].

Walker, Benjamin. *Beyond the Body: The Human Double and the Astral Planes*. Boston, London, and Henley, 1974.

Weiss, Jess E., ed. *The Vestibule*. Port Washington, N.Y., 1972; reprint ed., New York, 1974.

Weldon, John, and Zola Levitt. *Is There Life after Death?* Irvine, Calif., 1977.

Westoff, Clairann. In "Personal Accounts of Near-Death Experiences." *Anabiosis* (August 1980): 7–8.

Wheeler, David R. *Journey to the Other Side*. New York, 1976, 1977.

Wierenga, Edward. "Proving Survival?" *The Reformed Journal* 28 (September 1978): 26–29.

Wilkerson, Ralph. *Beyond and Back: Those Who Died and Lived to Tell It*. New York, 1977.

Witt, Linda. "Life after Death: Yes, Beyond a Shadow of a Doubt." Interview with Elisabeth Kübler-Ross. *People* (November 24, 1975): 66–69.

Woelfel, James W., et al. "Life after Death: Faith or Knowledge?" (Readers' Response.) *The Christian Century* 93 (July 7–14, 1976): 632–35.

Woodward, Kenneth L. (with bureau reports). "Life after Death?" *Newsweek* (July 12, 1976): 41.

———. "There Is Life after Death." *McCalls* (August 1976): 23–26.

Zaleski, Philip. "Elisabeth Kübler-Ross." *Social Issues Resources Series*, vol. 2, no. 58 [reprint from *New Age Journal* (November 1984): 39–44].

Zubek, J. P., ed. *Sensory Deprivation: Fifteen Years of Research*. New York, 1969.

Index

Note: NDE = near-death experience; OWJ = otherworld journey.